Steps to Recovery from Bible Abuse

Steps to Recovery from Bible Abuse

Rembert S. Truluck

2000
Chi Rho Press, Inc.
Gaithersburg, Maryland, USA

Steps to Recovery from Bible Abuse

Second Printing, March 2001

Printed in the United States of America.

ISBN 1-888493-16-X

Except where specifically noted, all of the Bible translations and paraphrases are by the author and are based on the original literal meaning of the Hebrew and Greek with special reference to the *New American Standard Version*, and careful attention to the way the meaning speaks in our language today.

Library of Congress Cataloging-in-Publication Data

Truluck, Rembert S.
Steps to recovery from Bible abuse / Rembert S. Truluck.
p. cm.
Includes bibliographical references (p.) and index.
ISBN 1-888493-16-X
1. Christian gays--Religious life. 2. Homosexuality--Biblical teaching. I. Title.
BV4596.G38 T78 2001
261.8'35766--dc21

2001028208

Chi Rho Press, Inc.
P.O. Box 7864
Gaithersburg, MD 20898, USA
301/926-1208 phone/fax
Orders@ChiRhoPress.com e-mail

Dedication

For Susan

And to All Gay, Lesbian, Bisexual, and Transgendered People Who Struggle With Self-Acceptance.

Contents

Publisher's Note

The publication of *Steps to Recovery from Bible Abuse* has been a long process for us. We have always been captivated by Dr. Rembert Truluck's erudition, scholarship, eloquence, and good humor. His *Invitation to Freedom*, which Chi Rho Press published in 1993, was very popular and *Steps to Recovery* is more of the same scholarship and good sense – much more. Part of the reason it has taken so long to get *Steps to Recovery* in print lies in its length.

Steps to Recovery is more than twice the size of any other book Chi Rho Press has published to date. It is packed with information, examples, anecdotes, vignettes, and Bible quotes, all of which has required careful presentation. It has been almost more than a small, religious, gay publishing house could handle.

So why did we undertake this Herculean task? Because *Steps to Recovery from Bible Abuse* is a groundbreaking book. It is the book for which the lesbian, gay, bisexual, and transgendered community and our families, friends, and supporters have been yearning. This book is going to be an essential volume for the library of every thinking person of faith who is concerned about the misuse of scriptures to foster hatred, discrimination, and exclusion of anyone.

For too long, the lesbian and gay religious community has been on the defensive. We have devoted most of our time reacting to attacks by the "Polyester Patriarchs" of the televised religious right. This is especially amazing since the ammunition they use against us is pitifully meager, just six small passages in the entire Bible! Seminal scholars from Derrick Sherwin Bailey (who wrote *Homosexuality and the Western Christian Tradition* in 1975) through the brilliant work of John Boswell and John McNeill, and to this day with the work of John Shelby Spong, Daniel Helminiak, and our own Michael England, have repeatedly shown that the few "clobber passages" used against us have been taken out of context, mistranslated, and falsified.

Despite the faulty rationale of the homophobic religious right, the LGBT faith community and our growing number of supporters have largely been reactive. We have limited our arguments to responding to the ignorant, hypocritical ranting of a small minority of people. With a few notable exceptions, the gay community has not written exegesis on scripture that has affirmed the truth of God's love to all people. In devoting so much time to reacting to those poor, six misused verses, we have ignored and abandoned most of the scriptures.

Dr. Truluck's work is different. While he spends time discussing the "clobber passages," the bulk of this book talks about how the Bible is the friend of lesbian and gay people, not our enemy. He writes about how God loves us, how God intends for us to be included in the broader community of faith, and he backs up all of what he has to say with dozens of examples from the Bible. Here is a book that will make you feel good about yourself as a member of a sexual minority. It will also make you feel good about being a Christian.

Dr. Truluck's Web site, also called *Steps to Recovery from Bible Abuse*, has received over two million hits in the last two years. I am constantly seeing his work being quoted throughout the Internet. Now much of the important work he had posted on his Web site has been removed from the Web and placed in this book, for all to enjoy and use.

I want to take a moment to thank Kevin Stone Fries, the assistant editor of Chi Rho Press, for working with me to prepare this manuscript for publication. Kevin's erudition, good sense, and excellent editing skills are not only a splendid addition to Chi Rho Press, but also make him a great pleasure to work with and have as a colleague. We also want to thank the people who have invested in and contributed to this important project.

R. Adam DeBaugh
Director, Chi Rho Press

Preface

This book is for people who have been abused and oppressed by religion, have been hated and rejected by their own parents, family, and friends, and who have suffered under the whip of distorted and manipulative uses of the Bible to condemn, humiliate, and invalidate them. This book is for lesbian, gay, bisexual, and transgendered people. I am not trying to change or preach to homophobic, legalistic, judgmental preachers and churches. Their minds are usually tightly closed to the material in this book. This purpose is complicated by the fact that there are many homophobic, legalistic, judgmental preachers and church members who are themselves homosexual. Of course, everybody is invited to use the book. You may find help here that you did not expect.

A New Reformation

We are living in a New Reformation that will challenge the churches for many years, probably for most of the next century, and may turn violent. The Old Reformation began in 1517 with the challenge of Martin Luther to the church to take a fresh look at the Bible and change its distortions of Scripture to teach damaging doctrines that were inconsistent with the gospel of Jesus. The church split into Protestant and Catholic and then into hundreds of other divisions and factions. Bloody religious wars were fought with great destruction to all sides.

This New Reformation is also grounded in a fresh look at the Bible. It is the warfare between pro-gay and anti-gay forces that cross all denominational lines, all levels of education, all religious traditions – both Christian and non-Christian, and all sexual orientations. As I write the final draft for this book, the war is just heating up. Joined in this deep division within the churches are the issues of women's rights and the separation of church and state. People who believe that religious political power should control what people do are among the leaders of the anti-gay forces in this struggle.

This book is a challenge aimed at the reactionary and regressive forces at work in our society and within the minds and hearts of people of all sexual orientations. The facts and Bible study materials in this book intentionally push the outer limits of what many church people and religious leaders have been willing to consider. As Bishop John Shelby Spong said in a recent book, "Christianity Must Change or Die."

A Fresh Look at the Bible

This book is a fresh look at the Bible from a gay Christian point of view. All Bible interpretations and applications are from somebody's point of view. The history of biblical interpretation is filled with examples of scholars who came to opposite conclusions about central teachings of the Bible. The individual interpreter's education (or lack thereof), personal history, religious background, personality, and prejudices guide the results.

My search for truth in the Bible for gay, lesbian, bisexual, and transgendered people has led to these studies. Others will probably disagree with what I have seen in the Bible that is supportive and helpful to gay people. I have looked at the evidence through eyes of faith in Jesus Christ as well as through the eyes through which I accept and affirm myself as a gay person.

My Bible study work on this book began in 1952 when I experienced a "call to the ministry" when I was 18 years old. My preparation continued through 14 years of formal education in college and seminary. Research, writing, teaching, and preaching as pastor of many churches from 1953 to 1973 continued my research and application of this material. Eight years of study and teaching over 5,000 students in 18 different college religion courses at Baptist College of Charleston have helped me to formulate this book. Attending writer's conferences and writing Adult Sunday School Lessons for the Southern Baptist Sunday

School Board for several years also helped to prepare me to write this book.

Studying, writing, teaching, counseling, and preaching in the Metropolitan Community Churches (MCC) since 1981 also focused my energy and experiences in the direction of this book. The actual writing of this material began in 1988 in Atlanta. My Web site on "Steps to Recovery from Bible Abuse" was published on the Internet on September 14, 1997 [www.truluck.com], and the steady flow of e-mail responses taught me many new insights and provided my most recent preparation for this book. The following studies contain some of what I have discovered and learned in the past 65 years.

What Prompted the Book at this Time

Many recent events related to Gay and Lesbian people have made the need for this book acute. National newspaper anti-gay ads in the summer of 1998, the vicious murder of Matthew Shepard in Wyoming in October, 1998, and the recent trials of his murderers made the information in this book more needed than ever before. Now, as I write these closing words of the Preface, four events are receiving national media attention.

The meeting of the Rev. Dr. Mel White with the Rev. Jerry Falwell in Lynchburg in October, 1999, to try to lower the level of violent anti-gay rhetoric captured public attention and raised the hopes for better relationships between the gay community and some religious fundamentalists.

The second trial and guilty verdict of the Rev. Jimmy Creech for performing a holy union ceremony for a gay couple resulted in the Rev. Creech being expelled from United Methodist Clergy.

The confessed murderer of two gay men asleep in their bed in Northern California tried to justify his crime by quoting the Bible as a basis for hating and killing homosexuals.

The Georgia Baptist Convention expelled two Atlanta churches for accepting gay people.

These events and an ongoing campaign against gay, lesbian, bisexual, and transgendered people on many levels in our culture cry out for the message that is in this book.

Victims of Misinformation

My friend Mel White in his Soulforce movement to challenge and correct the abusive use of religion against gay, lesbian, bisexual, and transgendered people calls homophobic religious leaders "victims of misinformation." Many gays and lesbians and their families also are victims of misinformation. The purpose of this book is to challenge and neutralize misinformation about gay people and about the Bible.

Jesus confronted religious leaders in Matthew 22:29 by saying, "You are wrong, and you do not understand the Bible or the power of God." This book is saying the same thing to people in and outside the churches who use the Bible and religion to demean, abuse, invalidate, demonize, condemn, and destroy people because of their sexual orientation or for other reasons that make them different.

Because of my web site, I have received thousands of letters from wounded gay, lesbian, bisexual, and transgendered people who have suffered vicious attacks by their own parents, family, friends, preachers, and churches based on ignorance and the oppressive use of the Bible. This book is a remedy for both sides in the homophobic wars. It is an "information atomic bomb" that could help to end this devastating war against gays and lesbians. I pray that it will.

Thanks and Acknowledgements

Special thanks go to my parents, my children, my sister, many friends over many years, and all of my teachers who helped to shape my mind and heart. Thanks to Amir Ragsac, who designed my Web site and gave unrelenting support and encouragement to me during this project. Thanks to Adam DeBaugh at Chi Rho Press, my editor and publisher, and to Kevin Stone Fries, assistant editor at the Press. Thanks also to so many people in MCC that I cannot possibly list all of them here. Some of them are mentioned in "My Story" and within some of the chapters and lessons. Special thanks also to my friend and pastor, the Rev. Barry Wichman, pastor of New Life MCC in Berkeley, California, for his support and encouragement. Every person who has touched my life has made a difference that helped me to see my own truth and to see clearly the necessity for this book.

Some of the people who have been my teachers and possibly never realized it are, Jim Mitulski, Frederick, Daniel, Allen, Shannon, Alvin, Eddie, Scott, David, Duncan, Chris, Tony, Paul, Valentine, Brandon, Ty, Jun, Kevin, Jay, Ricky, Ronnie, Carolyn, Dan, Barry, Brian, Russell, Jim, Bart, Susan, Bill, Deborah, and Jackque, and many others who have let me learn far more from their personal lives and struggles than I could ever have learned without them.

All Bible translations and paraphrases in the book are by the author with special attention to *The New American Standard Version* as the best and most accurate Bible presently in use.

Special People Who Helped

I extend my thanks to people of many sexual orientations who helped to make this book happen with special contributions to Chi Rho Press: my mother Mary Truluck, Anthony W. Sykes, Jim Ferguson, John L. Bennett, James Martin, and Edmund G. Good.

Rembert Truluck
www.truluck.com
November 20, 1999

AUTHOR'S PREFACE TO SECOND PRINTING

During the year since this book was published in January 2000, there have been many significant events relating to gay, lesbian, bisexual, and transgendered (GLBT) spiritual issues and religious oppression.

The largest church denominations in the U.S. held national conferences in which full participation by GLBT people in all of church life was debated at length without any positive results. Soulforce volunteers under the leadership of Dr. Mel White and Rev. Jimmy Creech protested anti-gay religious oppression and abuse at many of these national gatherings.

The election of a new U.S. President took place, and the new administration has vastly different attitudes towards GLBT issues and the separation of church and state. The long-term effects of these changes on GLBT people are yet to be seen. Religion remains the primary source for homophobia and the oppression of GLBT people. Misinformation about GLBT people in politics and religion is being challenged, but the results so far have demonstrated little or no change in religious and political actions.

The need for the information in this book is greater now than ever. An encouraging sign during the past year has been the development of many home study groups around the world using this book as a guide. I have visited many churches and conferences, leading workshops on this book which led to local study groups being started in many places. My web site on "Steps to Recovery from Bible Abuse" at www.truluck.com along with regular e-mail updates to thousands of readers have provided an on-going interactive dialogue and learning opportunity for many.

A series of GLBT Sunday School lessons is the next step in this ministry of information. I am preparing this series of lessons on Jesus to be published soon by Chi Rho Press and to be made available in the form of weekly group study materials.

A video to accompany *Steps to Recovery from Bible Abuse* will also be made available through Chi Rho Press. This video, produced by Adraine Bowie, will provide an inspirational example of the possibilities arising from the use of *Steps to Recovery from Bible Abuse.* The video was made during my visit to Resurrection MCC in Houston, Texas, in January 2001.

Contact the author by e-mail at rembert@truluck.com to be added to the e-mail list for updates related to the web site and book.

Rembert Truluck
February 2001

Part I

Introductory Material

Chapter 1

Why This Book is Here

Religious terrorists have distorted the Bible and used it to abuse, oppress, and hold hostage the spirituality and sexuality of gay, lesbian, bisexual, and transgendered people.

> "What Freud called religion, Jesus called sin."
> Harry Emerson Fosdick

This book is a weapon to fight back.

Steps to Recovery from Bible Abuse is intended to give encouragement and hope to the multitude of gay people and others who have suffered from unrelenting attacks by religious leaders. Jesus taught that God loves and accepts you as God's children, just as you are. Being gay does not cut you off from God.

The information in this book will help you to answer the ignorance that represses and wounds the human spirit. Give yourself the time it takes to study all of this material. It will equip you to feel good about yourself and to help others do the same.

Once at a home spiritual growth group, the question was asked, "How is Christianity different from all other world religions?" One answer was that Christianity is the only world religion that does not do what it claims to do. All other religions basically do what they claim to do, whether it is honoring ancestors, respecting nature, accepting all religions, or learning the teachings of a great teacher like the Buddha. Christianity claims to follow Jesus in giving and demonstrating God's unconditional love for all people. Christianity, however, does not carry out that claim and denies it in countless churches, councils, denominations, radio and television preachers, and a steady flow of books, magazines, and Web sites.

This book takes a fresh look at "The Bible as the Friend of Lesbians and Gays," which was the first working title for this book several years ago. This material is both new and old at the same time. My position that the Bible never discussed or condemned homosexuality is often called "revisionist." It is not. The revisionists are those who have read homosexuality and lesbian and gay people into the Bible through a few out-of-context and incorrectly translated verses and by incorrectly reading current sexual attitudes into the culture of Bible times.

This book attempts to do two basic things. It focuses on Jesus and the living Spirit of Jesus within every believer as the true and relevant guide to all scripture and all of life. It also gives detailed information and facts about Bible words and translations to clarify the truth as the Bible writers intended. In giving these details, this study brings out the cultural milieu in which Bible materials originated and which greatly influenced what was written and why it was written. Another primary purpose of the book is to show how the life experiences and teachings of Jesus apply directly to issues facing people today who have been abused and oppressed by sick religion.

The Gospel of John states that "these have been written that you may believe that Jesus is the Christ, the Child of God; and that believing, you may have life in Jesus' name" (John 20:31). Jesus, throughout all four Gospels, rejected and replaced the legalistic, judgmental religion of the Law with himself and gave the one consistent commandment, "Follow Me."

The warning in 2 Peter is still relevant today,

> Paul wrote things hard to understand, which the ignorant and unstable distort, as they do the rest of scripture, to their own destruction! You, therefore, beloved, knowing this beforehand, be on your

> guard lest, being carried away by the error of unprincipled people, you fall from your own steadfastness, but grow in the grace and knowledge of our Lord and Savior Jesus Christ, to whom is the glory, both now and to the day of eternity. Amen. (2 Peter 3:16-18)

Even during the time that the New Testament was still being written, the distortion and twisting of "scripture" was under way to be used by ignorant and unstable people against other people.

Steps to Recovery from Bible Abuse challenges and corrects current distortions and abusive uses of the Bible against gay people and all others who are different and do not fit in to the prevailing demands and expectations of fundamentalist religion.

Chapter 2

My Story

This book and the companion Web site, *Steps to Recovery from Bible Abuse* (http://www.truluck.com), are based on what I have experienced and learned from many sources. I grew up in a Southern Baptist home and church in South Carolina, a small town with cotton mills and a Presbyterian college. My parents taught me by example the family values of love, respect for all people, kindness, generosity, truth telling, fairness, self-respect, loyalty, and faith in God. "Finish what you start, always do your best work whether you feel like it or not, and take pride in your work" were the main features of the work ethic I learned as a child. I learned early that hate is not a family value. These family values continue to guide my life.

At about the time I started going to public school, I began to realize that I was sexually attracted to other boys and was not attracted to girls. This awareness grew stronger in high school and until I was 18 years old and graduated in 1952. Of course, I dated girls, pretended to be interested in them, and kept my homosexuality to myself except for the occasional sexual experiences that I had with other boys.

During the summer of 1952, I experienced God's call to the ministry and dedicated my life to serving Jesus Christ in whatever God led me to do. In 1956, I graduated from Furman University in Greenville, South Carolina. While attending college, I served for over three years as pastor of Beaverdam Baptist Church, a small rural church in Laurens County, South Carolina. There I began a lifelong emphasis on personal and small group evangelism and on Bible preaching. My home church ordained me when I was 19 years old.

Before I went to Furman University, I had pre-enrolled to major in art, then, after I decided to go into the ministry, I changed to a major in history and minor in English, which was the recommendation at the time for preparation for seminary. I also took a lot of religion courses with some outstanding professors. Sometimes I wonder how different my life would have been if I had stayed with art and become a flaming artist, cartoonist, or designer as I had intended instead of becoming a Southern Baptist preacher.

I entered The Southern Baptist Theological Seminary in Louisville, Kentucky, where I earned a Bachelor of Divinity degree (now M.Div.) in 1959 and a Master of Theology degree in 1962. I returned to the seminary after several years as pastor of Ingleside Baptist Church in Norfolk, Virginia, and earned the Doctor of Sacred Theology degree in 1968. Serving as student pastor of several churches in Kentucky and South Carolina during my seminary days, I learned about the destructive power of sick religion as well as the great power and love of Christ to change people into God's children.

My doctoral dissertation was on "Small Group Evangelism in the Local Church" and helped to prepare me for work in my churches, teaching at the college, and now in writing this book. My graduate studies and field experiences focused on group dynamics and the design and function of small groups for spiritual growth in and outside of churches. I prepared material, promoted, taught, and facilitated hundreds of small groups for inquirers, new members, Bible students, and others throughout my years as a pastor and as a professor at Baptist College and more recently in First Metropolitan Community Church (MCC) Atlanta, Golden Gate MCC San Francisco, MCC Nashville, and in dozens of other MCC churches and conferences.

My Struggle

During the years from 1952 to 1968, I wrestled quietly with my own sexual orientation without any counseling or helpful reading material. The present great wealth of books and articles on homosexuality did not yet exist. The Rev. Troy Perry began the first church for the lesbian/gay community, MCC, in Los Angeles on October 6, 1968. But I did not know about MCC until 1981.

In 1959, I married and began to build a home and family, just as I was expected to do as a Southern Baptist minister. We had three beautiful children, and everything seemed normal, but I was gay and frustrated and in secret pain that I could not discuss with anybody. I went to three different psychiatrists for help, including Dr. Corbet Thigpen, who wrote *The Three Faces of Eve*, but they told me that psychiatry could not change sexual orientation.

I served as pastor of South Main Street Baptist Church in Greenwood, South Carolina, from 1968 to 1973 and of First Baptist Church of Columbus, Mississippi, for part of 1973. Later in 1973, I joined the faculty of The Baptist College of Charleston, South Carolina, where I was professor of religion and developed a program of recruitment, church placement, and field supervision of ministry students until 1981. I visited over 700 South Carolina Baptist churches to lead revivals, Bible studies, pastors' conferences, and programs on church careers. For several years I also wrote adult Sunday School quarterlies for the Southern Baptist Convention.

Personal evangelism was an important emphasis in my entire ministry. Hundreds of young people in the churches and at the college learned to share their faith in Christ and went with me to churches and schools to tell about their personal experiences with Christ and to tell how they had witnessed to friends, classmates, and family members. I learned that the greatest influence on students is other students.

My Sexual Orientation Ended My Ministry

On March 3, 1981, the President of The Baptist College asked me to resign because the trustees had been informed that I was gay. I was outed by a long time friend and companion who was gay and a Christian and who said that God told him to do it. The college trustees had a secret meeting where no written record was kept. Even the college President was left out of the meeting and was informed by telephone to "secure my resignation immediately." I resigned "for personal reasons." Later, I was pressured by state Baptist leaders to resign my Baptist ordination to "protect my family from harassment." On March 5, 1981, I took my seven-year-old daughter to her second grade school, told her good bye as usual and said I would see her later. I was not allowed to see her again for five years. I moved to Atlanta to live with my sister, look for work, and start over.

Acceptance And Support From My Parents

My parents have been very supportive of my ministry in gay churches and as a gay activist and writer. My father died at the age of 87 in October, 1997. My mother is now 87 (in 1999) and lives in a retirement center in Laurens, South Carolina.

When I moved to Atlanta to live with my sister in 1981, my parents came to see me. My dad asked me if I could get some medical help in overcoming my homosexuality. I began to tell him that I had talked with three different psychiatrists about it and that there was no medical treatment to change a person from gay to straight.

As I began to tell him the details, my dad said that my mother needed to hear this also; so she came in and we sat at my sister's dining room table and for about three hours I told them the real story of my life as a gay person. After that, we never really talked in detail about it again. My mother's response after we finished talking was to say that she thought I was gay all along. She had noticed long ago how much more upset I was when one of my male friends could not come for a visit than I was when a female date did not work out.

From the time that we had that talk, my parents were as supportive, loving, and accepting of me as they could possibly be. I dedicated my first book, *Invitation to Freedom*, to them. My parents came to hear me preach and teach when I was pastor of Golden Gate MCC in San Francisco. They have taken a strong stand for accepting gay people in my home church of First Baptist Church in Clinton, South Carolina.

Painful Transitions

When I left the Baptist College, I had taught over 5,000 students in my religion classes and had seen hundreds of young people go into church-related careers. The sudden and total end to my ministry, family, career, and income on March 3, 1981, sent me into shock that lasted about seven years. Soon after I moved to Atlanta, I began to drink and became an alcoholic. My recovery from alcoholism began when I went with a friend to a gay Alcoholics Anonymous meeting, admitted that I was an alcoholic and needed help, and began the long road to recovery, sobriety, and health. I thank God for teaching me to live "one day at a time."

In Atlanta in 1981, I joined the MCC and found acceptance and encouragement as an openly gay Christian. Not until February, 1988, however, was I ready to resume church ministry. With the encouragement of Carolyn Mobley, Jimmy Brock, Chuck Larsen, Reid Christensen, John Hose, Jay Neely, Troy Perry, and others, I gradually resumed preaching and teaching. The studies in this book grew out of my personal experiences, counseling, Bible research, preaching, and teaching at First MCC Atlanta, Golden Gate MCC San Francisco, MCC Nashville and in many other MCC congregations from 1988 to the present.

Oppression is a Crazy-Making Place to Live

Low self-esteem among lesbian and gay Christians was the main issue that motivated my early Bible studies. Later Bible studies were developed to deal with many other pressures, problems, and issues faced by gay people in an environment of homophobic hate, religious oppression, abusive use of the Bible against gays, and the persistent problem of homophobia within the gay community. During my years of recovery and up to the present, I have experienced in myself and in many other people around me the prevailing self-destructive feelings and actions that try to control us.

We live in the midst of church and community alienation and suffer from chronic internalized and horizontal homophobia. The gay/lesbian world, including MCC, as I have experienced it is a social and spiritual war zone. All traditional churches carry the self-destructive virus of legalism and judgmental religion. I have no intention, however, of attacking or fighting churches or individuals. People and churches are not the enemy.

The enemy is Satan (meaning "the adversary" in both Hebrew and Greek). The enemy is not a class of people. The enemy is within ourselves in the form of idolatry, ignorance, fear, hate, anger, discord, disputes, greed, and the other works of the flesh ("human works") referred to in Galatians 5:19-21. The answer is the "more excellent way" of following only Jesus. The fruit of the spirit (in Galatians 5:22-23) is a description of the character of Jesus in the Gospels, "love, joy, peace, patience, kindness, goodness, faithfulness, gentleness, self-control."

For several years, I have seen my calling to be to help gay and lesbian people feel good about themselves and stop hurting themselves and each other. The only lasting solution that I have found is for individuals to invite Jesus into their lives and give up all other controls. Let go of everything else and follow Jesus. This was the first and the last message of Jesus in the Gospels. I have seen many people do this and experience the new life Jesus gives.

Evangelism and Bible Study

I am convinced that Christ-centered personal evangelism along with disciplined Christ-centered Bible study are the keys to success for gay and lesbian Christians in carrying out the call of Jesus to make disciples of all people. This book is an attempt to speak to our need for an approach to spiritual growth and personal evangelism that is sensitive to lesbians, gays, bisexuals, and transgendered people.

This means that we have to give careful attention not only to what we say but also to how we are heard when we talk about God's love in Christ for all people. This means taking a fresh look at how to translate many Bible words and ideas. It means taking seriously and listening to where people really are in their ideas and experiences. It means being far more flexible in "becoming all things to all people" than we probably were taught to be in our past religious traditions. I am convinced that reaching wounded and oppressed people with the gospel requires an accepting, non-judgmental, and non-threatening attitude that reflects the attitude of Jesus.

Many Problems at Once

We do not have the luxury of dealing with one problem at a time. Whenever we speak up for Jesus Christ in the gay environment, we are surrounded by a jungle of issues related to judgmental religion, HIV/AIDS, parents and family issues, Bible abuse against us, politics, self-esteem, and many more. Our mission is not hopeless. Jesus promised to give us the words when we appear before governors and kings, and I assume that includes queens, and even vicious queens! We also have each other. I thank God for what I learned through being in MCC. This book would not have happened without MCC.

We have the choice of selecting the people we want to be close to us and to influence our lives. Now is the time to get negative people out of your life so that you can go on to experience and enjoy the full and meaningful life and hope of glory that God has prepared for you now and in the world to come. Part of the joy of God in our lives is sharing our freedom, joy, love, and hope with others.

Legalistic, judgmental religion, however, is a deadly disease that spreads rapidly among religious people and that cripples and kills the spirit. Legalism is the enemy of the good news of Jesus Christ. Read Galatians to see how Paul saw the Law as the opposite of Gospel. Legalism is demonic. Legalism killed Jesus and will kill you if you do not resist it. The only cure for legalism is the new life and freedom that come into your life when you invite Jesus to take control.

My two years and three months as Senior Pastor of MCC Nashville taught me many hard lessons about religious abuse and the desperate need of gay and lesbian people to know and experience Jesus Christ. In Christ we can be set free and recover from Bible abuse, fear of religion, fear of sex, and internalized homophobia. Legalism and homophobia are social and religious diseases that have reached epidemic proportions. Legalism is "antichrist."

My experiences in Nashville taught me the liberating power of Jesus over legalism and sick religion. I learned how people grow spiritually and help each other in small group study and dialogue that is truly centered in Christ. For over two years I led a regular Wednesday spiritual support and Bible study group in my home. The sessions began at 7 p.m. and lasted for about an hour of study and formal discussion. Most of the study material is included in this book. Then a lot of the real healing, learning, and growing took place as we ate together and the people had the opportunity to share personally and informally with one other.

No attempt was made to control or guide this sharing time following the study. The Spirit of Christ seemed to be most active in liberating and healing ministry during these times when we shared in the "miracle of dialogue." People usually stayed until about 9:30 or 10:00 and some seemed to stay forever. We finally had to set a time limit that would give formal closure to the sessions.

Attendance varied, but the average was between 20 and 30. The last group that I led before leaving Nashville was attended by 31 people. Actually, I learned that groups of ten to 15 people experience more dialogue and healthier group dynamics than larger numbers, but we were reluctant to turn anyone away and could not find a convenient way to create more groups.

One of the most rewarding features of the small study group was that people would come seeking support and help and soon be giving support and help to others. Many people in the group personally shared Christ with their friends, brought friends to the sessions, and helped them become involved in the church. One man who came regularly to the group used the brochure, "The Bible as Your Friend, A Guide for Lesbians and Gays," to help his partner pray to receive Christ. Later I celebrated their holy union, and when I left Nashville, they both were leaders in the church and regularly shared their faith in Christ with their friends.

In this book, I hope to share with you what I have learned from my mistakes, from other people, from my own Bible study and personal experiences, and from my time spent in the trenches of spiritual warfare against "principalities and powers and the rulers of darkness" (Ephesians 6:12). My battle scars have been inflicted more by myself and by my friends than by outsiders. I have been deceived, betrayed, abandoned, and demonized by people I love. The enemy truly is within. Only Jesus can save us from ourselves. I pray for you that as you read and discuss this material, the Spirit of Christ will create in you a deeper understanding of your own experience with God in Christ and will clarify your own personal mission and ministry to change the world.

The Joy of Sharing Christ

The brochure, "The Bible as Your Friend," began as a Bible study at First MCC Atlanta in 1988. It developed through many sessions, feed back, and revisions. In 1990 in San Francisco, the Rev. Elder Don Eastman suggested that this study on how to become a Christian would be published by the UFMCC. It was published in 1991 and has sold about 6,000 copies each year since.

I sent copies of the brochure to a lot of people, including my ex-lover, Dan, who had constantly encouraged me in writing the Bible studies and was on the Board of Directors of First MCC Atlanta. Dan gave a copy of it to his new friend, David, who was not yet a Christian and had just begun to attend MCC with Dan. My thought at the time was that it would be great if my ex-lover could use my brochure to help his new lover receive Christ into his life.

David became a Christian, joined First MCC, and became an active member. In January, 1993, Dan and David were on the NBC television special on gays and lesbians hosted by Maria Shriver, who interviewed them in their home in Atlanta. Maria observed that they were active in church. David said, "Yes, we believe that God brought us together!" The next scene showed Dan and David taking Holy Communion with their pastor, the Rev. Reid Christensen, at First MCC Atlanta. When I saw this on national television, I was overwhelmed. I still am. Dan and David celebrated their holy union a few months later. With God, all things are possible.

You have only one decision to make. Are you willing to do the will of God? Once you make the decision to let go of everything else and follow Jesus, God will make the rest of the decisions for you.

My recent ministry has consisted of writing another book and several articles and brochures and publishing my Web site on "Steps to Recovery from Bible Abuse" at http://www.truluck.com on the Internet and answering e-mail responses from the Web site. I also have continued to write articles for the local gay paper in San Francisco, and for the on-line magazine, *Whosoever*.

I am an active member of New Life MCC in Berkeley, California, where I have led workshops and Bible studies and preached. I continue to lead church workshops and other conferences as I am invited to do so.

My current writing project is *Gay Sunday School Lessons* to be published by Chi Rho Press. Our goal is to provide regularly updated current materials for ongoing Bible Studies for gay, lesbian, bisexual, and transgendered people. These quarterly series of 13 lessons each will cover three months and will be available in 2000.

January 1, 2000
Rembert Truluck
www.truluck.com
P.O. Box 24062
Oakland, CA 94623

Chapter 3

Jesus Heals Sick Religion

This is the true personal story of a young man struggling with sick and abusive religion. His story speaks to me and to many others who face the same struggle in various forms. This book is intended as a response to his cry for help.

"I grew up in a very small rural southern town. When I was 16, I told my mother that I was gay. She passed it off and said I would get over it. But I didn't.

"At 19, I moved in with another guy and tried to be on my own, but my parents came and took me home and my mother took me to her Pentecostal church. I enjoyed church and accepted Jesus into my life. But I was still gay. I experienced the call to preach and began to preach whenever I could. I became a youth pastor, a mission pastor, and finally became pastor of my own little Pentecostal church.

"My church taught that being gay was demon possession. I prayed every day for deliverance from homosexuality. I could not understand why God would not do it. I joined the National Guard and spent four years in active service. I had to act 'butch' and be careful to hide my gayness. My community was very homophobic. I continued to preach at my church every week for six and a half years until I was 27. I stayed busy with revivals and a homeless mission as well as jail, nursing home, radio, and youth ministries. I worked nights at the local candy factory. But I was still gay and confused and in pain about it.

"I began to get depressed and went to a counselor, who told me to go to bed with a woman and I would not be gay! I didn't believe it and left his office. My depression got worse when two lesbians came to my church and I asked one of them to play for the service. The deacons told me not to let her play any more. They did not know that I was gay myself. I took a medical leave from work because of the depression. I became angry with God for letting all of this happen. I refused to read the Bible any more. I quit preaching.

"Finally, I took an overdose of pills. When I came to in the emergency room, my stomach was being pumped. I looked up and saw a big orderly holding my ankles and singing 'What a Mighty God We Serve!' Later, I told him that this was one of my favorite songs and asked him to sing it again. He did. This was the turning point in my life. I realized that God truly is a Mighty God who loves and accepts me just as I am.

"Later, I went to a psychologist and asked her to give me medicine or hypnotize me to make me straight. She said, 'You can't change your sexual orientation. You CAN be gay and a Christian!' Nobody had told me that before! She said, 'You ARE gay. Take off the mask. Be yourself and quit letting other people run your life. Move to the city and go to the church that will accept you.' Then she told me about Metropolitan Community Church. I did what she said. Now Jesus has set me free from self-hate and fear and I can accept myself and feel good about being me!"

July, 1994

Jesus Heals the Whole Person

"In Christ all things hold together" (Colossians 1:17).

Sharing Jesus with others is a healing ministry to the whole person. The word translated as "heal" in the Gospels means "to make whole" (John 5:1-18). Jesus practiced holistic healing. Jesus healed mind, body, spirit, and relationships. The "good news" of the Gospel of Jesus Christ is true liberation that brings freedom to live a full and meaningful life without fear.

Part of your own spiritual growth as well as your help to others is recovery from Bible abuse. Jesus said, "The thief comes only to steal, and kill, and destroy. I came that you might have life and have it abundantly" (John 10:10). The "thief" is Jesus' reference to judgmental and insensitive religious leaders. The good news of Jesus is liberation from sick and abusive religion.

Freedom from idolatrous and legalistic use of the Bible opens the way for you to follow Jesus as "the more excellent way" and to invite others to share in the same freedom that you have found. Until you are confident that God loves and accepts you regardless of your sexual orientation or anything else, you will hesitate to share the love of Jesus with others. Recovery from Bible abuse and religious oppression is essential for your motivation, your grasp of personal discipleship, and your outreach to others.

Many gay, lesbian, bisexual, and transgendered people have been so battered by legalistic, judgmental religion that they are in spiritual shock and cannot clearly see the goodness of the good news. When you have been told all your life by pastors, parents, and teachers that your sexual orientation is evil and separates you eternally from the love of God, you at least partly believe it.

The power and wisdom of the Holy Spirit can fully equip you to win this battle for yourself and for others you are called to help. Explanations seldom seem to be enough to overcome the homophobia (fear of homosexuality) and deep spiritual wounds created by years of negative religious conditioning against you. Your recovery from the damage caused by the abusive use of the Bible and religion against you can come to you as a gift from God, who has already given you life and hope through Jesus Christ.

Deliverance from the Idolatry of Legalism

Legalism is an idolatrous religion. Idolatry is the result of making anything other than God absolute. When laws and rules become absolute, the individual is absorbed into the system and loses identity and self-esteem. Legalistic religion is the mortal enemy of healthy self-esteem. Peace with God is a gift and not a work of law. "Christ is the end (or "goal," the Greek word *telos*) of the law for righteousness to everyone who believes" (Romans 10:4).

Legalism is always vague and confusing to the average person. An army of experts develops in legalism. As in the time of Jesus, average people cannot obey the law because they do not know or understand it. Legalism is always vague and inflexible. Such a demanding but unclear tyrant obviously creates tension, confusion, destructive behavior, and a constant battle for self-respect among the people. Jesus did not give a new list of rules about God but gave a new relationship with God that liberates.

Take the time to look up and study the following Bible passages to see how they relate to the problem of legalism in the culture of Jesus and Paul. Read Romans 5:1-10; Galatians 2:16, and 20-21; Galatians 5:1, and 13-15; and Ephesians 2:8-9 for the triumph of love and grace over law.

Legalism denies the love and power of God in Jesus in the Gospels. Legalism has certain distinct features in the Bible and today. (See Lesson 3 in Chapter 6 for a more detailed analysis of legalism.)

The awesome destructive power of judgmental legalism in religion should not be underestimated. Legalistic religion undermines self-esteem. The individual can never measure up to the absolute legal standards of "holy living" or "perfection" demanded by the legalists.

Jesus came to liberate people from hopeless bondage to legalistic, judgmental, abusive religion. "Since you are free in Christ, do not be bound again by a religious yoke of slavery" (Galatians 5:1). No matter how legalism is disguised, it is the enemy of Christ and of your self-respect and peace in Christ. Grow in Christ, and you grow in self-esteem and freedom.

The word "religion" is derived from a word that originally meant "to bind" or "to limit" and refers to ideas and beliefs that bind and control people. The New Testament idea of salvation, however, was expressed in Greek words that mean "liberation" and "freedom."

The Greek words for "save" and "savior" in the New Testament (Greek, *sozo* and *soter*) mean "to set free, liberate, rescue" or to be a "liberator" or "one who sets people free." In the time of Christ, the words were used for teachers, who liberated students from ignorance, doctors, who liberated people from sickness, or leaders, who liberated people from an enemy. The name "Jesus" is the Greek form of the Hebrew name Joshua, which means "deliverer" or "liberator." In this book, the author's translations reflect this more exact and accurate translations of the Greek words for save as "set free" or "liberate." (See Matthew 1:21; Luke 2:11; 19:10; John 4:42; 2 Peter 1:11; 1 John 4:14 and many other references in the New Testament.) See Lesson 3 in Chapter 6 for details on legalism as idolatry.

Freedom from Bible Idolatry

To make the Bible absolute is idolatry. The Bible is not the fourth member of the Trinity. It is a book. It can be translated incorrectly, distorted, twisted out of context, and made to say things that are the opposite of the original purpose of the text. Jesus has set us free from the idolatrous use of "biblical literalism" to provide religious weapons to hurt others and ourselves. (See the Special Study on "Homosexuality and the Bible" at the end of the book.)

John 1:1-14 tells of the coming of Jesus as the "Word of God" that "became human and dwelt among us." The word of God did not become words but became a human being ("flesh"). The Bible never calls itself "the word of God." The Bible calls Jesus "the word of God." Paul spoke of believers as "living epistles" (2 Corinthians 3:2-3) and saw that people who follow Jesus are "word of God" also. When we take our attention off Jesus and concentrate on the Bible as an end in itself, we ignore how Jesus used, interpreted, and corrected the scriptures. We create a new baalism, which like idolatry in the Hebrew Testament is manipulated to the advantage of the priests and to the abuse and oppression of everybody else.

Jesus did not say that all authority is given to the Bible but that all authority is given to him (Matthew 28:20). Jesus did not say to follow the Bible but "follow me." This does not mean that we abandon the Bible but that we never try to use it without the help of Jesus and the Spirit of Jesus, who has been given to us to be our teacher (John 14:26; 15:26; and 16:13-15) and who always bears witness to Jesus. Followers of Jesus are obligated to learn the content of the Gospels as their point of reference for everything else in and outside the Bible. Be free! Follow Jesus.

David and Sue

> Sue, a deacon at Golden Gate MCC in San Francisco, met David at a homeless shelter in 1992 and became his friend. She shared my brochure on "The Bible as Your Friend" with David and gave him a copy to keep. David had HIV/AIDS and was rapidly getting sicker. At midnight, David called Sue, told her that he was afraid, and asked if she would come to San Francisco General Hospital to see him. Sue found a neighbor to baby sit her young daughter and took the bus to the hospital.
>
> David was sinking fast and Sue realized that he did not have long to live. David said, "I am afraid to die. I don't know where I will go or what will happen to me." Sue reminded David of the good news of God's love in Christ that was in the brochure. David had read the brochure, but he said that he did not know how to pray. He asked Sue to help him. Sue suggested the words in the brochure, which David prayed to receive Jesus into his life. After he prayed, David leaned back on his pillow and said, "I think I have my purple angel wings now!"
>
> In a few minutes, David said, "Sue, I am tired. I want to go home. Can I go home now?" Sue said,

> "Yes, David. You can go home now." David died at 3 a.m. David was sixteen years old. Later, Sue called David's mother to tell her that David had died. Her reply was that as far as she was concerned, David died six months ago, when she learned that he was gay and had HIV/AIDS.

This book is intended to reach out to all of the Davids who have been rejected and hurt by abusive religion and ignorant parents. David probably would not read this book, but you will, and God will use you to love and help people like David.

Chapter 4

Guidelines for Small Groups

In the Gospels Jesus taught most of the time in small groups and to single individuals.

The "Jesus Group" was drawn from many ages, backgrounds, personalities, and points of view. We read that women were included in Luke 8:1-3. Variety in the group was both a source of great learning and a cause for tension that provided the setting for Jesus to teach and demonstrate love and truth.

The early church followed Jesus' same approach. Home-based spiritual growth groups do not require buildings, budgets, boards of directors, clergy, or any of the other features of traditional churches. House churches can move from place to place, as in Acts 2:46; 5:42; and Romans 16:5.

All that is required for a house church is people who will host, lead, and attend a small study group in someone's home and some study materials that are relevant, accurate, and interesting. Hopefully you will find this book helpful in your small group Bible study.

Some Basics for Successful Small Groups

Essential to healthy and healing groups is the development of an atmosphere of non-judgmental acceptance and trust within the group. Most religion tends to be judgmental and condemning of people who do not conform to the "rules." Successful spiritual support groups resist the pull of religion away from freedom.

◆ **Small group study and discussion should be simple.** Each group meeting will be different, even if the same people are present each time. No two meetings are ever exactly alike.

◆ **Make yourselves comfortable.** Everyone should be able to see everybody else. All studies of dialogue show that far more discussion takes place in a circle than when people sit in rows.

◆ **Encourage participants to talk without forcing them to speak.** People have to get into the discussion at their own pace and when they feel comfortable. People will probably remember what they said in a group even if they do not remember much else!

◆ **Actively develop an accepting atmosphere in the group.** Each person should feel safe from judgment and rejection.

◆ **The leader, teacher, or facilitator of the group sets the tone.** The leader should encourage all of the participants. Remember that "stupid questions" or "dumb comments" do not exist. There are no "stupid questions" or "dumb comments" in the group. It is the leader's responsibility to see that people in the group do not pass judgment on what others say. Allow each person to make whatever contribution they feel is appropriate. A good leader helps each member learn from the diversity of the group.

◆ **Maintain confidentiality.** In successful groups, individuals often feel free to become vulnerable and to bare their souls. Things shared in the group should never be discussed outside the group. To break confidentiality often is to repeat a remark out of context and change the meaning. It will take time for everyone to build an atmosphere of trust.

◆ **Model good listening.** God listens to us, we also show our love for others by listening to them.

◆ **Allow people to experiment with how they want to participate.** The various roles that people take in a group will shift from time to time. One person may be helpful in keeping the ball rolling one time and be a silent listener the next.

◆ **Know when to use prepared material** to keep the group moving both on a path toward recovery and growth and also in learning new and helpful information. Sometimes, however, the group may want to forget the prepared material and deal with a current issue that someone needs to bring up or the group may want to spend more than one session on a particular subject.

◆ **Each participant in the group should have a copy of the study material.**

◆ **Expect miracles**, but do not try to make them happen! God is the real leader of the group and God more than anyone else will help to keep the group on track. Needless to say, most groups will find time for group prayer sometime during the session.

◆ **Limit the study time to no more than an hour.** Usually the time limit of an hour is comfortable for most people. Everyone should be given the opportunity to leave at the end of the hour and refreshments. A lot of good discussion and sharing will take place during refreshment time. You can be flexible, but be sensitive to the needs and feelings of the people in the group.

◆ **Refreshments are not necessary, but they sure do help!** No one person should have to do refreshments every time. The group also may want to meet in various homes.

◆ **Keep it simple and flexible.** Flexibility and variety are assets. The group may want to set a limited length of time in weeks or months to meet. If interest begins to lag, do not be afraid to encourage the group to discuss what changes would help. Be willing and ready to start new groups when needed.

◆ **Remember, a group is not a church.** You do not have to have a building, budget, board of directors, clergy, ritual, or take an offering to be a recovery and spiritual support group!

◆ **The main ingredients** of successful, small study groups are the presence of Jesus, the guidance of the Holy Spirit, people who seek recovery and growth, people to host and lead, and good study material.

Do not be afraid to try new ways of doing things. Experiment. The Holy Spirit is with you to guide you as you go. Be free! Let go and move out into new territory. "Where the Spirit of Christ is, there is freedom!" (2 Corinthians 3:17).

When you discover a better or more helpful way of doing things in your group, write it down and send it to me in care of Chi Rho Press so that it can be passed on to others who are engaged in the same spiritual healing and growth ministry that you are!

A bewildering array of books on small groups has emerged in recent years. The best is still *The Miracle of Dialogue*: Seabury Press, 1963, by Ruel Howe.

Also see lesson 40 on "Group Dynamics According to Jesus" starting on page 338 in this book.

Flowers Are Red

(A Parable in Song from "Living Room Suite," words and music by Harry Chapin, © 1978 Chapin Music, used by permission.)

I played Harry Chapin's record of this song at the beginning of my Bible survey college courses. I think it speaks for itself. Play it for your group.

The little boy went first day of school
He got some crayons and started to draw
He put colors all over the paper
For colors was what he saw
And the teacher said... What you doin' young man
I'm paintin' flowers he said
She said... It's not the time for art young man
And anyway flowers are green and red
There's a time for everything young man
And a way it should be done
You've got to show concern for everyone else
For you're not the only one
And she said...
Flowers are red young man
Green leaves are green
There's no need to see flowers any other way
Than the way they always have been seen
But the little boy said...
There are so many colors in the rainbow
So many colors in the mornin' sun
So many colors in a flower and I see every one
Well the teacher said... You're sassy
There's ways that things should be
And you'll paint flowers the way they are
So repeat after me.....

And she said...
Flowers are red young man
Green leaves are green
There’s no need to see flowers any other way
Than the way they always have been seen
But the little boy said...
There are so many colors in the rainbow
So many colors in the morning sun
So many colors in a flower
And I see every one
The teacher put him in a corner
She said... It’s for your own good
And you won’t come out ’til you get it right
And all responding like you should
Well finally he got lonely
Frightened thoughts filled his head
And he went up to the teacher
And this is what he said... and he said
Flowers are red, green leaves are green
There’s no need to see flowers any other way
Than the way they always have been seen
Time went by like it always does
And they moved to another town
And the little boy went to another school
And this what he found
The teacher there was smilin’
She said... Painting should be fun
And there are so many colors in a flower
So let’s use every one
But the little boy painted flowers
In neat rows of green and red
And when the teacher asked him why
This is what he said... and he said
Flowers are red, green leaves are green
There's no need to see flowers any other way
Than the way they always have been seen.

Chapter 5

How to Use this Book

Much of this book is self-explanatory. The 52 lessons of Bible-based studies give spiritual growth and related information on spiritual and religious issues confronting gay, lesbian, bisexual, and transgendered people and all others who have been abused and oppressed by religion. This book is intended to provide a one year weekly cycle of studies for individuals and groups. The chapters and lessons are organized in units that speak directly to each of the thirteen Steps to Recovery. Special Studies are added at the end of the book to provide more detailed information dealing with issues that relate to all of the lessons.

Fear of religion and the Bible often develops among people who have been abused and oppressed by religion. Women, gay people, divorced people, racially mixed couples, people of color, children, and many others frequently have been singled out for attack by various judgmental, legalistic, religious leaders and churches.

Jesus came to liberate people from sick and abusive religion.

The studies in this book deal with the Bible and sexual orientation, God's inclusive love and acceptance of all people, how Jesus confronted religious abuse and other problems that we face today, and how we can help ourselves and each other to recover, grow, learn, and heal.

Steps to Recovery from Bible Abuse is designed for use in individual, couple, or small group study for building self-esteem and encouraging spiritual freedom and maturity. Recovering, learning, healing, and growth take time. Give yourself the time to study and share with others so that you can "always be prepared to explain to anyone who asks you to give a reason for the hope that is in you, yet with gentleness and respect" (1Peter 3:15).

You can read this book all the way through as you would any other to get an overview of the material. You can also use it as a workshop resource for discovery and growth over a period of time in disciplined study and sharing with others.

Home-based spiritual growth groups do not require buildings, budgets, boards of directors, clergy, liturgy, denominations, or any of the usual features of traditional churches. All that is required is people who will host, lead, and attend a small study group in someone's home and good study materials that are relevant, accurate, and interesting. The house church can meet from place to place, as in Acts 2:46; Acts 5:42; and Romans 16:5. Serving refreshments is optional. The home-centered ministries of Jesus and the early Christians are clearly the basic pattern of the beginnings of spiritual freedom in the New Testament. A vital feature of that freedom was liberation from oppressive and abusive religion.

This book is an invitation to return to the simple informal person-centered meetings and methods of Jesus and the first disciples. Effective small study group meetings in homes do not require that the leaders be experts. You can lead a group by reading and using the material in this book. Study the material in Chapter 4, "Guidelines for Small Groups." Here are seven simple suggestions for small group success.

1. **Prepare ahead of time for group meetings.** Prepare the meeting room by arranging comfortable seats in a circle so that each person can easily see and speak to everyone in the group. Each person in the group should have a copy of the book and read the lesson before the meeting.

2. **Prepare a simple lesson plan.** One or more members of the group can explore the suggested readings and Bible passages and prepare a brief report to share with the group.

3. **Questions** raised throughout and at the end of the lessons are intended to stimulate thought and discussion. Feel free to use them or raise other questions that are more relevant to your group. Disagree but do not argue.

4. **Think for yourself.** The lessons intentionally are thought provoking and encourage a free and open exchange of ideas.

5. **Listen and share.** Learn from yourself and from others.

6. **Be flexible.** Groups are dynamic and change constantly. Use more than one meeting for a lesson if needed.

7. **Be considerate of every person.** Avoid "cross talk," which happens when two group members begin to talk with each other instead of with the group. Since people usually share a lot of personal experiences in small group meetings, group members should respect the confidentiality of what is shared in the group and do not talk about each other to people not in the group.

Changing the way we see things that traditional religion has conditioned us to view in self-destructive and distorted ways takes time, knowledge, and thought. This is why these studies are given in a format that will encourage study, reflection, discussion with others, and further research in books, articles, and helpful Web sites on the Internet.

Related Resources

I published my Web site on *Steps to Recovery from Bible Abuse* on the Internet at http://www.truluck.com September 14, 1997. It has received over two million hits in the first two years. My Web site is a helpful resource to use in connection with this book, especially for updates that are frequently added and for up-to-date bibliography of books, articles, organizations, and links to other Web sites. If you want to receive regular updates related to the Web site, you can look at the site, send e-mail to me, and request to be on my mailing list.

Another new resource that continues the purpose of this book is my *Gay Sunday School Lessons* project that will be published by Chi Rho Press. These regular weekly lessons are calculated to deal with current issues of concern to GLBT people. They are published in the format of 13 lessons for a quarter (or three months) so that they follow the pattern already established by many churches. Regular publication every three months will make it possible for the *Gay Sunday School Lessons* to deal with developing events and news that affect our community. Contact Chi Rho Press for information about the *Gay Sunday School Lessons* project.

An Annotated Bibliography is included at the end of this book, but so many new resources are appearing on a regular basis that the only way to keep you informed of new books, articles, and other sources for information is through the material in my Web site. The Web site is available to you if you are on the Internet.

Use Your Bible

One of your most valuable resources to use with this book is your Bible. See my material on the Bible in the special study on Homosexuality and the Bible at the end of the book for information on how the author views the Bible and which Bible to use. The version that I use and recommend is the *New American Standard Bible* in a wide margin large print edition. Before you begin the book or your group meetings, find time to be alone and read through the Gospel of Mark all at one time. You will notice things about Jesus that you never saw before. Do this little exercise whenever you feel that you are losing a clear sense of direction in your study. Let the experiences and teachings of Jesus keep you on track.

Thirteen Steps To Recovery

1. Admit You Have Been Hurt by Religion
2. Turn to God for Help
3. Examine Your Faith
4. Face and Deal with Your Anger
5. Avoid Negative People and Churches
6. Confront The Scripture Used Against You
7. Find Positive Supportive Scripture
8. Read and Study the Gospels
9. Come Out and Accept Yourself
10. Develop Your Support System
11. Learn to Share Your Faith
12. Become a Freedom Missionary
13. Give Yourself Time to Heal and Recover.

Jesus Worked the Steps

"Steps to recovery" began with Alcoholics Anonymous (AA) as described in the *Big Book,* first published in 1939 and frequently revised and brought up-to-date in later editions. "Bill's Story" tells how the twelve steps to recovery began with a friend's suggestion, "Why don't you choose your own conception of God?" That was the idea that led Bill to take the first step of "being willing to believe in a Power greater than myself." This is also my suggestion to you in the First and Second Steps in beginning your own program of recovery from sick and abusive religion.

Many positive and healthy uses of steps to recovery have developed in support groups for codependents anonymous, narcotics addicts anonymous, sex addicts anonymous, and others. My friend Terrie Chan helped me to see the value of steps to recovery in helping people like myself who are codependent. Books by Melody Beattie (see Bibliography) have been very helpful to me personally both to understand the dynamics of codependency and to see the close connection between religious addiction and codependency.

Part II

Jesus and Spiritual Freedom

Jesus came to set people free. The Greek word translated "save" literally means "to set free" or "liberate." The name Jesus is the Greek form of the name Joshua in the Hebrew Testament. The names mean "deliverer" or "liberator" and are a reference to leadership that sets people free or saves them from an enemy. In the author's translations of Bible passages, the word used for "save" is usually rendered as "set free" or "liberate." "Set free" is more accurate than "save" and speaks more directly and clearly to people who have been oppressed and wounded by demanding, legalistic religion.

Jesus said, "You will know the truth and the truth will set you free," and added, "I am the truth." Read and meditate upon chapters 8 through 14 of the Gospel of John as a prelude to this entire book.

I have already suggested that you will profit from reading the Gospel of Mark all the way through at one time. You can do the same thing with Matthew, Luke, and John. You will find encouragement and spiritual growth by reading some every day in Luke and John, perhaps a chapter each day in each until you finish, and then start over. One reason for emphasis on Luke and John is that they are the most clear and detailed in telling of the inclusive ministry of Jesus. All four Gospels, however, emphasize the liberating work of Jesus in setting people free from abusive, sick religion.

Read Matthew 23 to see just how sick religion was in the time of Jesus. The word "gospel" means "good news." Freedom from abusive and oppressive religion is indeed good news.

Chapter 6

The First Step

Admit You Have Been Hurt by Religion

† **Preparatory Bible Reading**: Read Matthew 23:1-15, 24-28, and 33 to see how Jesus viewed religious abuse.

> Jesus came to set people free
> from sick and abusive religion.

For many people, this step is the hardest one. Religious abuse begins early in life and often is caused by parents, pastors, and teachers. We accept abuse as acceptable or deserved. Abuse is not acceptable and is not deserved. Many people see rejecting their childhood religion as being like rejecting their own grandmother. Our deep emotional ties with our childhood make it very difficult for us to be objective about the way in which religion was used to control and sometimes abuse us.

> Abuse is the use of power by the
> strong to control and oppress the weak.

What ***is*** sick and abusive religion? Sick and abusive religion is the judgmental legalism that Jesus came to destroy and to replace with himself. People can become addicted to abusive religion.

Have you ever been abused by religion? What is your earliest memory of religious ideas or religious experience? How would you describe the religion of your parents when you were a child? Can you recall any particular time when religion was used to punish or control you? How has religion affected your self-esteem? Answering some of these questions may be disturbing to you but may also help you to gain insight into why it is so difficult for you to face the damage that abusive religion has done to you.

Discussing and sharing these questions with others like yourself in a small group can be an enlightening and learning time of growth for you. You will discover how others have gone through many of the same problems and hurts regarding religion just as you have.

Jesus said, "All who came before me are thieves and robbers; but the sheep did not hear them. The thief comes only to steal and kill and destroy. I came that you might have life and have life abundantly" (John 10:10). "Thieves and robbers" are words that Jesus used for abusive religious leaders.

Additional Resources

Wayne E. Oates, *When Religion Gets Sick*: The Westminster Press, 1970 and reissued again in 1999.

David Johnson and Jeff Van Vonderen, *The Subtle Power of Spiritual Abuse*: Bethany House, 1991.

Lesson 1

Jesus Came to Replace Sick Religion

† Preparatory Bible Reading: Mark 3:1-6

We have no shortage of religion in America today. When I lived in Nashville, I could find religious preachers, music, and programming on several television channels 24 hours a day. Jesus was also born into an intensely religious culture. The Temple dominated the city of Jerusalem. The towns and villages were filled with synagogues, religious teachers, legal fanatics, and multitudes of people who were called sinners and unclean because they did not keep the religious laws, especially the Sabbath laws.

Jesus came to replace sick religion with something better: himself. Jesus came to show that people were more important than religion. He intentionally broke Sabbath laws to defy the bondage and abuse that the people suffered because of sick religion. Jesus broke the chains of legalistic, judgmental religion that oppressed the people and gave the religious authorities their power. Jesus challenged the religious system and said, "Follow me."

What passages in the Gospels do you think most clearly illustrate the attitude of Jesus toward abusive and oppressive religion? What passages demonstrate the way Jesus challenged the abusive use of Scripture to hurt people?

Look in Mark 3 and Matthew 23. When Jesus said, "Follow me," he was offering a way to escape from destructive religion. Read Luke 15 for how Jesus responded to religious leaders who wanted to define the people of God on the basis of who is left out.

How do you think that religion today has betrayed the liberating and inclusive life and message of Jesus? In what way have you personally experienced the destructive power of sick religion?

Jesus came "not to oppress the world but that the world through Jesus might be set free" (John 3:17). The words of Jesus and the words about Jesus in the Gospels were always life giving and healthy. Regarding some of the most difficult words of Jesus, he said, "The Spirit gives life; the flesh profits nothing; the words that I have spoken to you are spirit and are life" (John 6:52-63).

Healthy and Healing Words

The Pastoral Epistles spoke of "sound doctrine," which in Greek means "healthy teachings." See 1 Timothy 1:10; 4:6; 6:3; 2 Timothy 1:13; 4:3; Titus 1:9, 13; 2:1-2, 8. The word "sound" is Greek *hugiaivo*, meaning "to be in good health, healthy." Only Luke, a physician and companion of Paul who also probably helped Paul write the pastoral letters ("only Luke is with me," 2 Timothy 4:11), used the word elsewhere, Luke 5:32 and 7:10. The prodigal son was received back "healthy" (Luke 15:27). Religion can be sick, abusive, and unhealthy, but it does not need to be. This entire book focuses on the healthy and holistic ministry of Jesus as the cure for sick religion.

Deadly Words

Some of the most damaging and oppressive uses of religion that I have seen have been based on the legalistic and judgmental demand for "sound doctrine." When I resigned from Baptist College and moved to Atlanta, one of the church leaders where I had been pastor wrote to say that he and his family were praying that God would either change me (from being gay) or kill me! That prayer has not yet been answered with either of these choices. Their preachers have convinced many parents of gay and lesbian children that "sound doctrine" demands that they should reject their own children as better off dead than gay.

Children who are treated as "better off dead than homosexual" will all too frequently try to kill themselves or engage in self-hatred and self-destructive actions. The leading cause of death for gay teens is suicide. Sick religion has to take a lot of the blame for this tragic side of homophobia and gay bashing.

Do you know any gay people who have tried or succeeded in killing themselves? Read again the true story of the young man in "Jesus Heals Sick Religion" in Chapter 3. Do you identify with him in some of his frustration and pain? Have you found the kind of help and encouragement that he found?

Wonderful Words of Life

If you have accepted yourself as a child of God and know that God accepts and loves you just as you are, write out your experience and share it with at least one other person. If you feel comfortable doing it and you are part of a small Bible study group, tell the group about your struggles and experience of self-acceptance and inner peace with God. Sharing your experience can also encourage and help others more than you realize. It will also encourage and help you to build up your own self-esteem and confidence.

You are the world's authority on your own experience with God. If you are in doubt about what to speak or write about, think about Jesus and how Jesus has helped you. Jesus said, "It is not you who speak but the Spirit of God who speaks through you" (Matthew 10:20). You have spiritual help in thinking through and talking about your own experiences with God.

Miracles Happen

Adam DeBaugh, publisher of this book, told me of one such miracle. He was at Metropolitan Community Church (MCC) of Washington, DC one Sunday and noticed a man crying during the service. Afterwards, Adam talked with him and invited the man to lunch with him and his friends. The man expressed great need for spiritual help, and Adam went through the brochure, "The Bible as Your Friend," with him and he prayed the prayer in the brochure and invited Jesus into his life. He asked Adam for another copy of the brochure to give to his partner, John.

Several days later, John called the Rev. Larry Uhrig of MCC DC, and asked for an appointment to talk. John said that he had read the brochure his partner had give to him and was curious about it. Larry invited him to come to the church office, and they talked. John told Larry, "I want you to know right off that I am a Druid!" Larry said, "That's fine. I am a Christian." John replied, "But I really AM a Druid!" Larry said, "And I really AM a Christian!" John said, "But you don't understand. I believe that I can see God in the flowers, trees, and all of nature." Larry replied, "Well, so do I! Let's talk."

They had a thorough discussion of the brochure about Jesus and God's love. John decided to invite Jesus into his life and became active in the church.

Larry's approach included humor, taking the other person seriously, entering into his frame of reference, and listening without being judgmental. All of these things were natural to Larry. The Spirit of Jesus creates accepting and sincere attitudes in our hearts so that we say and do the appropriate things with each person to whom we tell our story.

Questions for Study and Discussion

1. What is your definition of sick religion? What forms of sick religion have you personally experienced? How do you think that Jesus would define sick religion?

2. How would you define healthy teaching? Can you think of anyone in your own life who has helped you to develop a healthy and positive spiritual life?

Additional Resources

Read all of Matthew 10:16-22.

A helpful book that gives an overview of many of the issues we face is Letha Scanzoni and Virginia Mollenkott, *Is the Homosexual My Neighbor?* (Revised and Updated): Harper San Francisco, 1994.

Bruce Bawer, *Stealing Jesus: How Fundamentalism Betrays Christianity*: Crown Publishing, 1997.

Lesson 2

Jesus Faced Religious Bigots

† **Preparatory Bible Reading:** Matthew 21:45-46; 22:15-22; 23:6-12, 27-33

Jesus was not killed by rowdy street gangs, pickpockets, prostitutes, hustlers, or crazy people. These all loved him. Jesus was tortured, mocked, and murdered by the most religious people in the world. Religious leaders killed Jesus to get rid of him as a threat to their power, wealth, and spiritual authority over the people. They were right to be afraid of Jesus, for Jesus came to destroy their sick oppressive religion. Jesus won. The resurrection of Jesus was the victory of Jesus over abusive religion.

Much of the life of Jesus in the Gospels is set in the midst of conflict between Jesus and religious bigots. Jesus faced most of the issues that you face today and demonstrated how to handle them. Many of these studies are based on the experiences of Jesus that show us how to handle the pressures and problems that we face today.

Destructive and abusive use of legalistic and judgmental religion to control weak and ignorant people has been a feature of every culture throughout the history of the human race. Jesus came to say, "Stop!" Jesus showed that you do not need over 600 laws to know the will of God. Jesus gave his followers only one commandment. "I give you a new commandment that you love one another just as I have loved you" (John 13:34).

Karl Marx called religion "the opiate of the people." He was too kind. Religion can be far more destructive than a sedative. Jesus called the most religious people he met "a den of snakes in danger of the pain of hell" (Matthew 23:33). This was an intense, scathing rebuke from the one whose spirit was gentle and kind. Jesus was acutely aware of the power of religion to confuse and destroy people. Whenever churches and leaders stray away from the clear and simple example of Jesus, abusive, destructive religion develops. Jesus predicted, "The time is coming for everyone who kills you to think that he is offering service to God. These things they will do, because they have not known God or me" (John 16:2-3).

Sick Religion Separates People

Jesus came to bring people together. As one woman said in the midst of a church fight, "Religion is meant to bring people together, not wedge 'em apart!" The history of the churches is the history of divisions and separations. I was surprised when I first learned that there were over 30 different denominations of Baptists. Now there are a lot more. Jesus predicted that the Temple would be destroyed because it was a symbol of separation of people from each other and from God. After Jesus cleansed the Temple, he began to teach and say, "It is written, 'My house shall be called a house of prayer for all the nations.' But you have made it a den of robbers." And the chief priests and scribes heard Jesus and began to seek how to destroy him; for they were afraid of him, for all the multitude was astonished at his teaching (Mark 11:17-18). The word "nations" (the Greek word *ethnos*) used in Mark 11:17 in a quote from Isaiah 56:7 is the word for "Gentiles" used throughout the New Testament.

Religion versus Spirituality

Jesus recognized the great difference between spirituality and religion. Most of the teachings of Jesus in the Sermon on the Mount (Matthew 5, 6, and 7) focus on this difference. For perhaps the most vivid teaching of Jesus about the contrast between religion and spirituality, see the story of two men who went to pray in Luke 18:9-14.

The only people that Jesus condemned and rejected were those who rejected and condemned other people who were different from themselves and who were viewed as inferior and worthless to them and to their god. Jesus never rebuked suffering people and never tried to lay blame on wounded people for their wounds.

A Definition of Bigot

The term "bigot" seems rather mild in view of the human suffering that bigots have caused. The dictionary defines a bigot as "hypocrite" and "one obstinately or intolerantly devoted to his/her own church, party, belief, or opinion." It is interesting that the next word in the dictionary after bigot is "big shot!" Jesus used strong language for bigots. He called them religious snakes on the way to hell.

Acceptance versus Rejection

Jesus faced a highly developed religious system of rejection and separation. Hundreds of laws and traditions were used to keep people in religious categories of "clean" and "unclean." The most easily enforced laws were those that were superficial and clearly visible, such as working on the Sabbath or eating the wrong food with the wrong people. Jesus repeatedly attempted to bring people out of obsession with religious trivia and lead them to freedom and spiritual joy by experiencing God's love and learning to love one another. Jesus accepted people that others had rejected. Jesus was crucified because he loved the wrong people. Jesus came to convert religion into love. Has your religion been transformed into love?

Where did some evangelists get the idea that their calling is to make people feel as rotten as possible about themselves and to see themselves as dirty, worthless spiritual scum so that they will turn to God? No basis for this exists in the Gospels. The old "sinners in the hands of an angry God" routine set America up for a distorted view of God and the gospel that has not diminished in the over 200 years since The Great Awakening, which was actually in many ways The Great Distortion.

Genesis 1:26-31 declared that God made people in God's own image and concluded that all that God had made was "very good." "You formed my inward parts; You did weave me in my mother's womb. I will give thanks for You, for I am honorably and wonderfully made! Wonderful are Your works, and my soul knows it full well" (Psalm 139:13-14).

Jesus echoed God's love and acceptance of all of God's children in his approach to the most rejected and despised people of his time. Jesus said that you are of more value to God than you realize. God gives love, acceptance, freedom, life, hope, peace, joy, and self-esteem to you because you are already valuable and wonderful in the sight of your Creator and not because you are a worthless worm. Religious abuse in the name of God denies God and dishonors Jesus. We have no choice but to challenge ignorant, homophobic distortions of the Bible and of the teachings and life of Jesus.

Changing the course of human history in the direction of respect for every individual as of equal value and to liberate people to be themselves without fear or shame will require changing the course of religion. To Jesus, all people have equal value. To religious bigots, people are all unequal and rejected on the basis of how they know and keep or disobey the laws and rules of the prevailing religious system.

You begin to make a difference in changing the world when you admit that you have been hurt by religion and set about to do something about it.

Questions for Study and Discussion

1. What form of protest against abusive and oppressive religion seems appropriate for you personally? How do you think Jesus would handle homophobic, legalistic religious leaders today?

2. Are you satisfied to go on searching for truth in traditional religious forms, teachings, and churches? What alternatives to traditional forms and programs do you think would be better for you?

3. Explain how sick and oppressive religion has hurt you. Have you ever used religion to hurt yourself or others?

Additional Resources

Many books have explored the problem of legalistic, judgmental religion being used to replace Jesus and the "good news" of the gospel.

John Shelby Spong, *Why Christianity Must Change or Die*: Harper, 1998. This is probably Spong's best book so far.

See also two great classics, Dietrich Bonhoeffer, *Letters and Papers from Prison*, and Soren Kierkegaard, *Attack Upon Christendom.*

Lesson 3

Escape from Idolatry

† **Preparatory Bible Reading:** Matthew 23:1-39

> I am the Sovereign your God, who brought you out of the land of Egypt, out of the house of slavery. You shall have no other God besides me.
>
> Deuteronomy 5:6-7

The Bible's main teaching is the sovereignty of God. "Hear, O Israel! The Sovereign is our God. The Sovereign is one!" (Deuteronomy 6:4). This verse, called the *Shema* (Hebrew for "hear" or "listen") is so important to the faith that it was contained in phylacteries, the little leather pouches worn by devout Jews during the time of Jesus. See also Deuteronomy 4:35 and Isaiah 44:6, which express the same ideas.

"I am the Sovereign your God" is the first commandment in the Hebrew list of the Ten Commandments. The second commandment is, "You shall have no other God besides me." "I AM" in Deuteronomy 5:6 is the Hebrew verb that is rendered as "Yahweh" (God) in the Hebrew Bible. See Exodus 3 for the story of how the name was first given. Jesus used "I am" as a reference to himself throughout the Gospel of John.

Idolatry was the problem most often addressed by the Hebrew prophets. Adultery and idolatry were often linked together. The prevailing Canaanite religions were expressed in sex acts with animals, men, and women at the "high places" devoted to sympathetic magic to influence the local gods, called "*baal*," who were believed to be rulers or lords of the flocks and the fields. The Book of Hosea links idolatry to adultery.

The prohibitions against "a man lying with a man as with a woman" (Leviticus 18:22 and 20:13) are references to fertility rituals that have nothing to do with sexual orientation or the private sex practices of two people of the same sex who love each other. This issue is treated more fully in Lesson 22 and in the Special Study on "Homosexuality and the Bible" at the end of the book.

Only God is Absolute

The religion of Israel was based on belief in a God who is above nature, whose will is supreme and not subject to compulsion and fate. The God of Israel could not be manipulated by magic, ritual, or nature. The Sovereignty of God was demonstrated in the Bible through a consistent emphasis on God's initiative in Creation, the call of Abraham, the Exodus, the choice of a king, the birth of Jesus, the resurrection, the sending of the Holy Spirit, and the end of the world. All of the major events in the Bible were seen as taking place at God's initiative and under God's control. God is God and there is no other. Idolatry is making anything absolute other than God.

What we face today in legalistic, judgmental fundamentalism and other abusive forms of church is parallel to the use of magic and ritual to try to manipulate God in Canaanite fertility worship of *baal*. Keep the rules and follow the correct rituals, and God is thereby obligated to give you what you want. Jesus challenged this entire point of view by showing and teaching that God already loves and accepts all people.

Many Idolatries Surround Us

Paul Tillich observed that God is "the ground of all being" and "ultimate reality" or else God is not truly God. (See Paul Tillich in the Bibliography.) Jesus came to challenge the idolatries of his time, and we are called to challenge the idolatries of today. The leading idolatry that Jesus faced was the dominant, entrenched, abusive, oppressive, judgmental, legalistic religion of his own people. How Jesus handled this problem tells us what we need to know to overcome the most powerful force being used today against gay, lesbian, bisexual, and transgendered people and all others who have been wounded and defeated by religion today.

This lesson is basic to your becoming equipped to overcome self-hate and self-rejection and to experience recovery from Bible abuse and oppressive religion. Religious leaders in many different traditions are trying to use politics and law to enforce their individual views of religion upon the entire nation. The religion that is most advocated by these people is judgmental legalism. The religion of judgmental legalism is based firmly in the selective use of biblical literalism. Biblical literalism is the use of the Bible to teach absolute rules and demands without regard for the history of the Bible, problems of translation, radical differences in the culture of Bible times and our culture today. Biblical literalism abandons common sense and objectivity and refuses to ask questions that challenge the views of the dominant religion in the community. Biblical literalism is based on and feeds upon ignorance.

For every hour and page that gay, lesbian, bisexual, and transgendered Christian activists have to tell our story on television, radio, newspapers, and magazines, the legalists have thousands of hours and millions of pages. We have watched while an army of religious terrorists have attacked and attempted to hold hostage the sexuality and human rights of multitudes of people because of their sexual orientation. Join me as we take a fresh look at how Jesus handled judgmental legalism.

Why Legalism Kills

Review what was said about "Legalism as Idolatry" in "Jesus Heals Sick Religion" at the beginning of the book. Here, the details will be spelled out. Legalism in Biblical times and now has these characteristics.

➢ **Legalism is Self-Centered.** Jesus described the legalist at prayer when he spoke of those "who trusted in themselves that they were righteous and viewed others with contempt. The Pharisee stood and was praying thus to himself, 'I thank Thee that

I am not like other people, swindlers, unjust, adulterers, or even like this tax collector. I fast twice a week; I pay tithes of all that I get'" (Luke 18:9-11). Jesus commented that the Pharisee had no contact with God in prayer because "he exalted himself."

Paul dealt with the same issue in Ephesians 2:8-9, "By grace you have been liberated ("saved") through faith; and that not of yourselves, it is the gift of God; not as a result of works, that no one should boast." Jesus said that we are to forsake everything and follow him, and he meant for us to let go of self-righteous legalism. When you follow Jesus, you do not say, "Look what I have done." You say, "Look what God has done for me." See also Philippians 3:9 and Romans 8:3.

➢ **Legalism Focuses on Externals and is Preoccupied with Trivia.** Jesus pointed out the desire of legalists for the public display of religious ornaments, the use of titles of honor, carefully cleaning the outside of the cup, and tithing the tiniest of herbs while they neglected justice, mercy, and fairness (Matthew 23:5-6, 24-25). Jesus concluded, "You outwardly appear righteous to other people, but inwardly you are full of hypocrisy and lawlessness."

Paul warns us against passing judgment on others for trivial and external expressions of religion, such as observing certain days and eating or not eating certain foods (Romans 14). In all of his letters, Paul fought an endless battle against superficial, legalistic, judgmental religion. We have to fight the same battle. My church experiences over many years showed me that people who tried to remove the pastor were consistently committed to a rigid formula of right and wrong. Often the most vicious opponents of the pastor and other leaders were meticulous tithers and regular attendees who complained about the people who did not do as much as they did for the church. Look at Romans 2:1-29; 2 Corinthians 4:7-18; Colossians 2:20-23.

➢ **Legalism Makes Things Other than God Absolute.** Read Mark 7:5-9 to see how Jesus responded to the religious teachers who criticized him for letting his disciples eat without first observing the ritual washing that the law required. Jesus said,

"You neglect the commandment of God and hold to human tradition instead" (Mark 7:8). Romans 10:1-17 shows how Paul dealt with legalism that made something other than God absolute, "For Christ is the end [Greek *telos*, "goal" or "completion"] of law for righteousness to everyone who believes" (Romans 10:4).

➢ **Legalism Obscures a Clear View of God.** Jesus said in Matthew 23:13-15 that the legalism of the Scribes and Pharisees prevented many people from being able to see and experience God for themselves. Paul in Romans 11:5-10 and throughout Romans 9 to 11 demonstrated how legalism keeps people from seeing the truth of God's grace and love for all people. Jesus faced that same problem that I faced when I taught Bible at college. The students had already made up their minds what the Bible said and meant. Students had to do a lot of unlearning to clear the way for honest, open, and objective study.

One of the greatest challenges faced by gay and lesbian Christians is to find effective ways to "speak the truth in love" about the deadly power of false religion based on judgmental legalism and to teach clearly the truth of God's love and acceptance for all people. The living presence of Jesus pushes out false legalism by replacing it with God's unconditional and all-inclusive love.

➢ **Legalism is Insensitive to Human Need.** Jesus frequently was condemned because he broke the traditional Sabbath laws by healing the sick and carrying out his ministry of compassion to outcasts and to the unclean. See Mark 3:1-6 and Luke 10:25-27. Galatians 6 is a helpful passage to see how Paul called on followers of Jesus to be responsive to human need because we are "a new creation" and not because of the demands of the law. Remember that to Jesus, people always were more important than religion. Jesus never said, "Sell what you have and give it to the church or to the building fund!"

➢ **Legalism Ignores Individuality.** In Matthew 23:1-4, Jesus showed how legalism ignores the individual differences in people and makes unrealistic demands that the legalists themselves cannot obey. In Matthew 11:28-30, Jesus said that he himself is the true meaning of the Sabbath ("rest"). "Come unto me all of you who are weary ["worked to exhaustion," perhaps in trying to know and keep all of the religious rules] and heavy laden [the same as religious "burdens" laid on people in Matthew 23:4], and I will give you rest" (Matthew 11:28). The word "Sabbath" means "rest." Jesus came to destroy sick religion and replace it with himself. Explore Paul's ideas on this in Romans 12:1-21 and 15:1-7.

God created you as an individual. Each person has equal value before God. There is nobody else exactly like you in the whole world. You are an individual with many features and abilities that God has given to you. In Jesus, you are invited to celebrate who you are and to follow the guidance and strength of the Spirit of Jesus to reach your fullest potential as a healthy mature person. Read Ephesians 4 for Paul's celebration of our unity in diversity in Christ.

➢ **Legalism Develops into a Religion of Experts.** Read Matthew 15:1-20 to see how Jesus repudiated the false power of the religious experts who confronted him. Jesus promised the gift of the Holy Spirit to be our teacher and to guide us into all truth (John 14:26 and 16:13-15). Learn to think for yourself. Nobody has the right to control your mind. Paul, who before his conversion was a legalistic religious expert, gave up all power and authority except Jesus. Read carefully Paul's description of his own escape from the idolatry of legalism in Philippians 3:4-14.

How has so much of the religion that claims to be Christian reverted into a destructive and deadly legalism that denies the very essence of the Gospel? Take the time to read Paul's words on this issue in 1 Corinthians 1:23-31; 2:1-16 and in all of the Book of Galatians, especially chapters 3 and 4. To Paul, following Jesus was to be "crucified with Christ; and it is no longer I who live, Christ lives in me" (Galatians 2:20).

In the time of Jesus, the average person could not read and did not know the great mass of religious legal details that the teachers had developed and demanded. The common people, who did not understand or try to keep all of the details of the law, were called sinners, not because they were evil people, but because they were not experts on the law like the Pharisees, Scribes, and Rabbis.

➢ **Legalism Condemns and Divides People.** Jesus in the model prayer in Matthew 6:5-15; 7:1-5 and in Luke 20:1-47 cried out against judgmental religion. Judgmental legalism always creates divisions between people. Read Paul's analysis of judgmental religion in Romans 14:1-23 and his clear conclusions in Romans 15:1-7. Jesus did not see his mission as judging people (John 3:17) and neither should we. Only God knows all of the facts and only God can see through eyes that are not distorted by sin. Only God is equipped to judge. We are not.

➢ **Legalism Always Needs More Interpretation.** See Matthew 23:16-23 where Jesus pointed out how laws always required increasingly complicated interpretations and creative applications. When legalism is in control, there is no end to the explanations, exceptions, and excuses that are used to get around the law or to apply it in ways that actually deny the original intention of the law. The Scribes and Pharisees devoted their full time to endless additions and applications of the over 600 laws that were found in the Hebrew Bible.

➢ **Legalism Denies Your Freedom in Christ.** "For freedom Christ set us free; stand firm so that you do not become oppressed again by a religious yoke of slavery" (Galatians 5:1). Yoke was a term used for the Law; therefore my translation of this verse makes the meaning clear by adding "religious." Read all of Galatians 5 and notice that Paul considered works of Law to be "works of the flesh" and in stark contrast to what Jesus has given in the "fruit of the Spirit, which is love, joy, peace, patience, kindness, goodness, faithfulness, gentleness, self-control. There is no law against these things" (Galatians 5:22-23). The presence of Jesus in your life produces the nine fruits of the Spirit, which are descriptions of the character of Jesus. Learn this list of nine results of the presence of the Spirit of Jesus. They all are gifts of God that cannot be earned or learned.

Your freedom in Christ is a gift from God. When Jesus told the disciples that he was giving to them a new commandment to love one another as he loved them (John 13:34), he knew that he was commanding the impossible. The only way that any person can love as Jesus loved is to have the Spirit of Jesus within. "The love of God has been poured out within our hearts by the Holy Spirit who was given to us" (Romans 5:5). The first evidence of the presence of Jesus is love. "By this all people will know you are my disciples, if you love one another" (John 13:35).

When we turn away from love and the presence of Jesus through the Holy Spirit and retreat back into judgmental legalism, we deny the truth of the Gospel and abandon our only hope for the freedom and joy that Jesus promised. Why would anyone abandon the good news of freedom in Christ for a prison of legalistic oppression and misery?

Why Is Legalism So Attractive?

Legalism offers a secure religious system without the risk of faith. Legalism appeals to our laziness. We often are willing to let others decide for us rather than having to work out our spiritual life for ourselves. Legalism allows us to keep self at the center of life. Legalism appeals to our pride in comparing our imagined correctness and goodness to the trashy and tasteless lives of others, who are beneath us and obviously inferior! Basically, the attraction of legalism is its offer of a tight system that does not demand that you think for yourself and that offers a way to serve God and still keep God at a safe distance from really interfering with your life.

Questions for Study and Discussion

This lesson is twice as long as most and probably should be covered in at least two group meetings. Stay with the material in this lesson until it is clear to you. In view of the kind of judgmental legalism that most often is used to attack and destroy people because of their sexual orientation, your mastery of this lesson is necessary preparation for your successful recovery from Bible and religious abuse.

Read and study all of the Bible references in this lesson so that you can be informed about the destructive power of legalism. Remember that homophobia is largely a product of legalism.

1. What has helped you to escape from judgmental, legalistic religion and to experience your freedom in Christ?

2. What do you still need to do to become free and help others to become free from the deadly grip of legalism?

Lesson 4

Keep Your Eyes on the Prize

† **Preparatory Bible Reading:** the Book of Philippians

> Forgetting what is behind and reaching forward to the future, I press on toward the goal for the prize of the upward call of God in Christ Jesus.
>
> Philippians 3:13-14

Children who have been abused by their parents often deny the abuse to such an extent that they cannot remember it when they become adults. Women who have been abused by their husbands often try to keep the abuse secret and firmly deny that it ever happened. Religious abuse by parents, teachers, and pastors is often very hard to admit, especially when it is indirect and subtle. Jim, a gay man, told me that his father often hugged his two brothers but never hugged him. When he was an adult he asked his father why he never hugged him. His father said, "I thought you were a sissy and if I hugged you it would make you worse!"

Another young man told of a father who was lot more direct. Dan was about 16 years old when he asked to talk with his father about a problem. His father was active in church. Dan told his father that he was gay and wanted his father to give him advice on how to handle it. His father told him to get a gun, put in his mouth, and pull the trigger! Needless to say, Dan was crushed by this and soon left home. He ended up hustling on the streets of San Francisco, where he contracted HIV/AIDS and an expensive drug habit.

This whole book could have been filled with horror stories about the abuse of gay men and lesbians by their own Bible-believing, church-going parents. Once you have admitted that in some ways you also have been abused and oppressed by others because you are gay, you can either wallow in self-pity, self-rejection, and self-destructive behavior, or you can turn your attention to God and catch a vision of God's love and acceptance of you. You can begin the new direction of following Jesus instead of religion and keep moving toward the goal of freedom and self-esteem that are your birthright as a child of God.

The Awesome Power of Abusive Religion

As long as any of us is oppressed because of our sexual orientation, none of us are free. The torture and murder of Matthew Shepard and dozens of other gay people in this country simply because they are gay has affected all of us. The suicide of every Bobby Griffith and thousands like him affects all of us. When a gay or lesbian person is abused by religion, many other people are hurt in the process. Family and friends often have to pay a high price for the tragedy of religious oppression of sexual minorities.

John was an active member of a fundamentalist church. John was gay but kept his sexual orientation secret. He attended church regularly with his wife and children. John got involved in a love affair with another man, and when it ended in a painful breakup, John went to his pastor for counseling. He told his pastor that he was gay and asked for prayer. The pastor rejected John, condemned him as an abomination to God, and demanded that he publicly repent and beg for forgiveness for his sin of homosexuality.

The next Sunday, John and his wife and children went to church. When the sermon began, the preacher called John by name and launched a vicious condemnation against him. The preacher demanded that John come to the front of the church and confess his sin of homosexuality and repent. John took his wife and children by the hand and they walked out of the church. Back at their home, John lingered in the garage while the family went into the house.

In a few minutes, a shot rang out and John was dead. John killed himself before he could know that immediately after he and his family left the church, the entire congregation got up and walked out, leaving the preacher raving and shouting to them to come back and not abandon God!

This kind of raw, dramatic confrontation between human need and powerful, judgmental religion is not as rare as you might think. According to the Centers for Disease Control in Atlanta, the suicide rate of gay men is three times the national average, and the suicide rate of men with HIV/AIDS is 60 times the average. Suicide is the leading cause of death of gay and lesbian teenagers. Some have responded to these terrible statistics by saying that being homosexual makes people depressed, but that is not the view of the American Psychiatric Association.

Being gay does not cause depression, but being rejected and treated like a sick and evil abomination would make anybody depressed. Being gay does not make people self-destructive, but being condemned and convinced that they are hopelessly lost and rejected by God can drive a person to devastating, self-destructive behavior. What self-destructive and self-defeating things have you done to yourself because of religious abuse and oppression as a result of your sexual orientation?

How Jesus Handled Religious Rejection and Abuse

During these studies we will take a close look at many of the ways Jesus handled rejection by his family and friends, betrayal by someone he loved, abandonment by his disciples, being misunderstood by everybody, loneliness, anger, and other pressures in his life that speak directly to us. Underlying the way that Jesus handled pressure was his guiding sense of mission and purpose in following the will of God. Jesus kept his eyes on the prize.

From the very beginning, when he was brought to the Temple at the age of 12, Jesus was obviously different. Throughout his life, Jesus was pressured by both friends and enemies to conform to the "normal" and "expected" behavior of other people. Jesus resisted the temptation to give in to being what others thought he should be and maintained his clear vision of his purpose in life. You also are different. God also has a purpose for you. Jesus can give inspiration and practical help in your life.

How Did Jesus Keep Focused on His Purpose in Life?

Jesus believed and trusted God completely. Jesus did the will of God. "I can do nothing on my own initiative. I do not seek my own will but the will of the one who sent me" (John 5:30). See also John 6:38. To follow Jesus is to seek, find, and follow the will of God in your life. What is the will of God for you? How does your God-given sexuality figure into your life's purpose and goals? Do you think that God wants you to be free from abusive religion?

Jesus always did the loving thing. Jesus believed in God's love and demonstrated God's love in all that he said and did. Love motivated every decision. Jesus gave his disciples various demonstrations of compassion and humble, loving service, as in the washing of the feet of the disciples in John 13. The ability to love as Jesus loved is a gift from God and not something that can be learned by purely human effort. You will never regret doing the loving thing.

Jesus stayed in constant communion with God. Jesus prayed and taught his followers to pray. The life of Jesus in the Gospels demonstrates a healthy balance between withdrawal for rest and prayer and intense ministry of compassion, healing, and teaching between outcast and wounded people. Jesus did not stay involved all the time nor did he stay withdrawn all the time. He practiced a healthy rhythm of withdrawal and involvement that kept him sane when everybody around him was falling apart.

Can you think of other methods that Jesus used to keep on track and to keep his eyes on the prize of the upward call of God? How did Jesus keep from being distracted by the abusive and dysfunctional religious oppressors around him? Have you learned yet how to keep other people's craziness from making you crazy?

Paul's Plan for Positive Thinking

The entire letter of Paul to the Philippians is encouraging, with the words "joy" and "rejoice" being used over and over. The fourth chapter has been of special help to me. I long ago memorized Philippians 4:6-8 and recite it to myself whenever I am frustrated and confused, "Be anxious about nothing, but in every thing by prayer and supplication with thanksgiving, make your requests known to God. And the peace of God, which surpasses all comprehension, will guard your hearts and your minds in Christ Jesus." Then Paul suggested the positive things we can think to keep our eyes on the prize, "Think about whatever is true, honorable, right, pure, loving, of good report, excellent, and worthy of praise."

In Philippians 3:13, Paul said that he let go of the past so that he could keep his eyes on the prize. What did Paul let go? Was it lying, stealing, cheating, drinking, sex, or other "sins?" No. Paul let go of religion in order to follow Jesus! Read Philippians 3:4-11. Paul let go of his past success as a zealous and blameless, legalistic, judgmental keeper of the Law, which he had come to realize was garbage compared to having Jesus Christ in his life. "I have suffered the loss of all things and count them but rubbish in order that I may gain Christ." For Paul, forgiveness, freedom, life, love, joy, and peace were all gifts from God. Paul was committed to Jesus Christ plus nothing.

Questions for Study and Discussion

1. What purpose have you found for your life so far? Have you found the freedom to love and accept yourself?

2. What most helps you to feel good about yourself now? What are your immediate and long-range goals in life?

3. Do you think that God has a mission for you to help other people who have gone through some of the same difficulties that you have faced?

Additional Resources

For help in dealing with issues in these first four lessons, read Bruce Hilton, *Can Homophobia Be Cured?*: Abingdon Press, 1992. This book was prepared in the form of questions and answers to be used in United Methodist Churches that were considering the acceptance of gay and lesbian people into full membership and leadership.

Now is a good time to become familiar with the writings of the Rev. Elder Troy Perry, Founder and Moderator of the Universal Fellowship of Metropolitan Community Churches. *The Lord is My Shepherd and He Knows I'm Gay*: Universal Fellowship Press, 1972 and 1994 and *Don't Be Afraid Anymore: The Story of Reverend Troy Perry and The Metropolitan Community Churches*: St. Martin's Press, 1990.

See an excellent recent book by Keith Hartman, *Congregations in Conflict: The Battle Over Homosexuality*: Rutgers University Press, 1996.

Chapter 7

The Second Step

Turn to God for Help

Pray and ask God to guide you into a healthy spiritual life and into a Christ-centered use of the Bible. God wants you to be happy and to feel good about yourself. God, as you understand and experience God, is very personal and individual. Nobody else can give God to you. This is why all recovery programs encourage you to turn your life over to your "Higher Power" or to God as you understand God. Your sense of self-esteem and self-worth depends on your view of God.

> Be anxious for nothing, but in every thing by prayer and supplication let your requests be known to God. And the peace of God, which surpasses all understanding, will guard your hearts and your minds in Christ Jesus.
>
> Philippians 4:6-7

> Cast all of your anxiety on God, for God cares for you.
>
> 1 Peter 5:7

Lesson 5

Jesus the Revolutionary Teacher

† **Preparatory Bible Reading:** Luke 4:14-30

> When Jesus finished teaching, the multitudes were amazed at his teaching; for he was teaching them as one having authority and not as their scribes.
>
> Matthew 7:28-29

Turning to God for help can be confusing and uncertain unless you have a reliable guide. Jesus came to be that guide. Jesus was viewed in the New Testament as "The word of God made human." Jesus said, "If you have seen me, you have seen God." Read John 1:1-18 and 14:6-20 now to catch a vision of how the early believers viewed Jesus as their guide and teacher.

My high school teachers that taught me the most were teachers who were themselves part of their lessons. Did you also have teachers who influenced your life far beyond the material that they taught in class? Jesus was both the messenger and the message.

Jesus was a revolutionary teacher in many ways. Jesus came not just to show the way but to be the way, not just to tell the truth but to be the truth, and not just to give life but to be life. The example of how Jesus handled stress and conflict is probably our most reliable guide to spiritual growth and recovery from religious abuse. In the midst of teaching humble service by washing the feet of his disciples, Jesus said, "I gave you an example that you also should do as I did to you" (John 13:15). "Gave you an example" means "to show under the eyes" in Greek and declares that Jesus intended for his followers to look at him and literally follow his actions.

Can You Let Jesus Be Your Teacher?

When I was a child, I was afraid of Jesus. My mental image was based on a faded yellow stain glass window of "Jesus in the Garden" in a dark hall in my church. I had to walk past that window to go to my Sunday School room when I was about five years old. It was spooky. Jesus in my mind had no connection with the fun things that we did in Sunday School, like planting grass seed to watch grass grow in little cups and eating bananas when we talked about missionaries in Africa.

I was also afraid of my public school teachers. They were nice people, but they had the power to judge me and pass or fail me. They also talked a lot to my parents and told them how bad (or good!) I had been in school. I never really thought of Jesus as my teacher. If I had, I probably would have been even more afraid of Jesus than I already was.

What do you think has kept you from letting Jesus be your teacher? As you go through this book and gain a more positive view of the love of God in Christ for you, think about how you are growing more open-minded and accepting of Jesus being your teacher. This book is just a beginning. Seeing Jesus as your reliable, trustworthy guide to God, life, love, hope, inner peace, your purpose in life, your happiness, and all of the other dimensions of your existence will determine a lot about your future.

Jesus said, "These things I have spoken to you that my joy may be in you and that your joy may be made complete" (John 15:11). Jesus wants you to be happy and to enjoy a full and meaningful life. Jesus offers you joy by offering you a new relationship with God, not by imposing on you a new set of rules about God, but by coming into your life and bringing Jesus' own relationship with you. Jesus' aim is to help you enjoy being yourself and to be happy with yourself, other people, and God.

How Revolutionary Was Jesus?

Jesus followed the traditional custom of sitting to teach. Sitting was the posture of confidence and authority. The content of Jesus' teaching was new and startling. Jesus said, "blessed are the poor." Some must have said, "Jesus, you have that backwards! Blessed are the rich." Jesus seemed to get a lot of things backwards, like teaching people to love their enemies and saying that you have to die to live.

Jesus broke with tradition by taking the initiative to seek out and call followers. The traditional teachers never selected their students. They had to wait for students to come to them. Jesus had women disciples (Luke 8:1-3). Mary was in the posture of a disciple "sitting at the feet of Jesus and listening to his word" (Luke 10:39). No traditional teachers had women disciples, and no woman was ever allowed to be a teacher. No teacher in the time of Jesus would give an opinion without quoting some ancient authority on the Law. Jesus regularly questioned traditional views and said, "but I say unto you. . . ." Matthew 7:28-29 tells of the amazement of the crowds at the authority of Jesus.

Jesus was new and creative, yet he was clear and easy to understand. He listened to the people and took them and their problems seriously to adapt his teachings to real human needs. Jesus was intensely realistic. He knew that learning takes time. He sat to teach, not only because that was the posture of authority and confidence, but also because Jesus knew that radical new truth of real value is not learned on the run. Jesus knew that the life-long "brainwashing" of the multitudes by an army of legalistic, judgmental Bible-abusing preachers and teachers could not be challenged and corrected in a hurry.

Jesus Called People to Become Disciples

Jesus called his followers to become disciples (students) and to make disciples of others, not just to make religious converts. Jesus led his team to commit time and energy to disciplined study and learning new information that was necessary for real freedom and truth. Hope for the healing of self-hate and low self-esteem that has been heaped upon gay people and on many others by generations of ignorant and abusive Bible preaching and teaching also requires time and concentration for serious study, reflection, and change.

Jesus Corrected the Abusive Use of Religion

Jesus' approach was new and inclusive, and it was costly. Review the story of the first teaching experience of Jesus at Nazareth in Luke 4:14-30 (the text suggested at the beginning of this lesson). When Jesus tried to show his people that God accepted and included outcasts and unclean people, the people tried to kill Jesus! The story ends by Jesus walking away and going back to his home in Capernaum. Whenever people try to define their religion on the basis of who is left out, Jesus leaves and goes home!

Women, youth, foreigners, the sick, the poor, Scribes, priests, Pharisees, and all kinds of people were included in the outreach efforts of Jesus as a teacher. The only requirement was an open mind. Jesus invited people to take a fresh look at Bible teachings as though they were seeing them for the first time without layers of interpretations and distortions. Much of the teaching work of Jesus was an attempt to cut through the misuse of the Bible that had obscured God's love and truth and that had made religion into oppression and fear. Jesus can help us accomplish the same goal.

Jesus as the Point of Reference for Bible Study

Paul said, "For me to live is Christ" (Philippians 1:21). Whatever you might think of Paul, his emphasis throughout his letters was centered in Jesus Christ, "in whom all things hold together [or find their proper place]" (Colossians 1:17). The life and teachings of Jesus in the Gospels gives meaning and purpose to everything else in the Bible and is the point on which Bible history turns.

Jesus saw everything in the Hebrew Bible as finding its fulfillment and completion in Jesus. Jesus said, "Search the scriptures, because you think that in them you have eternal life; and it is these that bear witness of me" (John 5:39). Read also Luke 24:27, 32, and 44-47, where after the resurrection, Jesus "opened the minds of the disciples" to understand all that scripture said about him.

What kind of God are you turning to for help in recovery from Bible and religious abuse? God has been called "the Unmoved Mover," "the First Cause," and many other descriptive names by ancient and modern philosophers. Jesus came to give God a clear new identity. To Jesus, God is the loving parent who already loves all of God's children equally and who has come to the people in Jesus to demonstrate what God is like. That is why Jesus said, "If you have seen me, you have seen God."

Turning to God

Recovery from any obsessive-compulsive destructive behavior requires turning to some outside "higher power" for help. How you view God is of great importance in your recovery. Recovery from alcoholism, co-dependency, addiction to abusive religion, or any of the other "unclean spirits" that can so easily derail our lives will be made more certain with God's help than without it. The Bible word "repent" means "to turn around" both in Hebrew and in Greek. Turning to God is a definite decision of will that only you can make. You can begin a new journey out of self-hate and self-rejection and into the light and love of growing self-esteem and self-confidence simply by turning to God and asking for God's help. Let Jesus help you do it.

Questions for Study and Discussion

1. Have you tried religion and found that it did not help you?

2. Why do you think that your previous attempts to try religion have failed?

3. How would you describe God now?

4. How does your view of God now compare to your view of God when you were a child?

5. What in this lesson was most helpful to you? What was most troubling?

Additional Resources

See a refreshing book by a famous black Christian teacher, Howard Thurman, *Jesus and the Disinherited*, Friends United Press, 1981.

See my Web site on "Jesus and the Bible" at www.truluck.com.

Lesson 6

Freedom to Rejoice in Hope

† Preparatory Bible Reading, 2 Peter 3:1-18

Jesus sets us free to trust God with our future and to "rejoice in hope" (Romans 12:12). Read Romans 5:1-9 and 12:9-21 for places where Paul sets "rejoicing in hope" in the context of our growth through adversities and at the center of our calling to love and accept each other and ourselves.

From Despair to Hope

The leading cause of death of gay and lesbian teenagers is suicide. The suicide rate for gay men with HIV/AIDS continues to be 60 times the national average. For every gay person who commits suicide, thousands more live in fear and despair that are self-defeating and unhappy. Individual loss of hope and the loss of the will to live are the bitter fruit of abusive, oppressive, legalistic, judgmental religion in our culture. Realize, however, that gay people are not depressed because they are gay but because of how they are treated for being gay.

The message of hope in 2 Peter 3:1-18 is that only God really knows and controls your future. Since God loves you, the future that God has planned for you is wonderful beyond anything that you might imagine or expect. One reason for turning to God for help in recovery is that God is Sovereign over time and eternity. God can lead you safely through tomorrow one day at a time and into the rest of your life and beyond.

Early Christians faced many pressures and disappointments. Much of the New Testament was written to give believers a basis for hope and encouragement in the face of what the writers called "tribulations", which is the Greek word "pressure." In his longest and most detailed description of hope in 1 Corinthians 15, Paul said, "We are not like those who have no hope." (See especially 1 Corinthians 15:54-58.) In Christ we shall finally be set free from all of the limitations of sick bodies and our fragile earthly existence. Recovery that does not take us into a sense of hope even beyond this life is incomplete. The letters of 1 and 2 Peter were addressed to "those who live as aliens" and who need encouragement and hope. So they speak to us as well.

Living in Hope

As I first began to write this lesson in 1996, I received a phone call from a friend in Nashville to tell me that my friend Bart had died. Bart was a 35-year-old gay man with HIV/AIDS who had recently come into MCC Nashville and began to attend everything, especially the Wednesday night supper and spiritual support group that I led in my home. Bart decided to turn to God for help in dealing with the many difficulties that he faced, and he asked to be baptized by immersion as a dramatic way to express his sense of new beginning in Christ. He was baptized in October 1995, and died in February 1996.

Bart became extremely weak, unable to respond to medication, and was in Vanderbilt Hospital for several days. His roommate called me one morning to tell me that the doctors had told Bart he could not live much longer; Bart wanted me to come to see him so he could say goodbye. When I saw him, Bart asked me if I had heard what the doctors said. I said yes. Then he brightened up and smiled and said, "I am so excited! I can hardly wait!" Then he talked about how he looked forward to passing over to the other side and being with God. He was far more cheerful when he thought he was about to die than later when he got a little better and had to linger for a couple of months in a nursing home.

Bart told me please not to let the doctors revive him if his heart stopped. He said he would really be angry if they brought him back when he was on the way out. He said that God had helped him to prepare to die and now had to help him adjust to life in the nursing home, which for him was very unpleasant. Bart was a great inspiration to me and to everyone who knew him. He begged us to take him to the Wednesday support group, even though it was painful for him to be moved and he had to be carried up three flights of stairs to get there.

When I learned that Bart had gone home, I felt the loss and sadness and also rejoiced with him that he finally had what he wanted so very much, to be in the presence of God. I am grateful that he found MCC and the people there to be his encouraging and supportive friends and that he let us get to know him and learn so much from him.

We Need Each Other

In the face of religious oppression, self-hate, HIV/AIDS, and the thousand natural and unnatural shocks that flesh is heir to, we need each other as we take the basic step of turning to God. After Bart was too weak to walk, others held him up and even carried him. He remained part of his group of friends as long as he lived. His presence with the people that he loved was part of what gave meaning and purpose to his life and to theirs. Members of the group visited him often, and one group member was with him all night during his last hours.

You may not think that you have much to give to others that will encourage them. But you do. You can give yourself. Take time to be with others who also are turning to God. Share your experiences and listen to theirs. From such a mixture God creates healing, hope, love, joy, and peace.

Clearing Up Confusion

The Second Letter of Peter was probably the last New Testament book written. It reflected on the rest of the New Testament and attempted to correct misunderstandings about the end of the world and the Christian hope for the future. In chapter three, the writer sought to correct wrong thinking about the future. This was done because much of the Christian teaching was already being taken out of context, turned into absolute laws and rules, and had developed into an emerging futuristic legalism that is still with us today.

Futuristic legalism has developed today into rigid competing systems of millennium expectations, an artificial separation of the Bible history into dispensations, and various extremist religious groups that abandon society and common sense to wait for an end to the world. Some, like David Koresh's "Branch Davidians" in Waco, Texas, and the suicidal followers of "Heaven's Gate" in San Diego have ended in disaster. The destructive potential of dysfunctional, legalistic, judgmental religion in futuristic sects has been demonstrated far too often.

The Bible has been twisted and distorted more in the study of the end of the world, called "eschatology," than in any other religious movement until the modern use of the Bible against lesbian and gay people by the self-righteous homophobic, religious fundamentalists of today. When homophobia is added to eschatology, it becomes a tragic stumbling block to spiritual health, hope, growth, and maturity. Some rabidly committed fundamentalists have disconnected Bible texts entirely from their original setting, twisted their meaning, and incorrectly translated them in order to maintain their complex religious agenda. Some have taught that homosexuality is a sign of the coming end of the world. Others have insisted that the end of the world and the Second Coming of Christ will be hastened by the killing of gay people.

Radio and television preachers often gain great financial support by offering an endless series of books, charts, and pamphlets about the end of the world to their loyal, gullible followers. Now anti-gay literature and videos have been added to the flood of self-serving propaganda that has been generated against people who are different and can be singled out as easy targets by the religious right. No two eschatology systems are alike. The element of speculation always creates confusion even for "experts" in the field. That is why there are so many books available on the end of the world. The religious specialists and experts cannot agree.

This same kind of confusion evidently was behind what the writer of 2 Peter 3 said. The writer's number one concern was to point out that God is the one in charge and only God knows the future. The Sovereignty of God was the basis for silencing fruitless and dangerous speculations. The Sovereignty of God also is seen as the basis for accepting each other and ourselves as people of value created by God in the image of God, no matter what our sexual orientation or other individual differences might be.

Problems with Understanding Paul

Second Peter 3:15-17 is very important for us in realizing that even the New Testament itself recognized how easily the writings of Paul could be distorted and used to abuse and confuse people. Paul wrote, "according to the wisdom given to him and spoke in all of his letters concerning things that are hard to understand. Ignorant and unstable people have distorted Paul just as they do other scriptures to their own destruction. You, therefore, beloved, knowing better, guard against being carried away by the errors of unprincipled people and shaken in your confidence and stability" (2 Peter 3:15-17). These verses are your keys to answering the abusive use of any of Paul's writings to hurt yourself or others.

The word "distort" in 3:16 is a Greek term (*streblousin*) meaning to "distort, torture, torment, twist something so that a false meaning results" and is used only here in the New Testament. It was also used in popular Greek for "crooked, perverted" persons. The real perverts are those who distort the Bible and change the Bible's meaning to hurt people!

Free at Last

Jesus promised freedom from pain, suffering, tears, separation, grief, loneliness, fear, and death. Romans 8:21 declared, "the creation itself will be set free." The creation includes all people and all things. 2 Peter shows that since all material things will be destroyed, our best investment is in loving one another and ourselves. 2 Peter 3:18 gives us the way to overcome Bible abuse, "Grow in grace and knowledge of our Sovereign and

Savior Jesus Christ, to whom be the glory both now and to the day of eternity." Christ in you is "the hope of glory" both now and in the age to come. As you turn to God for help, expect to be liberated from your past and be set free to rejoice in hope for your future.

Questions for Study and Discussion

1. What has helped you most when you have been depressed and tempted to give up?

2. Have you yet found a supportive person or group of people whom you can trust to share your feelings and ideas?

3. Who have you been able to help deal with despair?

4. How has your perception of God, Jesus, and the Bible been affected by this book so far?

Additional Resources

See Leroy Aarons, *Prayers for Bobby, A Mother's Coming to Terms with the Suicide of Her Gay Son*: Harper San Francisco, 1995.

A great classic study of despair and hope by Soren Kierkegaard, *The Sickness Unto Death*: written in 1849 and repeatedly published many times.

Challenge your mind with Paul Tillich, *The Courage to Be*: Yale University Press, 1952.

The chapter on "Legalistic Anxiety" in Wayne E. Oates, *Anxiety in Christian Experience*: Word, 1955, is relevant to these lessons.

Lesson 7

Do Not Give Up on God

† Preparatory Bible Reading, Luke 18:1-14

While reading the Gospel of Luke, we will find a few stories that Jesus told which illustrate God's presence. Read the parable that Jesus told "to show that at all times they ought to pray and not to give up [lose heart]" (Luke 18:1-14). An unjust judge finally gave legal protection to a widow because she "wore him out" with her constant requests for help. Jesus contrasted the judge's approach with that of God, who already wants to help the needy and will give help without your having to beg. Then Jesus continued to explain by telling the story about the self-righteous Pharisee who made no contact with God through his self-centered prayer, while a truly humble but despised tax collector was open to God and was heard and justified. These two stories say that God is available to you no matter what your circumstances in life might be. ***So do not give up on God!***

Why Gays and Lesbians Give Up on God

Mike Bussee and Gary Cooper helped to start "Exodus," an international chain of religious therapy groups that has developed into what is now an "Ex-Gay" industry that claims to use homophobic, fundamentalist religion to change sexual orientation from homosexual to heterosexual. For five years, Mike and Gary spent most of their spare time working, counseling, and promoting "Exodus" in churches all over the country. Mike was a family therapist, and Gary was a public school teacher. After five years in "Exodus", they began to realize that they had actually changed nobody's sexual orientation. They had, however, seen many people give up on God because God would not change them from gay to straight. They saw people mutilate themselves, attempt and commit suicide, and do many self-destructive acts because they could not change their sexual orientation. Finally, Mike and Gary realized that they were gay and fell in love.

Mike and Gary dropped out of church for eight years. They gave up on God. They sealed their Bibles in a taped box for fear that if they opened the Bible, something awful would attack them. In 1990, they came back to church. They came to the MCC in San Francisco where I was pastor and led a workshop on overcoming Bible abuse and religious oppression. When Mike came to me for communion in the worship service, he said, "This is the first time I have had communion in eight years!" Mike and Gary dedicated themselves to a ministry of helping lesbian and gay Christians accept and love themselves as children of God.

They were on several television and radio programs, and "One Nation Under God," a powerful 90-minute documentary that told their story, was shown on public television during gay pride week in 1993 and many years since. Mike and Gary demonstrated how people who have given up on God can turn back to God and recover from the abusive use of the Bible and religious oppression that create self-hate and self-destructive behavior.

Why We Should Not Give Up on God

Jesus revealed that God loves and accepts you just as you are. God loves the world, and that includes gay, lesbian, bisexual, and transgendered people, you, me, and everybody else. Jesus said that God loves you far more than your own parents love you. Read Luke 11:5-13 to see how God's love is greater than the love of parents for their children. God will give the Holy Spirit to whomever asks. God wants us to have God's help even more than we want it. O. Halesby, in a classic book on prayer, said that our needs are our most eloquent and persuasive prayers. A baby does not have to beg parents to give food, clothing, shelter, comfort, and affection. Parents love their children and meet these needs without being asked. We simply have to recognize and admit our needs and be open and receptive before God, and God will give to us abundant blessings beyond anything we can ask or think.

Jesus also gave us many reasons not to give up on God. The following list was developed in one of our groups as "The Eight Wonders of God" and clear reasons to trust God and not give up,

1. God always is greater than your need.
2. God always is greater than your enemy.
3. God always loves you more than you do.
4. God always has better plans for you than you do.
5. God always gives you what is good for you.
6. God always is available to you.
7. God gives you what you could never give to yourself.
8. Whatever God gives to you can never be taken from you.

How do you feel about these propositions about God? Do you think that these statements describe God as Jesus saw God? What main event or events in the life of Jesus do you think best illustrate how Jesus acted on these propositions about God?

God Always Has Better Plans for Your Life

This fact about God has helped me to keep turning to God and trusting God no matter what might be happening in my life. Many times I have been tempted to take things into my own hands and try to solve the problems, control other people, take over, and run things my way. Disaster usually follows my giving in to these temptations. Whenever I am tempted to take over and run things myself, dozens of scriptures come into my mind to turn me back to God. One of my favorites is, "Be still and know that I am God" (Psalm 46:10). The New American Standard Bible renders it, "Cease striving and know that I am God." Or, "Let go and relax! And know that I am God."

We never become so mature spiritually that we do not need to be reminded to turn to God for help. During my first year at the seminary, I took part in the month long Billy Graham crusade in Louisville, Kentucky, in October 1956. I learned more about follow-up evangelism than in any study I have done before or since. I served every night as a volunteer to talk with people who came forward to make decisions for Christ. That was the last big crusade when the leading fundamentalist preachers and evangelists supported Dr. Graham. The following summer, Billy Graham included all people who wanted to help sponsor the great New York Crusade, which lasted all summer in a packed Madison Square Garden and concluded with a full week of record setting crowds in Yankee Stadium. Roman Catholics, Jews, and many other religious groups along with previous sponsors joined. As a result, many of the leading fundamentalists like John R. Rice and Bob Jones called Dr. Graham a traitor, withdrew their support, and condemned him in their broadcasts and publications.

Many of the fundamentalists were close personal friends of Billy Graham. His old friends' opposition to his decision to include all people in his ministry profoundly hurt Dr. Graham. After the New York Crusade was over, Dr. Graham wrote a book about his experiences called *God in the Garden*. Something that he quoted from his diary just as the New York crusade began in 1957 has always stuck with me. I copied it onto a page at the end of my Bible and often have looked at it and used it in preaching and teaching.

Dr. Graham wrote, "My own attitude toward opposition has been one of quiet commitment to Christ. There were a few times, when I would hear some of the lies, distortions of truth and slander that I had a bit of resentment in my heart and was tempted once or twice to lash back. But then scores of Scriptures began to echo in my ears and penetrate my heart, such as 1 Peter 2:15, 'For so is the will of God, that with well doing you may silence the ignorance of foolish men.' I have thanked God a thousand times in the last few days that God gave me grace, during these months of severe attacks, never to answer back. I do not want to get my mind off Christ. We have been promised that if we keep our minds on Christ, the peace that passes understanding will prevail in our hearts. This has certainly been true."

These words by Billy Graham have been a sustaining inspiration to me through many years of tumultuous and frightening times and rapidly changing ministries. Billy Graham's determination not to answer his critics and enemies but keep his mind on Jesus may be one of the main reasons that 40 years later he is the most highly respected and best-known evangelist in the world.

Why Turn to God?

Turning to God always makes things better. Whatever you may think about God, you will surely handle things a lot better with God's help than without it. God can help you to be objective and logical when the pressures on you distort the way you see yourself, other people, and your situation. I am personally convinced that God can guide you through the Holy Spirit into a truly Christ-centered use of the Bible that is healthy, positive, uplifting, and realistic. You have to work out what works for you. You are an individual. God made you the way you are and God respects your individuality. One step in turning to God is to accept and respect yourself. You are God's child. That makes you special. Expect tangible help from God when you ask for help.

Questions for Study and Discussion

1. What is your earliest memory of God or religion? What was the view of God that you learned from your parents? How do these memories continue to affect you?

2. Has your conception of God changed any by reading these lessons? If so, in what way?

3. Exactly what do you think it means to "turn to God"? Have you had any experience with the steps to recovery in Alcoholics Anonymous or any other recovery program? Does any of what you have already experienced in recovery programs apply to what you are doing now in beginning the steps to recovery from religious abuse?

Additional Resources

Books that have helped me are,

John A. T. Robinson, *Honest to God*: Westminster, 1963.

The classic by Brother Lawrence (1666), *The Practice of the Presence of God*: many publishers, only 64 pages, but always rewarding reading.

Many of the works of Paul Tillich, especially *The Shaking of the Foundations*, *Dynamics of Faith,* and a more technical one, *Biblical Religion and The Search for Ultimate Reality.*

Father Leo Booth, *When God Becomes a Drug: Breaking the Chains of Religious Addiction and Abuse*: Tarcher/Putnam, 1991.

All of the books by John J. McNeill, especially *Taking a Chance on God*, 1988, and *Freedom, Glorious Freedom*, 1995, both published by Beacon Press.

Lesson 8

Things You Cannot Change

† **Preparatory Bible Reading:** Jeremiah 13:23; Luke 12:25-26; Ephesians 4:22-32; Colossians 3:1-17

Many of us have gained a healthy perspective on our lives with the serenity prayer, "God, grant me the serenity to accept the things I cannot change, the courage to change the things I can, and the wisdom to know the difference."

The Prophet Jeremiah asked, "Can the Ethiopians change their skin or leopards their spots?" (Jeremiah 13:23). Jesus said, "Which of you by being anxious can add a single inch to your height? If then you cannot do even a very little thing, why are you anxious about other things?" (Luke 12:25-26). The bottom line in the issue of the Bible and gay and lesbian people is that nowhere in the Bible is it written that gays can or should change their sexual orientation. The Bible never shows any knowledge or interest in sexual orientation. No word for "homosexual" exists in biblical Hebrew or Greek.

Nothing in the life and teachings of Jesus ever dealt with sexual orientation or homosexuality. All through the teachings and example of Jesus, however, we are taught to accept all people, including ourselves, as children of God with great value to God. If the rest of the Bible is to be tested and guided by Jesus, no basis exists to use the Bible to condemn and oppress gay men and lesbians or anybody else.

Psychiatry and Medicine

In 1998, the American Psychiatric Association took a strong stand against the so-called "reparative therapy" of a few renegade therapists who claimed to change the sexuality of their clients. This action was in keeping with the resolutions passed by the American Psychiatric Association in 1973 that removed homosexuality from their official list of mental disorders. The APA declared that "homosexuality implies no impairment in judgment, stability, reliability, or general social or vocational capabilities," adding "the American Psychiatric Association deplores all public and private discrimination against homosexuals in such areas as employment, housing, public accommodations, and licensing, and declares that no burden of proof of such judgment, capacity, or reliability shall be placed upon homosexuals greater than that imposed on any other persons and urges the enactment of civil rights legislation at the local, state, and federal level that would offer homosexual persons the same protections now guaranteed to others on the basis of race, creed, color, etc."

These decisions were made in 1973 and reaffirmed many times since then. In 1974, the American Medical Association and the American Bar Association agreed with the position of the psychiatrists. They added their approval of the "Model Penal Code" of the American Law Institute recommendation to legislators "that private sexual behavior between consenting adults should be removed from the list of crimes and thereby legalized." In 1975, the American Psychological Association also approved these declarations and "urged all mental health professions to take the lead in removing the stigma of mental illness that has long been associated with sexual orientations."

The continuous attempt by right wing political and religious groups to discredit the medical, psychiatric, legal, and psychological professions by charging that these leading experts and specialists caved in to gay activists in making these decisions is ludicrous and not supported by the historical facts. Continued defiance by homophobic, fundamentalist political and religious forces has distorted the truth and poisoned the minds of millions of people, including a tragic number of gay people. The ignorant, vicious leaders of the homophobic religious/political establishment are successfully pushing the whole country backward in the face of all of the scientific and practical evidence to the contrary.

Jesus Required No Change in Sexual Orientation

Jesus never used the word "sex" in the Gospels! That may come as a surprise, but the word "sex" was never used anywhere in the Bible. No biblical concordance has a listing for "sex" because there was no exact parallel word in Hebrew or in Greek for the Latin *sexualis*, from which our word "sex" comes. No Bible passage even mentions the idea of sexual orientation and no verse says that gays and lesbians can or should change their sexual orientation. The Bible gives no basis at all for the so-called "reparative therapy" of the discredited psychologists or conversion therapy of homophobic fundamentalists.

Scientists have not yet learned the origins of gender orientations, like homosexuality. Science continues to search for answers and to give new insights into human behavior. This scientific process of seeking new truth is an unending process. To remain scientific, science must always be open to new information. The search for truth is never over. I believe that sexual orientation is like other personality traits that a person is born with like talent for music, art, math, writing, creativity, leadership, and other similar characteristics that are impossible to predict or trace biologically. We just do not know why sexual orientation is different from one person to another.

For the most recent actions of the American Psychiatric Association and the medical profession regarding the causes of sexual orientation and the damage being done by "reparative therapy" that claims to change the sexual orientation of individuals, see the "ex-gay" material and references in my Web site, which is kept up-to-date.

Nothing Is Impossible With God.

God changes us in the ways that we need to change. "Nothing is impossible with God" and "nothing is too difficult for God" are ideas found in Genesis 18:14, Luke 1:37, Luke 18:27, Matthew 19:26, Mark 10:27, and elsewhere. The Prophet Jeremiah exclaimed, "Ah Sovereign God! Behold you have made the heavens and the earth by your great power and your outstretched arm. Nothing is too difficult for you" (Jeremiah 32:17).

Our encouragement and hope are based on God's unchangeable nature, "God desired even more to show to the heirs of the promise the unchangeableness of God's purpose. It is impossible for God to lie. We have strong encouragement who have fled for refuge in laying hold of the hope set before us. This hope we have as an anchor of the soul both sure and steadfast" (Hebrews 6:17-20). God is Sovereign and can do anything that God wills to do.

God decided what to do and not do in the life of Jesus. Many of Jesus' works seemed impossible, like raising the dead (John 11) and giving sight to one born blind (John 9). When Jesus prayed in the Garden of Gethsemane, he left to God the final decision of what to do, "If it is possible, let this cup pass from me; yet not as I will but as you will" (Matthew 26:39). Jesus demonstrated radical trust and obedience to God. Nothing is impossible with God, for God raised Jesus from the dead and gave victory and freedom through Jesus to all people. God, however, did not take away the cup of suffering, even though Jesus prayed for the cup to pass from him if it were possible. Of course it was possible, but it was not what God wanted to happen at that time. Jesus accepted the will of God and died on the cross.

God could change anyone's sexual orientation if God wanted to do so. Yet God has decided in God's perfect wisdom and love not to change gay people into heterosexuals. There is no credible scientific evidence that sexual orientation can be changed. Religious groups that claim to make such changes through various forms of religious behavior modification can only show that homosexuals can be conditioned to deny their real self and become celibate or to function heterosexually. These "converts" are then left to suffer whatever internal pain and torment that comes as a result.

I personally know of many people who have undergone years of counseling, intensive psychotherapy, and even electric shock therapy as well as years of tearful prayer that God would take away the "abomination" of homosexual orientation. But the change never came. Some of these people killed themselves or tried to. Some of them decided to fake it and live in the personal torment of the closet. Far too many tried to cure their homosexuality by getting married and lived to regret the agony and destruction that was caused down the road of deception and constant fear.

In response to my Web site, I have received hundreds of pleas for help from homosexuals who are married with children and who are in constant turmoil and fear with what seems to them to be a "hell on earth" with no way out. Some people, however, have learned in various ways to handle their sexual orientation with acceptance and love for themselves, for God, and for others.

The Christian Lifestyle

There is no such thing as "the gay lifestyle" any more than there is a left-handed lifestyle or a people of color lifestyle. The lifestyle of each individual is made up of many various experiences, choices, opportunities, pressures, and abilities. In our culture, the lifestyle of most people is determined by how much money they have. The lifestyles of the rich and famous are balanced by the lifestyles of the poor and unnoticed!

The parts of the New Testament that describe the characteristics of the Christian lifestyle never mention sexual orientation. The chief feature of Christian life is love. Take the time to look up and read the description of the Christian lifestyle in Ephesians 4:22-32. The conclusion is clear, "Let all bitterness and wrath and anger and clamor and slander be put away from you, along with all malice. And be kind to one another, tender hearted, forgiving each other, just as God in Christ has forgiven you" (Ephesians 4:31-32).

See again the "fruit of the Spirit" in Galatians 5:22-23 and the new lifestyle of believers in Colossians 3:1-17. Sexual orientation is never mentioned or implied. The main thing that the Holy Spirit changes is our ability to love ourselves and our attitudes and actions toward other people. In Romans 15:1-7, we "accept one another as Christ also accepts us." The Christian goal is to have the "mind of Christ" as described in Philippians 2:1-5. Read the conclusion of this powerful statement of the lifestyle of believers. "Do not do anything from selfishness or empty conceit, but with humility of mind let each of you regard one another as more important than yourself, not looking out for your own interests only but also for the interests of others. Have this mind in yourselves which was in Christ Jesus" (Philippians 2:5). The Christian gay lifestyle is like that of Jesus and all other Christians, which is expressed primarily through unselfish love.

What You Can Change

Jesus sets us free from trying to play God. We are not expected to do the impossible. We do not have to know all of the answers. Leave the impossible changes to God. Galatians 5:12-15 summed it up, "You were called to freedom, for the whole law is fulfilled in one word, love your neighbor as yourself. But if you bite and devour one another, take care lest you be consumed by one another." God is love. God always teaches us to love others and ourselves.

Turn To God With Confidence

This lesson encourages you to turn with confidence to God for help in your recovery from Bible abuse. It is sick religion that has used the Bible against you to abuse and hurt you because of your sexual orientation. You are made in the image of God. "It is God who made us and not we ourselves. We are God's people and the sheep of God's pasture" (Psalm 100:3).

Questions for Study and Discussion

1. Are you willing to trust God to guide you and take control of your life to shape your lifestyle into the most enjoyable and productive that is possible for you?

2. What do you think God would most want to change in you?

3. What do you most want God to change in you?

This lesson covered a lot of new material. You may want to read it over carefully again. Read carefully all of the Bible quotations and suggested readings. Look at the related Special Studies at the back of the book. Pray about it before you go on to the Third Step.

Chapter 8

The Third Step

Examine Your Faith

You cannot win the battle against abusive religion by yourself. Jesus won the victory for all people over oppressive religion.

Take a fearless objective look at your faith. It is really yours? Religion may have abused and oppressed you so that you have more doubts than faith. How can you regain your spiritual life and health? How can Jesus help? Jesus said, "Follow me" (Mark 8:34). What does following Jesus mean to you?

Every person experiences Jesus Christ in his or her own way. No two people have exactly the same experience with Jesus, because no two people are exactly alike. Attempts by religious leaders to expect and demand conformity to a standard kind of "experience with Christ" for everyone are unhealthy and usually lead to a shallow and hypocritical temporary religious fix.

Study the experiences with Jesus that are recorded in the Gospels and The Book of Acts and you will notice that no two experiences are exactly the same. Only Paul met Christ on the Road to Damascus. Your experience with God in Christ will fit you just as the biblical experiences always fit the personality and situation of each individual. Enjoy being yourself. Let Jesus be for you what truly fits you. You have the promise of the help of the Holy Spirit to guide you to discover and experience Jesus for yourself in the ways that best fit you.

Lesson 9

How to Become a Christian

When you take a good look at your own faith, what do you see? What is the practical effect of your spiritual life on the rest of your life? Have you found a path of faith that adequately equips you to deal with the doubts and fears that religious abuse and oppression have brought your way?

For many people, experiencing Jesus Christ in their lives has been the path to spiritual renewal, recovery, growth, and healing. This lesson explores how to become a Christian from an evangelical point of view. My own spiritual tradition follows this path. I recognize and respect the many other various spiritual directions that are available to you.

Since 1981, when I became involved in ministry in the gay, lesbian, bisexual, and transgendered community, I have wrestled with how best to share with others my own spiritual experience and the faith and hope that I have in Jesus. The material in this lesson is the product at this point of what seems to me to be a reasonable and clear way to invite Jesus into your life, if that is what you have decided you want to do.

One of the first Bible studies that I did when I began leading Bible Study at First Metropolitan Community Church (MCC) Atlanta, Georgia, in 1988, was the forerunner of the following material. That first Bible study was developed into the 1991 UFMCC brochure "The Bible as Your Friend: A Guide for Lesbians and Gays," that has been in print at this time for eight years. It has been used at the rate of about 6,000 copies a year throughout the world in personal evangelism in MCC and many other forms of spiritual outreach to the lesbian and gay community. Chi Rho Press published my first book, *Invitation to*

Freedom, in 1993 as a guide to how to use the brochure. It is used extensively as a group workshop and individual study guide to personal evangelism.

The brochure, "How to Become a Christian" has been revised several times. This present approach seems to be helpful to many, but I am always working on how better to word the message and make it more clear and useful. Let me know if you have suggestions.

Invitation To Freedom

For gays and lesbians and for all people
oppressed by sick and abusive religion

How to Become a Christian and Be Free from Religious Oppression

You Are Included in God's Love

"God loves you so much that God gave God's only child that you would not throw your life away but could have a life full of joy and hope now and for ever. For God did not send Jesus to oppress you but that you might be set free!" (John 3:16-17*)

Freedom Now!

Jesus said, "I speak to you so that in me you can have peace. In this world you live under pressure, but cheer up! I have won the victory over everything!" (John 16:33)

To live is to be under pressure and to have problems. Jesus' offer of help is available to lesbian, gay, bisexual, and transgendered people!

The Bible never discussed sexual orientation. The six Bible verses used to condemn us are twisted out of context,

---

* Bible quotations are translations by the author and are based on the fact that "save" in the Bible literally means "to set free" or "liberate."

distorted, and incorrectly translated to hurt people not intended in the Bible! There is no word for "homosexual" in the original languages of the Bible. No reference to sexual orientation exists in the Bible!

An army of ignorant religious terrorists has wrung fear and hate out of the Bible to use against us to try to take hostage our spirituality and our sexuality. Jesus faced similar kinds of Bible abuse and religious oppression.

Jesus came to set people free from abusive sick religion. He came to give us God's unlimited love and to invite us to live in the "truth that sets us free." (John 8:32; 15:11)

God Loves and Accepts You!
God Wants You to Love and Accept Yourself and Others!

You cannot "love your neighbor as yourself" until you love yourself! Remember that ***you*** are your own closest neighbor. The word "neighbor" in the Bible means "the one near by."

God Loves You Just As You Are!

The Bible nowhere says that you can or should earn God's love. God's love is a free gift that nobody can take away from you!

"God demonstrated God's own love for us in that while we yet were in rebellion against God, Christ died for us." (Romans 5:8)

"By grace you are set free [saved] through faith, not of yourselves. Spiritual freedom [salvation] is a gift from God and not a result of human effort. So not one of us can boast [before God]." (Ephesians 2:8-9)

The Liberating Promise

"You will know the truth, and the truth will set you free!"
(John 8:32)

Liberation From Sick And Abusive Religion

Jesus said, "I am the door of the sheep. All who came before me are thieves and robbers; but the sheep did not hear them. I am the door. The one who enters through me shall be set free and shall go in and out and find pasture. The thief comes only to steal, and kill, and destroy. **I came that you might have a full and abundant life**!" (John 10:7-10)

Jesus said that abusive and destructive religious leaders are thieves who came only to steal, kill, and destroy. This stark contrast between Jesus and sick religion is emphasized throughout the four Gospels. You also may have suffered under oppressive and abusive religion. Do not let sick religion keep you from God!

God's Gift To You

God's love and acceptance are available to you. God's love is inclusive and unconditional. God's love includes ***you***. Everyone needs and can enjoy God's "grace." The word "grace" means "unearned gift." Nobody can earn God's love, for God's love has already been given freely to all people.

God wants to set you free from the limitations and pain of "sin." The word "sin" in the Bible means "to miss the target." Sin is failure to hit the target of God's good purpose for your life to reach your greatest possible potential for joy and fulfillment.

Jesus defined "sin" as the failure to love. Jesus gave a new commandment to the disciples to "love one another just as I have loved you" and added, "By this everybody will know that you are my disciples [followers] if you love each other." (John 13:34-35).

Because God Accepts You, You Can Accept Yourself and Others!

"Therefore accept one another, just as Christ also accepted you to the glory of God." (Romans 15:7)

God Accepts You . . . But Have You Accepted God?

You can invite Jesus into your life now!

"If you confess with your mouth that Jesus is Sovereign and believe in your heart that God raised Jesus from the dead, you will be set free [saved]. Any person who calls on the name of God will be delivered!" (Romans 10:9 and 13)

Becoming A Christian Is Extremely Simple

*The only invitation that Jesus gave to people was "**follow me**."*

When you invite Jesus into your life, you receive the help of God in all of your other decisions. You have the Spirit "helper" promised by Jesus to all who follow Jesus. Jesus went about setting people free from abusive and oppressive religion. Becoming a Christian does not mean becoming religious! It means that you let God do for you what God already wants to do for you but cannot do without your permission! Let go and open up your mind and your heart to God's love! **Do It Now!**

Inviting Jesus to come into your life could be the most important decision you will ever make! It is the act of faith that can turn your life in a positive and healthy new direction.

Pray this prayer or use other words that are more comfortable for you.

Dear God,
I admit to you that I need your love and forgiveness.
I turn to you now and accept your love for me.
I invite Jesus to come into my life to be my savior and guide.
Show me how to live my life in your will and to love myself and others.
Thank you for setting me free to accept myself and to enjoy being me!
In Jesus' Name, Amen.

What Next?

Tell somebody about what you have experienced. Tell the person who is most important to you. Tell your friends.

Write out your experience of inviting Jesus into your life and be able to share it with other people.

Pray and ask for God's help to enter fully into your new life of following Jesus.

Read and study the life and teachings of Jesus in the four Gospels.

Find or Begin a spiritual support group for yourself and others.

You Have Begun The Steps To Recovery From Bible Abuse And From Sick And Oppressive Religion!

Questions for Study and Discussion

1. Did this lesson help you? If so, in what way? If not, why not?

2. What questions are still unanswered for you concerning your response to Jesus?

3. What effect has this lesson had on your progress in recovery from Bible abuse?

Lesson 10

The Truth Will Set You Free

† **Preparatory Bible Reading:** John 8:12-59

When Jesus said, "You will know the truth and the truth will set you free," (John 8:32) he was talking to people who were abused and oppressed by sick religion. Their first response to Jesus was to deny that they had a problem. They answered Jesus, "We are Abraham's offspring and have never been enslaved by anyone. How can you claim to set us free?" This was the sincere reply of people in denial. They denied their own history of slavery in Egypt and in Babylon, the present oppressive rule of the Romans, and the fact they lived in a suffocating oppressive religious environment in which nobody was free.

Many people have told me that as soon as they experienced God's presence by inviting Jesus into their lives they felt as if they had been let out of prison. Learning the truth that God does love and accept you as a gay person can be an overwhelmingly liberating experience.

A Dramatic Release from Sick Religion

John told me his story in San Francisco several years ago. He had grown up as a Roman Catholic, and when he was about 14 years old he began to tell his priest at confession that he was gay. His priest was accepting, understanding, and helpful. The priest routinely granted him absolution. John said that one day his regular priest was not there and another priest told him that he would hear his confession instead. John once again talked about being gay. The priest replied, "You are an abomination to God! You must repent and reject being a homosexual. Unless you do, God cannot love you and you cannot be forgiven of your sins.

Another priest may absolve you, but it will not be valid!" John left the confession booth that day and never went back to any church again.

Years later, John was invited by some gay friends to go to a new gay group meeting. When he got there, he realized he was in a church and started to leave. The speaker started to talk about God's love for gay people and John started to listen. He had been taken to one of the first meetings of Metropolitan Community Church (MCC) San Francisco, the new church for gay people. John said that he was overwhelmed by what he heard. He could hardly believe his ears. Here was a minister saying that God really did love and accept him as a gay person. John lost emotional control and fell to the floor.

John's friends helped him out to the car. John came back to MCC and began the road to recovery from religious abuse. John, who now is in his 60's, told me how much he has enjoyed the freedom and joy of knowing Jesus Christ in his life.

Lies, Denial, and the Devil

Read John 8:37-47 to see how Jesus put his finger on the problem of how people under oppression deny the truth. Something other than common sense and objective thinking was in control. Jesus called this destructive force "the devil." Demons were also called "unclean spirits" in the Gospels. "Unclean spirits" always caused people to be self-destructive. We do not use "unclean spirit" to speak of addictions today, but the effect is the same. My experience with alcoholism, co-dependency, and other obsessive-compulsive behaviors in myself and in others has convinced me that any addiction can be an "unclean spirit" that inappropriately controls and spiritually imprisons an individual and sometimes groups of people.

The account of Jesus and the angry mob in John 8 reveals clearly the intensity and insanity of mob thinking. The presence of inappropriate, excessive anger in addictive behavior is just as evident in religious addiction as in co-dependency, alcoholism, drug addiction, and others. Whenever I see inappropriate anger in a person, including myself, I look for the addiction that lies behind the anger. It usually is not hard to find. Alcoholics have a term for addiction-induced anger, "stinking thinking."

Just as a dysfunctional group can intensify and encourage denial and anger, so also a supportive group can help you to enjoy, develop, and sustain healthy self-esteem and recover from religious abuses and addictions. Groups can kill, and groups can heal.

What groups in your life have been destructive to you? What have you done about it? Groups can be family, friends, church and school groups, Alcoholics Anonymous (AA), clubs, informal gangs, etc. What groups have been a part of your recovery and healing?

The Price of Sustained Freedom

Constant vigilance is the price of freedom. To become apathetic and lazy about anything is to invite losing it. Freedom has many enemies. One of them is the great appeal of plain laziness. We often let others make decisions for us simply because we do not want to make the effort to become well enough informed to make our own decisions. Abusive and oppressive religion feeds on ignorance. Most people seem to be content to submit to abuse rather than break out of their religious stupor and fight back.

Jesus' call equips you to think for yourself. To let others decide what is right and wrong for you is to give up the guidance of Jesus in the Gospels and to abandon the leadership of the Holy Spirit in your life. Do not give up control of your life to ignorant and abusive teachings and demands of strong willed and often emotionally disturbed individuals who claim to speak for God. Have you ever known people who like to run other people's lives but who are an emotional mess themselves? Jesus had strong condemnation for people who specialized in running and ruining the lives of others. He called them "a brood of snakes headed for the fires of hell!" (Matthew 23:33).

Resist legalistic religion for the demonic addiction that it is. Jesus has set you free. "Don't let the world around you [including religion] press you into a mold that does not fit you" (Romans 12:1-2). Learn this verse, "For freedom Christ has set us free, therefore keep standing firm and do not be subject again to a religious yoke of slavery" (Galatians 5:1).

A New Beginning

Jim had not been to church for over 20 years when he came to Golden Gate MCC for the first time. He arrived in leather on his motorcycle and parked his helmet beside his seat in church. Jim called me the next morning, to say, "I want to be born again!" I had preached Sunday on the "new birth" in John 3:1-17. We made an appointment to talk on Wednesday evening. Jim came right on time on his motorcycle.

Jim had a big smile on his face. I asked if he had read the brochure, "The Bible as Your Friend," that he had received Sunday. (We gave a copy to each visitor.) He said, "Yes. I read it three times." I asked if he had prayed the prayer. He said, "Yes. I prayed it. I also cut the prayer out and keep it in my wallet now." Jim had already done it all himself. Then he said, "I want to join the church." He borrowed a copy of the MCC video, "God, Gays, and the Gospel," that all of our new members watched as part of new member training. Jim returned the video to me the next Sunday, and I asked if he had a chance to look at it. He said, "I watched it three times!" Jim became an enthusiastic member of the church.

Jim experienced a total change in his outlook, his feelings about himself, and his lifestyle when he invited Jesus to come into his life. He became active in all of the life of the church and began to encourage and help others in their spiritual growth. He learned to accept and respect himself and his spiritual gifts that God had given to him as a gay man. Jim found the freedom in Christ that had eluded him for many years of searching for freedom in behavior that was limiting and a lifestyle that was risky and self-destructive.

What Motivates You to Change?

Steps to recovery are always motivated by something. Some people hit bottom before they turn to God for help. Hitting bottom is different for different people. When I went to an AA meeting in August 1988, and quit drinking, I had come to the conclusion that I wanted to live my life sober and not as a drunk. Nothing special happened to make me hit bottom, but I woke up and faced the fact that I was ruining my own life. I had been lying to myself and telling myself and other people that I could stop drinking any time. But I did not quit until I realized that if I did not stop drinking I would destroy myself. I was never a quiet, mellow drunk; I was loud and obnoxious. I am still obnoxious some times, but at least I am not drunk!

When I quit drinking and started back into ministry after six years of active alcoholism, I asked God why it took so long for me to wake up and turn back to sanity and sobriety. The only answer that came to me then was, "Well, Rembert, it just did!" I do not understand why I descended into the depths or why I turned back around. It happened, and from this period of my life, I learned the dynamics of addiction and recovery and how to help other people also to see the light at the end of the tunnel.

During all of the years of the confusion and trauma of my pilgrimage through religious abuse and oppression, alcoholism, running from God, floundering in uncertainly, self-destructive behavior, and wanderings in the wilderness, I never doubted that God loved me and had called me into the service of Jesus in ministry. The Gospels, Acts, and the Epistles make clear the role of the Holy Spirit in convincing us of our need for Jesus in our lives. Many evangelists seem to feel that their calling is to try to work up feelings of guilt in their audiences and to make people feel like trash and spiritual garbage.

This was not the method of Jesus. The message of Jesus was filled with actions and words that consistently told people how valuable every person is to God. You do not turn to God because you are a horrible or evil person, but because God already loves you and wants you to enjoy a full and meaningful life. "Do you think lightly of the riches of God's kindness and forbearance and patience, not realizing that the kindness of God leads you to turn to God [repent]?" (Romans 2:4).

"Lower Than A Worm"

People at a recent Saturday workshop on "Steps to Recovery from Bible Abuse" shared their spiritual history and what they hoped to gain from the workshop. Pat described her experience of growing up Baptist, then going to synagogue, later becoming Catholic, and in her early 20's learning from her church that because she was a lesbian she was "lower than a worm!" Pat said she did not want to be where she felt like she was lower than a worm! So she left church and did not go back to church until many years later when she found God's love and acceptance at MCC in Houston. Pat and others in the group were my teachers. We all learned from each other and from our sharing. Nobody wants to be where she or he is made to feel lower than a worm.

Questions for Study and Discussion

1. Has religion ever made you feel "lower than a worm"? If so, how did you react?

2. What spiritual truth do you feel was kept from you by religious teachers and preachers as you were growing up?

3. Have you found a path to healthy and happy spirituality? What has helped you most to find the path to life and hope in your life?

Additional Resources

Mel White, *Stranger at the Gate*: Simon and Schuster, 1994.

Lesson 11

What the Crucifixion Says About You

† **Preparatory Bible Reading:** John 3:16-17 and Romans 5:6-11

You are very special. The New Testament teaches that Jesus Christ died for you and for all people. The Gospel is good news for all people. There are no exceptions. Your sexual orientation does not keep you from the benefits of what Jesus did for everyone. Jesus' death and resurrection speak powerfully to all people who have been oppressed by religion.

This lesson and Lesson 12 will help you to explore the basis for your faith in Christ that is given in the two main events in the Gospel story about Jesus, his death and resurrection. Some scholars have viewed the Gospels as "passion narratives" with long introductions. The Gospel of John, for instance, gives ten chapters about the life of Jesus leading up to the week before his death and then gives another eleven chapters about the events surrounding his death and resurrection.

We have already noticed how the actions and teachings of Jesus speak directly to many of the issues facing gay, lesbian, bisexual, and transgendered people. How Jesus handled issues similar to the pressures and problems that we face today is the most prominent emphasis of this entire book.

To refresh your memory and prepare for this lesson, read Matthew 27:45-56; Mark 15:33-41; Luke 23:44-49; and John 19:17-37. If you read all the way through the Gospel of John this week, you will notice how the impending death and resurrection of Jesus shapes all of the stories about Jesus. Read also the prophetic view of the cross in Isaiah 53.

Overcoming Fear of Jesus

Because of wrong information about Jesus and the Bible, many gay people have developed what one of my friends calls "Jesus-phobia." This fear of Jesus and the Bible has led many spiritual gay people to neglect Jesus and the Bible and to avoid talking about either one. Fear of rejection by Jesus has profoundly hurt and limited many lesbians and gays.

Tom called me from a small town near the city where I was serving as Pastor of Metropolitan Community Church (MCC). He was brought up in a Southern Baptist Church in a rural area, was married with children, and was deeply distressed because he was gay, isolated, and rejected. We talked about how God loves all of us regardless of our sexual orientation. Tom already knew and believed in the death and resurrection of Jesus. I asked Tom, "Have you ever invited Jesus to come into your life?" His reply made me cry. It still does. He said, "No, I never have. I did not think that Jesus wanted me." I asked Tom, "Would you like to ask Jesus to come into your life now?" He answered with a lot of enthusiasm in his voice, "Yes! But I don't know how to do it. Will you help me?" I read the prayer in the brochure to him, and he prayed the prayer himself, inviting Jesus to come into his life. We talked some more, and Tom expressed great joy that his feelings about Jesus had changed completely and believed that God accepted and loved him after all. Tom had experienced the liberating impact of the truth about God in Jesus.

Months later we talked again and Tom was still very happy and confident about having Jesus in his life. He still had a lot of problems and issues to deal with, but he had found inner peace with God. Tom continued to have trouble with "church-phobia" and the fear of going to any church, especially MCC, which was 30 miles away. He had made a new beginning, however, that brought about a great change in how he saw himself and how he felt about God.

Jesus Died for You

Jesus did not wait until we earned or deserved God's love before he died for us. Jesus died for us because God loves us and because we need help. “While we were still helpless, at the right time Christ died for the ungodly. One will hardly die for a righteous person; though perhaps someone would dare even to die for a good person; but God demonstrated God’s own love toward us, in that while we were yet sinners, Christ died for us” (Romans 5:6-8). The first and most obvious message of the death of Jesus for all people is that God loves gays and all people who are wounded and oppressed by religion.

Self-esteem and the Crucifixion

Jesus emphasized the great value of each individual before God. After describing God’s love for each little sparrow and how God notices each person, even to the number of hairs on each head (Matthew 10:29-31), Jesus concluded, “Therefore do not be afraid. You are of more value than many sparrows.” Homophobia damages gay people most by seducing them into lowering their own self-worth even to the point of hating themselves and engaging in self-destructive behavior. The main message of the New Testament is proof of the value that God has placed on you by sending Jesus into the world to demonstrate God’s love and acceptance for all wounded and oppressed people. The self-giving actions of Jesus for your liberation and healing are incentives for you to love yourself, others, and God.

Read 1 John 4:1-21 to see how God’s love for you leads you to love yourself, other people, and God. If you love other people, you also love yourself. You are people, too. If you love your brothers and sisters (John 4:21), you will also love yourself. You also are a “sister or brother.” Be kind to yourself. Be patient with yourself. Remember that the most important person in your life is you. Think about that for a moment. When we feel that we are weak and useless and see ourselves as victims, we often are drawn into being co-dependent in our relationships. We feel that we are inadequate without that special person in our lives. How would you answer if you were asked, “Who is the most important person in your life?” Many of us immediately think of someone with whom we are developing a sometimes-unhealthy co-dependency.

Accepting the value you have as an individual child of God

can equip you to trust your own judgment and ideas and not have to be dependent on someone else all the time. Some of us develop an unhealthy need to be needed. Our sense of self-worth is bound up in the weakness and dependence of "the most important person in my life." Resist the temptation to see yourself only in your relationship to someone else who "really, really needs me" or whom you "love more than life itself." Learn to respect your own need for space. A little humor can help. The most important person in your life will always be you.

Lifting the Burden

The word "sin" in the Bible means "to miss the mark" or "to fail to reach the goal." The high cost of missing God's purpose for your life is described in many ways throughout the Bible. See the "works of the flesh" (human works) in Galatians 5:16-21. (I hesitate to suggest this passage, because the translations often read "sex" into the words when there is no hint at sex in the original Greek. In no place in the New Testament does the word "flesh" mean "sex." See my material on The Bible and Homosexuality at the end of the book. For the best study that I know on this passage, read William Barclay, *Flesh and Spirit: An Examination of Galatians 5:19-23*: SCM Press, Ltd., 1962.)

After taking too many wrong turns in the road, you do not even realize what you have missed in life. One way to gain perspective on your need for God's love and help is to see clearly the meaning of the suffering and death of Jesus. The death of Jesus not only shows you how much God loves you; it also shows you how much you need God's love and acceptance.

The great theologian, Emil Brunner, in a sermon, gave a helpful illustration of the message of the death of Jesus. He told of a farmer driving a horse and wagon along a winding mountain road to market. The farmer came to a large stone that had fallen, blocking the road. The stone seemed to the farmer to be a minor hindrance to his trip. He put his shoulder to the stone and pushed with all of his might, but the stone did not budge. Another farmer came along and tried to help remove the stone. Several other people came on the scene and hitched their horses to the stone. Finally, with horses straining at their harnesses and farmers pushing with all their strength, the stone slowly moved out of the way. The road was clear. The true weight of the stone was shown by what was needed to remove it. Brunner's point was that only in the cross of Jesus do we see the depth of our own need for God's help. Our failures and wrong turns can be viewed as insignificant when we compare ourselves to what others do or make excuses about our own failures. In the light of what God did for us in the death of Jesus to remove the burden of our failure to hit the target, our need for God's help looms much larger than we at first imagined.

To live in denial about our need for God's lovc and forgivcness is to separate ourselves from the help that we need most. Read the passages about the death of Jesus in the Gospels and ask yourself what the suffering of Jesus says about your need for reconciliation and healing in your own life.

The Cross Is Always Voluntary

Jesus voluntarily accepted the way of the cross. He did not have to do it. The prayer in the Garden of Gethsemane shows that Jesus had a choice. Jesus accepted responsibility for sins that he did not commit and took the punishment for mistakes that he did not make. Jesus said, "Deny yourself, take up your cross daily, and follow me" (Luke 8:23). We often look at illness, loss of a job, break up with a lover, or other difficulties in life as "my cross to bear." These things are not things that we have chosen. They are not what Jesus meant by "take up your cross daily and follow me." But the cross of Jesus did not just happen to him. Jesus voluntarily accepted the suffering and death that resulted in the cross.

Taking up your cross daily to follow Jesus means that you voluntarily accept responsibility for other people when you do not have to. Identify with suffering people (which is what "compassion" means) and with God's help take up the burdens and pain of other people. With God's guidance and power, you lift up others so that they too can catch a vision of God's love and acceptance.

One detail of the death of Jesus was reported by all four Gospels in exactly the same way, Jesus "yielded up the spirit"

(Matthew 27:50; Mark 15:37; Luke 23:46; and John 19:30). Jesus said, "No one takes my life away from me, but I lay it down on my own initiative. I have authority to lay it down and I have authority to take it up again. I received this commandment from God" (John 10:18). Jesus gave up his life for you, me, and for all people. Jesus said that there is no greater love than the love of those who will lay down their life for their friends. Nobody can force you to follow Jesus. It is a completely voluntary choice that only you can make.

Law and grace are held in total contrast throughout Paul's letters, especially Romans and Galatians. "I have been crucified with Christ; and it is no longer I who live, but Christ lives in me; and the life which I now live in the flesh I live by faith in the child of God, who loved me and delivered himself up for me. I do not nullify the grace of God; for if righteousness comes through the law, then Christ died needlessly!" (Galatians 2:20-21). We cannot earn God's favor. We already have it.

Questions for Study and Discussion

1. As you review the passages about the suffering and death of Jesus, what details stand out most clearly to you?

2. How do you feel about the way the death of Jesus is pictured in art, movies, musicals, and in church? How would you make the popular images of the suffering and death of Jesus more truthful and meaningful?

3. Read the seven sayings of Jesus on the cross in Mathew 27:46; Mark 15:34; Luke 23:34, 43, 46; and John 19:26-30. How do these sayings express the inclusive good news of God's love for alienated and oppressed people? How do you view your own personal worth in the light of the crucifixion?

Additional Resources

William Barclay, *Flesh and Spirit: An Examination of Galatians 5:19-23*: SCM Press, Ltd., 1962.

Lesson 12

Hope and the Resurrection of Jesus

† **Preparatory Bible Reading:** Matthew 28; Mark 16; Luke 24; John 20-21

The first baptism service that I performed was in 1953 when I was student pastor of Beaverdam Baptist Church in Laurens County, South Carolina. Beaverdam was a country church over 150 years old. Baptisms had always been held in a nearby creek once a year after the summer revival. Just before I became pastor, the church built a concrete baptistry in the floor behind the pulpit. The church had no running water. Fifty gallon barrels of water were brought in a pickup truck to the church on Saturday to fill up the new baptism pool. By Sunday morning, most of the water had leaked out. Even with two more barrels of water poured in, the water was only about two feet deep.

Following the pattern I had seen other Baptist pastors use, I lowered each person into the water until they were completely covered by the water. Then I raised them up while saying, "You are buried with Christ by baptism into death so that just as Christ was raised from the dead by the glory of God, you too might walk in newness of life" (Romans 6:4). Later, when we had a full baptism pool, I realized that people bob back to the surface on their own and do not have to be lifted with so much strain and pain from lying flat on their back. My first baptism service convinced me that lying flat on your back under water is not much fun and is certainly a long way from the promise that "you can walk in newness of life!" The elements of burial and resurrection to a new life in baptism focuses not on the burial but on the new life. When religion is reduced to painful and miserable self-rejection and self-hate, the liberating happy experience of new life through the resurrection of Jesus is forgotten. The joy of freedom in Jesus along with any hope of an effective witness to others is never realized.

All of the Gospel of John was written from the point of view of the resurrection of Jesus. "Eternal life" is seen in the fourth Gospel as a present reality in Jesus from the beginning. (See John 5:19-26; 6:39-40; 10:1-18.) This is a good time to read quickly all the way through the Gospel of John. Give special attention to the last two chapters.

Born Again to a Living Hope

As a follower of Jesus, "You have been born again to a living hope through the resurrection of Jesus Christ from the dead" (1 Peter 1:3). Read 1 Peter 1:1-9. This is the Bible passage that I most often read at the "Celebration of Life" of someone when I became a Metropolitan Community Church (MCC) pastor. The passage is worth memorizing. The New Testament consistently sees the resurrection of Jesus as the basis for hope to all who are alienated and oppressed and who suffer misunderstanding and rejection. The resurrection of Jesus tells you to trust God and not give up no matter how low you might feel. The resurrection offers hope to you in the depths of the darkest night of your soul. The cross of Jesus says that God cares about you. The resurrection says that God's power is available to you.

The resurrection of Jesus was so essential to Paul's teachings about Jesus that he declared, "If Christ has not been raised, then our preaching is vain and your faith is vain [empty]" (1 Corinthians 15:14). The resurrection of Jesus offers hope. You do not have to stay the way you are. Read all of 1 Corinthians 15 for Paul's thorough analysis of the effects of the resurrection of Jesus. Jesus offers you a chance to start over. Discipleship in Jesus is the spiritual life of new beginnings. Every day can be a new beginning. To a person in recovery from addiction, every day is a fresh opportunity to live life successfully "one day at a time." Let go of the past, live in the present, and leave the future to God.

Romans 8:1-39 is probably the most convincing presentation of how Jesus' suffering, death, resurrection, and gift of the Spirit gives you love, joy, peace, and hope. Read the entire chapter and think about how the resurrection of Jesus undergirds and validates its great message. Romans 8 is worth the time it takes for you to memorize it. Give it a try.

God's Initiative in Resurrection

God's sovereignty and control are emphasized throughout the Bible from the creation to the end of the world. The birth of Jesus was at God's initiative "in the fullness of time" (Galatians 4:4), and so was the resurrection, for "God raised Jesus up again, putting an end to the agony of death, since it was impossible for Jesus to be held in its power" (Acts 2:24). Jesus is not pictured in the Bible as rising up from the grave as an act of his own will but "was raised from the dead by the glory of God." The resurrection of Jesus was an act of God at God's initiative just as your conversion and new life in Christ is God's gift to you as an act of God through the Holy Spirit and not something that you do for yourself.

All of the Gospel stories of the post-resurrection appearances of Jesus say that Jesus was not at first recognized by anyone until he took the initiative to identify himself. Peter said that the risen Christ did not appear to all the people, "but to witnesses who were chosen beforehand by God" (Acts 10:41). Mary thought at first that Jesus was the gardener until Jesus called her name. Disciples on the road to Emmaus did not recognize Jesus until he broke bread with them. Peter did not recognize Jesus after the resurrection at the lake until the miracle of catching fish was repeated.

Resurrection and the Inclusive Gospel

Women were the first to see the empty tomb and the angels. Mary was the first to see the risen Christ and the first to proclaim (preach) the good news (gospel); therefore a woman was the first apostle and the first preacher. Jesus appeared to over 500 people at once as well as to the twelve and to Paul (1 Corinthians

15:1-11). There is no record of Jesus appearing to priests, kings, rulers, or others in authority. Jesus appeared only to ordinary people, to rejected and oppressed people. No religious leader can give you Jesus Christ in your life. Only God can do that. In the same sense, no person or church can take away from you the love, acceptance, and spiritual power that God gives to you in Jesus.

The resurrection of Jesus is viewed in many different ways. How individuals perceive the risen Jesus is highly personal. No two people experience the living Jesus in exactly the same way. Bible scholars disagree about many aspects of the resurrection of Jesus as to how literal or symbolic the event was. The Gospel of John gives a highly spiritualized presentation of the life of Jesus, even changing the time of the cleansing of the Temple from the end to near the beginning of the story. In John, the suffering and death and resurrection of Jesus are anticipated as already present in the life of Jesus from the very beginning, from the Creation. Mark and the others take a more systematic and literal view. Both views are correct. You are free to view and experience Jesus in whatever way is most meaningful to you.

The inclusive good news of God's love for all people in Jesus leaves room for individuals to know and experience Jesus in whatever way works for them. The attempts of established religions to make following Jesus into a system of doctrines and rules that are then declared to be orthodox and necessary, can be confusing and create a complex distraction from simple faith in God. Jesus did not come to make God more complicated. Jesus came to make everything so simple that only a little child or one who became humble as a child could enter into the realm of God. Following Jesus is not the religion of experts. Jesus said that the greatest thing that you can do to be in the will of God is simply to love people.

Faith is not blind. Faith in Christ is based on reliable eyewitness reports of the resurrection of Jesus as recorded in the Bible. Christian faith is built on the evidence of many eyewitnesses whose testimony has been collected and preserved in the New Testament. See the explanation at the beginning of the Gospel of Luke, Luke 1:1-4. The New Testament is important because spiritual authority is based on evidence and not on speculation. Just as in a courtroom, hearsay evidence is not admissible. There is no substitute for the eyewitness accounts by the first followers of Jesus.

Eyewitness authority cannot be passed on to someone else who was not personally present for the event. Great spiritual writings of encouragement and hope have been written since the New Testament, but none can replace the authority of the New Testament. See 2 Peter 1:12-21 and many passages in Acts and the concluding chapters of the four Gospels for the New Testament emphasis on eyewitnesses.

Hope in the Midst of HIV/AIDS

Our community has been severely tested and oppressed by the HIV/AIDS epidemic. Pressures and stress from inadequate medical care, religious condemnation, ignorance, fear, isolation, alienation, pain, death, and grief may have led you and people you love to hunger for spiritual help and support. The good news of the Bible is the love of God and the power of resurrection to bring life and hope to all people now and in the world to come. Read Romans 6:1-23 to see how Paul viewed the resurrection as the triumph of God's grace over abusive, judgmental religion.

These first twelve lessons have intentionally been a basic review of the message of and about Jesus in the story that we call "the gospel." I hope that by now you are using a good, accurate, easy to read version of the Bible, preferably *The New American Standard Bible*, and that you are systematically looking up and reading carefully all of the Bible references included in these studies. Space prohibits our copying our own translations in every lesson, but I have given you my translations of brief sections that seemed to need the emphasis of being printed here.

Questions for Study and Discussion

1. How does the resurrection of Jesus influence the way you view the actions and teachings of Jesus? How did the resurrection change the way the first disciples saw Jesus?

2. How do you personally view the resurrection of Jesus? In what ways have you experienced the presence of the living Christ in your own life? (What evidence do you have in your personal experience that Jesus is alive now?) Try reflecting on your personal experiences to find evidence that Jesus already lives within you.

Additional Resources

For a very entertaining and inspiring story of hope under oppression, read Ernest Gordon, *Through the Valley of the Kwai: From Death Camp to Spiritual Triumph*: Wipf and Stock Publishers, 1997 (originally published by Harper). Ernest Gordon was a prisoner of war under the Japanese during World War II in Southeast Asia and was in the prison camp made famous by the movie, "Bridge Over the River Kwai." Gordon later became chaplain at Princeton University. His personal story of survival and spiritual awakening is awesome.

Part III

Eliminate the Negative

Negative people, thinking, and actions in your life will delay and limit your recovery from anything. Recovery from alcoholism means getting over "stinking thinking." Getting over addiction to abusive religion, drugs, sex, co-dependency, or anything else requires the same discipline. Three years ago I went through a prolonged experience of distress and grief over someone whom I loved very much betraying and hurting me. I wasted a lot of time and energy in anger, resentment, and trying to figure out "why he did it."

Then one day I suddenly realized that I had only so much energy. It was dumb for me to waste any of my energy in negative thinking. I also woke up to the fact that if I really follow Jesus, I cannot afford to let my emotions be controlled by how other people treat me. I do not want to let other people's craziness make me crazy! My only hope to resist anger and resentment seemed to be to focus on Jesus and get busy doing what I felt was God's will for me, which at the time was writing the first version of this book.

Follow these next three Steps to Recovery with prayer and great care. Negative feelings of fear, anger, hate, resentment, self-rejection, guilt, despair, self-pity, and a victim mentality are serious enemies to your joy and peace of mind. The key to success for me is to keep my eyes on Jesus and keep learning from Jesus how to handle my own feelings and the negative influences of other people. Jesus calls people to a positive and upbeat approach to life that is both realistic and hopeful. Do not waste your supply of energy dwelling on the negatives around you. One definition I heard of the closet is, "the closet is a dark place where negatives develop." Let God help you handle the negatives.

The next three steps focus on how to face and deal with three of the most troublesome issues that gay, lesbian, bisexual, and transgendered people face, anger, abusive religion and churches, and Bible verses that are used against us.

Chapter 9

The Fourth Step

Face and Deal With Your Anger

Anger toward people and toward God or yourself can delay your recovery. Resist seeing yourself as a victim.

> Let everyone be quick to listen, slow to speak, slow to anger; for human anger does not achieve the righteousness of God.
>
> James 1:19-20

How Jesus faced and dealt with his own anger is demonstrated in Mark 3:1-7, which is the basis for the first lesson in the Fourth Step. Jesus began dealing with anger by recognizing that he was angry and by taking appropriate steps to deal with it. The emotions of Jesus are given special attention in the Gospel of Mark. Read through Mark again and notice how often the human feelings of Jesus, such as compassion, grief, amazement, etc., are brought out. How Jesus handled his own feelings can be very instructive to us in equipping us to recover and heal from the abuses of sick, oppressive religion.

Anger is a prevailing feature of the current gay lifestyle. Oppressed, abused people are usually frustrated, and anger is the natural outgrowth of frustration. The second lesson in the Fourth

Step will explore the origins and dynamics of anger and suggest practical help in handling your anger.

The words "mad" and "anger" are used to mean the same thing, because anger makes us at least "a little bit crazy" and sometimes makes us into raving maniacs. We cannot over emphasize the importance of gay, lesbian, bisexual, and transgendered people learning to recognize and control their anger. Anger is a very natural and healthy emotion, but when it develops into a lifestyle or an expression of obsessive/compulsive behavior, anger kills.

Additional Resources

See a very helpful (and entertaining, with lots of cartoons) recent bestseller by Redford Williams, M.D. and Virginia Williams, Ph.D., *Anger Kills*: Harper, 1994.

Lesson 13

How Jesus Handled Anger

† **Preparatory Bible Reading:** Mark 3:1-35 (focus on verses 3:1-7); Matthew 12:15-45; and Luke 6:6-19

Sometimes I feel that my approach to handling pressure is like the office poster that read, "When in Danger, When in Doubt, Run in Circles, Scream and Shout!" Perhaps you also can identify with this poster. Our frustration and fatigue comes from trying to cope with the pressures of life and the aggravating and disruptive presence of other people in it. Jesus, like the rest of us, lived a life under pressure. There is no escape from pressure. To live is to be under pressures. The Greek work that is translated "tribulation" in the New Testament literally means "pressure." And we pray for God to deliver us from it!

How did Jesus handle pressure? The best example that I know also shows how Jesus handled anger. Mark 3:1-7 tells the incident. Read all of Mark 3:1-35 and notice the many forms of pressure on Jesus in just this one chapter. Mark frequently used strong words for the emotions of Jesus that are not used in the other three Gospels. For example, only Mark used "anger" in 3:5 and "astonished" (*King James Version*, "sore amazed" which in Greek means "to be surprised by something you did not expect") in 14:33. Neither of these highly charged emotional words are used about Jesus anywhere else.

Jesus clearly experienced the various emotional feelings of pressure that you and I feel. How did Jesus handle negative feelings? How did Jesus handle his own anger?

Facing the Fact of Anger

Jesus was moved to anger by the insensitive callous attitude of legalistic religious leaders who brought a disabled person into the synagogue on the Sabbath day to test Jesus to see if he would break the law and heal on the Sabbath. Remember that to Jesus, people always were more important than religion. When religion was used to oppress and control weak and wounded people, Jesus got angry.

The first response of Jesus to being angry was to face his anger and recognize that he was emotionally upset. His own emotions did not distract Jesus. His mission of healing and liberating people went on. Jesus healed the withered hand. Hard-hearted religious leaders succeeded in arousing anger in Jesus, but they did not stop Jesus. They became enraged at their failure to trap Jesus. Then they plotted to destroy Jesus. Read also the parallel accounts of this incident in Matthew 12:9-14 and in Luke 6:6-11, where in verse 11 the leaders were "filled with rage."

The Greek for "rage" is *sullupeo,* which means "folly" or "foolishness" and has the meaning of our word "madness." It is not the same word used for the anger of Jesus. The word for Jesus' anger in Mark 3:4 is Greek *orge*, which is the most common Greek word for anger and is the word from which we get "ogre." It is used only in Mark 3:4, Ephesians 4:31, and Colossians 3:8. *Orge* is the Greek word used to translate the many Hebrew Bible references to the anger of God.

Jesus Withdrew

The second step for Jesus in dealing with anger was to withdraw from the scene. All three Gospels say that Jesus withdrew at this time. A time honored approach to anger is to take time for everyone to "cool off" or to "count to ten" or do something to create space to think, calm down, and decide what to do next. The Gospel of Mark shows a healthy rhythm of withdrawal and involvement in the ministry of Jesus. Jesus did not stay involved with people all the time. Jesus at times drew away from the crowds to be alone. Read rapidly through the

Gospel of Mark, and you will notice this pattern of intense service to others balanced by times of regular periods of withdrawal for personal renewal, rest, and reflection.

Caregivers involved in demanding and exhausting support ministries to people with HIV/AIDS and other people under great pressure need to follow this particular example of Jesus. We could enjoy a longer and more fruitful ministry. We would avoid early "burnout," and we would be a lot easier to get along with as we grapple daily with the unavoidable pressures of frustration, pain, failure, fear, regret, and heaping helpings of anger.

Jesus Prayed

Luke alone noted at this point (Luke 6:12) that Jesus prayed all night. This third step in Jesus' response to his own anger and the rage of the leaders (Luke 6:11) was to pray. Prayer also was preparation for selecting special helpers, "the twelve." Jesus chose 12 primary disciples to symbolize their role as the new people of God, based on the 12 tribes of Israel and brought into a new beginning through the invitation of Jesus to "follow me."

Jesus used prayer to deal with emotional stress. The Gospel of Luke adds references to Jesus praying at baptism, temptations, questioning of the disciples, transfiguration, and on the cross. Luke gives more emphasis to the prayers of Jesus than any other Gospel. The most thorough look at how Jesus prayed is in the Garden of Gethsemane and in John 17. When the disciples saw Jesus praying, they asked Jesus to teach them to pray (Luke 11:1-13).

Prayer also provides time to calm down and think through how you will respond to anger. Prayer can help to clear your head and maintain self-control when "everybody around is losing theirs and blaming it on you." Prayer is unlikely to lead you to "run in circles, scream, and shout!" Prayer changes things, but more important, prayer changes you.

Jesus Used the Bible

Make no mistake about it, to abandon the Bible is to abandon following Jesus. To become enslaved to biblical literalism, however, and to use the biblical material as a legalistic, judgmental weapon to abuse and oppress people is to betray Jesus. Gays, lesbians, women, children, the poor and homeless, people of color, prisoners, mentally ill and retarded people, and anyone else who is different and not just like everybody else have been attacked, judged, and rejected by biblical terrorists. Religious leaders who use the Bible to betray the spirit, love, and purpose of Jesus become "anti-Christ" and deprive wounded and suffering people of the very spiritual food that they most need in their time of greatest need.

Jesus used the Bible from memory, as did all teachers. Only very rich people could afford to own a book. Scrolls of the Bible were kept protected and locked in a "tabernacle" in the local synagogue. Bible teaching and study were always done from memory. Disciples were expected to memorize the entire Hebrew Bible and the various interpretations of the law by the great teachers and authorities of the past.

Read Matthew 12:14-21, which is a quote from Isaiah 42:1-4, and is the fourth step in how Jesus handled anger. This particular prophecy focused on the non-violent and gentle approach of Jesus in his total dependence on God. Anger can distract us from our mission. Jesus resisted being distracted. As Jesus recalled the exact nature of his calling and purpose, he brought both himself and his disciples back to a clear and objective sense of purpose. Anger and other emotional pressures were resolved in this process.

Jesus Selected Helpers

Nobody likes to face stress and fear alone. Many gay and lesbian people feel isolated and alone in their struggle to survive. Jesus gathered around him the people of his own choosing to be with him and support him as the gathering storm of misunderstanding and violence against him approached. Jesus saw his disciples as his "family" ("Whoever does the will of God is my brother and sister and mother," Mark 3: 31-35). The story of Jesus' selection of helpers in Mark 3:13-19 and Luke 6:13-16 is set soon after the event of Jesus' anger in the synagogue.

The fifth step that Jesus took in dealing with anger within and against him was to choose friends to share his life and ministry. Having a friend or friends to talk to when you are under pressure from anger and other strong feelings can help you to become more objective about what is happening and about what to do. One of the most healing aspects of Alcoholics Anonymous and other recovery groups is the opportunity to tell your own ideas and experiences and to learn from the ideas and experiences of others who face the same kind of things that are happening in your life. Groups for recovery from Bible and religious abuse can offer the same help.

One of the main problems with anger is that it can cut us off from the people we most need in our lives. Our parents, friends, family, and others who love us, can because of their religious prejudice, lack of information, and misunderstanding cause us to become so frustrated that we just simply get angry and walk out. And I do not blame you for doing it, either. Sometimes it takes years to rebuild family ties that homophobia has shattered. Sometimes the family ties are never restored. In Mark 3:21, some of the family of Jesus decided that he was crazy and came to try to put him away! Does that sound all too familiar?

Jesus maintained a loving and close relationship with his mother and brothers while at the same time he selected helpers to be his friends and to be his "real" family. When Paul described "love" in 1 Corinthians 13:4, the first definition was that "love is patient." The Greek for "patient" is *makrothumei*, which the King James translation of the Bible rendered as "suffers long." The word is made up of two words, *makro* means "long" and *thumei* means "anger", more exactly "outbursts of anger." In other words, "it takes a long time for love to become angry." The same word is used in the "fruit of the Spirit" list in Galatians 5:22-23. The love that conquers anger is the love that Jesus experienced and has given to us.

Jesus Continued to Teach and Heal

Mark 3:10-12 shows that Jesus did not let anger derail him from God's mission of teaching and healing. Sometimes we handle emotional pressure best by simply keeping busy doing our work and carrying out our commitments. We do indeed have promises to keep. Jesus faced opposition with cool courage. Matthew 12:22-37 continues the story of how Jesus handled anger. After a time of withdrawal, prayer, Bible study, sharing with friends, and renewal, Jesus returned with confidence to face and deal with the misunderstandings and fears that fed the anger. The sixth step in how Jesus handled anger was to plunge back into his mission of teaching and healing.

Jesus Did Not Become Like Those Who Angered Him

The final, seventh step in how Jesus handled anger was his refusal to give in to demands that he should fight on the terms of his enemies. Read Matthew 12:38-45 to see how Jesus exercised self-control and clear thinking by resisting efforts by others to draw him into useless debates and speculations. Uncontrolled anger can draw us into a great waste of time and energy fighting the wrong battles. Loving and helping others experience the love and life of God in their lives is far more important than winning arguments.

Jesus was a teacher, and Matthew 13 continues the story of how Jesus responded to anger by teaching love, truth, hope, and faith. Learning takes time. Growing takes time. Healing takes a lot of time. But the time to begin to face and deal with anger is now. Anger can distract, weaken, cripple, and even destroy you. Anger can so dominate your personality that you become your own worst enemy. You simply must master it.

Questions for Study and Discussion

1. What is the most damage that your own anger has done to you?

2. What is the worst thing done to you in anger by others?

3. What spoke most directly to you personally in how Jesus handled anger?

4. What is the difference in anger and hate?

Additional Resources

See the end of the next lesson for books on how to handle anger.

Lesson 14

Overcoming Hostility and Violence

† **Preparatory Bible Reading:** Genesis 4:2-10; Proverbs 14:29; 29:22; James 1:19-20; and Ephesians 4:24-27

How do you react when someone gets mad at you and hangs up on you on the phone while you are still talking? If this makes you angry, what do you do? Do you call back immediately and if you get an answer, hang up on them? Perhaps you never acted in such a childish and immature way, but I have to confess that I have! Anger can make us do crazy things. That's why being crazy and being angry both are called "mad."

We took a close look at how Jesus handled anger in the last lesson. Now we take a look at the causes and dynamics of anger and some practical guidelines to how to deal with it. We are taught very early to deny and suppress anger. We transfer anger and misdirect it. We seldom face it cleanly and openly. When we are sad, we can say, "I am sad." When we are happy, we say, "I am happy!" But when we are angry, we say, "You are stupid!"

Anger alters our perception of others and ourselves. Anything like drugs, alcohol, co-dependency, religious oppression, or depression that alters our perception can make anger harder to handle. We speak of being in a "blind rage" or a "fit of anger" to express how anger can loosen our grip on reality. Anger is a powerful destructive force that can paralyze you and consume your energy. Learning how to recognize anger in you and in others is necessary for healing broken relationships.

Forms of Hostility

Anger takes many forms, can wear a mask, and sometimes be hard to detect even in ourselves. Three levels of hostility can be seen in "rage," "anger," and "resentment." Rage is undifferentiated and generalized anger. Rage is seen in early childhood in temper tantrums or fits. Anger is modified rage. Anger is hostility directed toward a goal. Resentment is concealed anger. Resentment can build until it openly explodes. Can you recall experiences of these three levels of hostility in yourself?

Some experiences, such as fatigue, pain, failure to communicate, candor, directness, and aggressiveness can be mistaken for hostility. We tend to respond to anger with anger. Our ability to distinguish real anger from experiences that can be mistaken for anger, therefore, helps us to cope with anger in ourselves and in others. Anger that is concealed or suppressed, however, can grow quickly into open hostility if it is overlooked or ignored.

The Hebrew word for "anger" used hundreds of times in the Hebrew Testament is the word that means, "to snort." Another word used frequently means "to become hot" or "to burn." "Angry" in Psalm 4:4, "be angry, but do not sin," is a Hebrew word for "tremble," and the word for "sin" is literally "do not speak." This is quoted in Ephesians 4:26 in the verse, "Be angry but do not sin. Do not let the sun go down on your anger." Read all of Psalm 4 to see how overcoming anger can help you to get a good night's sleep.

Causes of Hostility

All humans are destructive. "Original sin" in its original form contains anger and violence. Social psychology views hostility as a result of frustration, which can also be expressed in depression when anger is turned inward on the self. Harry Stack Sullivan saw hostility as a device to avoid the anxiety that comes from a lowering of one's sense of well-being. Wayne E. Oates said that the hostile self is the rejected self.

These causes for anger obviously speak directly to all abused and oppressed people. As gay people, we have experienced a lifelong barrage of criticism, misunderstanding, oppression, and religious condemnation that often results in frustration and rejection and in a dramatic lowering of our self-esteem and sense of well-being. Much of the abuse and pain that gays and lesbians inflict upon themselves and each other springs from anger. One of the persistent dynamics of oppression is for the oppressed to become oppressors when they can gain control.

Fear of closeness or of becoming dependent can produce hostility, especially for those who have already developed a suspicious personality under pressure. Resentment, anger, and even violent behavior can result from extremely dependent relationships and from forced but unwanted closeness. We can understand the feelings of angry young gay people who have been unfairly condemned, rejected, and isolated from other people. They often have suffered the loss of family ties and even career opportunities. We also can understand the feelings of angry older lesbians and gay men who have been rejected so many times that they have given up on being happy or having a partner or enjoying any of what is left in life for them. Smoldering resentment and pent up anger fester beneath the surface among gay people and like a hidden volcano keep us in constant danger of destructive and catastrophic explosions.

The Bible and Anger

The Book of Proverbs encourages self-control, "Whosoever is slow to anger has great understanding, but whoever is quick tempered [short of spirit] exalts folly" (Proverbs 14:29). "An angry person stirs up strife, and a hot tempered person abounds in transgressions" (Proverbs 29:22). The New Testament gave similar advice, "Let every one be quick to hear, slow to speak, slow to anger; for human anger does not achieve the righteousness of God" (James 1:19-20).

Ephesians warns against denial and anger, "Put on the new self, which in the likeness of God has been created in righteousness and holiness of the truth. Therefore, laying aside falsehood, speak truth each one of you with your neighbor [quoting Zechariah 8:16], for we are members of one another. Be angry, and yet do not sin; do not let the sun go down on your anger. Do not give the devil an opportunity" (Ephesians 4:24-27).

Cain and the Beginnings of Anger and Despair

Read Genesis 4:2-10 to see how Cain was the "rejected self" who became resentful and angry leading to violence and then to despair. The story of Cain and Able illustrates the causes of hostility that we have already listed. The roots of anger in Cain's experience of rejection, frustration, low self-esteem, and loss of self-respect grew into hostility, violence, murder, and then into depression. Cain first expressed his anger in resentment and frustration. Then his anger smoldered and accumulated until it exploded into violence.

Notice how Cain's anger toward God for rejecting the sacrifice was not directed against God, whom Cain could not reach, but was transferred to his brother, who had done him no harm. Observe also how Cain's frustration and anger were turned inward to create depression and despair at the end. What other causes and effects of anger do you notice in the story of Cain? Have you ever felt anger toward God for making you homosexual and not changing you when you begged for God to make you heterosexual? If so, you are not the only one to do this! Go back and read the testimony by the young Pentecostal preacher whose anger at God turned inward into depression and suicide (at the beginning of Chapter 3, "Jesus Heals Sick Religion").

How to Handle Hostility

First, learn to recognize anger in yourself. What is a clue to you that you are becoming angry? How do you handle your own anger? When someone is angry with you, ask yourself if you have done anything to cause hostility in the other person. Direct communication can sometimes clear up misunderstandings that breed hostility.

Look at the long-range emotional pattern of the angry person. Is the person angry with you or with everybody? Is the anger directed at you or at someone who looks like you or acts or talks like you? Transference is one of the most common ways that people try to avoid dealing directly with their angry feelings. If you are in a place of leadership, like clergy, some people may unconsciously transfer anger to you that they feel toward their father or mother, their boss, or even God! This is where you are to be "as wise as serpents and as harmless as doves" (Matthew 10:16). See all of Matthew 10:16-42 for a lot of practical insight and help from Jesus.

Humor can help if you include yourself. Know how much hostility you can absorb. That will depend on your relationship with the angry person. Facing hostility and dealing with it openly and objectively can strengthen relationships and draw people together.

My daughter gave me a huge poster to put in my office when I was teaching at Baptist College, where she was also a student. The poster was a picture of a big angry gorilla. Bold print said, "If I Want Your Opinion, I'll Beat It Out of You!" I thought it was very funny. Later, I wondered if she was trying to tell me something! Some people seem to go through life with a chip on their shoulder. Maybe you have done that at times without realizing it.

The Madness of King Saul

Suspicion, anger, and violence often go together. War between nations and between individuals can grow from suspicion and anger. Recall the link between King Saul's fear and suspicion of David and the king's attempts to kill David. Do you think that Saul understood his own anger? Saul's anger was finally turned inward upon himself in his suicide. 1 Samuel 13 through 31 and 2 Samuel 1 tell the saga of Saul, the first king of Israel. Read through this story and notice the intricate relationships of Saul, Jonathan, and David. Suspicion, jealousy, fear, and anger made Saul do many strange and self-destructive things.

The relationship of David with Jonathan will be explored in Lesson 26.

There are many other examples of concealed and misdirected anger in the Bible. Balaam's anger toward his donkey (Numbers 22), and Jonah's anger at God over a dying vine (Jonah 4) are examples of this kind of anger. The anger of the older brother when the prodigal son came home and was welcomed by the loving father (Luke 15) is one of the most powerful teachings of Jesus. Read these stories and see what they teach you about anger.

We can easily be drawn into the suspicion, homophobia, and anger of other people. When someone is angry and you refuse to join in and agree with the anger, then you become suspect and can become the object of anger yourself. For the sake of our own recovery from spiritual abuse, we simply must learn well the causes and effects of anger so that we can develop self-control and learn to deal effectively with hostility in ourselves and in others.

Questions for Study and Discussion

1. What is the clearest sign that you are becoming angry? What is your most effective approach to controlling your own anger? What most often makes you angry? Why?

2. When have you experienced or observed hostility transformed into friendship and an enduring relationship?

3. What is your customary response to people who are angry with you?

4. What are the results of your customary response to anger?

Additional Resources

James R. St. Clair, *Neurotics in the Church*: Revell, 1963, for a better understanding and coping with anger in the church.

Albert Ellis, *How to Live With and Without Anger*: Institute for Rational Living, 1977.

Dietrich Bonhoeffer, *Life Together*: many publishers, is a classic on interpersonal relationships for the followers of Jesus. It is a must-read book.

The autobiographical book by the Rev. Robert Williams, *Just As I Am: A Practical Guide to Being Out, Proud, and Christian*: Crown, 1992, contains powerful emotional reactions to abusive destructive religion. Several sections deal with anger. Robert Williams, who was raised a Southern Baptist, was ordained by Bishop John Shelby Spong of Newark and became the most famous and outspoken radical gay priest in America. His story is worth hearing and feeling.

Anger Kills, already recommended in the previous lesson, is the best current reading I know on the subject of anger. Redford Williams, M.D. and Virginia Williams, Ph.D., *Anger Kills*: Harper, 1994.

Lesson 15

Freedom from Fear

† **Preparatory Bible Reading:** John 6:15-21; 14:27; 20:19-23

Years ago, when I was at home from seminary for a few days, at about 2:00 a.m., I was suddenly startled awake by an ear-shattering noise. A huge wall mirror in my bedroom fell onto a tall lamp, shattering it, and then hit the tile hearth in front of a fireplace that broke up the mirror. The unexpected crashing sound scared me bolt upright in the bed. I lost my sense of where I was and was as terrified as I can ever remember being in my life. I ran into my parents' bedroom, who by then were also awake, and jumped into bed with them. For several nights, I could not sleep with the light off. When I went back to seminary, several weeks went by before I could sleep all night without waking up scared in the middle of the night. I finally got over it, but it taught me how fear can capture and paralyze our minds.

Fear is a terrible enemy. Anxiety and fear can distract us from our daily routine and can destroy our joy of living. Fear keeps many gay people away from all supportive gay groups and from any participation in encouraging activities, such as Metropolitan Community Churches (MCC). Many people have told me when I was an MCC pastor that they drove to the church and sat in the parking lot for several Sundays before they found the courage to come inside. They were afraid to risk being seen by somebody they knew. Fear saps our energy and distorts our perception of reality. I have found, however, that most of the things that I feared never happened. Fear makes us vulnerable. Fear is never our friend. Fear causes pain and torment.

Jesus frequently greeted his friends with the salutation, "Do not be afraid." See 1 John 4:1-21 for a wonderful expression of God's love overcoming fear. "There is no fear in love; but perfect love casts out fear, because fear causes pain and torment. The one who is afraid is not yet fully complete in love. We love because God first loved us" (1 John 4:18-19). 1 John 4 is the Bible chapter that twice says, "God is love." When "perfect love casts out fear," therefore, freedom and release are overwhelming.

How Jesus Liberates Us from Fear

When you know that people really love you, you are not afraid of them or what they will do to you. Perfect love really does cast out fear. The term "casts out" in 1 John 4:18 is a word that means, "to throw out" with great force. It was used for casting out unclean spirits. Fear is an unclean spirit that can control us and make us self-destructive.

Jesus' inclusive love and teachings in the Gospel of Luke demonstrate also the theme of freedom from fear. See the "do not be afraid" announcements by angels to Joseph (Luke 1:13 and in Matthew 1:20), to Mary (Luke 1:30), to the shepherds ("Do not be afraid; for behold, I bring you good news of a great joy which shall be for all of the people," Luke 2:10), and to the women at the empty tomb (Matthew 28:5). Jesus called Peter to become a fisher of people and said, "Do not be afraid" (Luke 5:10). When parents were told that their child was dead, Jesus said, "Do not be afraid anymore" and raised the child from the dead (Luke 8:50). When Jesus announced the equal value of all people, he said, "Fear not, for you are of great value"(Luke 12:7).

The Calming Effect of Jesus

Read about Jesus coming to the disciples during a storm in the middle of the night (John 6:15-21). They were rowing hard in the storm and getting nowhere. Jesus appeared and said, "Do not be afraid. I am here." They were immediately at land. Jesus came not only to calm their fears but also to bring them successfully to their goal of safety from the storm. When everything seems hopeless, Jesus is there to calm our fears and give us courage.

Jesus said "Peace I leave with you. My peace I give to you is not like the world gives. Do not let your heart be troubled or be afraid" (John 14:27). The term "afraid" here is a word that means "timid or cowardly" and was used for fear of wild beasts in the arena. Jesus makes you brave. After the resurrection, Jesus appeared with the familiar greeting, "Peace be with you" (John 20:19-23). The Holy Spirit was given to the disciples to continue the mission of Jesus. Fear was replaced with a mission from God.

The Awesome Power of Fear

Fear does not always paralyze. Sometimes fear energizes people to do things that they never thought they could do. Maybe you heard of the man walking through a cemetery late at night. He fell into a large open grave. He jumped and jumped but the grave was too deep and he gave up and decided to wait until morning and fell asleep. Along came another man who also fell into the grave. He jumped and jumped and could not get out. The first man woke up and said, "You can't get out that way." But he did!

Fear produces extra adrenaline, which gives your body a boost to help you run away from danger. Fear can produce noticeable physical problems, like uneasiness or a "knot in your stomach." Fear of being bashed can equip you to run and escape. Fear of failure and fear of what others will think or do to you produces fear in the form of anxiety. The long-term pain of anxiety can limit and distract us and reduce our ability to enjoy life. Paul said that in Christ he had "learned to be content" in all circumstances (Philippians 4:11). "Content" means "self rule" or "self control." Paul was at peace within himself no matter how he was treated. He had learned to resist letting other people determine and control his peace of mind. Even in prison, Paul had learned how to feel good about himself under pressure. Read all of Philippians 4.

Fear has been used to stir whole nations to war. Hitler used fear of the communists and fear of the Jewish people and others to galvanize the German people into a destructive war machine that left a path of devastation and horror that humanity can never forget. Fear of homosexuality and homosexuals is being used today in America to feed the religious and political ambitions of unscrupulous leaders. One of the main reasons for this book is to give accurate information that will help dispel the fear of homosexuality ("homophobia") that hurts all people, not just gay people.

Fear of Sex

In our culture, people have been conditioned for generations to fear sex. When I became a pastor in 1952 and began to guide couples in preparation for marriage, one of my religion teachers suggested that I should give engaged couples a little book called *Sex Without Fear*, which gave biological and psychological facts about sex. The book was needed because most people had learned a lot of incorrect information about sex and had been conditioned to dread and fear sex as something that was wrong but that they were expected to do anyway when they got married. This was before the so-called "sexual revolution" that flooded young people with all they wanted to know and a lot more.

The fear of sex has been fine tuned and greatly exaggerated in homophobia. A new edition of George Weinberg's book *Society and the Healthy Homosexual*, brings up to date the original definition of "homophobia," which Dr. Weinberg invented and first described in 1972. Homophobia is the fear of homosexuality in yourself or in other people. Many of the most homophobic people are closeted homosexuals. Fear of sex has grown into a formidable destructive force when combined with fear of God.

Fear of God

The Greek word for fear is *phobos*. The many phobias in medicine and psychiatry are built on this word. Weinberg considered homophobia to be a treatable mental disorder. He did not consider homosexual orientation to be a disorder. "Fear God" in the Bible means to "respect or honor" God. "The fear of God is the beginning of knowledge [wisdom]" (Proverbs 1:7). Psalm 23:4 used the same word to say "I will fear no evil." What does it mean to fear God? Does it mean to be afraid of God as we fear snakes, death, or heights? The idea of the holiness of God is behind the meaning of fearing God. The entire Temple system was based on the holiness of the unapproachable God, who dwelt in splendid isolation behind a curtain that was several inches thick. The Gospels say that when Jesus died, the Temple curtain was ripped in two. Jesus taught God's unconditional love and transformed fear into love, telling us to love God, one another, and ourselves.

Unhealthy Fear

When fear of God is coupled with fear that homosexual orientation is an abomination to God, it is not surprising that even loving parents learn with horror that their children are lesbian or gay. Parents must deny their own "natural love" for their children in order to abuse and reject them for being gay. "Without natural affection" in Romans 1:31 refers to abandoning the natural love that parents have for their children and not to homosexuality. Distortions of biblical material to condemn gay people as evil has set up an incredible situation where parents and others have been so afraid that they have treated gay children as if they were possessed by Satan.

When people truly are convinced that someone is under the control of evil or demonic forces, even the most terrible and destructive actions are justified, even in the minds of the people who think that they are possessed. Fear can blur the distinction between fact and fantasy. Vampires, werewolves, zombies, homosexuals, and other movie monsters are destroyed with dramatic violence "for their own good!" People have been burned alive as witches, and multitudes of gay men and lesbians have been subjected to electric shock therapy. As I write this, the murder trial is in progress for the two men who tortured and killed Matthew Shepard, simply because he was gay. The extreme horror of the crime sent shock waves and sparked outrage and hate crime legislation throughout the nation. But it did not change the conviction of homophobic religious fundamentalists, who remain sternly convinced that God hates homosexuality as a sin.

Religion has been enlisted as a powerful weapon against homosexuals in the "Ex-Gay" movement to judge, condemn, and then attempt to cure them in the name of God. The American Psychiatric Association in October 1998 condemned the ex-gay therapy as a dangerous distortion of medical practice that resulted in depression, despair, and suicide for many people. Yet the "ex-gay" industry continues to grow and thrive with the help and support of an army of preachers and churches.

Even the twelve steps of Alcoholics Anonymous (AA) have been perverted into a misguided program for the "recovery" of gay men and lesbians from their sexual orientation in "Homosexuals Anonymous." This organization has added three additional steps to the twelve steps of AA. These extra steps bring fundamentalist religious beliefs into the program and muddy the water for many people who honestly seek help in facing life more effectively as gay and lesbian people of many faiths.

Jesus came to set us free from fear. Freedom from fear of sexual orientation is long overdue. Sexuality is a gift from God to be celebrated and enjoyed. "You have not received a spirit of slavery and fear, but you have received a spirit of adoption as children; for the whole creation will be set free from its bondage to destruction into the freedom of the glory of the children of God" (Romans 8:15, 21). Fear and anger are the two most negative forces working against us. Jesus gives us victory over both fear and anger.

Questions for Study and Discussion

1. What have you feared most that never happened to you?

2. What is the worst thing done to you because you are gay? Why?

3. What help in dealing with fear have you found in the Bible?

4. How have your fears changed, as you have grown older? Make a list of things you fear and ask God to set you free.

Additional Resources

See practical and entertaining books by John Powell, *Why Am I Afraid to Love?* and *Why Am I Afraid to Tell You Who I Am?*: Argus Communications, 1967, 1969. These two books were required reading in my college courses on pastoral ministries.

Troy Perry, (with Thomas L. P. Swicegood) *Don't Be Afraid Anymore*: *The Story of Reverend Troy Perry and the Metropolitan Community Churches*: St. Martin's Press, 1990.

Lesson 16

Freedom to Live in Hope

† Preparatory Bible Reading: Matthew 26:31-39; Psalms 22 and 23; Romans 8:18-39

Depression is anger turned inward. To deny and conceal your anger can sour your disposition, drain your energy, and make you physically unattractive. A lot of the anti-social and self-destructive behavior of oppressed people can be traced directly to unresolved anger. Depression and suicidal thinking has taken an incredible toll of misery and wasted lives among us. What is the remedy for the mood of hopelessness that has frequently gripped many gay, lesbian, bisexual, and transgendered people and turned them against themselves and each other? This lesson explores how we can find the freedom to live in hope.

Finding Fresh Meaning in Life

Ed is a gay lawyer in San Francisco. He was not interested in religion and said that he was an atheist. He was a good friend of Jim, who had HIV/AIDS and was very sick. Jim was a Christian and active in Golden Gate Metropolitan Community Church (MCC), where I was pastor. Jim was in the hospital when I met Ed. As Jim became more ill, Ed took charge of Jim's business affairs. Jim thought that he was about to die. He was in a lot of pain. He wanted to kill himself and talked to me and wanted me to agree that he should commit suicide. I could not agree. I told him about the Rev. Troy Perry's suicide attempt and the start of MCC. I shared with Jim what Troy said about the temptation to end your own life that "you never know what might be around the next corner for you."

Jim decided that he did not want to die. He asked God to heal him. He got better. To everyone's amazement, Jim came back to church. Ed came with him to Bible study and to worship. Ed began to talk about inviting Jesus to come into his life. Several months passed and Jim came near death again. Ed read my brochure on how to become a Christian. Jim continued to pray for Ed. I went to see Jim at his home and we talked and prayed together. Ed came in. He said that he had read the brochure and wanted to become a Christian. Ed said he did not know how to do it and asked me to help him pray. We prayed together a prayer like the one in the brochure.

Ed was very happy about his decision. He said that he felt relieved and free. Ed said he could sum up his feelings now as "euphoria!" Jim was very happy also. He had lived to see his best friend become a Christian. We talked for a while about how Jesus set us free from oppressive and judgmental religion. Jim's love for Ed was part of the message of Jesus that reached Ed. Jim died about two weeks later. Ed continued to be enthusiastic and growing in his newly found faith. Jim taught me a lot about despair and hope.

What is Depression?

Depression is one of the most destructive negatives that can engulf us, distort our grip on reality, and blur our vision of hope. One reason that cheerful attempts to encourage depressed people do not work is that the underlying problem is not sadness but it is anger. The depressed person is "mad as hell" and cannot even see past the pain of anger. Well-meaning attempts to cheer up a depressed person often increase their anger and feeling that they are misunderstood. Intense long-term anger is hard to face and conquer and is more easily handled by denial.

Depression grows from any experience of loss, real or imagined. The loss can be the death of a lover, a parent, or a close friend. The loss can be a sickness that takes away one's health and mobility, an amputation, a loss of income or career, a loss of reputation or self-esteem, a divorce, separation, religious excommunication, or any other significant thing that changes the way one sees one's self. In depression, a slowing down is obvious. Eyes may look as though the depressed person has been crying even if they have not. The brow is furrowed. The corners of the mouth turn down. Life slows down. Hobbies, church, sex life, conversation, work, and other everyday activities slow down. Sleep is difficult. Chronic fatigue develops. The average depressed patient has lost 14 pounds by the time a psychiatrist is consulted. Relationships with people slow down. In acute depression, the individual will not respond.

When the depressed person does respond, the answers usually are expressions of hopelessness and preoccupation with guilt and self-depreciation that often are accompanied by negative religious thinking about the judgment of God and fear of the "unpardonable sin." The depressed person often turns belief in God's presence, which should be a source of comfort, into a threatening and judgmental presence. "God is watching you," can be an encouragement or a threat depending on your state of mind at the time. Imagined illnesses can accompany depression. You may have seen some of this in others or in yourself.

Causes of Depression

"Reactive Depression" is an individual's response to any significant loss. The grief process begins. Some day hope will return. The grief process after a great loss usually follows the following pattern,

1. **Shock and disbelief** (fairly brief).
2. **Numbness** (difficulty in feeling anything).
3. **A flood of grief** (may come after supportive people have gone away).
4. **Period of recall** (may take many days and gives opportunity for supportive listening).
5. **Acceptance of loss and period of adjustment** (can take months or even years).

A more troublesome form of depression is "Autonomous Depression," which has no observable cause, but in which a significant break in interpersonal relationships has taken place.

Here the individual cannot envision a time of hope for the future. The depression is an outward expression of internalized hostility. Depressed people are angry but turn it in on themselves. The greater the depression the greater the self-depreciation and loss of self-worth than can lead to self-destruction.

Depression is a bid for time. It helps to prevent violence. The depression should not be taken away too soon. This intense internalized anger should be approached with the guidance of a psychiatrist. Depression is by far the most common emotional illness. It is also fortunately the most treatable. Depression is a shield. The guilt that is expressed in depression is not the "godly sorrow that leads to repentance" but is the "sorrow unto death" (2 Corinthians 7:10). Read 2 Corinthians 7:2-16 for Paul's study of sorrow and depression

Clues to Suicidal Thinking

Classic depression has been described above. Two other types of depression, however, mask the obvious symptoms. "Agitated Depression" has many of the symptoms of classic depression, but the individual walks, wrings hands, and verbalizes a lot of anxiety. "Smiling Depression" is a concealment reaction. The person does not express the outward symptoms. The pain of a great loss and internalized hostility are still there. Superficially, however, everything is bright and pleasant. These variations on depression can mislead you into overlooking the self-destructive potential of a depressed person.

Obvious Clues to Potential Suicide

1. **An attempt.** This is a cry for help. It could backfire and succeed.
2. **Talk about suicide overtly or indirectly.** 75 percent of people who kill themselves talk about it first. Indecision about small matters can be symbolic of the ultimate question of living or dying. Indecision over suicide can cause headaches.
3. **The person plans for his or her death or absence.**
4. **The person begins improving after depression.**

5. **Self-Inflicted character assassination.** People throw away their success. A doctor might go on drugs, a minister might engage in socially unacceptable behavior. Depressed people use a change in behavior to tell the world that they feel worthless and deserve to die.

The idea that one can hurt others permanently through suicide is false and is based on a grandiose view of the Self. A baby sees itself as the center of the universe. To view Self as the center of the universe exemplifies severe regression as well as a profound rejection of God.

How to Help Depressed and Suicidal People

1. **Be familiar with the clues to suicide.**
2. **Avoid kindly assurances of God's forgiveness.** Guilt is not the basic problem, hostility is! Missing the basic issue increases the hostility.
3. **Avoid lengthy conversations and confessions** that can deepen depression. Do not listen endlessly to the depressed person tell and elaborate on their depression. It only re-enforces the distorted views that lie behind the depression. Avoid attempts to cheer them up with talk that misses the mark and infuriates someone who is already hostile. Make short frequent visits and calls.
4. **Share responsibility with someone** in the medical profession. Medical issues are also involved. Only with the help of a professional therapist can profound hostility be uncovered safely. There are many different kinds of depression that call for many different kinds of treatment.
5. **Give some responsibility to the depressed person** by making a covenant with them that they will not make major decisions without calling you or their doctor.
6. **Try not to leave the deeply depressed person totally alone.** Most suicides occur in private.
7. **Use brief prayer.** An early complaint can be, "I can't pray." You can offer, "Can I pray for you?"

The Bible and Depression

Matthew 26:31-39 tells how Jesus coped with despair in the Garden of Gethsemane. Jesus recognized and admitted his despair. He withdrew, prayed, turned to Scripture, shared with his friends, trusted in God, and kept his commitment to do God's will. Many have found encouragement in times of despair by studying the details of the trial, suffering, and death of Jesus and then going on to celebrate the victory of God for all people in the resurrection of Jesus from the dead.

The dynamics of despair are explored in the Book of Job. Read Job 14; Psalms 22, 23, and 103; 2 Corinthians 1:3-11; Romans 8:18-39; and Colossians 1:24-29.

Questions for Study and Discussion

1. How have you handled your own depression when you realized that depression was your problem?

2. How have you tried to help depressed people in the past?

3. What would you change in view of what you have learned in this lesson?

4. What Bible material has been most helpful to you in dealing with your own experiences of loss in your life?

5. Have you had the opportunity to give support and encouragement to others who have faced the same kind of loss that you experienced?

Additional Resources

Viktor Frankl, *Man's Search for Meaning* is the story that was first called *From Concentration Camp to Existentialism*. It is a psychiatrist's story of his life in four different Nazi death camps during World War II. In these intense experiences, Dr. Frankl developed "logo therapy," which means "meaning therapy" and has proved to be an effective approach to helping troubled people find health and wholeness. This book helped me.

Other classics are, *Sickness Unto Death* by Soren Kierkegaard.

The Dark Night of the Soul, by St. John of the Cross.

Confessions, by St. Augustine.

Chapter 10

The Fifth Step

Avoid Negative People and Churches

Listening to legalistic and abusive religious leaders can undercut and delay your recovery.

† **Preparatory Bible Reading:** Mark 7:1-23 and Colossians 2:20-23

Paul said in all his letters "some things hard to understand, which the untaught [ignorant] and unstable distort [twist and torture] as they do also the rest of scriptures, to their own destruction. You therefore, beloved, knowing this beforehand, be on your guard lest, being carried away by the errors of unprincipled people, you fall away from your own steadfastness" (2 Peter 3:16-17).

Many people are startled to learn that this warning about ignorant and unprincipled people who distort and twist scripture is contained in the New Testament itself. For a person who has been abused and oppressed by legalistic and judgmental religion to continue to go to an abusive church or tune in to abusive religious broadcasts is like an alcoholic going to bars. Family pressures, long term religious conditioning from childhood, and a desire to "fit in" can lead you into unhealthy religious situations. A friend recently told me that she grew up in a loving and healthy church where the pastor's first words to every baptismal class were, "Beware of any church that tries to tell you how to think."

Use your brain. Think for yourself. Jesus did not say, "Follow the rules, follow Paul, follow the traditions, follow the priest or preacher, follow the church, or follow the Law." Jesus gave only one invitation to all people equally, "Follow me."

Resist the spiritual virus of legalism. Legalism is alien to the life and teachings of Jesus Christ. Legalism is spiritual antimatter that dissolves the love, patience, and acceptance that God intends you to have towards other people. Exposing yourself to legalistic religion is like exposing yourself to a deadly virus. It is a chance you do not want to take! Review "Legalism as Idolatry" in Lesson 3.

Lesson 17

How Jesus Defined Family

† **Preparatory Bible Reading:** Mark 3:20-21, 31-35; 6:1-6; and Luke 4:16-30

The ugly duckling was rejected and oppressed by his own mother duck and his brother and sister ducks because he was different. He hated his own reflection in the water. He hated himself. He was different from the others. Later, the ugly duckling grew up and turned out to be a beautiful swan. His self-esteem soared and so did he. This delightful story is our special parable of the gay person in a straight world.

Pressures on children to conform to family and community traditions and values can be oppressive and overwhelming. The late Rev. James Brock, my first Metropolitan Community Church (MCC) pastor, told me that one problem for our church is that we try to become a family instead of a community. Many of us come from dysfunctional families, and when we create a church as family, we create a dysfunctional church. One reason for this is that the family always puts pressure on the family members to conform to whatever the family believes is normal. No member of the family is allowed to be really different and not suffer.

When a girl or boy growing up in the average home begins to realize that she or he is lesbian or gay, the fear and shame of being different can be devastating and paralyzing. Like any other childhood trauma, the development of homophobia in gay children can limit and distort their view of themselves and of their world. The claim that early childhood trauma causes homosexuality is totally unfounded and supported by no credible scientific research. Early childhood rejection and abuse of gay people does cause homophobia and self-hate in gay youth. Avoiding abusive parents is very difficult for gay and lesbian children, but many of them try.

Learning to fear and reject ourselves early in life causes many later developmental problems that plague us. We are not disturbed because we are gay but because of the way people and the churches have treated us for being gay. My parents have been wonderfully accepting and supportive of me as an openly gay man and a gay minister and teacher in gay churches. When I told my parents that I had gone to Alcoholics Anonymous and quit drinking, my mother's response was to be very happy and to say, "I was a lot more concerned about your drinking than about your being gay! You can do something about the drinking, but you can't do anything about being gay." Good for mom! I was and still am very proud of my mother. She is 88 as this book goes to press. Her love, acceptance, and prayers are still an important part of my life.

Afraid to Go Home

Many other lesbians and gay men are not as fortunate as I was in having family love, respect, and support.

Don cannot go home again. He was 17 years old and gay when I first met him. His parents refused to accept his long distance phone calls. He had little education and no job skills. He was immature and acted and thought like a 12-year-old. Don lived on the streets of San Francisco. All Don knew to do to survive was to look young and cute and to take whatever he could get from other people. For Don, life had become an elaborate hustle. Don had HIV/AIDS. He did not live to grow out of his teens.

I have known dozens of gay and lesbian youth who were thrown out of their own homes by their parents. Some have had their lives threatened by their parents if they ever came home again. Many have left home because of the unrelenting pressure and rejection that made life miserable for everyone. Some dropped out of school, gave up on life, and became part of the growing subculture of throwaway youth in the gay ghettos of our big cities.

As I write this in 1999, I have seen an increasing number of homeless gay and lesbian teens living on the streets of gay areas of San Francisco. The MCC of San Francisco now provides housing and meals for many of these young people. Far more is needed. The root causes of all of this misery are the erroneous religious teachings about homosexuality that the parents still accept in their home churches. When we discover the remedy for this social and human religious blight, we will be on the way to victory in Jesus!

Alienation from family often leads gay youth into hostility toward God and all religion. Who can blame them? The Bible tells children to honor their parents. We cannot cry out loud enough to plead with parents, "Love your children!" Just because a child is different does not make that child bad. That should be obvious. Insecure and ignorant parents, however, need information and encouragement to love, understand, and accept their lesbian and gay children. They should learn these qualities of love and acceptance in church, but all too often they do not. Instead, frequently parents are encouraged by churches and religious leaders to hate and reject their own gay children, just as gay children are taught to fear and hate themselves.

Jesus Felt Pressure from Family and Community

Read Mark 3 and count the different kinds of pressure that Jesus suffered in this brief chapter. In Mark 3:31-35, Jesus confronted family pressure by giving a new definition to the meaning of family. Some of his family actually came to "take custody of Jesus and were saying that Jesus had lost his mind!" (Mark 3:21). Following this, Jesus was accused by religious leaders of healing by the power of Satan and not by God. The pressure of family and community on Jesus built until Jesus finally declared that his true friends and family were those who do the will of God. This was not to reject family or friends but was to make clear that only God has the authority to control life and be the "mother" of the family. Jesus obviously marched to a different drummer than anybody else around him.

Read again Luke 4:16-30 for the story of how Jesus was received when he preached for the first time in his hometown of Nazareth. Jesus did all of the right things. He went to synagogue on the Sabbath, read the Bible, and then sat to teach. At first, all of the hometown people praised Jesus for his gracious teachings about God. Then Jesus pointed out to them that God loved and healed foreigners and unclean people. The hometown folks suddenly turned violent and homicidal. They tried to kill Jesus. Jesus escaped and went back to Capernaum. This dramatic beginning for the ministry of Jesus to his people revealed the destructive power of prejudice, religious abuse, and closed minds to change friends into a hostile mob.

The writer of the Gospel of John summed it up, "Jesus came to his own and they did not receive him. But to as many as did receive him, Jesus gave the right to become children of God, even to those who believe in the name of Jesus" (John 1:11-12). Mark 6:1-4 gives another story of Jesus being rejected in his hometown. The people "took offense" at Jesus. They said, "Isn't this the carpenter, the son of Mary and brother of James, Joses, Judas, and Simon? Are not his sisters here too?" "Took offense" is "scandalized," from the Greek word meaning "to be caught in a trap."

Jesus replied that a prophet is honored "except in his home town and among his own relatives and in his own house." Immediately after this incident, Jesus continued his ministry unhindered and sent out his disciples to represent him with authority and power to heal and proclaim the good news of God's love for everybody. When those who knew Jesus best rejected him Jesus turned his attention and energy toward others who were receptive and open to him. How does the way Jesus handled being belittled and rejected by those who knew him best speak to us when we are belittled, invalidated, and rejected by people who see us through the eyes of prejudice and erroneous distorted religious teachings? How much time and energy should we devote to trying to get through to abusive people with closed minds and arrogant attitudes about religion and the Bible?

Voluntary Association

You do not choose your relatives. They are given to you. You do not choose your childhood playmates or school classmates. They also are given. You may select some people to be special close friends from among relatives and neighbors. If you are gay, however, you might search in vain for someone who really understands you and makes you feel comfortable and safe.

Jesus carefully selected people to be close to him and share his life and the truth about himself. In the midst of misunderstandings about his work, intense pressure from family, and growing anger and threats of violence, Jesus made some careful choices of companions. "Jesus summoned those whom he himself wanted, and they came to him, and he appointed twelve that they might be with him" (Mark 3:13-14). Jesus was clear and confident about who he was and his purpose in life. He allowed only those who were compatible with his self-understanding and his goals in life to be really close to him.

Are you selective about letting other people into your personal, intimate space? People may have hurt you. Someone you trusted may have betrayed you. If you continue to let people who hurt you be close enough to you to damage your life, you are responsible for what happens. The Rev. Chuck Larsen chided me once about a very dysfunctional person whom I knew, "If you let him back into your life again, I will have serious doubts about your own self-esteem!" I am glad that I listened to that advice. One obvious way out of oppression and rejection by family and others is your own act of voluntarily selecting people who are right for you.

This can be very difficult if you are not really secure in your own identity or your reason for living. Do you love and accept yourself? One sure way to act out your own homophobia is to punish yourself and sabotage your life by allowing negative and destructive people to dominate and control you. Have you ever done that? How have you managed to remove negative people from your life?

Freedom to Choose Love

Freedom to love and to choose our companions has been at the center of our battle for gay rights. Gay, lesbian, bisexual, and transgendered people want and deserve the freedom to love and associate with those to whom their hearts might lead them and not to people forced on them by family, friends, or society. Gaining this freedom carries with it the responsibility to make good choices about who comes into our lives. The help that Jesus gives to us to handle rejection includes the example and teachings of Jesus through the Holy Spirit to help us make healthy and happy choices about the people we want to be with us.

Jean-Paul Sartre's conclusion in *No Exit* that "hell is other people" was prophetic for many gay people who have left or were driven from home and family only to find themselves in even worse destructive relationships of their own choosing. Spousal abuse within our gay community is a rapidly accelerating problem and one that is being addressed by many concerned groups, including sensitive and informed local police departments. The first line of defense against domestic violence for us is our intentional intelligent choices about people we let come into our lives and take over. Always remember that you are the most important person in your life. You cannot help anybody else unless you take care of yourself. Healthy relationships begin with your own self-worth and self-esteem.

Questions for Study and Discussion

1. What has family pressure and oppression done to you?

2. Have you tried to compensate for rejection at home by getting into codependent relationships that have let you down?

3. Have you attempted to make up for hurt from family and friends by wanting to rescue every troubled person who comes along?

Additional Resources

Melody Beattie wrote the pioneering books on codependency that are used in Codependents Anonymous groups, *Codependent No More* (1987) and *Beyond Codependency* (1989) plus a book that greatly helped me, *The Language of Letting Go: Daily Meditations for Codependents* (1990). All of the titles are published by Harper.

Lesson 18

Spiritual Warfare

† **Preparatory Bible Reading:** 2 Corinthians 10:1-18 and Ephesians 6:10-20

> Though we walk in the flesh, we do not war according to the flesh. For the weapons of our warfare are not of the flesh, but mighty before God for the destruction of fortresses. We are destroying speculations and every lofty thing that raised up against the knowledge of God and are taking every thought captive to the obedience of Christ.
>
> 2 Corinthians 10:3-5

Jesus was aware that his life and ministry were part of a great war between the forces of love and truth against the forces of deceit and violence. Many threats and attempts were made against the life of Jesus before he let go and allowed the enemy to take him and kill him. Paul also viewed his life and ministry as spiritual warfare, "Be strong in the strength of God's might. Put on the full metal jacket of God that you may be able to stand firm against the schemes of the devil. For our struggle is not against people [flesh and blood] but against the rulers, against the powers, against the world forces of darkness, against the spiritual forces of wickedness in the heavenly places. Therefore take up the full armor of God that you may be able to resist in the evil day and having done everything, to stand firm" (Ephesians 6:10-13). The pieces of armor that Paul then described are actually the armor that God was pictured as using in the Hebrew Testament. The first, not surprisingly, is truth.

Our Enemies Are Fear and Ignorance

The enemy is not Jerry Falwell, Pat Robertson, James Dobson, or D. James Kennedy. The enemy that hurts us most is ignorance. Ignorance of the truth about gay people and the Bible among church-going people and among lesbians and gay men is the enemy that sets us up to attack and fight ourselves and each other. Fear grows out of ignorance. A powerful parable of the disastrous mixture of fear and ignorance is seen in the biblical story of Gideon in Judges 7. Gideon raised a large army to fight the enemy. God, however, told Gideon to cut down the number of soldiers from 32,000 to 300. Then the 300 were armed with pitchers, torches, and trumpets. In the dead of night, the troops of Gideon silently entered the enemy camp. At a signal, they shouted, broke the pitchers, waved the lighted torches, and blew on the trumpets. The enemy troops were startled awake, and in fear and panic began to slash out at the dark, not realizing in their fear and ignorance that they were killing each other. So Gideon won and the enemy lost.

When fear and ignorance energize our fighting, we do ourselves more harm than good. Jesus said that we must be as wise as serpents and as harmless as doves. Being ignorant is never an advantage in any battle. Equip yourself with the truth as your primary weapon for human rights and against oppression and abuse. Jesus does not want you to be afraid anymore, but Jesus also does not want you to be ignorant any more.

How Radical is Your Commitment to Truth?

"Speak the truth in love" (Ephesians 4:15). Truth not spoken in love is not heard as truth. We speak the truth of God's love in Jesus for all people as "we grow up in all things into Christ, who is the head." Truth and love were the chief tools Jesus used. Whenever Jesus was taunted and harassed by the religious rulers, he always resisted fighting them on their own terms. One of the saints said to his enemies, "You can kill me, but you cannot make me hate you."

When I was a Metropolitan Community Church (MCC) pastor in San Francisco and in Nashville, I was given many opportunities to be interviewed on radio, television, and newspapers. I also spoke at several outdoor political rallies. Whenever I was given the chance to talk, I always talked about Jesus. At first, I was surprised at how quiet and supportive gay people became when I talked about Jesus and God's love and acceptance for us. I soon realized that Jesus is our greatest force for changing public opinion. Jesus was the most powerful revolutionary of all time. As Acts 10:38 says, "Jesus went about doing good."

We are frequently tempted to fight fire with fire. I was present in San Francisco for some destructive gay protests in the early 1990's. I never blamed or disagreed with gay people for fighting back with anger and violence against public attitudes and public policies that hurt and destroy gay people. I realized that some of the oppressive laws and political actions by public officials make life unbearable and even deadly for gay people. Denying adequate medical care, housing, and jobs to people because of their sexual orientation results in despair, suicide, sickness, and death. That is genocide. You cannot protest genocide too much! Though violence was not my style, I always supported the most radical of protests and protesters. Many of the violent protesters were my friends, and I found myself and others helping them get out of jail and getting their fines reduced.

Love as a Weapon of War

Angry protests can be destructive and get a lot of attention. The only way that we can win, however, is if we can change public opinion about us. How we see ourselves and how non-gay people see us will have to change in order for us to change the world into an accepting and affirming place for all people regardless of sexual orientation.

How do these words sound to you as effective weapons for spiritual warfare? "Let all bitterness and wrath and anger and clamor [shouting] and slander be put away from you, along with all malice, and be kind to one another, tender hearted, forgiving each other, just as God in Christ also has forgiven you" (Ephesians 4:31-32).

When I see and hear the lies and blatant distortions of truth about gay, lesbian, bisexual, and transgendered people on television talk shows, political speeches, and an endless parade of ignorant evangelists, I want to fight. This book is the best weapon I have been able to develop. It is the accumulated arsenal of spiritual weaponry that has come my way for the past ten years. As you read it, I pray for you that you will catch a vision of the victory that is within our grasp. I truly believe that if God is for us, nobody can stand against us, however, we have to fight God's way.

Zechariah saw victory to be sure "not by might nor by power, but by my spirit says the Lord of Hosts" (Zechariah 4:6). Paul grappled with spiritual warfare and said, "Where the Spirit of God is, there is freedom" (2 Corinthians 3:17). Liberation from sick, abusive, legalistic, judgmental, oppressive religion is God's gift to us through Jesus. God wants us to be truly free even more than we want to be free. The Spirit of Jesus equips us to become like Jesus. We cannot love one another as Jesus loves us unless the Spirit creates the new love within that we need in order to follow Jesus into any kind of victory.

My friend, Mel White, former ghostwriter for many famous homophobic fundamentalist leaders and author of *Stranger at the Gate*, has developed a ministry of "Soulforce" that draws on the non-violent protest work of Mahatma Gandhi and Martin Luther King, Jr. You can learn of this new power for positive change for us on the Internet at Web sites www.melwhite.org and at www.soulforce.org. Dr. White told recently of seeing a wall near his home in southern California that had been scrawled with the bold message, "Kill Jerry Falwell!" He had seen the signs that said "Kill a Queer for Christ" and others, but this was a shocking new turn of events. Mel said that we cannot win that way. He is right. We cannot. Read Matthew 5:9-16, 43-48, and 10:16-20 for clear guidance as to your most effective spiritual weapons and for a clue to where your real power comes from.

Leave the Results to God

Years ago I learned the steps to salvation in several tracts and brochures published by Baptists and others. The best advice that I can remember, however, was from Campus Crusade for Christ material that said you are to do your best to share Jesus with others and then "leave the results to God!" If the fear, anger, and hate that motivate gay bashing and homophobic preaching and teaching are to be changed, God will have to do it. I have not yet found any way to bash people into the truth and beat them into loving and accepting us.

Bible Abuse is the Enemy

The abusive use of the Bible and religion against gay people and the oppressive attitudes and policies of traditional churches against us have to be challenged. The question is by what means and weapons do we best fight and win. The question is not "Do we fight for our freedom?" but "How do we fight for our freedom?" To give up and go back into the closet is impossible. To ignore abuse and oppression is emotionally unhealthy and spiritually dead. We cannot turn back. This is war. There have been many casualties and there will be more. I have been a casualty of homophobia, misunderstanding, fear, and institutional terrorism myself several times. I have survived for a lot longer than I could have thought, but God was not through with me yet. God is still not finished with me. God is not finished with you either.

Learn the contents of this book and share it with others. Explore the resources and references here and in my Web site. Look up all of the Bible passages that are given and think about what they say to you personally. We have great spiritual resources and equipment to carry out our mission to open the eyes of those who do not see, to set at liberty those who are wounded, to lift up the brokenhearted, and to proclaim clearly and convincingly that now is the time when God truly and completely loves and accepts every person without exception.

Questions for Study and Discussion

1. Are you willing to go to war armed only with truth and love?

2. Can you think of any occasion when you did this?

3. What new information did you learn in this lesson?

Additional Resources

On political activism, see the academy award winning documentary, "The Times of Harvey Milk," or read the book about Harvey Milk, *The Mayor of Castro Street*, by Randy Shilts.

Mel White, *Stranger at the Gate*: Simon and Schuster, 1994. For more information about Dr. White's "Soulforce" go to his Web sites at www.melwhite.org and at www.soulforce.org.

See also, R. Adam DeBaugh, *Writing to Congress*: Chi Rho Press, 1982, for information about how to contact your legislators and an excellent Bible study on Ezekiel 34.

Also by R. Adam DeBaugh, *The Least of These: A Christian Social Action Bible Study*: Chi Rho Press, 1994, is a seven-part Bible study on Matthew 25: 31-46.

Lesson 19

Stinking Thinking and Gay Bashing

† **Preparatory Bible Reading:** Galatians 5:1-26; 6:1-18; Colossians 3:1-17; and 2 Corinthians 12:1-10

"Kill a Queer for Christ" was a bumper sticker used in a religious campaign against gay people a few years ago. More recently, "Stamp Out AIDS: Kill a Queer" was a bumper sticker in some church supported campaigns against civil rights protection for gays and lesbians in several states. The 1998 summer national newspaper ads against gays by the leaders of the homophobic religious right promoted the "ex-gay" industry and sent confusing and misinformed messages to the public. Anti-gay religious rhetoric continued to accelerate into the fall. Suddenly, an event rocked the nation and captured the attention of the media for weeks.

On the night of October 6, 1998, Matthew Shepard was tortured and beaten then tied to a fence in Wyoming to die slowly in sub-freezing weather simply because he was gay. Matthew was a gay 22-year-old college student who had hoped that he could become an activist in the fight for equal protection for gay people. Sadly, he probably accomplished more through his tragic death than by anything else he might have done. The national news media reported every detail of this horrible event. "The Advocate" put Matthew's picture on the cover of the November 24, 1998, issue with the statement, "The Ultimate Ex-Gay; His murder leaves blood on the hands of the Far Right: How their rhetoric kills; Why their TV ads won't work; How $$ are the bottom line." Many gay and lesbian activists in public rallies, candlelight vigils, interviews, and on the Internet reflected the sentiments of "The Advocate" all across the country.

Representatives of the homophobic fundamentalist religious establishment were quick to deny that Matthew's murder was their fault. Yet their anti-homosexual planning, preaching, and advertising continued. As I write this, the trial of the two men charged with the murder of Matthew Shepard is under way in Wyoming. The world is watching. Since Matthew's murder, cruel torture murders of other gay men have taken place. Billy Jack Gaither was beaten to death with axe handles by two men in Sylacauga, Alabama, simply because he was gay. Then his body was thrown on a pile of burning tires like garbage. Public revulsion and horror at this act of gay bashing again swept across the nation. The Rev. Marge Ragona, Pastor of Covenant Metropolitan Community Church (MCC) in Birmingham, Alabama, led a highly publicized memorial service for Billy Jack at the church. The 225-seat church was filled to overflowing by over 500 people and the event received national media attention. Other killings of gay men are coming to light and are under investigation.

Public Attention to Gay Bashing

Public attention has become focused on the oppression and bashing of gay people as never before. For the first time, leading national magazines have featured stories about anti-gay attacks that have been inspired by the Right Wing's warped and abusive use of the Bible. "Rolling Stone" magazine, in the March 18, 1999, issue, had a special report on "The Holy War on Gays" that reported in detail and with pictures the complex political/religious conspiracy against gay people that is gaining momentum. In March 1999, "Vanity Fair" ran an article about "The Crucifixion of Matthew Shepard." The April 1999, issue of "Seventeen" magazine ran an article with pictures and a list of helpful resources on "Coming Out in America: Gay Teens tell the world, Here I am, deal with me," by Robert Rorke.

In my Web site (www.truluck.com), I have placed articles about these current events and have included reviews of recent books by John Paulk and Joe Dallas, which have tried to sell the myth of the ex-gay ministry. See also my Special Study on "The Ex-Gay Fraud" at the end of the book.

A nationwide rush to add "hate crimes" legislation to state laws has produced more public attention and debate about protection from gay bashing. Such laws help, of course, and they serve to set the tone of public support for human and civil rights for gays and lesbians. Laws, however, do not shape public opinion. Religious teachers and preachers do. Television news does. The truth is our best weapon against the lies and distortions about the Bible that underlie most of the vicious and hateful bashing of homosexuals. The Bible does not condemn or even discuss homosexual orientation or romantic love between people of the same sex. (See Chapter 11, the Sixth Step, and the Special Study on "Homosexuality and the Bible" at the end of the book.) The true message of the Bible is God's unconditional love for all people.

Where Does Hate Come From?

"Stinking Thinking" is a term used in Alcoholics Anonymous (AA) for the resentment and anger that come from alcohol-induced distortions of reality. Alcoholics often hurt the ones they love. Frustration and self-hate can boil over into angry outbursts, hateful words, and violence. Alcohol is not the only power that can distort and blur one's vision of self and other people. Homophobia (fear of homosexuality) also produces "stinking thinking," and resentment, anger, hate, and violence against lesbians and gays and people who are thought to be gay. Internalized homophobia often leads gay people to hate themselves and engage in self-destructive behavior, including suicide.

Threats and acts of physical violence against gay people are only a tiny part of gay bashing. Anxiety and fear of being discovered to be gay and fired from work is a form of gay bashing. Religious condemnation and rejection by churches and church leaders is gay bashing. Discrimination in housing, inadequate and expensive medical care, and unfair law enforcement against gays and lesbians are gay bashing. Religious pressures to hate and reject yourself because of your sexual orientation are gay bashing. Pressure from family and friends to "change and be normal" is gay bashing. The varieties of gay bashing are as endless as the varieties of ignorance about human sexuality. Does the Bible offer any answers?

Bible Answers to Gay Bashing

Read carefully all of Galatians 5:1-26, which begins, "For freedom Christ set us free, therefore keep standing firm and do not be subject again to a religious yoke of slavery." Paul showed in the rest of this passage that the deadliest work of the flesh is angry, legalistic religion. Especially eloquent is, "The whole law is fulfilled in one word, 'You shall love your neighbor as yourself.' But if you bite and devour one another, take care lest you be consumed by one another" (Galatians 5:14-15). Legalistic, judgmental religion is a form of spiritual cannibalism. Resist the temptation to give in to the negative forces of low self-esteem and negative self-image demanded by legalistic religion.

The most damaging form of gay bashing is fear and hate by gay people against themselves and each other. If you are ridiculed by your friends, harassed by your family, and cursed by your church for being gay, which you cannot change, it does not take long for you to begin to hate and despise yourself and to sabotage and destroy your own life and happiness. Internalized gay bashing takes a far greater toll on gay people than any other negative force in their lives. The leading cause of death for gay teens is suicide, which is just one of the horrors of homophobia and one reason that the answer to gay bashing must be found.

Eliminate Your Negative Self-Image

Accept and respect yourself and expect respect and acceptance from others. Jesus tells you to love yourself, for how can you love your neighbor as you love yourself unless you first love yourself? Take a quick look again at 1 John 4. Paul gave a clear answer to internal and horizontal hate and gay bashing in Galatians 5:14-15 (quoted above). Paul then concluded, "If you are led by the Spirit, you are not under the Law" (Galatians 5:18).

Most people assume that the word "flesh" in the Bible means "sex", but that is not true. There is no word for "sex" in the entire Greek New Testament. "Flesh" (Greek *sarkos*) never means sex. It means human in contrast to spiritual. Works of the flesh are those attitudes and behaviors that demonstrate our human frailties and our "missing the mark" of God's purpose for us in our relationships with other people. The list of 15 works of the flesh Galatians 5:19-21 say nothing about sexual orientation but say everything about hostility, anger, and hate. Read the list, which begins with "immorality" (Greek *porneia*, built on *pernumi* meaning "to sell"). It sets the stage for the rest of the list that describes ways in which we use people as things rather than relating to others as persons. The list continues, impurity, sensuality (literally "not caring"), idolatry, drug abuse (*pharmakeis*, "drugs," from which we get the word "pharmacy"), enmities, strife, jealousy, outbursts of anger, disputes, dissension, factions, envying, drunkenness, carousing. This list is a clear description of the "stinking thinking" of ignorance, fear, and hate that produces homophobia and gay bashing.

Replace Negativity with Life

Memorize the list of "fruit of the Spirit" in Galatians 5:22-23. Notice that the words describe the character of Jesus in the Gospels. When the Spirit of Jesus is within you, the fruit of the Spirit is expressed through your personality. The words in this list need no explanation beyond the picture of Jesus presented in the Gospels. "Love, joy, peace, patience, kindness, goodness, faithfulness, gentleness, and self-control" give the other side of hate, anger, and fear.

After giving the "fruit of the Spirit," Paul said, "Those who belong to Christ Jesus have crucified the flesh with its cravings and desires. If we live the Spirit, let us also walk by the Spirit and not be boastful, challenging and envying one another" (Galatians 5:24-26). Read Galatians 6:1-18, where Paul interpreted his contrast of flesh and Spirit by talking about overcoming boasting and jealousy. See the same approach in 2 Corinthians 12:1-10. When most preachers talk about the sins of the flesh, they usually mean sex. When Paul talked about sins of the flesh, he meant anger, hate, conflicts, discord, jealousy, boasting, alcoholism, drug abuse, oppression, and legalistic, judgmental religion. How could churches and their leaders so totally miss the point?

Neither Jesus nor Paul condemned private, personal sex practices. Neither of them ever commented on sexual orientation or discussed romantic love of same-sex couples. Both of them repeatedly condemned anger, hate, violence, and deceit. To see the issue of homophobia and gay bashing in biblical perspective, ask the question, why do we say that loving same-sex couples who express their love sexually are "the abomination of God" and the military leaders who order the bombing of innocent people are "patriotic"?

Our Weapons of War Against Hate

Jesus did not call for weak submissive acceptance of abuse and oppression. Jesus never taught his followers to give up and quit in the face of religious abuse. Jesus calls you to fight ignorance, not people. You destroy errors and lies that hurt and oppress people by your living and teaching the truth of God in Christ. As the slogan for winning against HIV/AIDS says, "Fight AIDS, Not People With AIDS!" Victory over gay bashing begins within each of us. Self-hate is the worst form of gay bashing because it never stops. You can move away or run away from ignorant, homophobic bullies, but you cannot run away from yourself. Read Colossians 3:1-17, in which Paul writes, "Put on love and let the peace of Christ rule in your hearts" (Colossians 3:15). Peace in Christ is the hope for disturbed minds and hearts, "Peace I leave with you. My peace that I give to you is not like the peace that the world gives. Let not your heart be troubled, don't be afraid anymore" (John 14:27).

Questions for Study and Discussion

1. Have you ever feared for your job or your safety because of prejudice against you? How did you handle it?

2. How have you resisted homophobia in yourself?

3. Why do you think that church leaders have placed so much emphasis on sex as sin and so little on anger, hate, oppression, injustice, and the other evils that get about 99 percent of the attention given to "sin" in the Bible?

Additional Resources

William Barclay, *Flesh and Spirit: An Examination of Galatians 5:19-23*: SCM Press, Ltd., 1962.

Wayne E. Oates, *When Religion Gets Sick*: The Westminster Press, 1970.

Ronald M. Enroth, *Churches that Abuse:* Zondervan, A Division of HarperCollins Publishers, 1992.

Lesson 20

Free to Feel Good About Yourself

† **Preparatory Bible Reading:** Matthew 16:1-28 and Luke 9:18-36

My chief prayer and hope is that you will feel good about yourself. I have seen far too much self-hate and self-destructiveness in our community. I have seen the lingering face of HIV/AIDS and suffering and death. I have witnessed and experienced the internalized and horizontal homophobia and far too much religious abuse and hate. It is time for the tide to turn. The time has come for us to rise up and say with one voice, ***Stop! This is enough!*** We will not stand for any more unfair discrimination and violence against us. We also are the children of God, made in the image of God. Respect us, for we respect ourselves!

All of this is easier said than done. The most frequent kind of the thousands of pieces of e-mail that I have received in response to my Web site in the almost two years that it has been on the Internet is an expression of "praise God" or some other word of gratitude for learning the truth about God's love and acceptance. Most people have expressed joy for the freedom and hope that they have experienced. Many others send e-mail to explain and ask for prayer in their situation of living in the closet under the unrelenting abusive use of religion against them by their families and churches.

A third group of responses has to be called hate mail in which committed, homophobic Bible abusers feel obligated to tell me how evil I am and that I am going to hell for what I am doing to try to encourage and help gay people. Usually the hate e-mail is anonymous and is sent with a nonexistent return address.

Recently someone sent me an envelope with no return address that contained only a copy of all of Romans 1:1-32 from the *NIV* Bible with verse 26 highlighted in bold type. I have been impressed by the determination of ignorant fundamentalists to engage in one-way conversation. They refuse to listen and are committed to having the last word.

Self Respect

When religion, family, and people in power keep telling you that as a gay person you are the abomination of God and that you do not deserve fair treatment, you eventually begin to believe it. When you are reminded every day that your sexual orientation is a dirty secret that is better kept hidden, you begin to believe that you really are inferior. When you hear lies over and over about lifestyle and sense the disgust of many people around you who despise you for who you are, you cannot help feeling that some of it must be true.

None of it is true! Lies about who you are as a gay person are dangerous and false. The abusive use of the Bible to condemn you is a false and evil religion that denies the Spirit of Jesus and the facts about Jesus in the Gospels. You are not a monster. You are a child of God. You can hold your head high and be yourself. Together we are far stronger than our enemies. We are committed to the truth of who we are. You are part of one of the greatest movements for freedom and equality in history. Jesus Christ is our leader. The way of the cross leads home. Jesus lived, died, and was raised from the dead in total victory and final triumph over the binding and oppressive forces of this present age in order that in Christ we might enter into the liberty and joy of the children of God now and forever.

The View from the Mountaintop

We have been to the mountaintop and have seen the Promised Land. We have had a taste of hope and freedom. We have made giant steps of progress in gaining respect and acceptance as gay, lesbian, bisexual, and transgendered people of God. We are God's special children with a mission from God to change the world. We will never turn back. There can be no retreat. God is on our side, for God is on the side of truth. You have much to celebrate. You have much to be proud of.

We join together with the saints of all the ages who sing with us, "Lift up your heads, O gates, and be lifted up, O everlasting doors, that the ruler of glory may come in! Who is the ruler of glory? The Sovereign of hosts is the ruler of glory." We are God's people. The victory of God is our victory too. We are more than conquerors through the Christ who loves us. Since God is for us, who can stand against us?

Self-Denial and Self-Esteem

One of Jesus' most famous sayings is, "If anyone of you desires to come after me, deny yourself, take up your cross, and follow me. For if you want to save your life, you will lose it, but if you lose your life for my sake, you will find it" (Matthew 16:24-26). How can self-denial build your self-esteem? "Denial" usually means that we fail to face reality. To be in denial is a serious obstacle in recovering from any addiction. How can "self denial" be healthy?

The term "deny self" in Matthew 16:24 means "to act in a totally selfless manner." The word is the same term used in Matthew 16:23 for "get behind me" when Jesus rebuked Peter for trying to tell him what to do. Self-denial simply means putting Jesus first in your life as your leader and guide. Read the parallel accounts of this incident in Mark 8 and Luke 9 for further understanding.

Self-denial is not a rejection of your own value and abilities as a person. It is an affirmation of your personal worth and potential as a follower of Jesus. Like all religious terminology, self-denial has its proper and healthy meaning only when it is understood in relationship to Jesus. Self-denial out of the context of following Jesus can become unhealthy and self-destructive. Self-denial becomes an expression of sick religion when it says, "Look at what I have given up for God!" The pride that accompanies self-conscious denying of self as an end in itself is evidence of dysfunctional, legalistic religion. Read all of Matthew 16:1-28 to see the setting of self-denial in contrast to the legalism of the Pharisees.

Follow Jesus

The first invitation of Jesus in Luke 5:1-11 was to offer to make the disciples become like Jesus and to become "fishers of men and women." The disciples "left everything and followed Jesus." At the end of the Gospel of John, Jesus said three times to Peter, "Feed my sheep," and in John 21:22, he gave the absolute call to Peter, "You follow me." In the Gospel of John the terms "believe" and "follow" were used interchangeably. Read all of John 21 to see the context of this final "follow me." See the use of "follow" in Matthew 4:19; 8:19-22; 9:9; and 19:21. The Greek word for "follow" is *akoloutheo*, which was a very flexible word that could mean to follow an argument, to follow a law, to follow the instructions of a particular teacher, to follow a leader, and to get up and physically follow another person from place to place. All of these uses were implied in the invitation of Jesus to "follow me."

Letting go of the past and the attractions and addictions that have controlled our lives is part of our decision to follow Jesus. Following Jesus in the Gospels is seen as a positive and healthy move toward self-esteem and self-respect. Jesus said in Matthew 18:1-5 that true greatness is to become like a little child. Read this wonderful story and consider what it is saying to you personally. A little child is humble, trusting, vulnerable, dependent, honest, and teachable, which are the qualities that make one an effective disciple of Jesus. Self-esteem is God's gift to us through the presence of Jesus in our lives. Denying Self and following Jesus sets us free and empowers us to become our best self.

Lift Me Up So I Can See Too

In 1953, I was at a Baptist summer assembly program in North Carolina and heard a preacher tell a story that has remained with me ever since. The preacher had gone with a group of volunteers to pre-Castro Cuba to help with local church programs. The group was in Havana at the time of a parade and everyone went to the celebration. The preacher was watching the parade when a little boy touched his arm and said something to him in Spanish. The Guide had told the group that the children would ask for money but not to give it to them. He assumed that the boy was asking for money and told him, "No." In a few minutes the little boy pulled on the preacher's coat and asked the same thing in Spanish. Again the preacher said a firm "No." Finally the boy pulled harder and said the same words. The preacher was irritated and pushed the boy away with a harsh "No!" Later at his hotel, the preacher looked up the Spanish words that the boy had said three times. He was deeply touched by what the boy had been saying. He was not asking for money. Three times he had begged, "Please, mister, lift me up so I can see too!"

The most important thing that we can do for other people is "to lift them up so they can see too." If we have found acceptance and love from God in our lives, we can help others to see what we have found. We cannot lift up anyone if we are standing in quicksand ourselves. To be able to give a lift to others, we stand on solid ground and are unafraid to listen and really hear what others are saying. Telling people how stupid they are or avoiding them altogether cannot possible change them from despair into hope.

Grow in Jesus Christ and your self-esteem will also grow. The better you feel about yourself, the more confidence you will have in sharing with others the love and truth that you have found. Nobody can force you to lift up others so that they can see what you see. Only your love and compassion for people can motivate you to humble yourself to lift up and encourage wounded and abused people.

When the Spirit of Jesus lives within you so that you really do accept yourself and feel good about yourself, you will want to share your happy discovery with other gay, lesbian, bisexual, and transgendered people. Few things will ever make you as happy as helping other people feel good about themselves.

Overcoming the Hate

Dr. C. Everett Koop, former U.S. Surgeon General, said that we need a stronger word than homophobia to describe the hate against homosexuals that he has seen in religious extremists. Dr. Koop said that his national efforts to educate people about HIV/AIDS have been met with opposition by some preachers who would gladly push a button that would instantly destroy all lesbians and gay men. Dr. Koop is a very spiritual man, and his disappointment at the unloving and hateful attitude of many church leaders toward gay people has discouraged him from going to church, which he does not attend now nearly as much as he once did.

How does Jesus liberate and heal us from such blatant religious abuse as Dr. Koop encountered in his travels around the country? One step on the road to recovery is to recognize and accept the fact that homophobic, legalistic, judgmental religion is wrong and does not accurately reflect the attitude and teachings of Jesus. Learn and remember the truth about the Bible and homosexuality, which is included as a Special Study at the end of this book. Then go on to develop your own spiritual life in positive and constructive ways. Accept God's unconditional love for you. Rejoice and be glad that you are a child of God, and nobody can ever take that away from you. Jesus said, "I have spoken these things to you that my joy may be in you and your joy may be made complete. This is my commandment that you love one another, just as I have loved you" (John 15:11-12).

This would be a good time to read all of John chapters 13 through 17.

Questions for Study and Discussion

1. What religious experience has most abused you and made you feel bad about yourself?

2. What has most made you feel good about yourself?

3. Why do you think that some people who know the gospel still are attracted to judgmental legalism and oppressive religion?

4. How can you work out your own spiritual life without somebody else telling you what to do?

5. What did Jesus do to lift people up so that they could see and experience God's love and acceptance?

Chapter 11

The Sixth Step

Confront the Scripture Used Against You

Learn the facts about homosexuality and the Bible. The truth will set you free.

Jesus said, "You search the Scriptures, because you think that in them you have eternal life; but it is these that bear witness of me. . . . You will know the truth and the truth will set you free" (John 5:39; 8:32).

Jesus frequently showed how the Bible had been used incorrectly to hurt people. In Matthew 5:17-48, Jesus said that he had come to fulfill the Law, not that he had come to force you to keep the Law! In this passage Jesus corrected several mistakes in the Old Testament by saying repeatedly, "you have heard it said, but I say unto you." Things that Jesus corrected were based on quotations from the Bible. **Jesus corrected mistakes in the Bible.**

Jesus spent most of his time dealing with abusive and oppressive religion and showing how he had come to replace law with love. He taught his disciples to think objectively and logically about their relationships with God and with other people.

The burden of proof concerning Bible condemnation and rejection of gay people is upon those who use incorrectly translated and out-of-context passages to hurt people who were not intended in the original texts. Frequently I have been asked to prove that the Bible does not condemn homosexuals. That question is backwards.

No word for "homosexual" exists in biblical languages. No reference to sexual orientation exists in the Bible. Of the six Bible passages used against gays, three of them, Genesis 19:5; 1 Corinthians 6:9; and 1 Timothy 1:10 are translated incorrectly, and three, Leviticus 18:22; Leviticus 20:13; and Romans 1:26-27 are taken out of their correct context of condemning idolatrous religious practices and applied incorrectly to people of the same sex who love each other. The Bible nowhere condemns love, affection, or sex between people who love each other. In fact, no word for "sex" exists in the Bible.

When the verses that are used to condemn people for their sexual orientation are examined carefully in their context and with the accepted methods of academic research and logic, there is no evidence that the Bible says that gay people are evil and hated and rejected by God. No evidence exists in the Bible to prove God's rejection of gay men and women. The case against gays and lesbians is dismissed for a lack of evidence.

Jesus never mentioned homosexuals or any issue related to sexual orientation. If you follow Jesus, you accept everyone equally. Jesus is proof that God loves and accepts all people, including you.

Before you begin to study the four lessons in this Sixth Step, turn to the back of the book and read and study carefully "Homosexuality and the Bible" with special attention to "Hebrew and Greek" and "Six Bible Passages Used Against Homosexuals."

Author's note: This material on the Sixth Step was the most difficult part of the book to write. When the Rev. Chuck Larsen first invited me to begin research, writing, and teaching

Bible studies for gays and lesbians at First Metropolitan Community Church (MCC) Atlanta in 1988, he suggested that we look at the positive use of the Bible to help encourage and strengthen the spiritual life of our people and call the studies, "The Bible as the Friend of Lesbians and Gays," which was the first title of the material in this book.

Most of this book is about the positive use of the Bible as a guide to Jesus and the good news of God's love for all of us. Dealing with the abusive misuse of the Bible against gay people is necessary, however, because much of the oppression of gay men and lesbians springs from the errors and mistakes that have been read into the Bible in six obscure and questionable passages, and none of it comes from the life and message of Jesus. The basic problem in answering the verses that are used against us is that it is a negative task. We have to show what the passages do not say, partly because the six verses used against us do not make any reference to sexual orientation and partly because the verses all are relatively obscure and are usually used only as a weapon to attack gays.

Jesus said nothing against gay people, though homophobic legalists have looked long and hard trying to find something. The bottom line is that if Jesus is our true and only reliable guide to understanding the Bible, there is no evidence at all in the Bible to condemn us for our sexual orientation. Praise God!

Lesson 21

Gay Pride Day in Sodom

† **Preparatory Bible Reading:** Genesis 19:1-38 and 38:1-30

The true story of Sodom is just the opposite of what homophobic religious leaders have made of it. The Sodom story is the first demonstration of God's love and protection for misunderstood minorities who were feared and hated because they were different. Read Genesis 19 with new eyes. Lesbian, gay, bisexual, and transgendered people are the people of God. We are the church behind closed doors. We are kept imprisoned by our fear of what hateful people will do to us if they know us! God's judgment on fear, hate, and violence is dramatic and complete in Genesis 19.

Bible Abuse of a Christian Lesbian

Kim began to come to Metropolitan Community Church (MCC) Nashville and to our Wednesday night spiritual support group. She asked to see me and showed me a letter she had received from her uncle, a local Baptist pastor. In the letter, he attacked Kim's attempt to answer his condemnation of her for being a lesbian. He was particularly vigorous in his attack on Kim's saying that Jesus did not mention homosexuality. The letter said, "Kim, the Bible is God's Holy Word. All of it is equally Inspired and Preserved of God. Jesus' words are not more inspired than Paul's or Moses' words, and what you do with the Bible will determine what God does with you."

None of this is true. The Bible never claims that it is the "word of God." The Bible does, however, teach that Jesus is "the word of God" (John 1:1-18). Jesus not only corrected abusive use of the Bible against people, but Jesus also corrected mistakes in the Bible. Jesus showed that it was a mistake for Moses to allow divorce (Matthew 19:1-12). Jesus disagreed with Leviticus 19:18, "You shall love your neighbor and hate your enemy" (Matthew 5:43-49).

Jesus said many times, "You have read" and then added, "but ***I*** say unto you. . . ." To say that Jesus is no more inspired than the rest of the Bible contradicts the teachings of Jesus and turns biblical literalism into an idolatrous religion. Remember that the Bible is not the fourth member of the Trinity.

Happily, Kim was able to overcome the religious attacks by her uncle and develop her own personal experience with Christ. She felt good about herself as a Christian lesbian.

Homophobic Distortions of Scripture

The Bible nowhere says that lesbians and gay men can or should change their sexual orientation. "Sodomy" is not a biblical word. No words for gay, lesbian, or homosexuality existed in biblical Hebrew or Greek. Sexual orientation is never discussed or implied in the Bible. In these four lessons, we will take a close look at the main facts about the Bible and homosexuality. For detailed information about this subject, look at the material in "Homosexuality and the Bible" at the end of this book.

We all need to understand how the Bible has been intentionally distorted, twisted, incorrectly translated, and taken out of context in order to condemn and oppress a group of people never intended in the original texts. We need to know the truth about the Bible, not to attack the homophobic fundamentalists, but to gain self-acceptance and self-esteem for all who have been hurt by the abusive use of the Bible and religion.

Where to Begin

Trying to understand sexual ethics and customs in the Hebrew Bible is a formidable task. For instance, women were property. They belonged to their father or husband. The value of women was in their ability to produce children for the men who owned them. The only away that a man could continue to live after his death was through his children ("seed"). There was no belief in heaven at that time. There is no word for "bachelor" in biblical Hebrew. Everyone got married as soon as possible. The average life expectancy even in the time of Jesus was 25 years. Parents chose marriage partners for their children, and romantic attraction had nothing to do with marriage. Men usually married at about 16 years of age and women at about 14. Were you ever told any of these facts in Sunday School? Why not? These facts have everything to do with your understanding the truth about sexuality and sex ethics in the Bible.

Read Genesis 38:1-30 and notice the view of women, the double standard for men and women, and how the view of marriage and sex were totally unlike the way we view these experiences today. I have never seen a Sunday School lesson on Genesis 38 and Tamar, yet Tamar is listed in Matthew 1:3 as an ancestor of Jesus. Genesis 38, however, is a clear window on the real views of the Bible about women, marriage, inheritance, sex, male dominance, and a lot of other issues.

Read Genesis 19:1-38. If the translators would leave the word "know" in Genesis 19:5 as it is in Hebrew and in the *King James Version* and the *Revised Standard Version*, the message would be a lot clearer. Modern translators, however, have added words, interpretations, opinions, and explanations that distort the meaning and import homophobic and homosexual ideas that were not stated or implied in the original text. Some, like the Good News Bible, add an entire sentence, "The men of Sodom wanted to have sex with them."

The angels of God were aliens and strangers in a tiny fortress called Sodom. Lot, whose traditional family values included respect and honor of strangers and others who were different from him, protected them behind closed doors. Lot, like his Uncle Abraham, had caught a vision of God's love for all people. He extended hospitality to strangers.

What Really Happened in Sodom

The angels in Lot's house were like Christian gays and lesbians who are behind closed doors because of the fear and hate against them by ignorant unloving religious bigots and their obedient sheep. The mob in the street, banging on the closed door and demanding that the strangers "come out" so that the mob can know who they are and take control of them, are like a mob of fanatical fundamentalists, who out of ignorance and fear are hostile to gay people and want to expose, control, humiliate, and destroy them.

The story of Sodom has no connection with sexual orientation. Sexual orientation was never mentioned in the Bible. The Bible knows no more about sexual orientation than it knows about germs and viruses. Our understanding of homosexuality as a sexual orientation is less than 40 years old. Reading current cultural and medical ideas into the Bible is an absurd misuse of the Bible and a guarantee that truth will suffer.

What Does the Story of Sodom Teach?

One proof that Genesis 19 does not deal at all with sexual orientation, is that no later biblical discussions of the Sodom story mention homosexuality. All later biblical references to Sodom emphasize the general wickedness and idolatry of the people or else see Sodom as a symbol of desolation and destruction. (Deuteronomy 29:22-28; 32:32; Ezekiel 16:49-50; Jeremiah 49:18; 50:41; Isaiah 13:19-22; and Matthew 10:14-15, where Jesus said that inhospitality was the sin of Sodom. Jude 7 speaks of "strange flesh" which is a reference to foreign gods or people and not to sex. "Strange" is the Greek word *hetero*, which is the Greek part of the word "heterosexual." No Jewish teachers viewed the sin of Sodom as homosexuality until after the time of Jesus.

The story of Sodom has no bearing on the issue of God's acceptance or rejection of gay people. To twist the story to say what it does ***not*** say is to miss what it ***does*** say. The story clearly teaches that evil and violent people who attack aliens and strangers whom they do not know and do not understand simply because they are different and not known ("in the closet") deserve and get God's quick and terrible judgment and punishment.

The Story of Sodom is About Fear

Why were the people of Sodom so afraid of strangers and so violently hostile to unknown aliens? Sodom was a small fortress. It was one of four small forts along the southern edge of the Dead Sea, Sodom, Gomorrah, Admah, and Zeboiim (Genesis 14:8; Deuteronomy 29:23; Hosea 11:8). Little forts like Sodom were repeatedly attacked and destroyed by enemies who then rebuilt on the old ruins to try to protect trade routes and tribal territory.

In Palestine many mounds of these ancient forts can be seen. The ruins of an ancient town are called a *tell*, from the Arabic word for hill. They are like layer cakes that archaeologists can cut through to study the many levels of destruction and rebuilding. These mounds are only a few acres in size. The ancient site of Jericho is not larger than a football stadium. Sodom may have been smaller than one city block in size. The four "cities" of the plain destroyed in Genesis 19 are now under water in the Dead Sea, which has slowly grown in size over the centuries.

The Dead Sea is about 1300 feet below sea level, has no outlet, and is the lowest point on the earth. The land around the Dead Sea is desolate and barren. The southern end is still isolated and desolate. The people of Sodom lived in a hostile environment along a trade route that was constantly under threat of attack and destruction by hostile tribes. No wonder they were afraid of strangers.

To read homosexual orientation into the story to explain the fear, violence, and destruction of the Sodomites is to invent nonexistent evidence and to overlook and deny the real evidence both in the Bible and in studies of the geography and history of the region. Ignorance, however, has never stopped religious fanatics. People resist what they do not want to hear. The absurd idea that sexual behavior between same-sex loving adults is "sodomy" and should be a felony punished by long prison sentences is a blatant disregard of the constitutional separation of church and state in the United States and is based on faulty biblical study, prejudice, and ignorance. The reply of Jesus to people who distorted the Bible to teach lies was, "You are wrong! And you do not understand [know] the Scriptures or the power of God!" (Matthew 22:29).

What Jesus Said About Love for Strangers

Jesus said, "I was a stranger and you invited me in" (Matthew 25:35). Gay and lesbian people are the strangers and aliens in our culture. What you do for lesbians and gay men you do for Jesus.

Dan is gay. Over twenty years ago when he finished high school at the age of 17, Dan moved to Atlanta to escape harassment and rejection by people in the small town where he had grown up. Dan knew nobody in Atlanta. He got a job with a tailoring shop and moved into a hotel room. He knew nothing about the gay community in the city. Dan was an alien in a strange land. Lonely days and nights stretched into weeks and months. Dan finally heard about the gay nightspots and met Steve. Life took a great turn in a new direction when Steve took Dan to the MCC that had recently begun in Atlanta. Dan found a place to belong, to be accepted, and to be himself.

Dan has served on the Board of Directors of MCC Atlanta and for many years directed the Names Project sewing bee in Atlanta. Over the years, Dan has helped many gay people accept themselves and make the best of their lives in the alien and often hostile atmosphere of a big southern city. He frequently gave homeless gay people a free, safe place to stay. He encouraged people who were discouraged and down on themselves. He never gave up on himself or others. Dan was my partner for two years in Atlanta and never gave up on me. He is one of the main reasons that I am sober and writing this book today. Dan serves Christ in church and community in a ministry of love and encouragement because he never forgot how it feels to be a stranger.

The Bible View of Strangers

Understanding the story of Sodom in Genesis 19 is linked to the meaning and treatment of "strangers" or "aliens" in the Hebrew Bible. Strangers and travelers were and still are vulnerable. In the first century, travel was slow, usually on foot, and risky. In Luke 10:30-37, the Good Samaritan helped someone who was beaten, robbed, stripped of clothes, and left for dead beside the road. The victim was a typical stranger on the 17-mile, steep, isolated road between Jericho and Jerusalem. There were no hotels or hospitals. Travelers were at the mercy of robbers. People were suspicious and afraid of strangers.

In the Hebrew Bible, the plight of strangers was linked with the helplessness of widows and orphans. Read Deuteronomy 27:19; Isaiah 1:23; 10:1; Amos 5:24; Habakkuk 2:4; and Micah 6:8 to learn about God's concern for justice and fairness toward strangers. The biblical word translated as "stranger" means "foreign, different, alien" and is a word that describes the way many people see gays and lesbians today.

The story of Sodom has been turned around backwards because of homophobia, Bible ignorance, and the growing cancer of legalistic, judgmental religion. As we have seen, no reference to homosexuality as we know it today is found anywhere in the Bible. Sexual orientation was never discussed or even implied anywhere in the Bible. None of the verses used against lesbians and gay men hold up under close examination. The Bible is our friend, not our enemy.

The call of Jesus to minister to the stranger clearly includes the call to accept and minister to gay people as a way to accept and help Jesus. Jesus said, "I was a stranger and you invited me in." Including lesbians, gay men, bisexuals, and transgendered people at every level of church life and leadership, in the community, in society, in the military, and in all of life is to invite Jesus to come in. The irony of the situation is that lesbians and gay men already are in churches, politics, medicine, education, society, the military, law enforcement, business, and industry as well as in the arts and entertainment. The freedom to be honest and tell the truth about sexual orientation, however, is not yet enjoyed by the majority of gay people.

A powerful statement of Jesus' point of view is given in the Letter to the Hebrews, "Let love of the brothers and sisters continue. Do not neglect to show hospitality to strangers, for by this some have entertained angels without knowing it. Remember the prisoners, as though in prison with them; and those who are oppressed, since you also are in the body" (Hebrews 13:1-3).

Questions for Study and Discussion

1. Has this lesson helped you to be more accepting of yourself?

2. Why do you think that Bible translators and publishers have continued the use of wrong translations against gay people even though objective scholarship contradicts these translations?

Additional Resources

Read the article on "Sojourner" in *The Interpreter's Dictionary of the Bible*: Abingdon, 1962, 1990, R-Z, 397-399.

Some of the books that I have found helpful on the subject of the Bible and Homosexuality include,

John Boswell, *Christianity, Social Tolerance, and Homosexuality*: University of Chicago Press, 1980. It won the 1981 American Book Awards for History and is still the most helpful single source for objective study of the Bible and homosexuality.

George R. Edwards, *Gay/Lesbian Liberation: A Biblical Perspective*: The Pilgrim Press, 1984. Edwards' book is a further study based on Boswell's pioneering work, and provides an historical perspective and bibliography.

John J. McNeill, *The Church and the Homosexual*: Beacon Press, 1976, 1985, and 1988. John McNeill was one of the first biblical scholars to challenge the modern misuse of the Bible against gays and lesbians. His work, as an openly gay Catholic priest, has been revised and updated as he continues now at the age of 72 to be a powerful voice for freedom and fairness for homosexuals in the churches. See McNeill's other books in Bibliography.

Michael E. England, *The Bible and Homosexuality* (fifth edition): Chi Rho Press, 1998. First published in 1977, this book has been revised several times and has been used extensively in Metropolitan Community Churches and in many other churches.

Sylvia Pennington, *Good News for Modern Gays*: Lambda Christian Fellowship, P.O. Box 1967, Hawthorne, CA 90250, 1985. A highly personal and interesting approach by a former Pentecostal preacher who came to accept homosexuals as her Christian friends. Also by Pennington and the same publisher, *But Lord, They're Gay*, 1978, and *Ex-Gays? There Are None!*, 1989.

L. William Countryman, *Dirt, Greed and Sex: Sexual Ethics in the New Testament and Their Implications for Today*: Fortress Press, 1988. Dr. Countryman is the openly gay professor of New Testament at the Church Divinity School of the Pacific (Episcopal) in Berkeley, CA.

Bruce Hilton, *Can Homophobia Be Cured?*: Abingdon Press, 1992. Brief but very helpful answers to basic questions about Homosexuality and the Bible in chapter 4.

Daniel A. Helminiak, Ph.D., *What the Bible Really Says About Homosexuality*: Alamo Square Press, 1994.

Lesson 22

What About Leviticus?

† **Preparatory Bible Reading:** Leviticus 18, 19, and 20

One Sunday evening I was giving a Bible study entitled "The Bible as the Friend of Lesbians and Gays" at Atlanta's First Metropolitan Community Church (MCC). An unidentified man walked in the back door of the church and shouted, "What about Leviticus?" He left immediately. A deacon followed him and told him if he did that again he would be arrested. (It is a felony to interrupt a religious service in the state of Georgia.) The man did not return, but he had made his point. ***What about Leviticus?***

Two verses in Leviticus say the same thing. Leviticus 18:22 and Leviticus 20:13 both call the ritual act of sex between two men "an abomination." These statements are part of a long list of *baal* religious rituals that were condemned as idolatrous in what is commonly called "the holiness code." Sex practices in *baal* rituals were viewed as "sympathetic magic" to influence the spirits or gods (*baal*) who were believed to control the fertility of crops and flocks.

Neither verse has anything at all to do with sexual orientation. They were addressed to heterosexuals who defied God by turning to *baal* fertility religion to insure good crops and healthy flocks. Since the economy of the people was based on the fertility of land and animals, the Israelites were frequently drawn into the various Canaanite sexual rituals in *baal* worship. God's prophets called the people to repent and turn back to God. The cycle of repentance from idolatrous lapses into baalism is often repeated in the Bible.

That is it. That is all there is to the two terrible anti-gay verses that are used to clobber gays and lesbians.

What Is An Abomination?

Leviticus always uses the word "abomination" to refer to idolatrous practices that were forbidden as a rejection of God. The death penalty was imposed on those who committed any of the many "abominations" listed in Leviticus 18 and 20. Even cursing one's parents was punished by death! (Leviticus 20:9). Sexual orientation was never a biblical issue. When Jesus quoted from Leviticus, the only reference that he used was 19:18; "You shall love your neighbor as yourself." (See Matthew 19:19; Mark 12:31; Luke 10:27; and Romans 13:9-10; Galatians 5:14.) Jesus used Leviticus to teach love. Many modern preachers misuse Leviticus to teach hate.

Proverbs 6 gives a list of "abominations" that clearly defines what an abomination is in the sense of what we mean by an abomination today. Notice how much this list sounds like the characteristics of homophobic, legalistic, judgmental religion, "There are six things which God hates, Yes, seven which are an abomination to God: haughty eyes, a lying tongue, and hands that shed innocent blood, a heart that devises wicked plans, feet that run rapidly to evil, a false witness who tells lies, and one who spreads strife among friends" (Proverbs 6:16-19). Homosexuality is not mentioned, but hateful acts of abuse and violence against other people are what the list is all about.

The only term for sexual intercourse used in the Hebrew Bible is "to lie with," which is used in Leviticus 18:22 and 20:13. It does not imply any sexual orientation. Our problem is heightened by translations like the Living Bible, which paraphrased Leviticus 18:22 as, "Homosexuality is absolutely forbidden, for it is an enormous sin (Hebrew "abomination")." Leviticus 20:13 was paraphrased as, "The penalty for homosexual acts is death to both parties." Homosexuality is our term for same-sex sexual orientation, not just for a sex act. The interpretation of "lie with" as "homosexuality" is not based on the meaning or intention of the Hebrew words that were used. No word for homosexual existed in ancient Greek or Hebrew.

Unexpected Support

When I was on a radio talk show in March, 1993, in Eugene, Oregon, I explained the verses in Leviticus. A caller said, "I am Jewish, and my son just had his *bar mitzvah.* He had to read the passage you just explained from Leviticus when it was his turn to read in the synagogue. My rabbi gave the same explanation that you gave. I just wanted to tell you it is good to hear a Christian telling the truth about the Bible for a change!"

The requirements in the Book of Leviticus are totally bound up and determined by the culture in which they were written. To ignore or be ignorant of the cultural setting of ancient biblical writings is to miss the original meaning and to discount any value whatever in the writings for today. One of our problems in interpreting Leviticus is that we actually know very little about the cultural setting of the book.

The only reason that Leviticus 18:22 and Leviticus 20:13 have received so much attention in recent years is because the are the only places in the entire Bible where a legal requirement can be found and taken out of context to be used to attack and destroy Gay people. In doing this, the homophobic, fundamentalist, legalists ignore all the rest of Leviticus as if it were not even in the Bible. No other teaching in the history of the church has ever been based on such flimsy and obscure evidence. Fear of homosexuality is perceived as such an awful threat to homophobic, biblical legalists that they are willing to stop at nothing to find or create biblical texts that support their fears.

Jesus Replaced the Law and the Temple

Jesus was seen in the entire New Testament as the fulfillment and replacement of the Law and the Temple. The four Gospels, the Book of Acts, and the letters of Paul leave no doubt that the New Testament authors viewed Jesus as the fulfillment and replacement of the Law and the one whom believers follow in place of laws and their interpreters. The Letter to the Hebrews is clear that Jesus also fulfilled and replaced the Tabernacle, the Temple, and the sacrificial system. In both Law and Temple a primary concern was deciding who should be left out and who could be included. Jesus challenged and shattered the exclusive view of God that dominated religion at his time. He said clearly that God is for every person and that God unconditionally accepts and loves all people.

I have frequently been amazed at the extent to which some Bible teachers are willing to distort and pervert the plain meaning of verses in order to leave gay people out of the love of God. After one Bible study that I did in Nashville on Gay Cable Television, I got a phone call from someone who was an avid listener to a fundamentalist preacher who came on Public Access Television immediately after my program. He said, "I'll bet you believe and teach that God loves homosexuals, don't you?" I said, "Yes, I do. John 3:16 says that God loves the world and that includes lesbians and gays also." He replied, "No it doesn't. Do you know the word for world?" I said, "Yes. It is *cosmos*. We get cosmic from it and it means the entire created order." He jumped on what I said and argued; "God loves the orderly universe, not those who are not part of God's order, like homosexuals!"

I listened to him rave on for a lot longer than I should have. I was fascinated by anyone who could twist the most powerful Bible statement of God's love for all people into a verse that excluded gay people. He had found a biblical basis for keeping out the undesirables that he feared and rejected. I recalled the Letter of Peter speaking of some things that Paul wrote "which are hard to understand, which the ignorant and unstable distort, as they do the rest of Scriptures, to their own destruction" (2 Peter 3:16). This man, however, took something that is perfectly clear and easy to understand and twisted it into a denial of the basic purpose of Jesus.

The Holiness Code and Religious Isolation

The main message of Leviticus is the "holiness code" that was intended to set Israel apart from all other people. It spelled out in great detail what the people of Israel could and could not do to remain distinct from the native people of Canaan. Any hint of idolatry or worship of *baal*, which dominated local culture, was forbidden to Israel.

Everything was classified as either clean or unclean, this included various foods, clothing, people, places, physical conditions, and an endless list of practices and everyday activities. This harsh separation of people from other people was based on religious uncleanness and set up hostility and frequent violence between Israelites and the people who already occupied the land. It created constant conflict among the religious leaders over what was clean and what was unclean. This religious struggle continued into the time of Jesus and dominated the religious system that challenged and rejected Jesus.

Jesus cut through the entire legal system of separation, especially the provisions of Leviticus, and invited outsiders and outcasts to follow him. Jesus violated the Law by touching lepers, eating with sinners, healing on the Sabbath, and constantly breaking down the artificial legal barriers that separated people from each other and from God.

Jesus quoted Leviticus only once to say that you shall love your neighbor as yourself (quoting Leviticus 19:18), which gives as much force to the idea of loving yourself as to loving your neighbor. The Scribes and Pharisees and official teachers asked Jesus, "Who is my neighbor?" The word in Hebrew and in Greek simply means "the one nearby." The religious authorities argued endlessly about how to define neighbor. They decided that the neighbor had to be someone of their own race, sex, religious party, social class, and as near to being just like them as possible.

Jesus told the story of the Good Samaritan in Luke 10:25-37 to define "neighbor" as the one who needs you, no matter what race, religion, sex, sexual orientation, or other defining factors might be. The victim beside the road had been stripped of his clothes, which were the badges of identity in those days. The victim was a completely unidentified person. His only cry for help was his desperate condition. The word used in the parable for the feelings of the Good Samaritan for the victim is "compassion." This word is the strongest word for human feeling in Greek. It means to feel the pain of another person just as much as they do. The word is used in the Gospels only of Jesus and two people who represented Jesus or God in parables, the Good Samaritan and the father of the Prodigal Son (Luke 10:25-37 and Luke 15:11-32).

Jesus challenged and upset the whole social and religious system when he taught and acted on his belief that all people have equal value before God. Jesus demonstrated and proclaimed the unconditional love of God for all people. For this crime of breaking the tradition, Jesus was persecuted, rejected, and finally crucified.

Questions for Study and Discussion

1. What other stories in the Gospel of Luke can you recall that demonstrate the inclusive mission of Jesus to outcast and rejected people? Review the first sermon by Jesus in his hometown of Nazareth in Luke 4:16-30.

2. Why do you think that churches and church leaders still cling to a legalistic, judgmental, abusive form of religion in the name of Jesus, especially regarding sex?

3. How can you challenge and change the legalistic, abusive use of the Bible and religion against homosexuals and others who do not comply with the expectations of the majority of churches today? What have you already done to make a difference?

4. How have you personally separated yourself from the destructive and demeaning use of religion to hurt yourself and others?

Additional Resources

John Shelby Spong has written several books that ask these same questions, *Living in Sin? A Bishop Rethinks Human Sexuality*: Harper, 1988; *Rescuing the Bible from Fundamentalism: A Bishop Rethinks the Meaning of Scripture*: Harper, 1991; and *Why The Church Must Change or Die: A Bishop Speaks to Believers in Exile*: Harper, 1998. Become familiar with all of these revolutionary works.

Lesson 23

Discovering the Truth in Paul

† **Preparatory Bible Reading:** Romans 1, 2, and 3

Paul's writings have been taken out of context to punish and oppress every identifiable minority, Jews, children, blacks, slaves, women, people of color, politicians, divorced people, intellectuals, the ignorant, poor people, convicts, pro-choice people, lesbians, gays, bisexuals, and transgendered people, religious reformers, and the mentally ill. The list could go on and on.

Taking anything that Paul said out of its context is like trying to drive a car blindfolded! You don't know where you are, where you have been, where you are going, or whom you just ran over!

Paul, like all of us, was a child of his culture and time in history. He started, visited, and wrote to new Christians in all parts of the world. Usually he wrote from one group of people to another group of people. Sometimes these helpers were named, sometimes not. We do not know for sure who really wrote down most of the things in the letters of Paul, because Paul did not write himself but used a scribe to write for him, probably due to his bad eyesight, which he mentioned several times. Paul, like all of us, used colloquial and idiomatic figures of speech that would have been clear to his readers but which confuse and puzzle us.

Saint Augustine of Hippo (396-430) said that every Christian should memorize the Letter to the Romans, be able to recite it word for word, and spend some time with it every day. In *The Confessions*, the best known work of Augustine, Romans was quoted frequently throughout. In the time of Jesus, all biblical scholars and students did their study from memory. Students of a rabbi had to memorize the Hebrew Bible and all of the official interpretations. Memorization guaranteed accuracy and credibility; it meant that the context was always part of the teaching and interpretation.

When I taught a course on Paul's Letter to the Romans at the Baptist College, I decided to memorize Romans as Augustine suggested. I nearly ran some of my friends crazy by having them follow along in the Bible as I recited the sections I had memorized, but the effort paid off. Being able to visualize the message of Romans as a whole immediately cleared up a lot of Paul's thought that I had not been able to untangle before. It helped so much that I set out to continue memorizing the books of the Bible that I taught in college courses. The last book that I memorized and taught before I left the college was Philippians, which I also taught in over 40 pastor's conferences in South Carolina.

Paul used Greek with great skill. One sentence, however, could go on for more than a full page of the text. Paul also used many of his letters to answer questions that people at a distance had asked, and most of the time we do not know what these questions were and can only guess at them. Reading Paul is like listening to only one side of a telephone conversation. For these and many reasons having to do with translation problems and our still limited certainty about what a lot of words and expressions meant, we have difficulty in understanding Paul. Remember the warning in 2 Peter 3:16-18 about distorting and twisting what Paul had said. If you do not remember that passage, stop and read it now.

The Context of Romans 1:26-27

Many people have told me emphatically that Paul said, "Homosexuality is an abomination to God." They do not know where, but they know that he said it somewhere. Of course, Paul never said it, and that statement is not found anywhere in the Bible. The context of Romans 1:26-27 is a long discourse that shows that all people equally need Jesus and that the gospel of which Paul was proud was "the power of God for liberation [salvation] for ALL who believe" (Romans 1:16). Paul's gospel was always inclusive of all people. He said it simply and eloquently, "There is neither Jew nor Greek, neither slave or free, neither male nor female; for you are all one in Christ Jesus" (Galatians 3:28).

Paul's vigorous denunciation of idolatrous religious worship is the context of Romans 1:26-27. The sexual practices that Paul denounced in these verses are part of his rejection of all forms of idolatry. Paul believed that all people have broken God's law and need to be set free, and all people have been given God's kindness, forbearance, and patience. Read all of the first three chapters of Romans in order to see the context of Romans 1:26-27.

Problems of Translation

Romans 1:26-27 is a difficult passage to translate. Some words are used nowhere else by Paul, and familiar words are used in unusual ways. We are not certain what some of the words mean in the context of these verses. Paul's letter is clearly directed against some form of idolatry that would have been known to Paul's readers. To us the argument is vague and indirect. Verse 25 is clearly a denunciation of idolatrous religion, "For they exchanged the truth of God for a lie, and worshiped and served the creature and not the Creator, who is blessed for ever. Amen." Then follows Romans 1:26-27,

> For this reason God gave them over to degrading passions: for their women exchanged the natural use for that which is against nature. And in the same way also the men abandoned the natural use of the woman and burning in their desire towards one another, men with men committing indecent acts and receiving in their own persons the due penalty of their error.

These two verses contain some of the most difficult and obscure uses of words that Paul ever wrote. Some of the words are used only in this passage, and others are used with different meaning than in other passages. We study each word in detail in the Special Study on "Homosexuality and the Bible" at the end of this book.

After this passage, Paul gave a list of sins that people commit against each other because of the fear and anger that flow from "a depraved mind" (the Greek word means "a mind that does not measure up"). At no point in his writings did Paul deal with same-sex orientation or the expression of romantic love and affection by same-sex couples. Romans 1:26-27 is an indictment of the many religious cults, temples, and rituals that had developed to provide entertaining and erotic experiences for the people in the name of religion.

Here, as in Leviticus 18:22 and Leviticus 20:13, the context of the verses is idolatrous religious rituals that have nothing to do with sexual orientation but have everything to do with abandoning God for other gods.

Paul Never Was Vague or Indirect About God's Love

Paul was a brilliant intellectual and a master of the Greek language. If he had wanted to condemn homosexuality as the most evil and monstrous sin in the world, he could have done so with no doubts about his intentions. He clearly denounced legalistic religion as a threat to the followers of Jesus in many places and at great length, especially in Romans and Galatians. In Romans 1:26-27, Paul was not talking about homosexuality. He was talking about idolatry and radical emotional excesses in local religious cults.

Paul wrote to the Christians in Rome from Corinth, the second largest city in the Roman Empire and a crossroads of world trade and culture. Pausanius observed at about the same time as Paul was there that there were over 1,000 religions in Corinth. The most prominent religions in Corinth were the fertility cult of Aphrodite, the worship of Apollo, and the Delphic Oracle, which was across the bay from and within sight of the city of Corinth. The Delphic Oracle was the best-known religious shrine of prophecy in the ancient world. Women prophets went into a trance with the aid of drugs and uttered difficult sayings in response to questions. The women prophets were called *python*, the name of the sacred snake that symbolized the knowledge of secret wisdom given by the god Apollo. The Temple of Apollo is the most imposing ruin left on the site of ancient Corinth.

Paul's readers would have been well aware of the religious climate from which he wrote to the Romans. Romans 1:26-27 probably was a lot clearer to them than it is to us. Gallio, the Roman ruler in Corinth at the time of Paul's visit to Corinth, became a friend to Paul and defended Paul against the attacks by local Jewish religious leaders (Acts 18:8-17). Gallio's brother was Seneca, the teacher and tutor of young Nero. Seneca was in Rome when Paul wrote Romans and later may have been the "Most Excellent Friend of God (Theophilus)" addressed at the beginning of both the Gospel of Luke and Acts. Scholars have noticed how much some of the writings of Seneca sound like the writings of Paul. When Nero became insane, he ordered Seneca to commit suicide, after that, Nero changed from being an efficient ruler into a dangerous and vicious tyrant who was finally killed himself.

Paul Was Clear About God's Unconditional Love

Paul's great exposition of love in 1 Corinthians 13 was written to believers in the city from which he had written Romans. When Paul talked about the main thing, Jesus and God's unearned favor and love given to all people through Jesus, Paul was perfectly clear and there was no confusion or vagueness about what he meant. See Romans 5 through 8 and Ephesians 2 and 4.

To take two very difficult and unclear verses in the midst of Paul's denouncement of idolatry in Corinth and use them to construct a whole theology of homosexuality and sexual depravity is ludicrous and would not be tolerated in any other area of biblical studies except that these verses give the meager fuel that homophobic biblical legalists need to fan the abusive flames of fear and hate toward gay and lesbian people.

Paul nowhere said or even hinted that gays and lesbians should or could change their sexual orientation. Paul had nothing to say about romantic love between two people of the same sex. Romans 1:26-27 turns out to be a blunt instrument to batter and wound people with no redemptive qualities and no reconciling force. The use of Romans 1:26-27 to judge and condemn gay people overlooks the great body of writing from Paul that clearly teaches God's freely given and all inclusive love for every person on earth. God offers through Jesus the free gift of liberation (salvation) that cannot be earned or bought by human effort or by religious works. Paul summed it up in Romans 10:4, "Christ is the end of the law for righteousness to everyone who believes."

Questions for Study and Discussion

1. What have you learned in this lesson that helped you to feel better about yourself?

2. How personally have you taken the statements in Romans 1:26-27 as a judgment of God against you? Has anyone ever used Romans 1:26-27 to rebuke you for being a lesbian or gay person? How did you handle it?

3. Why do you think that churches and church leaders have been willing to develop an absolute anti-homosexual legalism based primarily on these two verses?

Lesson 24

Homosexual Ghosts

† **Preparatory Bible Reading:** 1 Corinthians 6:1-20 and 1 Timothy 1:1-20

Ghosts may not hurt you, but they can make you hurt yourself! What I call homosexual ghosts in 1 Corinthians 6:9 and 1 Timothy 1:10 were created by inaccurate and intentionally misleading translations. The incorrectly translated words are an obscure and difficult Greek word and another familiar Greek word that simply does not mean what the translation says. The word translated "effeminate" does not mean effeminate or contain any sexual implications at all. The word translated "homosexual" is the obscure word that was not used outside of the New Testament in the time of Paul as far as we know, and we do not know what it really means. New Testament Greek has no word for "homosexual." The translation is a grave mistake.

We have to look at these two verses, however, because 1 Corinthians 6:9 is probably the most often quoted biblical passage that is used to condemn and reject gay people. It cannot be ignored. A typical modern translation of each passage follows, (both the following translations are from the *New American Standard Version*),

> The unrighteous shall not inherit the kingdom of God. So do not be deceived; neither fornicators, nor idolaters, nor adulterers, nor effeminate, nor homosexuals, nor thieves, nor covetous, nor drunkards, nor revilers, nor swindlers, shall inherit the realm of God.

Parallel to this is 1 Timothy 1:9-10,

> Law is not made for a righteous person but for those who are lawless and rebellious, for the ungodly and sinners, for the unholy and profane, for those who kill their fathers and mothers, for murderers and fornicators and homosexuals and kidnapers and liars and perjurers, and whatever else is contrary to sound teaching.

These two passages seem very convincing in including lesbians and gay men in the most dreadful lists of depraved human behavior imaginable. The problem is that the word that is translated "homosexual" does not mean homosexual!

There is no word for homosexual in New Testament Greek. Homosexual is a composite word made from one Greek word and one Latin word. It is of modern origin and was not in use at all until the late 19th century. No word for homosexual exists in biblical Hebrew either. The word translated "homosexual" is the Greek word *arsenokoite* and was formed from two words meaning "male" and "bed." The word is found nowhere else in the New Testament and has not been found anywhere in contemporary Greek of the time of Paul. We do not know what the word means, it appears only in these two lists of sinners.

Arsenokoite is of obscure origin and uncertain meaning. It probably refers to male prostitutes with female customers, which was a common practice in the Roman world. When early Greek-speaking Christian preachers condemned homosexuals, they did not use this word. John Chrysostom (345-407) preached on homosexuality, but he never used this word. When he preached on 1 Corinthians 6:9-10 and 1 Timothy 1:10, he did not mention homosexuals. (Read my discussion of this issue in the Special Study on "Homosexuality and the Bible" at the end of this book.)

Soft Does Not Mean Effeminate

The word translated "effeminate" in 1 Corinthians 6:9 is the Greek word *malakoi* and means "soft," "weak," or "vulnerable." It contains no sexual implications. It was translated as "soft" in reference to king's clothing in Matthew 11:8 and Luke 7:24 and as "illness" in Matthew 4:23 and 9:35. It is used nowhere else in the New Testament and implies no hint of reference to sexual orientation or to sex. The translation of "effeminate" is incorrect, ignorant, degrading to women, and impossible to justify on the basis of ancient usage compared to the meaning of "effeminate" today.

No Bible version before the 1946 translation of the *Revised Standard Version* translated *arsenokoite* as "homosexual."

Why have modern Bible translators given in to this incorrect and damaging use of homosexual in these two verses? Any Greek scholar good enough to participate in the translation of the Bible for publication already knows all of the above information. Why is the error not corrected?

The incorrect use of *malakoi* and *arsenokoite* as references to homosexual orientation has been disastrous for millions of lesbian, gay, bisexual, and transgendered people. This translation mistake has enlisted a great army of ignorant, homophobic, religious zealots against gay people and has turned many lesbians and gay men against the Bible. The result has been to alienate multitudes of gays from the Bible and the good news of Jesus and to deprive gay people of the comfort, encouragement, strength, and hope in Christ during the HIV/AIDS epidemic and in other times of greatest need.

Challenge and Stop the Hate

The holocaust of hate and violence against lesbian, gay, bisexual, and transgendered people and by gay people against themselves and each other is the continuing horror resulting from this evil mistake in translation. How can Bible translators publish and continue to print lies about gay men and women in the Bible?

Homophobic Bible "translations from hell" must not go unchallenged. There is no clear and unambiguous reference at all to gay people or homosexuality in the Bible. To build the tragic doctrine of God's hate for and rejection of gays on the flimsy evidence in the Bible is to invalidate the Bible itself as an effective guide to anything. Many of the people who claim most frequently to believe that the Bible is the "word of God" have distorted the message of the Bible to create a message of ignorance, fear, hate, and human destruction that contradicts everything that Jesus did and stood for. This abusive use of the Bible is not limited to the oppression of gay women and men. Anybody who gets in the way of the legalistic, judgmental, biblical literalists gets the same hateful treatment.

It is time for this perversion of spirituality to stop. The use of wrong translations and out-of-context twisting of the Bible to incite fear and hate towards gays and lesbians and others demands a clear, academically sound, credible, and easily understood response. Every biblical word that has been used to wound, alienate, and oppress people must be examined in detail and carefully defused. God has called us to return the Bible to the outcast and oppressed people for whom it was written in the first place.

Build Your Own Case for the Truth

Find as many different translations as you can of Genesis 19:5; Leviticus 18:22 and Leviticus 20:13; Romans 1:26-27; 1 Corinthians 6:9; and 1 Timothy 1:9-10. Compare the contrasts and contradictions in the various translations. Notice particularly how many different ways 1 Corinthians 6:9 has been translated. Why do you think so many different ways of translating this verse have developed?

Take as much time as you need to study and learn the material in "Homosexuality and the Bible" Special Study at the end of this book. This material is the result of over ten years of special research, study, and writing to try to clear up the confusion and misunderstandings that have been imported into the Bible itself to distort the original message of good news for all people in Jesus.

Read carefully John Boswell's study and explanations of the biblical material that is used against gay people. It takes time and patience to work through Boswell's material, but it is the best and most thorough source that is available on the background and history of the words and phrases that have been used to condemn and destroy gay people. Look up and read whatever is helpful to you from the other books in the list at the end of Lesson 21.

Do not leave this Step until you are clear and confident in your own mind that the Bible gives no basis for condemning and rejecting people on the basis of their sexual orientation. Your self-esteem and confidence as a gay, lesbian, bisexual, or transgendered Christian as well as your ability to share your faith with others depends on your knowing beyond a shadow of a doubt that God is your friend and not your enemy.

Feel free to contact me through the publisher of this book or write to me at my mailing address at the end of "My Story" in Chapter 2 if you have further questions about the Bible and homosexuality.

Explore my Web site at www.truluck.com for updated information related to these issues.

Our Enemy Is Formidable

In the spring of 1993 a reporter for a newspaper in Florida called to interview me about homosexuality and the Bible. I gave him over the phone much of the material in these four lessons. After he interviewed me, he let a famous local pastor see what I had said and respond to it before he printed the story. I was not given an opportunity, however, to respond to him. The pastor was a very well known television preacher heard over hundreds of stations. His response to what I said was to ridicule me. He said that nobody who said what I did about New Testament Greek could pass the first seminary Greek course!

This particular preacher likes to give his name on television with a long list of degrees attached. He did not deal with what I said about the Greek words. He simply declared that he had read from the Greek New Testament every day for the past 25 years, and he knew that I was wrong. This preacher did not know the Bible any better than the religious teachers who opposed and condemned Jesus. The Pharisees had memorized every detail of the Bible. Being informed about the details in the Bible does not make a person right in their legalistic, judgmental interpretations. You can live in a barn, but that does not make you a cow.

I really do not expect to change the way this powerful, rich preacher sees gay people. His mind is completely closed to any truth that he himself does not create. He produced and offered on television a truly horrible and inaccurate video about gay people. The video was full of lies, distortions, and speculations. He sold copies of the video, which I saw on seven different Nashville cable television stations one Sunday, and used the money from the sales to fight against gay and lesbian legal rights.

The anti-gay newspaper ads in the summer of 1998 that promoted the false and misleading claims to change homosexuals into heterosexuals through therapy and fundamentalist religion were planned and financed by this preacher and his Coral Ridge Presbyterian Church organization. This preacher will not listen to the truth. Many gay people and their families and friends hear his spiritual garbage and are confused and misled by it. This book is only a small response, but it is a response.

Share What You Are Learning

If this material is in any way liberating and encouraging to you, please share it. You can start a spiritual recovery support group yourself. See the material in Part V "Reach Out," in this book and the material on "Guidelines for Small Groups" in Chapter 4. As you read and discuss the material in this book, let me know what you think and any suggestions that you have. We absolutely must act to help ourselves. The religious establishment will not help us. Homophobic, legalistic fundamentalists already have far too much money, politics, institutions, and resources invested in their commitment to exterminate gay people for them to back down now.

The President of the Southern Baptist Theological Seminary in Louisville (my seminary) recently made public pronouncements against gay people and viewed us as the greatest threat to American civilization today. Religious leaders and denominations that once fought for spiritual and religious freedom and fair play have sold out to homophobia and have adopted rigid positions against gay people.

Our conflict is spiritual. Our tools are given to us through the truth and love that we experience in Jesus. The first thing that we are called to do is to help each other to see the truth of God's love for all of us. Helping other gay people to feel good about themselves is never a waste of time.

Questions for Study and Discussion

1. What experience have you had trying to change the minds and hearts of homophobic, legalistic fundamentalists?

2. What in this lesson most clearly spoke to you? Why?

3. Have you found a supportive group of people with whom you can share you own personal, spiritual pilgrimage and search for truth and the love of God in your life?

4. Have you prayed about the things discussed in these lessons? If so, what has been the effect of your prayers?

Additional Resources

John Boswell, *Christianity, Social Tolerance, and Homosexuality*, Appendix I, "Lexicography and Saint Paul," pages 335-353.

Part IV

Accentuate the Positive

People frequently have asked me, "What in the Bible is supportive of gay and lesbian people?" We have taken time to respond to how the Bible is used against us, but what in the Bible is for us? What do you think? What can you think of in the Bible that supports lesbian and gay people? Actually, there is a lot more than you might think. The Seventh, Eighth, and Ninth Steps take a look at positive biblical material that gives encouragement and helpful information to all oppressed and misunderstood people.

We have spent four lessons looking at the six Bible passages used against us. Can you make a list of six Bible passages that support and encourage lesbians and gay men? Our Wednesday night group in Nashville came up with these seven passages. You probably can add others.

Know that the Mighty God is truly God; It is God who has made us, and not we ourselves; We are God's people and the sheep of God's pasture. **(Psalm 100:3)**

God loves you so much that God gave God's only child that you would not throw your life away and die but that you might have life full of joy and hope now and forever. For God did not send Jesus to oppress you but that through Jesus you might be set free! **(John 3:16-17)**

Jesus said, "I speak to you so that you may have peace. In this world you will live under constant pressure, but cheer up! I have won the victory over everything!" **(John 16:33)**

Jesus said, "All authority has been given to me in heaven and on earth. As you go, make disciples of all people, baptizing them in the name of God, Jesus, and the Holy Spirit, teaching them to observe all I taught you, and behold, I am with you always for ever." **(Matthew 28:18-20)**

For freedom Christ set us free, therefore keep standing firm, and do not be subject again to a yoke of religious slavery. **(Galatians 5:1)**

Cast all of your anxiety on God, for God cares for you. **(1 Peter 5:7)**

There is neither Jew nor Greek, slave nor free, nor male nor female, for you are all one in Christ Jesus. **(Galatians 3:28)**

The following lessons address only a few of the Bible passages that are for us. You can think of a lot more, I am sure.

Chapter 12

The Seventh Step

Find Positive Supportive Scripture

Make a list of the Bible passages that especially speak to you and give you hope and encouragement.

John 3:16-17 is a good beginning, "God so loved the world [YOU] that God gave God's only begotten child, Jesus, that whosoever [YOU] believes in Jesus should not perish [throw away your life], but have eternal life. For God did not send Jesus into the world to condemn the world but that the world through Jesus should be set free [saved]."

See also Psalm 100; the Book of Ruth; the story of David and Jonathan in 1 Samuel 18:1 through 20:42 and 2 Samuel 1:1-27; John 14 through 17; Matthew 28:1-20; Galatians 3 through 6; 1 Peter 3 through 5; Romans 5:1-11; 8:1-4, 14-39; 15:1-7; and all of Romans 5 through 8.

Many other Bible passages are helpful and encouraging to people who are abused, misunderstood, outcasts, and oppressed. Discuss the Bible in your group and encourage people to suggest Bible passages that have helped them.

Lesson 25

Death Alone Shall Part Us: Ruth and Naomi

† **Preparatory Bible Reading:** The Book of Ruth

At the Academy Awards presentation on March 30, 1992, Bill Lauch accepted the Best Song Award for his late lover, Howard Ashman, who had died of HIV/AIDS. Debra Chasnoff thanked her lesbian life partner in her acceptance speech for the award for best documentary film. The audience accepted and applauded this unprecedented open expression of same-sex committed relationships.

Marriage in the Bible

Modern marriage customs have little to do with marriage practices in the Bible or in the early church. John Boswell concluded, "No marriages in ancient societies closely match their modern equivalents. Most cultures regard marriage as a private arrangement negotiated between two families" (John Boswell, *Christianity, Social Tolerance and Homosexuality*: University of Chicago Press, 1980, p. 26). Romantic love as the basis for marriage is absent in the Bible. The only way that people of equal rank and freedom of choice could enter into a lifetime covenant commitment in biblical times was for the partners to be two women or two men. A woman was the property of a man, her father, brother, or husband. Women were not free to make a marriage choice based on romantic love. The Greek word for romantic love, *eros*, is not used at all in the New Testament, though *eros* was the most common word for love in use at the time.

The most prominent Bible examples of commitment between two people based totally on individual attraction and free choice are Ruth with Naomi and David with Jonathan. Read the Book of Ruth and 1 Samuel 18 through 20 and 2 Samuel 1 to become familiar with these important Bible stories of same-sex, loving, committed couples. The Bible gives no basis for most modern heterosexual marriages, divorces, and remarriages. Yet the Bible stories of Ruth and Naomi and Jonathan and David paint a beautiful picture of same-sex loving and loyal, committed relationships entered into voluntarily before God and the community "until death alone shall part us."

Gay Marriages

For over 30 years, the Metropolitan Community Churches (MCC) have celebrated same-sex loving, committed relationships for gay and lesbian Christians in ceremonies of blessing and Holy Union. Recently, other Christian denominations have begun to accept and celebrate the life commitment of lesbian and gay couples. During the HIV/AIDS epidemic, thousands of gay men have cared for their life partners with HIV and AIDS and have been faithful care-givers over months and years of illness.

One of the greatest things that traditional churches can do for lesbian and gay Christians is to recognize, accept, and celebrate same-sex marriages. Lesbian and gay couples deserve and have the same right to the respect, community support, and protection under law as heterosexual couples.

Fairness and honesty demand that same-sex, committed couples should have legal protection of their property rights, medical coverage, social security, death benefits, job and housing security, and community encouragement and support. To deny basic human rights to any person because of sexual orientation is a blatant violation of the spirit of the United States Constitution and is given no support at all in the Bible.

Ruth and Naomi

Ruth forsook all others and committed herself to Naomi,

> Do not urge me to leave you or turn back from following you; for where you go, I will go, and where you live, I will live. Your people will be my people and your God will be my God. Where you die, I will die, and there I will be buried. May God's worst punishment come upon me if anything but death alone shall part us. (Ruth 1:16-17)

Many modern marriage ceremonies contain ideas from this speech. Most people, however, choose to ignore the fact that these promises were made first by a woman to another woman!

Ruth and Naomi were brought together in loving commitment to each other by the death of their husbands, which left them alone and vulnerable as widows. The Hebrew word for widow is "mute" and is a heavy reminder of the weak and defenseless condition of unmarried women in Old Testament times. The name *Naomi* means "pleasant," but after she became a widow, Naomi said, "Call me *Mara* [meaning bitter], for the Almighty has dealt very bitterly with me . . . and has afflicted me" (Ruth 1:20-21).

Being helpless and vulnerable in the face of social and economic pressures has also brought many gay and lesbian couples together. Living in the closet makes most gay people mute and defenseless about their deepest feelings and needs. Lesbian and gay couples can identify with the fears and dangers faced by widows in ancient times.

Gay men and lesbians can also appreciate the many references in the Bible about legal protection from abuse and injustice against widows, orphans and aliens. "Cursed is the one who distorts the justice due an alien, orphan, and widow. And all the people said, Amen!" (Deuteronomy 27:19).

Community Approval

The relationship of Ruth and Naomi was accepted and approved by family and friends. Community appreciation and encouragement for the love and faithfulness between these two women was expressed in Ruth 2:11-12, 22-23, 3:17; 4:13-17. Ruth and Naomi developed healthy and inclusive loving relationships with other people in their lives. But, the Book of Ruth never says that Ruth loved Boaz, her second husband, but frequently says that Ruth loved Naomi. It is obvious that Ruth cared very much for Boaz and also that Ruth and Naomi loved Ruth's baby, who was named Obed, the father of Jesse, the father of David. Ruth was David's great grandmother. Read Ruth 4 for details of the arranged marriage of Boaz to Ruth. Notice the interesting reference to Tamar in Ruth 4:12 and look up and read the story of Judah and Tamar in Genesis 38, where continuing the family line was far more important than issues of sexual practices, sexual morality, or sexual orientation.

Personal Choice and Mutual Responsibility

The 1990 San Francisco Domestic Partners ordinance respects and protects the committed relationships of same-sex couples and defines domestic partners as "two adults who have chosen to share one another's lives in an intimate and committed relationship of mutual caring, who live together, and who have agreed to be jointly responsible for basic living expenses incurred during the Domestic Partnership." The basis for the partnership is a free decision of choice by consenting adults.

The Hebrew word for love is *ahab*, used to describe Ruth's love for Naomi (Ruth 4:15) and of Jonathan's love for David (1 Samuel 18:1; 20:17). *Ahab* means, "electing or selecting love." *Ahab* is the word used for God's choosing love for Israel (Jacob) instead of to Esau in Malachi 1:2, which Paul quoted and developed in Romans 9:13. The love of Ruth and Naomi was freely expressed romantic love that could not be forced on them or arranged by parents or other authorities. The love shared by Ruth and Naomi was like the romantic love that draws two people together to be married today, whether they are heterosexual or homosexual. This kind of love clearly was not the basis for biblical marriages, which were always arranged by other people than the married couple.

Ruth and Naomi took care to see that they each had food and shelter. Naomi's scheme to provide security, protection, and support for Ruth by arranging Ruth's marriage to Boaz is the main plot of the story. The Book of Ruth never says whether the loving, committed relationship of Ruth and Naomi was or was not a lesbian relationship. The Bible never discussed same-sex sexual orientation either to condemn or to commend it.

Ruth and Naomi stuck together through great adversity. They traveled a long distance to stay together, looked after each other when they were hungry, and protected each other from danger. They expressed their love through physical affection in kissing and holding each other (Ruth 1:9, 11). They respected family and community customs and still maintained the integrity of their love for each other.

The Bible is Clear

Lifelong committed partnerships of loving same-sex couples are clearly supported in the Bible. Nowhere does the Bible condemn same-sex romantic love. Neither homosexual nor heterosexual romantic love was ever discussed in the New Testament. Homosexual love was not condemned; it was never mentioned. The Bible encouraged loving commitments between people who freely choose their partners in life. The Bible's emphasis is on God's "faithful" and "steadfast" love and on human love that demonstrates the character of God. Reread Ruth 4:13-17. Ruth was David's great grandmother; and I wonder what David called Naomi!

Questions for Study and Discussion

1. How has love developed in your life?

2. When did you first realize that you loved someone other than your parents or family? Who first aroused your sexual interest? What control did you have over your feelings?

3. Do you know any loving same-sex couples? Should they be accepted and protected by legal marriage? Why or why not?

4. Genesis 2:18 says people should not be alone. People need helpers who "correspond to themselves." How should gays and lesbians interpret this? What does it say to you?

Additional Resources

Read John Shelby Spong, *Living in Sin? A Bishop Rethinks Human Sexuality*: Harper, 1988.

Karen Thompson, *Why Can't Sharon Kowalski Come Home?*: Spinsters/Aunt Lute, 1988.

Malcolm Boyd and Nancy L. Wilson, Editors, *Amazing Grace: Stories of Lesbian and Gay Faith*: The Crossing Press, 1991.

Contact the UFMCC Web site (http://www.ufmcc.com) to locate the MCC pastors and congregations near you that can give you up-to-date information concerning planning a Holy Union (same-sex wedding).

Lesson 26

What Love Has Joined: David and Jonathan

† Preparatory Bible Reading: 1 Samuel 18:1 through 20:42 and 2 Samuel 1:1-27

The loving relationship of Jonathan and David got off to a highly dramatic public beginning.

> Jonathan made a covenant with David because he loved him as himself. And Jonathan stripped off the robe that was on him and gave it to David, with his armor, his sword and bow and belt.
>
> 1 Samuel 12:3-4

This extravagant display of public affection by Jonathan for David was remarkable in that the clothes he gave to David signified his rank as heir to the throne of Israel. No wonder Jonathan's father, King Saul, got so angry that he tried to kill both David and Jonathan.

Saul's feelings about Jonathan's love for David are clear, "You son of a perverse and rebellious woman! Do I not know that you are choosing the son of Jesse to your own shame and to the shame of your mother's nakedness?" (1 Samuel 20:30).

Upon saying this, Saul tried to kill Jonathan. The love of David and Jonathan was so unacceptable to Saul that he was willing to kill his own son to end it! Saul and David also loved each other, which further complicated the whole situation.

The covenant between David and Jonathan was renewed in 1 Samuel 20:17 and 20:23, "As for the agreement of which you and I have spoken, behold, God is between you and me forever." The same-sex committed relationship of Jonathan and David was made under God and for life. The loyalty of David and Jonathan was a central theme of their story.

Even though David and Jonathan loved each other in an oppressive environment and under the threat of violence, they did not waver in their commitment to each other. Perhaps one reason that David was called "a man after God's own heart" (1 Samuel 13:14) was because David's love was steadfast and enduring. God's covenant love is steadfast and dependable.

Jesus "loved his own who were in the world and loved them to the end." In 1 Corinthians 13:8 the climactic statement about love is that "love never fails." The word "fails" means "to come to an end or to collapse." Love never gives up under pressure. Jonathan and David pledged durable and unswerving love for each other that will never end.

"Gadal"

Unlike Ruth and Naomi, David and Jonathan had to meet in secret because of Saul's anger. (Is this an early example of being in the closet?) Jonathan escaped from Saul's wrath to meet David in an emotional farewell, "When the lad was gone, David rose from the south side and fell on his face to the ground, and bowed three times. And they kissed each other and wept together, until David was satisfied [or "fulfilled"]" (1 Samuel 20:41). The Hebrew word at the end of the verse which says David "was satisfied," which is my translation of *gadal*, literally meaning "to be or to become large or great." *Gadal* was used in a great variety of ways in the Old Testament.

Some readers believe *gadal* has sexual connotations and is evidence that David made love to Jonathan until achieving erection and orgasm. There is no basis in this use of the word to say whether or not a sexual encounter took place. Like most Hebrew words, *gadal* was used with many meanings depending on the context. The *King James Version* of the Bible says "wept one with another, until David exceeded." The *KJV* also rendered *gadal* as "exceeded" in 1 Kings 10:30 where "Solomon exceeded all the kings." The word also was used for intense emotional "grief" in Job 2:13 and for "mourning" in Zechariah 12:11. It is translated "to grow up" in 1 Samuel 2:26 and "to be great, magnificent" in victory in 1 Samuel 19:5. In 1 Samuel 26:24 *gadal* was used twice to speak of David's life being "highly" valued to Saul and to God.

The word *gadal* is flexible enough to refer in 1 Samuel 20:41 to David's great and overwhelming emotions. Physical love and affection are clearly indicated, but a sexual encounter is neither required nor ruled out by this use of *gadal*. The Bible never described details of private sexual practices of people who love each other, straight or gay.

Arranged Political Marriages

The same Bible materials that describe the loving same-sex commitments of Ruth to Naomi and Jonathan to David also tell of arranged marriages for political and economic reasons for Ruth and Boaz and for David and Saul's daughter Michal. The Bible stories show that the same-sex partnerships of Ruth with Naomi and David with Jonathan were far superior to the arranged marriages, because they are based in love.

David described Jonathan in a wonderful outpouring of emotional fervor in 2 Samuel 1 when David was told of the death of Jonathan and Saul. David's words of lament would be appropriate for a gay lover who has died of HIV/AIDS. This is the first "psalm" (song) of David recorded in the Bible. David lamented the death of Jonathan and cried out, "I am distressed for you, my brother Jonathan. You have been very pleasant to me. Your love to me was more wonderful than the love of women! How the mighty have fallen! The weapons of war have perished" (2 Samuel 1:26-27). David's eloquent poem of grief and loss over his beloved young companion Jonathan is filled with beauty, pathos, and inspiration.

David as a Biblical Ideal

The Gospel of Matthew begins by calling Jesus the "son of David" and then gives the ancestry of Jesus in three groups of 14 names in each group. Jesus was called "son of David" in the gospels. "Son of" meant, "to be like" someone as well as to be a biological descendent.

David represented the ideal of being "after God's own heart." David loved many people with great emotion and at great cost. David was well known for his love for his several wives, for Bathsheba, his baby that died, his soldiers, his rebellious son Absolom and even his greatest enemy Saul. Nathan, the prophet of God, challenged and condemned David for his love for Bathsheba, which led to the murder of her husband Uriah. General Joab criticized David for loving his son Absolom to the neglect of his own loyal soldiers.

David's inclusive love was illustrated in many ways in the Book of Psalms. David loved God and David loved people. The deepest and most profound love of David for any person in the Bible was for Jonathan. As David said in his final song of praise and appreciation for his dead lover, "Jonathan's love was wonderful!"

Holy Union and Gay Marriages

Today, only a few countries permit same-sex marriages. Other countries are considering it. A growing number of cities and states in the United States have established public policy that respects same-sex "domestic partners" in regard to certain limited job and medical benefits. In 1990, San Francisco was the first city anywhere to approve a same-sex domestic partner ordinance by popular vote. It marked a revolutionary beginning for same-sex couples to celebrate their loving life commitment to each other in the context of public acceptance and support. Now the City and County of San Francisco will do business only with companies that provide the same employee benefits to domestic partners as to married couples.

Much of the material in these studies of Ruth and Naomi and David and Jonathan was printed and used in the campaign for approval of the Domestic Partner proposition in San Francisco in 1990 and for reaffirmation in 1991. At the San Francisco City Hall celebration of the first registration of Domestic Partners on February 14, 1991, several lesbian and gay couples rejoiced to announce publicly for the first time their committed partnerships of twenty-five years or longer.

Challenges and opposition to justice and fairness for gay men, lesbians, and bisexuals at state and local levels continue to be fueled by the fircs of fear and hate generated by ignorant and abusive religious leaders. Biblical facts do not support negative religious and political campaigns against gay people. The Bible gives support and encouragement to loving committed same-sex couples who want to celebrate their "holy union" before God in Christian marriage, with their congregations, and in the presence of their families and friends. Fairness and justice for all people will eventually legalize gay and lesbian marriages.

Fear, ignorance, anger, and hate should not be allowed to determine the spiritual validity of gay marriages. The human need for respect and fairness is the basic issue. Many same-sex couples in committed partnerships suffer under public policies that are inconsistent with Christian and civilized principles of fair play.

Holy Union and Evangelism

Frequently at Holy Unions for Christian lesbians and gay men, we have given copies of my UFMCC brochure, "The Bible as Your Friend," to the guests at the request of the celebrating couple. The ceremony of holy union is a witness to God's love and acceptance and a powerful testimony to the gift of freedom in Christ.

Questions for Study and Discussion

1. Is it fair that loving same-sex couples cannot share in family health plans, visit their partners as family in many hospitals, receive death benefits, or have their community property rights protected?

2. Is it fair to deny to gay and lesbian couples the family and community support that friends and neighbors and family always give to heterosexual couples at times of sickness, death, and grief?

Additional Resources

Eric Marcus, *The Male Couple's Guide to Living Together: What Gay Men Should Know about Living Together and Coping in a Straight World*: Harper, 1988; (this book personally helped me).

Larry J. Uhrig, *The Two of Us: Affirming, Celebrating and Symbolizing Gay and Lesbian Relationships*: Alyson, 1984.

Keith Hartman, *Congregations in Conflict: The Battle Over Homosexuality*: Rutgers University Press, 1996. Mentioned earlier in lesson 4, this book tells the story of Dr. Mahan Siler and the Pullen Memorial Baptist Church in Raleigh, North Carolina, where the first public celebration of a same-sex marriage was performed in a Southern Baptist Church. It led to the expulsion of the church from the Southern Baptist Convention and the change in bylaws by that denomination to exclude any local church that accepted openly gay people into the church.

Lesson 27

God Knows Your Name

† **Preparatory Bible Reading:** Exodus 3:13-15; Philippians 2:1-11

In the next few lessons, we will study how the Bible gives help and support in many of the issues faced by gay people and others who have been oppressed by religion. The Names Project HIV/AIDS Memorial Quilt is one of the ongoing events that has had profound positive impact in the lesbian, gay, bisexual, and transgendered community, as well as in the lives of people of all gender orientations. This lesson will help us to explore the Bible basis for the Names Project.

Names in the Gay World

In the beginning, gay people always gave false names in the bars, in the park, to our gay friends, and even at church in Metropolitan Community Church (MCC). In a gay place, you would never dare risk giving your real name to a stranger. Many gay people still give a fake name when they fear exposure. One sign of progress and change in our community is the "Names Project" that celebrates the names of those who have suffered and died from HIV/AIDS.

When I was in Buenos Aires, Argentina, in 1972 to lecture at an international pastors' conference at the Baptist Seminary, the students had a favorite gospel song with the title, "God Remembers My Name." It was truly beautiful sung in Spanish to the usual accompaniment of four guitars. It expressed their faith that God cares about each of us as individuals, knows our names, and loves us as God's own children. Many of the students were from other South American countries far from home and in a strange land. We also, as strangers and aliens, take great comfort and encouragement in our belief that "God knows our name" too.

Bible names have symbolic meanings and were given to express the character of the individual. The Bible also makes much of remembering. One of the Ten Commandments begins with, "Remember the Sabbath Day." Jesus at the Last Supper, said, "Do this in remembrance of me." Peter said in 2 Peter that his eyewitness experiences of Jesus were being written in order that people might remember what Jesus did.

The Names Project

The Names Project quilt was begun to help us remember those who died of HIV/AIDS. Names are important things to the writers of the Bible. On November 27, 1985, during the annual candlelight march commemorating the murders of Mayor George Moscone and San Francisco's first openly gay supervisor, Harvey Milk, mourners covered the walls of the old Federal building with placards of the names of people who had died of AIDS. The many different sizes, shapes and colors of the cardboard signs reminded Cleve Jones of a quilt and inspired the idea of an AIDS memorial quilt.

My first contact with the Names Project came in 1988 in Atlanta. Dan Lewis was a tailor and had begun to work on a number of quilt panels. He invited me to go with him to a quilting bee. I had heard of the quilt but did not know much about it. When I first saw a panel hanging on the wall, I was struck by the large size. I had imagined small panels, like the ones in quilts my grandmother made. I asked why it was so big. Dan said, "It is three by six feet, the size of a grave." I still feel the emotional impact of that moment.

The Names Project quilt often produces a powerful emotional effect whenever it is experienced. As I write this material with an open copy of the book, *The Quilt: Stories from the Names Project*, before me, I am choked up again as I remember people and miss them. To remember is to reflect on the image of God who remembers. Memory helps make us human. Remembering the course of human and natural history is what education is about. The Bible is a book of remembering. Read 2 Timothy 1:3-5; 2 Peter 1:13-15; John 14:26; and Luke 22:19 for special passages on remembering.

Names in the Bible

The Bible is a "names project." From Adam, meaning "dirt," to Jesus, meaning "liberator, savior," names in the Bible help to tell the story of the acts of God. Read Philippians 2:5-11 to see how Jesus by humility and obedience reversed the sin of Adam's pride and disobedience. God gavc to Jesus "the name which is above every name."

Matthew and Luke gave lists of names of the ancestors of Jesus as part of identifying Jesus. The special nickname of Peter (the Rock, or as we might say today, "Rocky") was given to Simon. The disciples called Joseph of Cyprus by the nickname of Barnabas ("son of encouragement"). Each of these names had great significance. Paul wrote his letters recalling groups of people to other groups of people, and his letters were full of names. Read Romans 16 to see how important names were to Paul and notice how many women were named in Paul's greetings to the leaders of the church at Rome. Four of the first seven people named were women.

A Christian missionary was trying to explain to a new convert why Christians have so many different names for God. "Why do you call God by many different names like Father, Lord, Savior, Shepherd, King, Prince of Peace, etc.?" The missionary replied, "I guess we call God by whatever name describes what we let God do in our lives." Each of us is a unique person unlike all other people. Each of us has a name that is important to us. Remembering names is biblical and respects the value of each person. The Names Project is a way for us to celebrate life and to honor our individuality a gift from God to us.

Honoring and Remembering Individuals

No two Names Project quilt panels are exactly alike. Many are elaborate and highly individual. Most panels are made by close friends, lovers, or family and include pieces of clothing and other personal items. Robert is a child who died with AIDS and Robert's panel has on it the little teddy bear that was all that Robert had at the end and to which he clung as he died.

The profound love that goes into making the panels can be overwhelming and can provide a tremendous release of pain and grief. When the quilt was shown for the first time in Atlanta in 1988, I had the privilege of attending as a volunteer. Some times the most appropriate act of emotional support was to weep with those who weep. The most frequent comment that I heard from gay, lesbian, and straight people was, "There is so much love here!" The Names Project quilt has been a wonderful means of bringing people together and dissolving barriers.

Letting Go

For many panel makers, the hardest part of the Names Project was giving up their panel in the presentation ceremony. It was hard for people to let go of something that represented so much love. All who witnessed the closing ceremony were deeply moved. Tears flowed as each panel was given up to become part of the national quilt. Hugs were given and received and love was there. Read Philippians 3:12-14 for a Bible passage on letting go in order to move on with life.

To symbolize the letting go, the final event of each display of the quilt on tour is a release of hundreds of colorful balloons by everybody at the same time. As the great mass of balloons floated up and scattered in the wind, all of us who watched felt a surge of emotion, letting go of the pain and loss of seeing friends and loved ones leave this world.

Gays and lesbians have given to the world some new, creative, and positive ways of remembering and dealing with grief. When the Names Project quilt came to Atlanta in 1988 and was displayed at the massive World Congress Center, filling the entire space with panels, less than 2,000 panels were shown. They seemed endless then. Now, over close to 100,000 people have been memorialized in quilt panels. More panels are being made each day around the world. The HIV/AIDS epidemic continues. Progress in treatment and prevention has been made, but the epidemic is not over. Pain, oppression, and death continue, but love and care and support also continue.

Coming Out

HIV/AIDS has brought many people out of the closet. The quilt contains panels for some people who fought very hard to keep their sexual orientation secret. When I helped with the quilt showing, the panels most people wanted to see were those made for Liberace and for Rock Hudson, both of whom might have been very upset to be remembered as gay and included in the quilt. Years ago, the Rev. Troy Perry said he wished all gay people would suddenly turn purple so that the world would realize how many we are and that we really are everywhere. Later, Troy Perry said that HIV/AIDS-related Karposi's Sarcoma lesions did that for many of us in a tragic and unexpected way.

Coming out as lesbian or gay is simply a matter of facing, living, and telling the truth. But the misunderstanding and oppression of gay people have forced many to hide and even to deny their sexuality. The Names Project has encouraged lesbians and gay men to come out and to stand together in love, in grief, in pain, and in power.

Coming Together

One effect of the Names Project has been increased cooperation between various gay, lesbian, bisexual, and transgendered people and groups. One of the most dramatic results of the showing of the Names Project in Atlanta in 1988 was the remarkable beginning of close cooperation between lesbian and gay organizations in the city. The Lesbian/Gay Pride Parade a month after the showing of the quilt was the largest ever in Atlanta and set the stage for political activism and accelerated progress in human rights for gays and lesbians in the city. I had been to pride parades in Atlanta in the mid 1980's when less than 1,000 people took part. One year the parade was cancelled because of a lack of local cooperation. The pride parade participation after the first showing of the quilt was 6,000. The gay pride event in Atlanta is now one of the largest in the United States with around 200,000 people taking part.

Gay, lesbian, bisexual, and transgendered people compose a vast cross section of America and the world and include every race, culture, social status, occupation, income, age, national origin and language. The Names Project reflects and celebrates our diversity and has as a result helped to teach us more respect and care for each other.

The Names Project also has provided a setting for many Christian ministries in local MCC congregations and other affirming and accepting churches where space for Names Project sewing sessions has been provided along with other resources and lots of encouragement. These congregations also have been available for emotional and spiritual support both for people with HIV/AIDS and for their loved ones during the severe stress of life-threatening illness as well as during times of grief and loss.

Questions for Study and Discussion

1. How has this lesson influenced your opinion of the Names Project?

2. How would you compare the Names Project to traditional forms of bereavement and grief?

3. One observer said the quilt was a "portable cemetery." Is it? Have you seen the quilt or any part of it?

Additional Resources

The Academy Award Winning (1989 Best Feature Documentary) video, "Common Threads: Stories from the Quilt."

You can get more information about the Names Project on their Web site at http://www.aidsquilt.com or by telephone to Names Project Foundation in San Francisco at (415) 882-5500.

See the book of pictures and stories about the quilt by Cindy Ruskin, *The Quilt: Stories From the Names Project*: Pocket Books, 1988.

Lesson 28

Jesus and Same-Sex Love

† **Preparatory Bible Reading:** John 12:3-8; 13:1-35; Matthew 26:6-50; 27:1-10

Charles Haddon Spurgeon was Pastor of the London Baptist Tabernacle and the most famous preacher of his time. Sometimes he was quite controversial. He told a lot of jokes in his sermons. Some complained, and when he was asked if he thought Jesus ever laughed, Spurgeon replied, "I don't know if Jesus laughed or not, but Jesus sure fixed me up so I could!"

Was Jesus gay? I do not know. But Jesus sure fixed me up so I could feel good about being gay!

Jesus as the Standard

The life and teachings of Jesus are the standard by which all Christian beliefs and practices are tested. This is consistently the view of the New Testament. Paul concluded in Colossians 1:17, "In Christ all things hold together [find their proper place]." Take the time now to read and reflect on Colossians 1:15-22.

Jesus declared love to be the greatest good by which all behavior should be tested. Jesus defined love in terms of his own example. Read John 13:1-35 and spend some time meditating and thinking on the events and teachings that represent a great turning point in the history of all religion. All of the parables about love in the teachings of Jesus are about same-sex love, but Jesus never mentioned homosexuality or said anything about sexual orientation.

Romantic love and personal sexual practices are never even hinted at in the Gospels. Homophobic religious attacks on gays and lesbians have to find their evil ammunition outside of the Gospels and the life of Jesus. To scour difficult and obscure biblical material to find legalistic grounds on which to condemn and destroy gay people violates the principle of Christ-centered Bible study that fundamentalists and other biblical literalists claim to follow.

Jesus Was Selective

Jesus could not talk about everything. He was very selective about what he used from the Hebrew Bible to throw light on his own life and work. The four Gospels also were highly selective in telling the good news of Jesus. More was left out of the story than was included. Though the public ministry of Jesus lasted approximately three years, biblical scholars have estimated that the material recorded in all four Gospels could have taken place in less than three months. The Gospel of John concluded the world could not contain the books if every detail of what Jesus did and said was written. Why was so much left out and many things repeated over and over in the Gospels?

The Gospel of John gives an answer, "Many other signs therefore Jesus also performed in the presence of the disciples, which are not written in this book; but these are written in order that you may believe that Jesus is the Christ, the child of God; and that believing, you may have life in the name of Jesus" (John 20:30-31). The careful selection of gospel material was made to provide what disciples needed to know to "follow Jesus" in response to Jesus' invitation.

The New Testament views Jesus as the final filter of all spiritual truth. For the believer, no higher authority exists than the Gospel record of Jesus of Nazareth. Many critical and academic problems and questions about the Gospels continue to be unresolved. The necessity for Christians to test all things by the life and teachings of Jesus, however, is clearly the point of view taken by the New Testament itself. Jesus is the basis and center of all things, the point of reference for all salvation history.

Jesus said, "The Scriptures bear witness of me" (John 5:39). Luke 24:13-49 records how Jesus after the resurrection taught the disciples how the entire Hebrew Bible was fulfilled in himself. Religious speculation that builds fear and hate for gay people is the kind of abandonment of Jesus Christ that Paul rejected, "We are destroying speculations and every lofty thing raised up against the knowledge of God, and we are taking every thought captive to the obedience of Christ" (2 Corinthians 10:5).

Several gay and lesbian Christian organizations have published little folders that say on the cover, "Everything that Jesus Said about Homosexuality." Inside, the folder is blank.

A Grandmother Is Convinced

Sherry has been in a loving committed relationship with her lover for seven years. Sherry is a Christian and has suffered greatly from the abuse and rejection heaped on her by some of her own family. Searching for help, Sherry read carefully all of the words of Jesus that had been printed in red in the Bible that her grandmother gave to her years before. She told her grandmother, "I read all of the words of Jesus in the Bible you gave me, and not one word of Jesus condemned me for being lesbian or for living with Carla." Sherry said that this not only made her grandmother think and stop condemning her, but it also helped Sherry to accept herself and love herself as a lesbian. Sherry is an attorney. She has continued to press for acceptance of her sexuality and her committed relationship with Carla by all of her family. Recently after six years of hostility and rejection, Sherry's father, also an attorney, wrote her a beautiful, reconciling letter apologizing for his attitude in the past and inviting Sherry and Carla to come for a visit.

What Jesus Taught and Did About Love

Jesus did not condemn lesbians and gay men, but how does Jesus encourage and support homosexual love, "the love that dare not speak its name?" Jesus clearly loved and had an affectionate and emotional relationship with his disciples. Every example of love by Jesus in the Gospels is love for other people of the same sex. This does not imply homosexuality, but it does not exclude it either. Jesus broke many of the rabbinical traditions about the relationship of a teacher with his disciples. Jesus took the initiative to call young people to follow him. Traditional teachers had to wait for students to choose them. The first disciples were probably teenagers still living at home with their parents. Read Matthew 4:18-22; Mark 12:16-20; Luke 5:2-11; and John 1:37-51 for the story of how Jesus attracted his young followers and led them to abandon everything and go with him. Jesus said, "You did not choose me, but I chose you and appointed you that you should go and bear fruit and that your fruit should remain" (John 15:16).

Can aspects of being gay be seen in some of the attitudes and actions of Jesus and the disciples? What was the role of physical affection? What prompted jealousy and personal conflicts among the closest friends of Jesus? Why did the love of Judas for Jesus turn to hate, betrayal, and suicide? Can answers to these and similar questions help lesbian and gay Christians to accept and understand themselves better and know more clearly how to follow Jesus by growing up with love that is healthy and healing?

Jesus Taught Same-Sex Love

The best-known parables of love like the Good Samaritan and the Prodigal Son (Luke 10 and 15) are about love between people of the same sex. The giving and receiving of love that Jesus taught and demonstrated were always in the setting of same-sex relationships. Jesus, however, never mentioned romantic love in any of his teachings. Jesus never mentioned sex or used a word that meant sex.

The Greek word for romantic love is *eros*, and this word is not used even once in the entire New Testament, yet it was the most common word for love in the Greek world. The Greek word that is used for the love of Jesus and the love that Jesus taught is a rare Greek word, *agape*, that is seldom found outside of the New Testament.

The definition of *agape* is the example and teachings of Jesus. *Eros*, the common Greek word for love that is never used in the New Testament, means love that takes and controls. *Agape* is the love that draws you to others because they need you. *Agape* is unselfish and is the word used for God's love. *Agape* is liberating and accepting love that seeks to help the beloved to reach the fullest possible potential for a full and meaningful life. The New Testament sees God as the definition of *agape,* "The one who does not love does not know God, for God is love [*agape*]." The characteristics of *agape* are spelled out in 1 Corinthians 13 and give a description of the love of Jesus as demonstrated in the Gospels.

Competition Among the Disciples

Read Matthew 20:16-28 to see the immature bickering of the disciples over positions and rank with Jesus. In Matthew 12:46-50, the circle of disciples was like a special family with Jesus as the authority figure. Jesus warned in Matthew 23:8-9 against the disciples calling him father, as was the custom of rabbinical disciples.

Touching and physical affection were expressed between Jesus and his disciples. In Matthew 16:21-23, Peter "took hold of" Jesus. That means to take to one's self in a possessive and affectionate way. It was used of Barnabas and Paul (Acts 9:27) and of Jesus rescuing Peter in the storm (Matthew 14:31). Peter was probably used to "taking hold of" Jesus in this way, but this time Jesus pulled back and rebuked Peter for trying to persuade Jesus to go against the will of God.

Read Matthew 26:6-13; Mark 14:3-11; Luke 7:36-39; and John 12:1-8 for the story of Jesus letting a woman touch and kiss his feet. See also John 13:18-30 and 20:20-22 for the story of the beloved disciple leaning on the breast of Jesus at the Last Supper.

The relationship of Judas and Jesus is mysterious and yet revealing as to how Jesus handled extreme pressure from some one he loved and called to follow him as a disciple. Judas and his strange and special relationship with Jesus will be discussed in

Lesson 38, "Love in Action." The emotional and affectionate expressions between Jesus and his disciples are revealed indirectly and directly in many places in the Gospels. Read through the Gospel of Mark again and notice the demonstrations of love by Jesus for the men in his life. There is a moving portrait of the love of Jesus for another man, in John 11.

Hebrews 4:15-16 portrays Jesus as standing where we stand and experiencing the kind of feelings and pressures that we face, "We do not have a high priest who cannot sympathize with our weaknesses but one who was tested in all things as we are tested, yet without sin. Let us therefore draw near with confidence to the throne of grace that we may receive mercy and may find grace to help in time of need." Hebrews 2:17 says, "Jesus had to be made like his brothers and sisters in all things." Jesus really does know what you are going through. He has been through it all himself.

Questions for Study and Discussion

1. Why did Jesus not discuss romantic love? Why do you think that no reference to sexual orientation is found in the life and teachings of Jesus?

2. How do the teachings of Jesus about love apply to gay people?

3. Do the statements in Hebrews 2:17 and 4:15-16 mean that Jesus experienced all sexual orientations and knew what it was like to have homosexual feelings?

Additional Resources

One of the most influential books in my education was Anders Nygren's *Agape and Eros*, which is a careful analysis of the differences between the kind of love that Jesus demonstrated and taught and the kind of emotion that we mean by love today.

Another more recent book by the Rev. Michael S. Piazza, Senior Pastor of the Cathedral of Hope MCC in Dallas, *Holy Homosexuals*, has been helpful to me partly because of Michael sharing his own struggle as a gay Christian so clearly and honestly. Also the book grapples with just what it means to take seriously the humanity of Jesus and yet follow Jesus. (Sources of Hope Publishing, 1997.)

As this lesson is being written, the story and mission of the Cathedral of Hope MCC, "the world's largest gay and lesbian church," is being broadcast in historic television shows on WBN Chicago in April, 1999, after a legal battle that tried to stop the showing of the program. A lot of people are learning for the first time that gay Christians love and serve Jesus also!

Chris Glaser, *Come Home! Reclaiming Spirituality and Community as Gay Men and Lesbians, Second Edition*: Chi Rho Press, 1998.

Henry Drummond, *The Greatest Thing in the World.* The most famous devotional study of 1 Corinthians 13.

Chapter 13

The Eighth Step

Read and Study the Gospels

† **Preparatory Bible Reading:** Read the four Gospels.

Learn the content of the Gospels, especially Luke and John. Saturate your mind with the life of Jesus. Become your own expert on what it means to follow Jesus. Many people have found that they gain a better picture of Jesus by reading through the Gospel of Mark (it is only 16 chapters) in one sitting. Use a good modern language translation for this exercise. You will notice things about Jesus that you did not realize before.

My friend Paul, who was director of an HIV/AIDS support ministry in San Francisco, was going through a lot of stress about his work. He agreed to read through the Gospel of Mark and let me know what he learned. When we met a couple of days later, Paul said he read Mark and did not like what he learned! I asked, "Why?"

Paul answered, "Jesus also had volunteers who did not show up!" The last time I read all the way through Mark, I was struck by the attitude of urgency in the mission of Jesus. It made me aware that I needed to become more urgent about getting this book written so that you might have it today. Please read through Mark and see what you learn about Jesus that speaks directly to you.

> These have been written that you may believe [continuously believe] that Jesus is the Christ, the child of God: and that believing [following] you may have life in Jesus' name. (John 20:30)

Studying and learning the story of Jesus in the Gospels is necessary if you really want to follow Jesus in your spiritual recovery and growth. Learning the content of Luke and John will take time and discipline. Learning these inclusive and Jesus-centered documents can be made easier by sharing your study with at least one other person.

Lesson 29

Jesus Made All Things New

† **Preparatory Bible Reading:** Luke 4:16-30; Matthew 25:31-46; Mark 6:30-44; Romans 15:1-7

There are two chief characteristics of the life and ministry of Jesus in the Gospels. First is the revolutionary and inclusive emphasis that brought new and often unexpected actions and teachings. Second is the equally unexpected compassion and action of including people that had always before been left out.

Jesus defined his ministry in terms of who was included. In his first sermon (Luke 4:16-30), Jesus said that he came to carry out the prophecy in Isaiah 61:1-2. It is impossible to give too much attention to this section of Luke. The careful beginning of the public ministry of Jesus sets the stage for the whole body of Luke's writing in the Gospel and the Book of Acts, which ends with the inclusive "unhindered gospel" being proclaimed freely by Paul in Rome. The prophecy in Isaiah that Jesus quoted was highly suggestive of what every Christian's mission is to be as we follow Jesus,

> The Spirit of God is upon me, because God anointed me to proclaim the gospel [good news] to the poor [outcasts]. God has sent me to announce release to the captives and recovery of sight to those who cannot see, to set free those who are downtrodden [kicked and stepped on], and to proclaim the year [time] of God's acceptance of all people.
>
> Isaiah 61:1-2

[As always, this is the author's translation and is based on the literal meaning of the Greek words and a careful use of them in a way that speaks in our language today.]

After reading this passage, Jesus told how God sent Elijah to a foreign widow to help her and sent Elisha to a foreign leper to help him. The reaction of Jesus' hometown neighbors was to rise up in anger to try to kill Jesus because he included people that they considered to be unclean and outcast from God in much the same way that many people today feel about gay and lesbian people. "But passing through their midst, Jesus went his way" and returned to his home in Capernaum. Whenever Church is defined on the basis of who is left out, Jesus walks out.

Jesus defined the people of God as those who helped Jesus by accepting and helping rejected, "unclean," and outcast people, saying,

> I was hungry, and you gave me food. I was thirsty, and you gave me drink. I was a stranger, and you invited me in, was naked, and you clothed me. I was sick, and you visited me. I was in prison, and you came to me. . . . Inasmuch as you did it to one of the least of these, my brothers and sisters, you did it to me. (Matthew 25:35-36, 40)

The strict legalistic religious leaders carefully rejected each of the six categories of people that Jesus identified with himself as unclean and outcast from God. Poor, needy, naked, alien, sick, and imprisoned people were called sinners, being punished for their sins by an angry and stern God. Jesus completely rejected this view of God. Instead, Jesus lived and died to include the very people that the prevailing religion rejected. What does this say to you about the relationship of Jesus to transgendered, bisexual, lesbian, and gay people today?

Look for New and Inclusive Actions by Jesus

Everything that Jesus did was new simply because of who he was. Never before had God become human and lived as a fellow human among us. No teacher had called students to follow him. No leader had included women as disciples. No teacher had taught on the basis of his own authority. Jesus touched the untouchable lepers and healed them, gave sight to people who were born blind, raised the dead, and most startling of all (at that time) ate with sinners. Jesus was so busy loving and accepting unclean, outcast, oppressed people that he became tired and occasionally had to get away from the crowd to rest and pray.

From beginning to end, the Gospel of Luke emphasizes the new, inclusive approach of Jesus. Luke begins by telling the story of the birth of the Messiah, which was announced by angels and the entire heavenly host not to kings, priests, or religious leaders but to unclean shepherds keeping watch over their flock by night. Shepherds were one of the many classes of people that the religious teachers called sinners because their work kept them from keeping the Sabbath laws. Never mind that David was the shepherd king and that God is called our Shepherd in Psalm 23 and elsewhere. Luke ends his Gospel with a convicted murderer on the cross, who turned to Jesus to ask him to "remember me" [accept me]. Without hesitation, Jesus said, "Today you will be with me" [I accept you].

Feeding the Five Thousand

Probably the most significant new and inclusive event in the daily ministry of Jesus was the feeding of the 5,000. This is the only mighty work ("miracle") of Jesus that is recorded in all four Gospels. Read the story in Matthew 14:13-21 (repeated in Matthew 15:32-38); Mark 6:32-44; Luke 9:10-17; and John 6:1-13. The emphasis given to this event is unusual and intentional. In being so distracted with trying to explain how the food was multiplied, most people have overlooked the real meaning of this story. When you begin to look for the new and inclusive themes in the work of Jesus, the meaning of stories like this one will jump out at you and you will wonder why you never noticed it before.

The clue that led me to take a fresh look was the comment in John 6:23 that the feeding of the multitude took place near Tiberias, which is on the southwestern shore of the Sea of Galilee and was the Roman capitol of the province. Jews would not live in Tiberias, for the city had been built on a site where ancient tombs were built. Jews still would not live there when I visited Tiberias in 1958. The location of the feeding of the people near Tiberias meant that the multitude would have included Jews, Samaritans, Gentiles, Romans, soldiers, slaves, slave owners, women, children, lepers, the sick, Pharisees, priests, and a great variety of the people called unclean and sinners. The crowd was a cross section of people from all walks of life.

Jesus told the people to sit down to eat together. The word "sit" is the word "recline" (Mark 6:39), which was used to describe the posture of the disciples at the Last Supper. People would not eat with those who were not of their same social rank, race, politics, religion, class, race, or gender. To recline to eat made a person vulnerable to others. One of the most persistent customs of the Arabs in Palestine today is the practice of not eating with anyone who is a stranger or who might not be trustworthy.

The new thing that Jesus did was not the multiplying of food. Moses had given manna in the wilderness, and Elijah had multiplied food for the widow. The new thing was that all of the people from widely diverse lives and lifestyles for the first time sat down together to eat. This had never before happened in the history of Israel. It was the truly remarkable new beginning of including everybody in Christ.

The disciples gathered twelve baskets full of fragments, a reminder of the twelve tribes of Israel, which indicated that the crowd was the "New People of God," brought together in unity because of Jesus. The fragments were gathered in order that nothing should be lost. Nobody was left out of this magnificent feast with Jesus. To become distracted by trying to figure out how five loaves and two fishes fed so many people is to miss the real meaning of the story as a clear demonstration and proclamation of the inclusive gospel of Jesus for all people.

Jesus Accepted the Unacceptable

Lepers had to wear a sign that said "Unclean!" and when they came within 50 feet of people, they had to cry out "Unclean! Unclean!" They could not go into the Temple or synagogue.

They were thought to have leprosy as punishment for their sins. (Leprosy was the name given to any illness that caused skin sores, blemishes, etc., and it was not necessarily what is known as leprosy today.) Jesus had compassion for lepers, touched them, healed them, and especially commended a Samaritan leper who showed gratitude for Jesus' ministry to him (Luke 17:11-19). Imagine being a leper and a Samaritan in Israel during the time of Jesus!

Jesus accepted and taught women as disciples and he called outcasts and hated misfits to be his disciples. Jesus even prayed that all of this mixed crowd of followers would become united just as Jesus and God are one "so that the world will believe in God's love" (John 17:20-23).

Perhaps the greatest challenge to the inclusive gospel of Jesus is the gay, lesbian, bisexual, and transgendered community. I remember well the first time I ever went to a gay bar by myself in Atlanta in 1981. I felt like wallpaper. I did not talk to anybody and nobody talked to me. I felt lonely, rejected, depressed, and completely left out. I had to wonder, "What's so gay about being gay?" Later, I learned to handle the gay scene a little better, but some sense of alienation from my own people persists. We know well how to read people and make jokes about everything that others say, but sometimes we have a hard time accepting ourselves and others as acceptable people.

Building Community

The presence of Jesus in our gay gatherings can make a positive difference. One of the great features of our Wednesday night spiritual recovery and study group was how people in the group accepted, loved, and tried to be helpful to each other. A number of people came to the group directly from their regular Alcoholics Anonymous (AA) meetings and usually brought new people with them. A profound sense of acceptance developed in the group.

One member of the group, Bill, had been sober for over a year. He went through a very severe personal crisis and got drunk. Instead of going home, Bill came to the group. He showed up almost an hour late. We were wondering where he was, because he never missed the group and was never late. All of the approximately 28 people in the group that night rallied around Bill to show their love and acceptance of him and to welcome him. When he got to the group, he apologized for coming in drunk, but he said that he did not know anywhere else he could go and be loved and welcomed except here. No hint of judgment or condemnation was ever expressed to Bill. We felt honored and affirmed that he came "home" to us. We made him stay until he had sobered up with lots of coffee, and we made sure that he got home safely.

To me, this kind of acceptance and encouragement is what following Jesus is all about. How has it been possible for traditional churches to abandon the inclusive and accepting ministry or Jesus and replace it with legalistic, judgmental abuse and oppression? What kind of perverted view of the gospel makes people reject and hurt the people who most need love and acceptance?

Encouragement, Perseverance and Acceptance

Paul's Letter to the Romans sums up how Jesus' followers relate to other people in new and liberating ways. Encouragement and perseverance come from God and through the Bible. "We who are strong ought to bear the weaknesses of those without strength and not just please ourselves. . . . Wherefore accept one another, just as Christ also accepted you to the glory of God" (Romans 15:1 and 7).

Questions for Study and Discussion

1. Why do you think that some lesbians and gay men have so much prejudice against other gay people who are different from themselves?

2. What do you think is the reason why some gay and lesbian people criticize and put down others as a habit?

3. What liberated you from acting like a vicious queen? Maybe you still do! How can you love your enemies if you do not like yourself?

4. Explore the four Gospels, try to find as many places as you can where Jesus was new and inclusive.

Additional Resources

R. Adam DeBaugh, *The Least of These: A Christian Social Action Bible Study*: Chi Rho Press, 1994, is a seven-part Bible study on Matthew 25:31-46.

Lesson 30

How Women Disciples Changed the World

† Preparatory Bible Reading: Luke 8:1-3; 10:38-42; 23:49 through 24:12; John 20:1-18; Romans 16:1-6

No message in the four Gospels is more revolutionary than the attitude of Jesus regarding the role of women as disciples and ministers. The Bible has been used for years to oppress and limit women. Jesus, however, clearly elevated women from property to partners in ministry. No basis exists in the Gospels for denying leadership to women in ministries of evangelism, preaching, teaching, and pastoral care. Some of Paul's opinions have been taken out of context and distorted to oppress and alienate women. Jesus and Paul both were revolutionary in their acceptance and respect for women. Jesus included women as disciples and in everything that the male disciples did. There is no evidence to the contrary in the Gospels and much evidence to show how thoroughly Jesus included women in all aspects of the invitation, "Follow me."

Women in Bible Times

Women in the synagogues were neither seen nor heard. They were required to sit behind a screen when the law was read for fear that angels, thought to be present at any reading of the law, might be seduced. Rabbinical traditions about Genesis 6:1-8 blamed the union between "the daughters of men" and "the sons of God" (angels) and the Great Flood on the seductive powers of women, which is a constant theme in the Old Testament. See Proverbs 7:1-27; 9:13-18. This is why Paul said in 1 Corinthians 11:10 that women should cover their heads "because of the angels."

Religious laws in the time of Jesus forbad women to read the law or speak in the synagogues. No woman could be a rabbi or the student of a rabbi. Women could not be Priests, Pharisees, Scribes, Sadducees or Levites. Women could not go to the synagogue during their menstrual flow. When a woman had a baby, she was "unclean" and could not go to the synagogue for a month. If the baby was a girl, the woman was unclean for two months!

A rabbi would not speak to any woman in public, not even to his own mother. Some Pharisees would not even look at a woman in public; so they shut their eyes whenever a woman came into view! A woman was the property of her husband. Adultery was against her husband or father, not against the woman. But Jesus said, "Whoever divorces his wife and marries another woman commits adultery against her" (Mark 10:11).

Devout men prayed three times a day to thank God that they had not been born slaves, Gentiles, or women! Because a woman could not be circumcised with "the sign of the covenant," she was included in the community of faith only by her relationship to her husband, father, or brother. Paul clearly challenged this, "There is neither Jew nor Greek, slave nor free, male nor female, for you are all one in Christ Jesus" (Galatians 3:28). Many other rules and traditions made religion totally "a man's world" in the time of Jesus, and Jesus turned that tradition on its head.

Jesus Shattered Tradition

Jesus talked to women in public, such as the woman at the well in John 4 and the woman accused of adultery in John 8:1-11. Jesus touched and healed the "unclean" woman with a flow of blood in Luke 8:43-48. In Luke 21:1-6, Jesus said that a poor woman gave more than rich men gave, because she gave all that she had. Then he went on to predict the destruction of the whole Temple system that wounded and oppressed weak and vulnerable people like the poor widow.

Read through the Gospel of Luke and notice the role of women. Luke 1 and 2 tell of Mary, the mother of Jesus, as well as Elizabeth and Anna, who emerge as more open than the men to knowing and doing the will of God. Women disciples of Jesus are listed in Luke 8:1-3 and mentioned in 23:49, 55-56; 24:10-11, 22-24 and in Acts 1:14.

Mary the Disciple

Jesus' visit to the home of Mary and Martha, as told in Luke 10:38-42, reveals the most about Jesus' revolutionary treatment of women. "Mary was listening to the word of Jesus, seated at Jesus' feet." These few words announced the dramatic revolution of the role of women in the life and ministry of Jesus. Each word is powerful. "Listen" is the first word in the Hebrew *Shema* (which is Hebrew for "hear") in Deuteronomy 6:4, "Hear O Israel, your God is One." This verse was included in phylacteries that were worn by devout men. "Listen to Jesus" is the instruction of the voice at the Transfiguration in Luke 9:35, which recalled Deuteronomy 18:15 and 18, where a prophet like Moses will come and the people will "listen to him."

When someone sits at the feat of another it signifies their being a disciple of that person. Thus Luke is saying here that Mary was a disciple of Jesus. Paul uses "sit at the feet" to tell of his being a disciple of Gamaliel (Acts 22:3). The sight of Mary in the posture of a disciple was very threatening to her sister Martha. Jesus' words to Martha were intense, "Martha! Martha! You are anxious and bothered about so many things! Mary has chosen the good thing, which will not be taken away from her." The church, including many sisters like Martha, has been trying ever since to deny Mary and all women the freedom to be disciples of Jesus!

Challenging and correcting the misuse of the Bible against women helps all minorities to overcome Bible abuse. A fresh look at the role of women in the life of Jesus and in the mission of the church speaks directly to acceptance and freedom for gays, lesbians, and all people alienated and oppressed by religion.

The First Apostle Was a Woman

Jesus appeared first to a woman, Mary, after the resurrection, and she was the first preacher of the good news of the victory of Jesus over sin and death for all people (John 20:11-18). According to Paul in 1 Corinthians 15, seeing the risen Christ was what made a person an "apostle," from the Greek *apostello*, meaning to send on a mission representing the sender. So the first apostle and preacher of the resurrection was a woman.

The appearance of Jesus to Mary was no accident. Peter said to Cornelius in the first preaching of the gospel to Gentiles (in Acts 10:34-43) that God does not show partiality. Everyone is welcome. "God raised Christ up on the third day, and granted that he should become visible, not to all the people, but to witnesses who were chosen beforehand by God" (Acts 10:40-41). God selected a woman to be the first witness to the resurrection, the first preacher, and the first "living stone" in the Church (1 Peter 2:1-10).

Widows As Leaders

The word "widow" in Hebrew means "mute, silent." It was a term that focused on the weakness and helplessness of a woman that resulted from not having a man to protect and support her. A great deal of the ministry of Jesus in the gospels, especially Luke, addressed the special needs of widows. Later, the first serious problem in the church was the equal distribution of food to needy widows in Acts 6.

In the Pastoral Letters, a great shift took place. Widows changed from being weak and needy into strong ministers of Christ. They carried out arduous tasks of pastoral and practical care to people in need. They were described as "washing the feet of the disciples" and "praying all night" just as Jesus was described in the gospels. Widows were expected to meet the same requirements as other ministers in the emerging church. See 1 and 2 Timothy and Titus. Jesus and the early church recognized that women had undeniable gifts of ministry, just as men did.

Women Leaders in the Early Church

Women were prominent in the early churches as leaders and ministers. They were part of the praying group on which the Holy Spirit came at Pentecost in Acts 1:14; 2:1-6; 4:31-33 and were included among the first preachers who gave witness to Jesus. Paul called a woman, Phoebe, "the minister of the church at Cenchrea" (Romans 16:1). The word translated as "minister" is the Greek word *diakonos* (deacon) and was used to describe Paul and Christ in Romans 15:8, 25, 27, 31 as "ministers" to the Gentiles. Paul called Phoebe "my sister." The word "sister" and "brother" are the same in Greek, like our word "sibling." "Brothers," as a reference to believers, should always be translated "sisters and brothers" to be accurate. If a male pastor had led the church at Cenchrea, Paul surely would have greeted him.

Four of the first seven leaders of the church in Rome whom Paul greeted (Romans 16) were women. Paul said "Greet Mary, who has worked hard for you" (Romans 16:6). I imagined Mary working hard doing domestic chores, but that was before I looked up "work hard" in Greek. The word is used in Romans 16:12 for another woman, Persis, and in 1 Corinthians 15:10 and 16:16, Galatians 4:11, Philippians 2:16 and Colossians 1:29 for "hard work" in preaching and teaching by Paul and others. 1 Thessalonians 5:12 uses the same Greek word for those who "give you instruction." 1 Timothy 5:17 uses it for elders "who rule well who work hard preaching and teaching." So Mary was no domestic servant, but a teacher and preacher! Careful examination of the Bible text shows that women were indeed Christian disciples and leaders who changed the world.

To obscure the role of leadership by women in the New Testament is to perpetuate a lie that distorts the Bible and denies the fullness of salvation and service given to all believers through Jesus Christ. Women's issues, like lesbian, gay, bisexual, and transgendered issues, should be everybody's issues. As long as the abuse of the Bible is allowed to oppress and to deny full discipleship to lesbians, gays, bisexuals, women, or any other group, the good news of the gospel of Jesus Christ is distorted and diminished.

Slow Progress for Women in Ministry

Many religious denominations still do not allow women to be pastors or priests. Two traditions as opposite as Southern Baptists and Roman Catholics agree on rejecting women leaders. Southern Baptists have traditionally refused to allow women to be pastors. Recent actions by the President and trustees of the Southern Baptist Theological Seminary in Louisville, Kentucky, (my seminary) got rid of all of the women on the seminary faculty and removed professors if they believed that God called women to be pastors! The argument against women priests in the Roman Catholic Church is based on "the fact that God is a man, and Jesus is a man, and they can be represented adequately only by a man!"

Church leaders who are trying to get fair treatment for women also are often in the fight for acceptance and affirmation of gay people at every level of church life. 2000 years after Jesus opened the doors to acceptance and ministry for all who follow him, churches continue to struggle and strangle on their legalistic, judgmental, biblical literalism that keeps them from reflecting the life and mission of Jesus in their institutions and in their church polity. These churches also resist becoming part of the modern world and they drive their people backwards in retreat into a paralyzing irrelevant "past shock" that leads nowhere but further away from the realities of Jesus for the twenty-first century.

Questions for Study and Discussion

1. Have your own ideas about the role of women in Christian ministry changed in recent years? How have your views changed? What brought about the changes?

2. What connection do you see between feminist issues and gay/lesbian issues? How does religious oppression of one person hurt everybody?

3. Why do you think that Luke emphasized the role of women in the life and ministry of Jesus?

Additional Resources

Nancy Hardesty, *Inclusive Language in the Church*: John Knox Press, 1987.

Virginia Ramey Mollenkott, *Sensuous Spirituality: Out From Fundamentalism*: Crossroad, 1993

Elizabeth Stuart, *Religion is A Queer Thing*: The Pilgrim Press, 1997.

Lesson 31

Jesus Was Misunderstood

† **Preparatory Bible Reading:** Matthew 27:39-50; Mark 4:1-20; and Mark 7:7 through 9:13

Jesus was constantly being misunderstood. His mother and family, his disciples, the crowds, and especially his enemies frequently misunderstood Jesus. This lesson is about how Jesus handled being misunderstood and what that says to us.

Sometimes after I explain how Bible translations have distorted the original Hebrew and Greek to create oppression and rejection of gay people, people react as if I was speaking in a foreign language. Some close their minds to any new evidence that might challenge their fears and prejudices. They maintain their former opinions and attitudes unhindered by the facts. They reply to what I have said about the Bible as though they had not heard it. Some, who do not understand, simply do not want to understand.

Since September 14, 1997, when my Web site on "Steps to Recovery from Bible Abuse" was published on the Internet, I have received thousands of e-mail responses. I have been grateful for the many positive and encouraging letters. The hate mail and letters that misunderstand and reject my material, however, also have come frequently. People glance at the Web site and do not really read any of it and get angry and throw an e-mail letter at me; or some read it and just do not comprehend it. This misunderstanding of the truth that is in the Web site are frustrating, because I seldom have an opportunity for any dialogue in response. Many of the most severe critics leave a message with a false return address. Many also "shout" (in all capital letters) and rave emotionally at me with more anger than common sense. Being misunderstood is always a frustrating experience!

Stress and Misunderstanding

People under great emotional stress often are irritated and angered by being misunderstood. This is why depressed people frequently become angry when their anger is misunderstood as sadness or guilt, as discussed in Lesson 16. As gay people, we are under various degrees of stress from just being on the earth in an alien and oppressive environment. When we are misunderstood in some significant matter, we can easily overreact and cause ourselves even more stress.

This lesson deals with only one of the aspects of the life of Jesus that speaks directly to us on our road to recovery from Bible abuse and religious oppression. There are many other examples of Jesus that speak to us. We are better equipped to face life if we learn how Jesus handled helpers that let him down, friends who ran away, and partners who denied and betrayed him. Jesus shows us how to handle fatigue, hunger, temptations to distort his own mission or just let go and quit, and the charges from religious authorities that he was evil, demonic, crazy, and unfit to live! Many of these themes will be considered later.

The Ultimate Misunderstanding

One can hardly imagine a greater stress for Jesus than the crucifixion. Read carefully Matthew 27:39-50 and notice how Jesus was misunderstood as to who he was, what he had taught, what was happening in his death, what his death meant, and even what he said as he died. Not surprising, the final word about Jesus on the cross is, "Jesus cried out again with a loud voice and gave up the spirit."

What else could he do? He had everybody's undivided attention. He was fulfilling a thousand years of prophecy. His hour had come. He was doing the ultimate will of God on behalf of all humanity. And they all misunderstood everything. No wonder darkness descended upon the scene at midday.

Getting Used To Being Misunderstood

Does anyone really get used to being misunderstood? I have not. I wonder if Jesus ever did. Most gay people I know never do. Jesus was misunderstood from the beginning. When Jesus was taken to the temple for the first time at the age of twelve, his parents "did not understand" him (Luke 2:50). Jesus' mother, his friends and neighbors, his disciples, religious leaders, legal experts, political authorities, and the crowds all misunderstood Jesus.

Jesus constantly confronted misunderstanding. Soon after beginning a ministry of teaching and healing, Jesus told the parable of the different types of soil (Mark 4:1-20) to deal with the problem of people not listening and comprehending what he said. Read all of Mark 4 to see how this theme is spelled out. A constant emphasis in Mark is the failure of the disciples to understand Jesus. Read Mark 7:7 through 9:13 to see how those who were closest to him misunderstood Jesus. Jesus had to face and deal with many kinds of misunderstandings.

Mark 8:14-21 gives a summary of the mood of the whole section. Jesus said to his disciples, "Do you not yet see or understand? Do you have a hardened heart? Having eyes, do you not see? And having ears, do you not hear? And do you not remember?" (Mark 8:17-18); and "Do you not yet understand?" (Mark 8:25). The intensity and repetitions of these quotes seem to indicate a lot of frustration felt by Jesus in coping with misunderstanding by his own disciples. I doubt that Jesus ever really got used to this kind of misunderstanding by his disciples, especially when Peter misunderstood what Jesus said about having to be crucified and tried to talk him out of it (Mark 8:31-33).

The Destructive Power of Misunderstanding

Misunderstandings are part of life. Communication breaks down. We hear what we want to hear or expect to hear. Uncertain messages are given. Words are taken out of context. We jump to conclusions. Everybody talks, nobody listens. Jesus lived in the same kind of world that we do. Part of being human is dealing with being misunderstood.

Wars, divorces, murders, riots, religious persecutions, and a lot of other forms of human misery have been caused by misunderstandings. The entire "ex-gay" industry is based on misunderstanding the Bible and psychology. The Bible has been misunderstood and distorted to feed the fires of homophobia. How have misunderstandings affected your life? Gay men and women suffer a lot of misunderstanding simply because so many of us are at least partly still in the closet. When people do not know the truth about you, they fill in the blanks with their own feelings and prejudices. It is easy to get discouraged when your love is misread as lust, your kindness is seen as gullibility, your explanations are dismissed as selfish, and your honesty is interpreted as anger.

Misunderstandings are usually due to our telling or being told half-truths, but a half-truth is also a half lie. Jesus promised that you will know the truth, and the truth will set you free. Growing in self-understanding and in the ability and desire to understand and be understood by others can carry us a long way toward the freedom that truth gives. Jesus was like a small island of self-understanding and self-acceptance in a sea of self-deception and hypocrisy.

Causes of Misunderstanding

Others can fail to understand us when we ourselves are unclear about how we feel or think. Our vagueness can allow others to read their own ideas into our actions and words, especially if they are already suspicious and hostile toward us. Another cause of misunderstanding is our inconsistency in what we say and what we do. Mixed messages are confusing to others and create misunderstanding. Transference of previous experiences and feelings into new relationships is a major cause of misunderstandings. "You sound just like my mother!" "You are acting just like my ex-lover!" Most of the time we just act out such feelings without saying them. I have not yet figured out how to avoid this kind of thinking myself. If you discover the secret formula for conquering destructive transference, please let me know!

As gay and lesbian Christians, we have to deal with a lot of misunderstanding from other gay, lesbian, bisexual, and transgendered people, who transfer bad church experiences and painful religious abuse to any form of Bible study or spiritual encouragement that we might offer. Misunderstandings are not always out in the open. Sometimes they go on for a long time before we realize what is happening. Like resentment, misunderstanding can be hidden and build up pressure until violent actions finally explode with sudden and unexpected destructive force.

Reactions to Misunderstanding

The three least productive reactions to being misunderstood are getting angry, arguing, and giving up.

- The frustration that comes from being misunderstood can easily make us angry, which usually works to increase the misunderstanding.

- To argue in a verbal battle of more heat than light can wear us down without producing much understanding. We present our views and rather than listening to the other side, we use our time trying to figure out what to say next when we get our turn. Learning to listen would be a great help in building better understanding in tense relationships.

- Giving up is the third reaction to being misunderstood. If efforts to clear up misunderstandings do not succeed, we are tempted to give up and break off contact. Sometimes this can mean destroying a valuable relationship or can lead to an uneasy and tense relationship that is not fun anymore.

How Jesus Handled Misunderstandings

1. **Jesus did not ignore misunderstandings.** He acted quickly to clarify his teachings and actions.

2. **Jesus remained calm and in control.** He resisted the temptation to become angry or give up.

3. **Jesus explained things.** He was a teacher and took the time necessary to help people learn and grow.

4. **Jesus was consistent with his words and loving actions.** This gave greater understanding to those who wanted to know and be clear about what Jesus meant.

5. **Jesus continued on his mission.** He did not let misunderstandings or rejection stop him.

6. **Jesus was willing to wait.** He knew that his death and resurrection would explain many things that were misunderstood during his ministry. He had faith that God would vindicate and validate his life and work.

7. **Jesus promised to send the Holy Spirit to give understanding to his followers** (John 14:26). After the resurrection, Luke's Gospel tells us Jesus "opened their minds to understand" (Luke 24:45).

Love and Understanding

Only God has perfect understanding. We never fully understand ourselves or anybody else. Yet we learn to accept and care for each other and ourselves because of the love that God has placed in our hearts. We are all different from each other. The differences make us special and give us value to ourselves and to each other. The differences also, however, create misunderstandings. Love gets us through this jungle. "Love never gives up" (1 Corinthians 13:4-8). When you love someone, you give her or him the benefit of the doubt. You can trust the people who love you, even though you do not always understand them. Love covers a multitude of sins. "Love casts out fear."

Questions for Study and Discussion

1. What is the worst misunderstanding you ever had? How did you handle it? How would you handle it differently now?

2. How has understanding and accepting your sexuality helped you to deal with misunderstandings by other people? What do you still have difficulty understanding and accepting about yourself?

Lesson 32

Jesus and HIV/AIDS

† **Preparatory Bible Reading:** John 9:1-38

No issue has challenged the gay community, the churches, and the whole world like the HIV/AIDS epidemic. Jesus said and did many things that have a bearing on how we see HIV/AIDS. The example and teachings of Jesus can help us to become more effective in our understanding and practical help to people with HIV/AIDS and their friends and families.

Roy was a 30-year-old gay man who lived in a small town near my home in South Carolina. When Roy discovered that he had HIV/AIDS, he reached out for help to a county nurse, who put him in touch with the minister of education of a local church. The minister had no experience with gay people or with HIV/AIDS and asked me to go with him to visit Roy. I gave Roy my brochure on "The Bible as Your Friend," which was the only material he had seen on how the Bible does not condemn gay men and lesbians and how God's love includes him also. Roy had many questions about the Bible and homosexuality and was searching for support in dealing with his illness.

Roy did not know anyone else with HIV/AIDS and had no support group. He had never heard of Metropolitan Community Church (MCC). Roy began a search for spiritual encouragement and hope and found some practical support from a newly organized Laurens County AIDS Task Force. He became weaker and had to deal with a lot of frustration and anger. As I was writing the first draft of this lesson, I learned that Roy had died. This experience forced me to realize that many of the victims of HIV/AIDS live in small towns and rural areas where they feel alone and isolated. The highly developed HIV/AIDS services in cities like San Francisco and Atlanta do not exist for thousands of people with HIV/AIDS, who suffer alone and in secret.

Jim was 21 years old when he learned that he was HIV positive. Fear, self-hate, and confusion overwhelmed him. He abandoned the church that he had been attending and left school. He began to sink rapidly into drugs, heavy drinking, and self-destructive and irresponsible behavior. He refused to tell his family about his illness or accept any offer of help from people who cared about him. Jim lives in San Francisco, where the best medical and supportive services anywhere in the world are available for people with HIV/AIDS. Jim gave up. Nothing seemed to slow his headlong plunge into the abyss of self-destruction. Jim is not an isolated case. Thousands of gay men like Jim sink into lives of quiet desperation. How can Christian lesbians and gays reach out effectively to the great multitude of people like Roy and Jim? What kind of help does Jesus offer? Does the Bible have any real answers?

Jesus the Healing Teacher

Read through John 9:1-38 and notice the striking parallels between the treatment of HIV/AIDS patients today and the treatment of the one born blind 2000 years ago.

Jesus and his disciples saw a blind person on the street. The disciples asked Jesus, "Who committed the sin that this one should be born blind?" They assumed that all suffering and sickness were the result of sin. They were wrong. Jesus replied, "Neither this one nor his parents sinned." Nobody was to blame. Jesus had no interest in trying to decide whose fault it was. Jesus was saying, "This gives us an opportunity to demonstrate God's love and power." Then Jesus gave sight to the blind person. Read carefully through John chapter 9 and notice the many parallels to HIV/AIDS issues in the story.

Jesus was surrounded by sickness, suffering, pain, and death. The average life expectancy was 25. No effective medical treatment existed for most illnesses. Most diseases were fatal. Treatments often were worse than the sickness. The woman in

Luke 8:43-48 who touched Jesus for help had "suffered at the hands of many physicians."

Jesus Had Compassion

Jesus was motivated by compassion. The Greek word for compassion is built on the word for the viscera and was used to express feeling the pain and suffering of someone else "in the pit of your stomach." It was the strongest word in Greek for human feeling. It expressed Jesus' real identification with the wounded and suffering people around him. Jesus had compassion for lepers, whose painful and disfiguring disease kept them away from all other people. It was commonly thought that leprosy was punishment for sin. Lepers were called "unclean" and were not allowed in the synagogue or Temple. HIV/AIDS is much like leprosy in the way people have reacted to it. Jesus loved, touched, identified with, and healed lepers then, and he does the same for people with HIV/AIDS today.

Spiritual help can be elusive for those who already feel alienated and isolated from the church. Religious bigots and ignorant Bible abusers frequently distort the "good news" of the gospel of Jesus Christ. They make it an insensitive and destructive tirade of condemnation, rejection, and guilt aimed at the very people who most need love, tenderness, acceptance, and understanding.

HIV/AIDS is a medical, political, legal, economic, social, spiritual, and religious issue. Most of all, HIV/AIDS is a human issue. Mental, emotional, and physical pain engulfs victims of HIV/AIDS. Desperation and fatalism often blur the vision and dull the senses of people with HIV/AIDS and those who are close to them. The compassion of Jesus, who identified with and felt the pain of others, is perhaps the most needed spiritual ingredient in our war against HIV/AIDS.

Jesus Healed the Whole Person

Jesus' holistic ministry of healing is described in this way, "Jesus was going about all the cities and villages teaching in their synagogues and proclaiming the reign of God and healing every kind of disease and every kind of sickness. Seeing the crowds, Jesus felt compassion for them, because they were distressed and downcast like sheep without a shepherd" (Matthew 9:35).

Jesus healed the whole person. Holistic medicine began with Jesus, who combined compassion with teaching, healing, and helping people to live at peace with God, others, and themselves. Jesus gave wholeness and health to all in body, spirit, mind, and relationships with others. Jesus never condemned or blamed people for their pain or sickness. Jesus' angry judgment was aimed only at those who were insensitive to human suffering and who condemned the people who most needed love and encouragement. To Jesus, human pain and suffering were always seen as opportunities to do the work of God and to demonstrate the love and power of God.

Jesus Broke Religious Laws to Help Outcasts

Healing was so important to Jesus that he did it on the Sabbath, breaking the law by making clay and by healing the blind. The rest of John 9 after the first five verses is the story of stormy conflict over legalistic religion. The issues in this story are amazingly contemporary. The story deals with incurable illness, family rejection, conflicts over religion, fear of authority, ignorant and heartless religious leaders, misplaced judgment, and the determination of Jesus to cut through all of the confusion to accept and encourage the sinner. Jesus accepts us when religion does not.

The parents of the one born blind avoided defending their own child for fear of offending judgmental religious leaders. Sometimes the greatest pain of HIV/AIDS is being rejected and abandoned by family and friends. Religious leaders rebuked the rebels and threw them out. Jesus searched for the religious rejects, found and encouraged them. Rejected people need someone to care for them. All of us need encouragement.

Jesus did not waste time trying to decide who is to blame for sickness and pain. Jesus was motivated by compassion and love. He calls us to follow him and do the same. When we help people with HIV/AIDS by giving our time, practical care, food, financial help, clothing, shelter, transportation, friendship, love, encouragement, and the simple gift of being there, we truly are following Jesus.

Jesus cleansed the Temple as a dramatic act of defiance against the abusive and oppressive legalistic religion that left out marginal and undesirable people. "Jesus began to teach and say to them, 'Is it not written [Isaiah 56:7], "My house shall be called a house of prayer for all the nations [the Greek word *ethnos*],"' But you have made it a robbers' den" (Mark 11:17). The word *ethnos* is the New Testament word used for Gentiles.

The part of the Temple that Jesus cleansed was the part that was set aside for the use of foreigners and non-Jews. It had become a place of commerce and greed. Jesus attacked the abusive use of religion in the special place that was intended to make faith in God inclusive of all people. This turned the politically powerful priests against Jesus and led directly to his death.

Throughout the ministry of Jesus, his actions were consistently aimed at including the people that religion had left out. Jesus included women, children, foreigners, sinners, the "unclean," outcasts, the sick, and even outlaws and murderers (the thief on the cross) at a time when the basic thrust of religion was to divide people into insiders and outsiders, the clean and the unclean. Not much has changed.

Help Yourself As Much As You Can

Jesus never encouraged people to sink into self-pity and give up. Jesus expected sick people to do something. Jesus told the blind man to "go wash in the Pool of Siloam." He ordered them to "Stretch forth your withered hand;" "Go and show yourself to the priest;" and "Take up your bed and walk!" Applying for assistance, taking necessary medication, and allowing others to help can be difficult for those who are ill.

Feeling good about yourself is a great step toward healing and hope.

As I write this in the spring of 1999, great progress is being made in funding and research for treatment of HIV/AIDS. New, powerful, and effective drugs are being developed, and hope for prevention and cure continues in the field of medicine. But the need for spiritual truth and compassionate support for people with HIV/AIDS never lets up. Do what you can. Become informed about HIV/AIDS. Join with others who give special care to people with HIV/AIDS. Be part of the solution and take care of yourself. Be here for the cure!

Questions for Study and Discussion

1. Why do you think that some religious leaders ignore Jesus' refusal to blame sick people for their illness? How have you answered the claim of some preachers that HIV/AIDS is God's punishment on gay people?

2. What teachings of Jesus have been most helpful to you in times of great stress?

3. Do you know people with HIV/AIDS or other life threatening illnesses or serious physical difficulties? What can you do to give them your encouragement and support?

4. What has been the source of greatest strength to you when you have been sick? How has your own sickness and stress prepared you to help others who go through the same things?

Additional Resources

Many books have helped us to understand and give practical help and encouragement to people with HIV/AIDS. Some that have helped me include, Stephen Pieters, *I'm Still Dancing! A Gay Man's Health Experience*: Chi Rho Press, 1991.

John E. Fortunato, *AIDS: the Spiritual Dilemma*: Harper, 1987.

Perry Tilleraas, *The Color of Light*: Harper, 1988, and *Circle of Hope*: Harper, 1990

Letty M. Russell, editor, *The Church With Aids: Renewal in the Midst of Crisis*: Westminster/John Knox Press, 1990.

Randy Shilts, *And the Band Played On*: St. Martin's Press, 1987. This book was made into an HBO movie about the beginnings of the HIV/AIDS epidemic in San Francisco. It is available on video.

Chapter 14

The Ninth Step

Come Out and Accept Yourself

You cannot change your world from a closet! Accept yourself and connect with others like yourself. Coming out is facing and accepting the truth about your sexual orientation and telling at least one other person. The most difficult person to come out to is yourself. The life and ministry of Jesus gives a great deal of emphasis to telling and living the truth. Each gay and lesbian person, however, deals with coming out in his or her own personal way. No two people have exactly the same experience of coming out.

Jesus dealt with every human problem that we face today. One of the most significant features of the way that Jesus handled stress was how Jesus came out. We have no evidence that Jesus was gay, of course, (any more than there is direct evidence of Jesus being heterosexual – the Gospels simply do not address Jesus' sexuality) but we can see how he struggled and handled coming out and letting people know the truth about himself and how different he was from everybody else. Jesus came out to his parents in the visit to the Temple in Luke 2:39-52 and said that he must be doing God's business and acting on who he really was and not what his parents might expect of him.

Jesus later came out again to the people at his baptism in Matthew 3:1-17; to his closest friends in Mark 8:31-38; and to the world in his triumphant entry into Jerusalem in Matthew 21:1-17. Then Jesus came out in a new way to his followers in his resurrection in John 20:1 through 21:25. Read Luke 2:39-52, Matthew 3:1-17, Mark 8:38, and Matthew 21:1-17 to prepare for the next four lessons.

Two strong Bible texts that relate to coming out are, "Let your light shine before the people in such a way that they may see your good works and glorify your God in heaven" (Matthew 5:16) and "Speak the truth in love. . . . Laying aside lies, speak truth each one of you with your neighbor, for we are members of one another" (Ephesians 4:15, 25).

No problem so tests and challenges gay people as the decision to come out. The following four lessons deal with various dimensions of the coming out process, drawing on biblical materials and the experiences of Jesus along with practical suggestions and guidelines. Read the material carefully; not only to find your own guidance and help, but also to become better equipped to help others who face the challenge of coming out.

Lesson 33

The Bible Basis for Coming Out

† **Preparatory Bible Reading:** Matthew 5:14-16, 37; John 8:32, 40-46; John 18:37-38; Ephesians 4:15, 22-25

Coming out to yourself and to others as gay or lesbian is not easy. Living in the closet of denial limits our lives and undercuts our self-esteem. Coming out as both Christian and lesbian or gay is part of being prepared. Coming out is essential for full recovery from Bible abuse.

Coming Out Can Be Painful

Tony is a 30-year-old black gay man who came out to his family years ago. His father is a wealthy contractor who is divorced from Tony's mother. Tony is the only child, and his father loves him. Tony's father hates gay people and has refused to help Tony financially. His father told Tony that he would give him a nice condo and all of the financial support he needed if he were living with a woman instead of with a man. Tony works part-time at a restaurant and uses drugs and alcohol much of the time. He barely makes enough money to survive.

Was it a mistake for Tony to come out? Tony's situation unfortunately is not unusual. What would you have done in Tony's place? Does the Bible offer any help?

Coming out means to admit to yourself and accept the fact that you are gay and to tell at least one other person. Coming out is not easy. It is often a painful and frustrating process. For a gay person not to come out is to stay in the closet. That too can be frustrating and painful. The hardest person to come out to is you.

Homophobia and Coming Out

If you are like most people, you have been conditioned to think that homosexuality is "the abomination of God" or a form of mental illness. As a result, most people fear homosexuality in themselves and in others. This fear is called "homophobia" and was first discussed by psychotherapist Dr. George Weinberg in *Society and the Healthy Homosexual*, (published in 1972 and 1983 by St. Martin's Press). Weinberg began his book by saying that he did not consider patients to be healthy if they had not overcome their prejudice against homosexuality.

Coming out is a formidable task. Fear, confusion, great emotional stress, mixed feelings, denial, self-hate, and an army of other enemies battle against your healthy self. When you discover that you are gay, you wrestle with what it means and who to tell. Does truth set you free if you are gay? Or does it destroy you?

Amy's family is very religious and conservative. Amy carefully hid her homosexuality, though she and her lover had a holy union at the local Metropolitan Community Church (MCC). Amy had an accident in her car, and her sister found pictures of the holy union service in the glove compartment. The sister told the rest of Amy's family that Amy is a lesbian and arranged for Amy to undergo psychiatric therapy to cure her of being homosexual. Amy has always been very close to her family, but now she dreads and avoids seeing them.

Was it a mistake for Amy not to come out earlier? How does the Bible provide help for Amy and her lover?

You Cannot Come Out to God

God already knows you. God created you just as you are. God loves you, for God made you to be an individual unlike any other person who ever lived. You can either celebrate your identity or deny and reject who you are. Read Psalms 100, 103, and 139 (Note 100:3; 103:2-3, 11-14; 139:1, 13-14) for help in understanding how and why God made you as you are. Begin by remembering that "God didn't make no junk!" Your sexual orientation is a given. You cannot decide to be straight or gay. You can only decide how you will handle it. The Bible offers help to you if you decide to face, accept, and tell the truth.

Jesus Celebrated and Lived the Truth

Jesus rejected violence and deceit. He lived to help others love and to find their personal truth. Jesus said, "I am the truth" and "the truth will set you free" and he declared to Pilate, "I came into the world to bear witness to the truth" (John 14:6; 8:32; and 18:37). Read in John 8:34-47 what Jesus said about the evil origin of lies in contrast to the truth from God. To live a lie is to live outside of the will of God. Lying to yourself and to others about who you are is spiritual self-sabotage.

The Sermon on the Mount (Matthew 5, 6, and 7) is about being honest with yourself, with God, and with others. Self-acceptance and self-esteem begin with being willing to face and admit the truth about yourself. You cannot "love your neighbor as yourself" until you love yourself, and you cannot be honest with others until you are honest with yourself. Read through Matthew 5, 6, and 7 and notice the many references to living in the truth. Mark or write out the statements of Jesus that most clearly speak to you about being honest.

The call to follow Jesus is the call to become like God. "Be perfect as God is perfect" (Matthew 5:48). "Perfect" is the Greek word *telios* and means to reach a goal and be complete or mature. It is the word Jesus used on the cross in John 19:30, usually translated as, "It is finished." To be like God is to be honest. "It is impossible for God to lie" (Hebrews 6:18). Throughout the Bible, God is faithful and consistent.

The Sermon on the Mount was directed to the disciples who had left everything to follow Jesus. It was not directed to the multitude, though all of the people listened along with the disciples. See Matthew 5:1-2. As you read through all of Matthew 5, 6, and 7, you will be struck by how demanding and absolute the teachings of Jesus are. But Jesus' teachings are not a new legalism of unrealistic demands. They form the pattern for all believers, like the disciples, who have been forgiven their sins and have entered by faith into a fresh new relationship with God. The Spirit of God empowers this new life in Christ. "The Spirit of God speaks in you" (Matthew 10:16-20).

Your witness as a lesbian or gay believer depends on your coming out to yourself and to the world. "Let your light shine before all people in such a way that they may see your good works and glorify God in heaven" (Matthew 5:16). The hope that lesbian and gay Christians will demonstrate God's love and turn the tide of religious oppression and homophobic hate can happen only if lesbian and gay believers come out. God is on the side of truth. God will empower you to "speak the truth in love" (Ephesians 4:15).

Taking Off the Mask

The word *hypocrite* is the Greek word for "mask" and means to pretend to play a part that is not yours. *Hypocrite* is a transliterated Greek word. Jesus used the word to mean insincere giving in Matthew 6:2, empty praying in Matthew 6:5, superficial religion in Matthew 6:16, and judging others in Matthew 7:5. *Hypocrite* was the harshest label Jesus used for religious leaders who were dishonest, insensitive and judgmental of others and blind to their own faults. Trace the word *hypocrite* in Matthew 15:7; 22:18; 23:13-15, 23, 25, 27-29; and 24:51.

In Galatians 2:11-14, Paul points out how Peter's fear of others led him to the hypocrisy of refusing to eat with foreigners and how this failure influenced others, including Barnabas, to be afraid and dishonest. First Peter 2:1-2 shows that honesty is basic for spiritual growth. Jesus simplified the issue of truth, saying, "Let your word yes mean yes and your no mean no. Anything beyond that is evil" (Matthew 5:37).

Love Casts Out Fear

No matter how we try to justify staying in the closet, the closet is still a lie. Lying can become a way of life. We can become addicted to lying. We lie to our parents and family, to our friends and even to ourselves. We hide our true feelings for others of the same sex. We boldly lie when we are asked about our sexual orientation. We develop skills in deception and misdirection. We justify lying by saying that we do it to protect our family and friends from being hurt. But whom are we really trying to protect? And how can we be sure that we are loved and accepted as we are if we lie about whom we are? We cannot. We convince ourselves that too much is at stake to face and tell the truth about our being homosexual. Actually, too much is at stake to lie about it!

Lying about being gay re-enforces your fear of being different and unacceptable. This fear, homophobia, can have a paralyzing effect on your life. Here is a wonderful verse for us, "There is no fear in love; perfect love casts out fear, because fear causes torment" (I John 4:18). Read I John 4:1-21. Since God loves you, you also ought to love other people and yourself. This is truly good news!

Once we become conditioned to lying consistently about our sexual orientation, lying about other things gets easier. We make a habit of lying to get out of difficult situations. Even when we do come out and begin to develop gay/lesbian relationships, we have to work hard to break the habit of lying. Deception and dishonesty threaten our most cherished and intimate relationships. The stress produced by trying to sustain lies and deception in our daily relationships with people takes a heavy toll on our energy and health.

Coming out is facing and telling the truth. God helps us face and tell the truth. Coming out sets us free, for "the truth will set you free." You can with God's help break the chains of deception and dishonesty. You can face the truth and begin to live your own reality one day at the time.

Facing and sharing your personal truth is part of your testimony for Christ as a Christian lesbian or gay man. God is on the side of truth. Your truth is your greatest asset. Through Christ, you can become free to be yourself and to enjoy life without fear.

Do Not Let Others Make this Decision for You

As I write this lesson, I am in correspondence with a closeted gay man who is a high official in a very conservative Christian denomination. A few friends know that he is gay, but he has one friend who is putting a lot of pressure on him to come out to the world and let everybody know that he is gay. This official is grappling with a difficult choice, remaining closeted in the influential position that he has and trying to change his church, or coming out, knowing that he would be fired and have no further opportunity to make a difference in his denomination. This is not an easy decision to make.

I remained in my denominational job with the Baptist College until someone else outed me in 1981 and I did not have any control over how or when I came out. Many others more recently have come out and suffered the consequences. What would you suggest to the high denominational official?

Questions for Study and Discussion

1. Have you come out yet? If you have, what prompted you to decide to come out? If you have not, what is keeping you from doing it?

2. Have other gay people put pressure on you to come out? How have you handled pressure from others to come out beyond the level at which you feel comfortable?

3. Have you been "outed" (your sexuality revealed by somebody other than yourself)? How did you handle it? Why did you wait until somebody else told your secret rather than telling it yourself?

4. What advice would you give to other gay people about coming out?

Additional Resources

See the autobiography of the Rev. Troy Perry in his first book, *The Lord is My Shepherd, and He Knows I'm Gay*: Liberty Press, 1972 and later editions.

See stories edited by Malcolm Boyd and Nancy L. Wilson, *Amazing Grace*: The Crossing Press, 1991.

Lesson 34

Singing in the Rain

† **Preparatory Bible Reading:** Philippians 4:1-23

The Bible Basis for Gay Pride

"Rejoice in Jesus Christ always; again I will say, Rejoice!" (Philippians 4:4). Paul wrote to the Philippians to thank his friends for a gift that they had sent to him in prison. Have you ever given gifts to someone in prison? Even the most insignificant and tiny gift takes on great meaning to someone in prison. A pack of cigarettes, old magazines, a little bag of candy, a letter, or just a brief phone visit can be the greatest thing that happens all day to someone in jail. I have had close friends in prison, and they have told me that most prisoners never have any contact at all from anybody on the outside. Paul had learned to be happy and rejoice under pressure.

Even in prison, Paul knew how to "sing in the rain," because Paul had found inner peace in Christ. After thanking his friends for their gift, Paul said, "Not that I speak from want; for I have learned to be content in whatever circumstances I am. I know how to get along with humble means, and I also know how to live in prosperity; in any and every circumstance I have learned the secret of being filled and going hungry, both of having abundance and suffering need. I can do all things through Christ who strengthens me" (Philippians 4:11-13). Paul then added, "Nevertheless, you have done well to share with me in my affliction" (verse 14).

Pride Under Pressure

Gene Kelly's performance of the title song in the movie "Singing in the Rain," is a classic. It is memorable because it shows that you can be happy and sing even in adversity and trouble. Lesbian/gay pride day and parades have become annual celebrations for gay people and their supporters throughout the world. Pride Day, or Freedom Day as it is called in San Francisco, is usually celebrated one of the weekends of June each year to recall the riot at the Stonewall Inn in New York in 1969, which was the beginning of public resistance by gay men, many of them drag queens, against abuse and harassment by the police. The modern national gay rights movement is usually traced from this violent dramatic beginning. Stonewall was the historic beginning of Gay Pride.

My first Gay Pride Parade was in 1981 in Atlanta. Charles was a member of Metropolitan Community Church (MCC) and wore a paper sack over his head in the parade for fear that he would be fired if his employer recognized him. He was a recruiter for a church-related college. He was celebrating and hurting at the same time. He was "singing in the rain." We have made a lot of progress since 1981. Now Charles not only marches without the paper sack; he was recently chairperson of the parade.

1981 was before the widespread public consciousness of HIV/AIDS. Since then, the parades have featured many reminders of the HIV/AIDS epidemic in support groups, the Names Project Quilt, and many protests and demonstrations for better medical and other community support for people with HIV and AIDS. If we sing at all, we always are "singing in the rain." It never stops raining on our parade for lesbian, gay, bisexual, and transgendered people.

Contentment in Christ

Paul learned to be "content" (Philippians 4:11), the Greek word *autoarkes*, which is *auto* (self) and *arkes* (rule or control). It was the key word in Stoic teaching. It was used to speak of the state of mind that one reaches when no outside events or pressures are allowed to disturb one's happiness or peace of mind. Paul had found calm inner security and self-control in Christ and was not shaken by what others might do to him.

What makes you happy and keeps you singing? Who or what do you let rattle your cage and ruin your day?

Paul also felt good about himself and could rejoice because all things came together in harmony with Christ at the center of his life. See the frequent use of "all," "all things," and "everything" in Philippians 4, verses 4, 6, 7, 8, 11, 13, 19, and 22. You are encouraged to "Be anxious for nothing, but in everything by prayer and supplication with thanksgiving let your requests be known to God, and the peace of God, which surpasses all comprehension, shall guard your hearts and your minds in Christ Jesus" (Philippians 4:6-7). The promise in Philippians 4:19 is wonderfully inclusive, "My God shall supply all of your needs according to God's great abundance in glory in Christ Jesus."

The Power of Positive Thinking

"The peace of God, which is far beyond all human understanding, will guard your hearts and your minds in Christ Jesus" (Philippians 4:7). The "heart" was thought of as the center of human will and decision-making. The "mind" was the center of reason and thought. Christians have "the mind of Christ" (1 Corinthians 2:16). You are what you think about all day long. You cannot control a lot of what happens to you, but you can decide what you will think about it. To change your thoughts is to change your life.

"What happens to you is not nearly as important as what you do about what happens to you!" (a quote from Dr. Roy O. McClain in 1956). Lesbian, gay, bisexual, and transgendered people and all other alienated people are tempted to search for someone to blame or blame themselves for their problems and the pressures that they face. Negative thinking produces negative results. Paul encouraged positive thinking in Philippians 4:8, "Finally, brothers and sisters, think about whatever is true, honorable, right, pure, loving, attractive, and what is excellent and worthy of praise."

Read now Philippians 2:1-11, where Paul described the "mind of Christ" that is in you and me if we follow Jesus.

Whenever you feel sorry for yourself and sink into self-pity, you focus on your failures and hardships. You are tempted also to focus on the failures and mistakes of others. You can generate a lot of negative energy for yourself and everybody else around you. How can you break out of this gloomy downward spiral?

Mrs. Wilson was 75 years old and still very active in the church I served as pastor in Greenwood, South Carolina. She brought a car full of other older people to church activities and to our regular Senior Citizens Meetings. One day we were discussing what we have learned from our pain and hardships in life. I asked Mrs. Wilson what she had learned from having back pains for years, spending months in the hospital, and having to wear a heavy back brace all the time. She fired back an immediate answer, "I learned that other people don't want to hear about it!" We all laughed, but we knew that Mrs. Wilson had learned something that most of us have not. Nobody really wants to hear you recite yet another rendition of "Woe is me!"

Whenever I would whine and complain about how bad things were going for me in Atlanta, the Rev. Jimmy Brock would laugh and say, "Now don't throw another pity party!" The Rev. Marge Ragona would simply tell me, "Get over yourself!" They were not being mean, just realistic.

Sometimes I feel like the little man in the cartoon under about ten feet of water who complained, "Into each life a little rain must fall, but this is ridiculous!" Multitudes of lesbian, gay, bisexual, and transgendered people celebrate the fun and festivities of gay pride each year, but many are smiling through tears. A lot of us are grieving over the loss of friends and partners to HIV/AIDS. Many are hurt and wounded by religious abuse and by rejecting families. Many do not march because of fear.

Many are living with HIV/AIDS. Floods of fear, rejection, oppression, injustice, sickness, poverty, and loneliness never seem to subside. Yet in rain and through tears, we continue to celebrate who we are.

Self-esteem and Self-respect Come from God

What others think of you is not nearly as important as what you think of yourself. Do you really love yourself? At this point, lay down this book and read carefully and thoughtfully through the Book of Philippians. It is only four chapters and will not take long. Mark or copy each of the statements in Philippians that help you to feel good about yourself. Take a moment to pray and thank God for what good things you have discovered about yourself.

You are blessed. Do you usually see the glass as half full or half empty? This depends on how you think about it and how your mind works. Sometimes you may feel abandoned, and perhaps you are. God loves you anyway, however, and with God's help you can love yourself and the other people around you.

Make a list of the things you like about yourself. (I hope it takes you a long time!)

Learn to be your own best friend. Let Jesus come into your heart and mind to direct your thoughts to the "upward call of God in Christ Jesus" (Philippians 3:1-16). Let God love you and build your self-esteem and self-confidence. Let go of the baggage of past religious abuses that made you feel bad about yourself and go on to something better and spiritually healthier for you and for the people around you.

Philippians is a happy book about joy and rejoicing under pressure and oppression. Let it lift you up and help you to build pride in yourself. Self-worth can free you from destructiveness and also free you from letting others hurt you. Paul told us a lot about himself in Philippians. Even in prison and under great stress, Paul was happy and at peace and reached out to give love and encouragement to others.

Generous Under Pressure

Billy was five years old. His sister was in the hospital and needed surgery. Billy's blood type was the same as his sister's rare type. Billy loved his sister very much; so when his parents asked him to give blood to his sister, he thought about it for a while and then said, "Yes." Arrangements were made for Billy to go to the hospital the next day to donate blood. That afternoon, his mother noticed Billy going out of the house several times with arms full of his toys. She asked what he was doing. Billy said, "I am giving away my toys to my friends before I die tomorrow when I give my blood to my sister!" His mother said, "Oh, Billy, you won't die! You will give only a little bit of your blood to your sister, not all of it!" Billy was very relieved and said, "Whew! I thought I had to give it all!"

Do fear and pressure make you more loving and generous? You do not have to lay down your life to give yourself to your friends! Help others to feel good about themselves. You will like yourself better too.

Stress, pressure, and fear have often brought out the best in people in our community during the HIV/AIDS crisis. Care givers have worked themselves into exhaustion and chronic "burn-out" and some have demonstrated the willingness to lay aside their own needs to give their lives in service for their loved ones and partners in months and years of tender loving care. Many gays and lesbians have rallied all of their personal time and resources to do whatever it takes to lengthen the lives and sustain the quality of life for people with HIV/AIDS. Whatever else the HIV/AIDS epidemic has taught us, it has showed us how much love was there that we did not even realize we had. God is love, and God has been with us and loved in and through us even when we were not aware that God was present at all.

Questions for Study and Discussion

1. What have you given away under pressure that made you feel good about yourself? What most makes you glad? Why?

2. How has stress brought out the best in you?

3. Have you learned to celebrate who you are and your sexual orientation even in the face of oppression and abuse? How have you helped others to do the same?

Additional Resources

For lesbian and gay role models, see, Eric Marcus, *Making History*: Harper, 1992.

Troy Perry and Thomas Swicegood, *Profiles in Gay and Lesbian Courage*: St. Martin's Press, 1991.

Lesson 35

How Jesus Came Out to the World

† Preparatory Bible Reading: Matthew 21:1-17; Mark 11:1-18; Luke 19:28-48

Jesus entered Jerusalem in the "Triumphant Entry" to be greeted by multitudes of oppressed people. During the Passover season once a year, the population of Jerusalem grew from several thousand people to as many as two million pilgrims from all parts of the world. People camped on the hillsides and valleys around the city. The slope of the Mount of Olives that leads to the eastern wall of the city was filled with thousands of people. No teacher could address such a crowd. Jesus did something that everyone could see and understand. This lesson gives us an opportunity to see how one of the great events in the life of Jesus speaks to all people.

Doing the Unexpected

Jesus carefully prepared to create the maximum dramatic effect when he entered the city during Passover. Disciples were sent to find a donkey that Jesus had already arranged to use. Matthew 21:5 includes the prophecy from Zechariah 9:9, "Your king is coming to you, gentle and mounted on a donkey." Read Matthew 21:1-7. Conquerors rode a horse into a defeated city as a sign of military victory. A ruler on a mission of peace rode a donkey, "a beast of burden." Every action and word of Jesus taught the good news of God's love for and acceptance of all people. No gesture was wasted.

People were expecting a deliverer to come and set them free, a military messiah who would drive out the Romans and free the country from their oppression. Jesus did not plan to do that.

Jesus had no intention of killing soldiers. He had no intention of attacking and killing the hypocritical religious leaders who opposed him and engineered his death. His coming out to the world in his Triumphant Entry into the city was a clear challenge to the common ideas about the Messiah and what the Messiah would do. We know from the Dead Sea Scrolls some of the popular military expectations that were associated with the coming of the Messiah. Jesus rejected them all.

Jesus was a revolutionary Revolutionary! He neither supported nor identified with any of the revolutionary movements of his day. He had settled in his mind the kind of Messiah he was to be. Read again Matthew 12:14-21, which Jesus quoted earlier when he was under pressure to abandon his original plan. The people saw Jesus as a king. Jesus had to make it plain, however, that he was not the kind of king that they expected. His actions tried to make his real mission clear. The people misunderstood Jesus. So did the religious leaders.

"Hosanna"

"Hosanna to the son of David. Blessed is the one who comes in the name of God. Hosanna in the highest," (Matthew 21:9), is a quote from Psalm 118:26 (which was from the part of the Bible that was read in synagogue during Passover). "Hosanna" means "deliver or save now" and was a shout of hope and longing. This response of the crowds revealed that they saw the mission of Jesus as a promise of peace and liberation. They entered into the celebration of the coming of Jesus by shouting and waving palm branches that expressed joy at the coming of the Savior who would set them free. Jesus came out and identified with oppressed people. Coming out as gay people is also identification with all oppressed people.

Hope for Oppressed People

The people were oppressed. They were under the tyranny of the Roman Empire. Their lives were controlled by the military forces of a foreign power and by religious leaders who worked in partnership with that power. Priests and teachers enforced a legalistic, judgmental religion of rigid laws that alienated and wounded the majority of people. Only a minority of the people tried to keep the whole law. Most people were seen and saw themselves as sinners and outcast. They were unable to understand or keep all of the laws, especially the detailed laws against work on the Sabbath. The crowds saw Jesus as a way out of the heavy oppression from soldiers and from religion that dominated their lives.

Pressures of Poverty and Sickness

Few of the people in Jerusalem were Roman citizens. Paul was a rare exception. Most of the people lived in incredible poverty by our standards. A day's wage was about 16 cents. The diet commonly consisted of bread, water, and occasional vegetables. Meat was seldom available. No effective medical treatment existed for most illnesses and life expectancy was 25 years. All serious sicknesses were fatal. Illness was viewed as God's punishment for sin. Poor, sick, and afflicted people not only lived in miserable conditions; they were also condemned and rejected as unclean.

Oppression was added to poverty and pain. No social contact was allowed between Jews and foreigners, men and women, slaves and free, rich and poor, religious and the non-religious. The people of the land were aliens in their own country and among their own race. God's special care for aliens and outcast people is a theme throughout the Bible. Psalm 137:4 lamented, "How can we sing the Lord's song in a foreign land?" This reminder that God's people had been aliens and strangers in Egypt and in Babylon was a painful prophecy of the current situation where the majority of the people were strangers and foreigners in their own land and society.

Exodus 22:21 required, "You shall not wrong or oppress a stranger, for you were strangers in the land of Egypt." See also Leviticus 19:33-34. Deuteronomy 27:19 declared, "Cursed is the one who distorts the justice due an alien, orphan, and widow. And all the people shall say, Amen."

When the Oppressed Become Oppressors

One of the most painful aspects of the people's suffering was that their own religious leaders condemned and oppressed them. The Romans were cruel and effective in keeping subject people under control. Crucifixion was utilized to isolate and destroy any troublesome traitor to the system. The threat of death hung over all people ruled by Rome. A Roman soldier could kill any subject who refused an official order. Local religious and political leaders cooperated with the Romans and exerted whatever pressure was necessary to control their own population.

The common people welcomed Jesus into Jerusalem with great joy and celebration. Jesus represented their only hope for deliverance and change from corrupt political and religious oppression. The oppressed had become the oppressors. This tragic dynamic of oppression is painfully evident in every minority, even today. Abuse and oppression are especially damaging when it comes from the people closest to you.

Oppression in the Church

Very early in the history of the church, minorities were being oppressed. Discrimination against Greek widows during community meals led to the selection of special helpers to wait on tables in order to be sure that everyone received fair and equal treatment (Acts 6:1-7). Paul confronted Peter for refusing to eat with foreigners because he was afraid of religious abuse by prejudiced believers from Jerusalem (Galatians 2:11-14). All of 2 Corinthians grappled with legalistic conflicts among believers. Descriptions of the early church are filled with stories of divisive conflicts among believers and the struggle to resolve these conflicts.

One of the most vigorous and vital struggles is recorded in Acts 15 at what is commonly called the Jerusalem Conference. The issue was the acceptance of Gentiles into the church without requiring that they first become converts to Judaism. The decision of the conference to accept Gentiles as Christians based only on their faith in Jesus was a significant turning point in the history of the church and led to the missionary journeys of Paul and others.

Religious Opposition to Jesus

The crowds sang and praised God in welcoming Jesus. The religious leaders resented and rejected Jesus and considered him a nobody with no official standing or recognition. His followers were from among the poor, the street people, the outcasts, the disinherited, and sinners. The leaders ordered Jesus to make the crowds stop calling him "the blessed king who comes in the name of God to bring the peace of heaven and glory in the highest." Notice the similarity of the crowd's praise and the announcement of the birth of Jesus by the angels to shepherds (Luke 2:14). Jesus answered the demands of the rulers by saying, "If the crowds are quiet, the stones will cry out!" (Luke 19:40).

Jesus wept over the city that he came to deliver from oppression. Read Luke 19:41-44. Their own religious leaders were leading the people to destruction. Jesus then went into the Temple and drove out the merchants and the moneychangers from that part of the Temple that had been reserved for "all nations" (the Greek word for Gentiles). Read Mark 11:15-18; Matthew 21:2-17; and Luke 19:45-48. Jesus consistently took the side of those who were alienated and oppressed by religion. The rulers plotted to kill Jesus because he had attacked their evil and ungodly system. Jesus died to set all people free from sick, destructive religion.

Celebrating in the Midst of Pain

Christians learned early in their history to celebrate and rejoice in times of persecution. Acts 16:25 tells how in prison in Philippi "about midnight Paul and Silas were praying and singing hymns of praise to God, and the prisoners were listening to them." Paul's letter to the Philippians was written from prison and developed the themes of joy and rejoicing more than any other of his writings.

The crowds saw the entry of Jesus into Jerusalem as a sign of hope. The religious rulers saw it as a threat to their power. The people praised Jesus and proclaimed him to be the king sent from God. The rulers hated Jesus and decided that he must die. The rulers won and Jesus died. His followers ran away and hid in fear. That seemed to be the end of it. The whole story, however, was not over yet.

Passive and Active Resistance

Jesus came out to the world in the dramatic entry into Jerusalem on a little donkey as an act of humility and a fulfillment of prophecy. This was a clear act of protest against the pride and pretense of the prevailing religious establishment. The crowds loved it. The leaders resented and hated it. Jesus later cleansed the Temple and called the traditional abusive religious leaders a den of robbers. The first action was passive activism. The second was a direct attack upon a corrupt religious system that had lost touch with God and the people. We face much the same challenge today. How can we effectively come out and change abusive, destructive religion?

Questions for Study and Discussion

1. What has it cost you to resist abusive and oppressive religion? What price have you paid for coming out and revealing who you really are and challenging the twisted use of the Bible against you? Why do the oppressed become oppressors? Have you ever used religion to try to control others?

2. How has the coming out of Jesus to the world spoken to you? Do you see the coming of Jesus as hope for healing and life or as a threat? How much prior planning should you do in your own coming out process?

3. Why were such educated and experienced religious leaders unable to recognize their own Messiah in Jesus?

4. What are the features of religion that make it destructive and oppressive?

Additional Resources

See the great work on Jesus as a revolutionary by Oscar Cullmann, *Jesus and the Revolutionaries*: Harper, 1970.

Lesson 36

A Practical Guide to Coming Out

† Preparatory Bible Reading: Matthew 10:1-42

Telling other people that you are gay is called coming out. It is something that can and will totally change your life. You need and have God's help to do it. Pray about it before, during, and after you come out. Be prepared for unexpected responses. You never know ahead of time how others will react. You cannot control how other people will react. You cannot assume that your parents, family, friends, boss, church friends, pastor, fellow workers, or anyone will understand what you mean by saying that you are gay. You can usually assume that non-gay people will have an entirely different picture than you do about what being gay or lesbian means.

Coming out can be a minefield of dangerous and explosive possibilities. Coming out is the field that all of us have to cross eventually, however, on our road to self-acceptance and recovery from Bible abuse and religious oppression. You need God's protection and encouragement on this journey. You also need friends who are accepting and supportive. Coming out does not necessarily mean telling everybody you know. Coming out begins with you and then is shared with others in a very selective way. Tell others only on the basis of their need to know. Be intentional and cautious.

Why Come Out?

This is a good question in view of the sometimes disastrous consequences of coming out. One simple answer could be, "the truth will set you free." Coming out is far too complex and threatening to be answered so simply. The people who know and love you the most, such as your parents, family, and best friends, do not really know you if you are not out to them. Whenever gay women and men come out to parents and family, they risk rejection and even danger. Some lesbian and gay people have told me of coming out to their parents and being told to leave home and never come back. Some had their lives threatened. Often, however, even the most hostile attitude of parents will change over time and their gay children and their life partners will be loved and accepted back into the family. Unfortunately, however, this can take a long time.

At a Metropolitan Community Church (MCC) district conference in Tennessee a few years ago, Mary shared her experience with the group. She told how her son, who was living in San Francisco, told her that he was gay and had HIV/AIDS. She asked him how long he had known that he had HIV/AIDS. He responded that he had known for about a year. Mary was surprised and said, “Why didn’t you tell me before now?” He said, “Because I was afraid you would reject me.” Mary was shocked. She said, “How could I reject you? I am your mother. I love you!” As a result of this conversation, Mary was able to be with her son and help him live with HIV/AIDS and leave this life with courage, hope, and a lot of loving support. Mary has developed the first support team for people with HIV/AIDS in her part of the state.

Do not expect the worst when you come out. Just be ready for the reaction to be different than you expected. Mary’s reaction to her son coming out was encouraging. Many parents, however, react to their children telling them that they are gay by saying typical responses, “What did I do wrong” or “How could you do this to me!” or “What will the neighbors think?” All of these responses center attention on the parents and not on the children, who are sharing their innermost feelings and hurts with their parents. Sometimes the response is a pleasant surprise of support and love.

One of my neighbors told me of a visit from his mother who had once told him that she never wanted to hear him tell her that he is gay! He was uneasy about his mother visiting him at his apartment. She was relaxed and enjoyed the visit and so did he. In the conversation one night, his mother asked, "Well, are you gay?" He said, "Yes, I am." His mother's reply was, "I love you and accept you and will support you any way I can." It was such a smooth and easy experience that my friend was happy, relieved, and feeling especially good about himself when he told me about it a few days later.

Why We Are Afraid to Come Out

When John Powell wrote his book, *Why Am I Afraid to Tell You Who I Am?* (Argus, 1969), he was discussing the book with a friend. The friend said, "I can answer that question for you, John. I am afraid to tell you who I am because if I tell you who I am, you may not like who I am, and that's all I have."

Telling your personal truth to others makes you vulnerable. Who do you trust enough to give your most intimate personal information? Be very selective about coming out. Be intentional and in control. Do not just let it slip out. Tell others only on the basis of their need to know and your need to tell them.

Being outed can be a very traumatic experience. Some gay people have been far too eager to tell others about someone else who is gay. When someone tells people that another person is gay, it is called outing, and it has destroyed careers, marriages, homes, and lives. I was outed by another gay person and lost my job, home, career, and much more. Just the accusation of being gay is enough to cost gay people their jobs in church work. I know dozens of gay and lesbian people who have been fired from Baptist churches and from Baptist institutions because other people outed them.

Levels of Coming Out

Coming out takes courage and time. Most of us come out in stages. We first come out to ourselves and admit and face the fact that we are gay. That first step may take years. After this first step, we usually do not plan the rest of the coming out process. We just let it happen and pay the continuous price that society demands. We allow events and other people to control how, when, where, and to whom we come out. Do not let chance control anything in your life as important as your coming out as a lesbian or gay person. Be thoughtful and intentional as well as prayerful about how you come out. God wants to help you face, understand, and share who you are. Coming out is part of your recovery and your foundation for personal spiritual growth. It is a necessary ingredient in your successful witness to your faith among other lesbians and gays.

Here are some practical guidelines to coming out that seem to help a lot of people.

Some Practical Guidelines for Coming Out

1. You Cannot Predict How Others Will React.

Coming out can be very scary and threatening to you. It can also be very difficult and threatening to the persons to whom you come out. Pray about it. Ask God to give you the words and to show you how to handle it. Remember that when you tell your parents, family, boss, and others that you are gay or lesbian, they do not have the same mental picture that you do. Their minds have been filled with homophobic images from preachers, talk shows, and anti-gay propaganda. Prepare to be surprised. With God's help you can handle it! Sometimes the reaction is pleasant, sometimes not. Joe said that he dreaded telling his mother that he was gay. When he finally told her, she responded by saying, "I understand. Years ago I was in love with another woman my-self!" Allen, however, said that when he was 16 years old and asked his father for advice about how to handle being gay, his father said, "Put a gun in your mouth and pull the trigger!"

2. Find Caring and Supportive People.

You need acceptance and encouragement in coming out. Find other lesbian and gay people and develop a support network. Join or start a spiritual support group. Remember that other people need your encouragement too.

Coming out is a process that takes time. You begin by facing and accepting the truth about yourself. Then you tell at least one other person. When you finally settle this in yourself, you will feel so much better! As you gain self-confidence, you can help others who face the same issues and problems.

3. Come Out on the Basis of a Need to Know.

Before you come out to others, consider carefully why you are doing it. Why do they need to know? Why do you need to tell them? Coming out can hurt you and others. Can you handle the results? Think through how you will tell your truth. God will empower you to tell your truth. Remember, however, that the truth is seen as true only when you "speak the truth in love."

4. You Cannot Go Back into the Closet.

Once you are "out of the closet," you cannot really turn back. Some people try to deny their sexual orientation and play a game of hide-and-seek with themselves and others. You may have done this for a while yourself. Many of us have. If you are uncertain of your sexual orientation, work through it before you come out, even to yourself.

If you need counseling to deal with your sexual orientation, find a gay and lesbian friendly counselor who will help you to face and deal with your issues without judging and condemning you. Contact the nearest Metropolitan Community Church (listed in the local phone directories) or UFMCC Headquarters (310/360-8640) or at www.ufmcc.com for information, or you can contact the author of this book. Knowing and accepting your sexual identity sets the stage for your future self-esteem and peace of mind. Do not panic, but do not neglect dealing with it, either.

No matter how you feel about your sexual orientation, you are not alone! God loves you, accepts you, and is always with you. Read Philippians 4:6-7 for encouragement.

5. Feel Good About Yourself.

Once you have come out, feel good about yourself. Celebrate! You have crossed a great barrier. Good for you! Stop and thank God for helping you do it. There are many levels of coming out. Go on to the next level. Be intentional about who you will tell next. Think it through. Be in control. Do not let other people or unexpected events push you out. Enjoy being yourself. God wants you to be happy and to love yourself. God will help you to know what to say and how to say it. Always speak your truth in love.

Questions for Study and Discussion

1. What kept you from coming out before you finally did? What prompted you to come out when you did? What would you go back and change about your coming out experience if you could?

2. What advice would you give to a gay or lesbian friend who was wrestling with whether or not to come out to parents or to friends? Have you ever helped someone else come out? What happened?

3. What are the advantages or disadvantages to staying "in the closet"? What are the advantages or disadvantages of "coming out"?

4. How is lying about your sexual orientation different from lying about other things? Is living "in the closet" a form of lying?

Additional Resources

Many helpful books on coming out have appeared in recent years. None existed when I was growing up and trying to deal with my own homosexual orientation. I never even heard the word gay until after I finished graduate school. One of the most helpful books is Chris Glaser, *Uncommon Calling: A Gay Man's Struggle to Serve the Church*: Harper, 1988. The emphasis of Glaser's book is on coming out.

Also see Malcolm Boyd, *Take Off the Masks*: Harper, 1978; Revised Edition, 1993.

See my Web site at www.truluck.com for recent helpful literature.

Part V

Reach Out

Once you have discovered your own self-esteem and found hope, healing, growth, and recovery from abusive, oppressive religion, you will want to reach out to others and share your good news. Reaching out to others is an important and enjoyable part of recovery. Jesus regularly encouraged people to share their good news of God's love and acceptance. Gospel stories like the woman at the well (John 4) and the call of the first disciples to become fishers for people (Luke 5:1-11) focus on the action of reaching out to others as a follow-up to spiritual renewal and recovery.

Do a fresh read through of the Gospel of Mark and notice how much of the work of Jesus consisted of preparing and sending people out to tell others of the wonderful things that God had done for them. Notice the special emphasis on this theme in Mark 5:1-20. See also Matthew 9:35-38 and Matthew 10:1-42. Take a look now at the Great Commission at the end of Matthew 28:18-20. Read again John, chapters 17, 20, and 21.

Jesus intended that those who followed him would also become teachers and makers of disciples. One reason for this is the joy people have in sharing good news with other people. Read John 15 for the clear instructions of Jesus to disciples to produce "fruit" by helping other people also to become disciples.

Reaching out involves inviting other people into your life who can be encouraging and supportive to you as well as offering yourself in support and encouragement to others. The basic reason for Alcoholics Anonymous meetings is the simple fact that we need each other. We need re-enforcement to keep our recovery program working and not to slip back into self-destructive and self-defeating negative attitudes and behavior.

As you work through these final Steps to Recovery, search for practical and workable ways in which you can reach out and include other people in your progress and growth in healthy and encouraging activities. Becoming healthy is important, because we can become overly dependent on others and because unhealthy codependency is always a threat to our recovery and healing. Reaching out to others is the best way we have to resist falling back into legalistic, self-destructive, judgmental religion.

Jesus has set us free from sick and abusive religion.

Now we are in a position to rethink our spiritual lives and help to bring shape to healthy spiritual recovery and outreach. We can share with others to develop working models of community and life that are free from oppressive religion and are truly new creations in Christ.

Jesus said that new life requires new forms, "Nobody puts new wine into old wineskins, for the wine will burst the skins, and the wine is lost as well as the skins, but one puts new wine in new wineskins" (Mark 2:22). Paul abandoned the unworkable, inadequate religious forms of his past and "pressed on toward the goal for the prize of the upward call of God in Christ Jesus." Read again Philippians 3:1-14.

Chapter 15

The Tenth Step

Develop Your Support System

Find accepting and affirming people who can encourage you and share in your spiritual life and recovery. Others also need your support. Start your own Spiritual Recovery Group.

> We who are strong ought to bear the weaknesses of those without strength and not just please ourselves. . . . Therefore accept one another just as Christ also accepted you to the glory of God.
>
> Romans 15:1, 7

All recovery programs include a time and place for people in recovery to meet and share with others who are dealing with the same issues and problems. You need and can help others who are facing and dealing with recovery from abusive and oppressive religion. You can learn from the experiences of others and they can learn from you.

Finding an appropriate and supportive group can be difficult. Churches usually are indifferent or even hostile to gay and lesbian people who are dealing with how the church has hurt them. Some churches, such as the Metropolitan Community Churches (MCC) and a growing number of traditional churches, are reaching out in love and acceptance of gay people without judgment or condemnation.

You can start your own group. You do not have to have a large group of people to begin. Two people can develop a time and place for dialogue and sharing that will be encouraging and supportive to them. Do not be discouraged if you never move beyond two or three people in your group. Keep it simple.

Jesus met with his group of close friends outdoors, in homes, and in a variety of places. Meeting in a home or in a public place like a coffee shop or at local gay, lesbian, bisexual, and transgendered centers are some of the various settings for many kinds of recovery programs. As in all recovery programs, the purpose of a group is not to preach or promote any organization but to be open, accepting, and nonjudgmental. Creating an atmosphere of mutual respect and acceptance encourages growth, self-esteem, and healthy, healing dialogue.

Lesson 37

Stand By Me

† Preparatory Bible Reading: John 14:12-27; 15:26; 16:13-15, 32-33; Psalm 23; Acts 4:3-37; 9:26-28; 11:19-30; and 2 Corinthians 1:3-7

Stephen King's story, "The Body," was made into a delightful movie about a group of boys on a great adventure to locate a body in the woods. The movie explored dynamics of growing up as the boys stood by each other in a series of exciting and threatening events. The movie and the hit song from it were titled, "Stand By Me."

During my ministry as Pastor both in Southern Baptist and in Metropolitan Community Churches (MCC), I visited people in hospitals and at home in times of serious illness, grief, and bereavement. The usual response to my visit was, "Thank you for coming. Thank you for being with me." People seldom commented on what I said. They simply said, "Thank you for being here." I learned that often when people are under severe stress, the less said the better. Often a loving hug and to "weep with those who weep" says far more than words. Pastoral care Professor Dr. Wayne E. Oates at seminary taught the symbolic role of Christians "being there." We represent God's love and presence. Dr. Oates cautioned us not to talk too much or try to explain everything but to let our presence speak for itself.

The Spiritual Gift of Being There

"Thank you for being here when I needed you." "I just want somebody with me. I don't want to go through this alone." "Where is everybody?" "Please come to see me." "Will you go with me? I can't face this by myself." Do these words sound familiar? Have you said them yourself? Everybody needs somebody sometime. Many gay people and people with HIV/AIDS and those who care for them often go through loneliness, isolation, and feelings of abandonment. For many in our community, the greatest spiritual gift of all is the gift of showing up.

You may have helped with volunteer support ministries or sat with a friend or lover for many weeks and months simply "to be there." Loneliness and isolation are the most frequent sources of distress for many of the gays and lesbians who contact me for help and encouragement. When I was a volunteer for emotional support at the showing of the Names Project Memorial Quilt in Atlanta, in May, 1988, I stood with Barbara as she stooped down to attach a "Be a Buddy" pin to the quilt panel she had made for her brother. It was the pin that had been worn by the friend who stood by her brother and cared for him in the final months of his life.

Barbara and I stood by the quilt panel for several minutes and held hands and cried. Nothing was said. Nothing needed to be said. Ten years have passed, and I am choked up again as I write this. I still feel Barbara's pain and sadness. The gay, lesbian, bisexual, and transgendered community is gradually learning the healing power of just being there.

Jesus and the Ministry of Being There

Jesus invented the buddy program. Jesus' final promise in Matthew 28:20 was, "I am with you always." Read John 14:16-17, 26-27; 15:26-27; and 16:13-16, 32-33 for the words of Jesus about the Holy Spirit as the one who is "called alongside." The Greek word translated comforter in *KJV* is *paraklete*, made up of two Greek words, *para*, meaning alongside and *kalleo*, meaning to call. The word is also translated as helpers, consolation, encouragement, exhort, and other English words that try to convey the idea of a person standing alongside another. In John 14:16-17, after calling the Holy Spirit the "one called alongside" whom God would send in the name of Jesus and who would "abide with you and be in you," Jesus added, "I will not leave you as orphans; I will come to you" (John 14:18). The Spirit clearly is also Jesus. B. H. Carroll called the Holy Spirit "the other Jesus."

In John 17:18-26, Jesus prayed that his followers will be as close together and united with each other as Jesus is with God. This remarkable prayer of Jesus reminds us that we have the same help to handle stress as Jesus had. We have each other, and we have God. Jesus declared, "I am not alone, because God is with me" (John 16:32). In John's Gospel, Jesus identifies with God and with his disciples in an absolute way. "If you have seen me, you have seen God" (John 14:9 and John 1:1-14). "As God sent me, so send I you" (John 20:21).

Jesus carefully and prayerfully selected a group of intimate friends "that they might be with him" (Mark 3:14; Luke 6:12-16). Jesus had special people with him when he had to cope with the mounting hostility of religious leaders against him and the threats to his life that led quickly to his arrest, trial, and crucifixion. What a personal loss it was to Jesus when he was arrested and "they all left him and ran away" (Mark 14:50). Jesus knows what it is like to be abandoned by your friends and he knows what it is like to have friends who stay with you through it all, as the women did (Matthew 27:55-56).

A Man Named "Encouragement"

Barnabas was a model disciple. Read the story of Barnabas in Acts 4:32-37; 9:26-28; 11:19-26; 12:25; 13:1-5; 15:30-41. Barnabas means "son of encouragement," which is the word translated as son, which means, "to be like" something and the word *paraklete*, which is exactly the same word used for the Holy Spirit in John 14:16, 26; and John 15:26. It is the nickname given to Joseph the Levite from Cyprus by the apostles (Acts 4:36). Barnabas was a person you could count on to stand by you and be with you when you needed him. His story illustrates his character.

Barnabas stood with Paul and identified with him to encourage the apostles to trust and listen to Paul, who was a recent convert and a former enemy (Acts 9:26-28). The term "take hold of" in Acts 9:27 where Barnabas took hold of Paul in the presence of the apostles the same word that was used of Peter taking hold of Jesus (Matthew 16:23) to rebuke him. It is used of Jesus taking hold of Peter to rescue him from the stormy water (Matthew 14:31) and Jesus taking hold of a disabled person to give healing (Mark 8:23). The word translated "take hold" literally means "to draw to one's self" and was used to express affection and close identification by one person with another. Without Barnabas, we might never have heard of Paul.

Years later, Barnabas was being true to his name in "a ministry of encouragement (*paraklete*)" to new believers at Antioch, the third largest city in the Roman Empire (Acts 11:19-24). Barnabas left Antioch to look for Paul, found him at Tarsus and brought him to Antioch to help teach the new converts, who were first called "Christians" (Christ-like) at Antioch (Acts 11:25-26). The story of Barnabas reveals his strong role in expanding the inclusive gospel to all people. In Acts 15, the gospel of Jesus was finally seen to be the good news of God's unconditional love for all people. Nobody was left out.

It is fitting that the last mention of Barnabas tells of him standing by a young man named Mark, whom Paul did not like and did not want to take with them on their next trip. Barnabas left Paul and took Mark with him. Much later, Mark was reconciled with Paul (Colossians 4:10) to share in ministry with him again. Mark went on to give us the first written gospel of Jesus Christ. The "called alongside" ministry of Barnabas was incredibly important. When you stand with someone who really needs you as a friend, you never know what God might do through that person's life in the future.

Your Ministry of Encouragement

Read 2 Corinthians 1:3-7 for an impressive summary of the believer's call to "stand alongside" those who suffer pain and oppression. In this passage, the word "comfort" is *paraklete*, "called alongside." The word "tribulation" is the Greek word for "pressure." Our source of encouragement is God and our "being there" for each other is possible because God is within us. Read

Romans 15:1-7 for a powerful reminder that encouragement and perseverance in the Bible come from God, "May God, who gives perseverance ["super remain" or "never give up" in Greek] and encouragement [*paraklete*], grant you to be of the same mind with one another according to Christ Jesus. Therefore accept one another just as Christ also accepted you to the glory of God" (Romans 15:5-6).

The presence of the Spirit of Jesus in our lives gives power and wisdom to be a supportive friend in times of stress. As Benjamin Franklin said to John Hancock at the signing of the U.S. Declaration of Independence, "We must indeed all hang together, or, most assuredly, we shall all hang separately!"

Faithfulness Under Fire

The Hebrew Bible pictures God as steadfast, dependable, and unchanging. Frequently the terms "steadfast love" or "faithful love" are used to translate the Hebrew term *hesed*, meaning God's "covenant love" to all. The Greek word *paraklete* ("called alongside") was used in translating Isaiah 40:1, "Comfort ye, comfort ye, my people, says your God." Read Isaiah 40:1-11 and notice close relationships with the Gospel of John.

Studying the meaning of *paraklete* in the Bible, I was curious about how the Septuagint (Greek version) of Psalm 23:4 rendered "comfort" in "Your rod and your staff comfort me." I was not really surprised to see that it was *paraklete*. I looked up the Hebrew word that was being translated into *paraklete*. It is *naham*, which is an intensive form that means, "to console, comfort" from a word that means literally "to draw breath forcibly, pant, sigh, groan." This was an exciting discovery. God's comfort as God stands alongside us is given to us as we "breathe in" or receive encouragement from God. The Hebrew word for Spirit is *ruach*, which means "to exhale, breathe out forcibly." See Genesis 2:7 and Ezekiel 37, where breath, wind, and spirit are all the same word, *ruach*.

Psalm 23:4 paints a beautiful word picture of our comfort coming from God as God breathes out to us the life-giving Spirit and we breathe in and receive the Spirit. Jesus made this explicit after the resurrection, "Jesus breathed on them and said to them, receive the Holy Spirit" (John 20:22). When we faithfully stand with one another, we continue the work of the apostles, the ministry of Jesus, the mission of the Holy Spirit, and the comforting work of God.

"Comfort" originally had the primary meaning "to make courageous, brave, strong," from Latin *fortis*, from which we get, "fort, fortress, fortification, etc." Now, however, "comfort" implies soft and frail. We use "comforter" for a soft pliable bed covering. *Paraklete* means "to be called alongside" others, not to make them dependent and weak but to encourage them to be strong and brave and not to be victims. *Paraklete* equips you to live in hope, love, joy, and peace in Christ.

Has God's presence encouraged you lately? Has your presence with a friend given encouragement and courage to stand firm and not give up? One MCC called its outreach and support ministry for People with HIV/AIDS the "*Paraklete* Project." How can you and your group earn the nickname Children of *Paraklete*?

Questions for Study and Discussion

1. How has this lesson helped you to clarify the meaning and purpose of following Jesus in ministry to others?

2. What special skills and abilities do you have that will help you to lift up and encourage people who have been oppressed and put down by sick and destructive religion?

3. What is the most encouraging and helpful ministry that you ever received from someone else?

Additional Resources

How to give courage and support to others is the subject of many recent books. The HIV/AIDS epidemic in our community has given rise to a great many carefully researched and prepared guides for caregivers. *The Aids Caregiver's Handbook*, ed. Ted Eidson, St. Martin's Press, 1988, published at the height of the HIV/AIDS crisis.

A book that helped me is Wayne E. Oates and Kirk H. Neely, *Where to Go for Help*: Westminster, 1972.

See also Louis F. Kavar, Ph.D., *Families Re-Membered: Pastoral Support for Friends and Families Living with HIV/AIDS*: Chi Rho Press, 1993.

Also by Louis Kavar, *To Celebrate and to Mourn: Liturgical Resources for Worshiping Communities Living with AIDS*: Chi Rho Press, 1989.

A. Stephen Pieters, *"I'm Still Dancing!" A Gay Man's Health Experience*: Chi Rho Press, 1991.

Lesson 38

Love in Action

† **Preparatory Bible Reading:** John 13:1-35; Philippians 2:1-13; Romans 15:1-7

Child abuse, spousal abuse, alcohol and drug abuse, and abusive use of the Bible and religion all have been called "love." So-called "tough love" has been used to justify parents casting their gay children out of their home and abandoning them to the streets of big cities. Child abuse has been the result of the kind of twisted thinking that says, "I love you; so this is going to hurt me more than it does you." Distorted destructive expressions of love abound in the world, including the world of gay, lesbian, bisexual, and transgendered people and their families and friends.

One of the most destructive attacks upon gay people has been the use of fundamentalist religion in the "ex-gay" ministries to torture gays and lesbians with religious "reparative therapy" to offer "the cure" and try to change gay people into heterosexuals. Many bruised and broken lives have been the result. Depression, isolation, and self-destructive behavior including suicide have been the sad results of this fraudulent industry. The American Psychiatric Association in October 1998 issued a strong rebuke against the "ex-gay" abuses and declared that there is no evidence that anyone's sexual orientation can be changed.

Love in Action as a Movement

One of the earliest "ex-gay" movements, which Kent Philpot began in Marin County, California, was called Love in Action, which now has joined with Exodus International. The story of Love in Action was told by the founder, Kent Philpot, in a book called *The Third Sex?*, (Logos International, 1975). The following statement was released shortly after the publication of the book,

"With deep regret it has come to our attention that Logos Press is continuing to publish and sell a book titled *The Third Sex?* by Kent Philpot. This book in its cover subtitle says, 'These six stories of how homosexuals were changed through Christ will save our children' and its contents, falsely and erroneously used our testimonies as its proof. Nothing could be farther from the truth, and we are appalled at the deceit involved in using false claims, false examples, and false hopes to entice people from all over the country to join Love in Action with the appeal of 'hope and change' used in their brochure and the examples in this book used as their proof.

"We cannot with good Christian conscience allow these falsifications to continue. Too many lives are at stake, and these claims must be amended, indicating that none of us have ever changed our homosexual orientation. We are living at this time satisfying Christian lives with our mates. As ex-charter members of Love in Action, it is imperative that we make public the true facts so that possibly fewer people will be lured into a situation that at best may prove detrimental and untenable if not out-right damaging."

The statement was signed by four of the six people described in the book. A court ruling forbade the book being published in the United States. It is still available in England.

This information was made available through the ministry of Evangelicals Concerned, founded by Dr. Ralph Blair, (who can be reached at 311 East 72nd Street, New York, NY 10021 and at Web site www.ecinc.org). One of my best friends, John Evans, was one of the founding members of Love in Action and left the program when his best friend killed himself because he could not make the changes demanded by the group. John was featured in the Rev. Sylvia Pennington's book *Ex-Gays? There Are None* (Lambda, 1989), and has appeared frequently on national television and in documentaries to tell the truth about the destructive results of the "Ex-Gay Fraud."

John told me that the hardest thing he ever did was to break up with his lover of 14 years because the preacher told him to. (The preacher, not Jesus, told him to do it!) John is a well-known and successful artist in the Bay Area. John introduced me to the Rev. Sylvia Pennington and arranged for me to be in the documentary "One Nation Under God" with him and to be in a "Good Morning America" special with him when I was Pastor of Golden Gate MCC in San Francisco.

Another survivor of "Love in Action" is also a friend of mine in San Francisco who has recently put his story and many helpful links on the Internet in his Web site, "Ex-Gay Nomad." Other Web sites for "Ex-Ex-Gays" and many other similar groups are available.

"Love in Action" According to Jesus

We "love" coffee, movies, food, each other, our parents, our mates, and God. One word has to do too many different things. To define love, Jesus said, "Look at me and do what you see me doing." Jesus gave himself as the definition of love for those people who believed and followed him. To follow Jesus is to accept the life of Jesus as your guide and pattern for life.

The foot washing experience in John 13 is filled with important details and high drama. Stop and read John 13:1-35 a couple of times and let the actions and teachings sink in.

Love Never Gives Up

Jesus loved his own that were in the world and "loved them to the end." The word "end" is the Greek word *telos* and means, "to reach a goal." It is also the cry of Jesus from the cross, "It is finished" (John 19:30). It means that Jesus did not quit loving until his goal was reached. No matter what others did, Jesus kept on loving. Jesus never said, "I do not love you any more," not even to Judas!

Do you put a price tag on your love? Do you directly or by implication tell those you love that your love depends on what they do for you? If so, your love has yet to grow up and become like the love of Jesus. When you receive Jesus into your life, God's love is "poured into your heart by the Holy Spirit given to you" (Romans 5:5). See Paul's description of "the mind of Christ" in Philippians 2:1-11 and in Romans 15:1-7.

Self-Confidence and Practical Support

Jesus, "knowing that God had given all things into his hands and that he had come forth from God and was going back to God, rose from supper and laid aside his robe; and taking a towel, girded himself about" (John 13:3-4). Jesus knew why he was there. Emphasis is placed on Jesus "knowing" in John 13:1, 3, and 11 and when Jesus said, "I know where I came from and where I am going" (John 8:12-15). Do you? When you are confident of who you are and why you are here, you can humble yourself and be a "slave" along the way. Our self-conscious uncertainty about our own identity and personal value undercuts our ability to be humble and to give ourselves in service to others.

The Highest Rank is Slave

Jesus laid aside his outer cloak and was dressed as a slave without the identifying clothing of a teacher. The great outer cloak was designed to indicate a person's rank and profession. Soldiers gambled for this robe at the cross. "Laid aside" is Greek *tithame* and was used also of Jesus "laying aside" his life in John 10:11, 15, 17, 18, and 15:13. To "take up" is Greek *lambano* in 13:12 and was used of Jesus "taking up" life again in John 10:18. Jesus was in total control. Confidence in your purpose in life and in your worth as an individual gives you the freedom to put your love into action no matter what that love demands.

Custom required that the host of a banquet should provide someone to wash the feet of guests. Usually the task fell to the lowest rank of slave. Dust from the streets was "unclean" because of contact with unclean animals and people. Washing the feet was of great religious importance in preparation for eating. According to religious law, a teacher could not require disciples to wash his feet. This is why Peter protested when Jesus stooped down to wash his feet. The word "clean" in John 13:10 and 15:2 is Greek *kartharos* from which "catharsis" comes and it usually meant religious, ceremonial purity. Giving and receiving cleansing in "you ought to wash one another's feet" (John 13:14) seems to refer to the continuing need for disciples to give and receive forgiveness and acceptance from each other. Jesus gave a dramatic, unforgettable demonstration of humble service as the highest expression of "love in action."

Can You Accept Help?

Love in action requires someone to love and some to receive love. Do you resist letting people help you? Why? Some times accepting help is harder than giving it. Accepting forgiveness is as important as giving forgiveness. I have always had more trouble letting people do something for me than doing things for others. Sometimes it is because of pride, but low self-esteem can also make us feel unworthy of help from others.

Who was more humble, Jesus for washing Peter's feet or Peter for letting Jesus do it? It took both of them for the foot washing to happen. When we celebrated the ancient ritual of foot washing in our church, we learned that washing someone else's feet is a lot easier and more comfortable than letting someone else wash your feet.

Jesus said finally, "I gave an example that you also should do as I did to you." The word "example" means, "to show under the eyes" from the Greek *hupodeiknumi* and was used in the Papyri for "illustration, example, warning." Jesus was saying, "Do not just read my lips. Read my actions." Jesus demonstrated that even the most humble act of service to others could be an act of God. Jesus used the Hebrew Bible idea of "Suffering Servant of God" to illuminate his own sense of mission in Matthew 12:18-21 and 20:17-28. See also Isaiah 42:1-4; 49:1-6; 50:4-9 and the great "Servant Song" in Isaiah 52:13 to 53:12.

Isaiah 55:11 spoke of "word of God" in the same terms as "servant of God." John 1:14 expressed the same idea of combining the "Servant" and "Word" of God, "The word became flesh and dwelt among us." The highest rank in the realm of God is slave. "Truly, truly I say to you, a slave is not greater than the owner; neither is the one who is sent greater than the one who does the sending. If you understand these things, you are blessed if you do them" (John 13:16-17). Jesus announced later, "As God sent me, I also send you" (John 20:21).

Contrast of Judas to Jesus

John 13:18-30 draws a sharp contrast between the humble act of Jesus in washing the feet of his friends and the decision of Judas to betray Jesus. Even Peter who boasted of his faithfulness was revealed to be vulnerable to denying Jesus under pressure. The contrast between Jesus and Judas is emphasized in the Gospels. Judas is the Greek form of the name Judah, from which the term "Jew" comes. On the cross, Jesus, a Jew, was labeled "the king of the Jews." Judas, however, is pictured as the hostile and resentful man who betrayed another Jew, Jesus. Was Judas angry because Jesus accepted the affection and loving care of Mary washing and kissing his feet? Judas condemned Mary for her waste of money and then went to the priests to betray Jesus. Read John 12:1-8; Mark 14:1-11; and Luke 7:36-50.

Judas betrayed Jesus with a "kiss" (Matthew 26:49; Mark 14:45), which in Greek is a special intensified word for kiss, *kataphilesen*, meaning "a passionate or lover's kiss." This special, intense word for "kiss" was used only two other times in the Gospels. One is in Luke 15:20 for the extravagant welcome of the prodigal son by the loving father, where the intensity probably indicated kissing repeatedly. The other is in Luke 7:38, 45 for the woman who anointed and "fervently kissed" the feet of Jesus. Jesus predicted the betrayal of Judas by quoting, "Even my bosom friend in whom I trusted, who ate of my bread, has lifted his heel against me" (Psalm 41:9).

Guests at the Last Supper "reclined" on their left side to eat from a low table in the middle of the room. The reclining guests leaned against each as they ate. They were arranged like the spokes of a wheel with their heads near the table and their feet stretched out behind them. This is how Jesus was easily able to get to their feet to wash them. The beloved disciple rested his head on the breast of Jesus, which placed him to the right of Jesus. Jesus could speak to Judas without the others hearing; so Judas was on Jesus' left, which was the place of greatest honor and meant that Jesus was leaning on Judas' breast when he leaned back to speak to him. The intimate relationship of Jesus to God was expressed in John 1:18, using the same Greek word to speak of Jesus being "in the bosom [breast]" of God.

Jesus loved Judas to the end. Judas was still in the place of the most intimate friend at the supper. Had Judas once been "the beloved disciple?" The Gospel of John calls someone else (probably John) the beloved disciple, five times beginning with the Last Supper, in John 13:23; 19:26; 20:2; 21:7, and 21:20. Read John 21:15-25 and notice how the disciples misunderstood what Jesus said about the beloved disciple. Also note the detailed description of the beloved disciple as "the disciple whom Jesus loved; the one who also had leaned back on Jesus' breast at the supper and said, 'Lord who is the one who betrays you?'" Why do you think that this detailed identification was given?

Pilate said that the priests delivered up Jesus for envy. Did envy also motivate Judas to deliver up Jesus to the priests? We do not know what went on in the heart and mind of Judas. Judas' passionate lover's kiss of Jesus, however, cannot be ignored. What did it mean? Was Judas mocking the love that he once had shared with Jesus? Judas was clearly disappointed in Jesus for not winning the effort to save his life. Was he also a disappointed lover, angry that Jesus had let a woman passionately kiss and love his feet and angry that another disciple was beginning to get attention from Jesus that Judas resented?

Judas sold Jesus to the priests for "30 pieces of silver" (Matthew 26:6-16, see also Exodus 21:32 and Zechariah 11:12-17), which was a highly symbolic amount, "the price of a wounded slave." Was Judas' selling price the value that the angry, rejected Judas wanted everybody to know that he placed on this man that he once loved and admired? Judas regretted his betrayal and killed himself in a dramatic suicide in which his body fell and splattered on the rocks. The dynamics of these dramatic events speak volumes about men loving other men and having to face and deal with misunderstandings, rejection, and disappointments. It does not say whether there was a gay dynamic at work with Jesus or his disciples, but Jesus and his friends were truly human. They were loving, affectionate, sensitive, and caring. They lived in a threatening atmosphere of fear, hate, violence, and death. How Jesus and the disciples handled stress and conflict is given in the Gospels to instruct and help us and all other alienated and oppressed people as we attempt to put our "love in action."

Questions for Study and Discussion

1. Who do you most identify with in the foot-washing story? Why? What have you most resisted letting others do for you?

2. Do you see any gay attitudes in Jesus and his friends? What does the foot washing tell you about Christian ministry? What in John 13 made you the most uncomfortable?

3. Reflect on John 13:34-35. Why do you think that Jesus replaced all Law with one new commandment, "Love one another just as I have loved you?"

Additional Resources

This lesson is longer than most because of the importance of the information included in order to make clear the distinction between destructive "support" groups and the kind of healthy and healing group that Jesus led during his ministry. You may want to devote two sessions to it.

M. Scott Peck, M.D., *The Road Less Traveled*: Touchstone, 1978; and *People of the Lie*: Touchstone, 1983.

Read the material abut Judas and the Last Supper in William Barclay's great *Daily Study Bible Series*: Westminster (revised edition, 1975) on Matthew, Mark, Luke, and John, where he gives startling and informative details that set the physical and cultural stage for the events surrounding the Last Supper and the betrayal by Judas. Special help is given in his description of the setting of the Last Supper in the Gospel of John.

This *Daily Study Bible Series* by William Barclay covers all of the New Testament books and is the best brief commentary I know. Unfortunately Barclay is homophobic and imports anti-gay ideas into the three "clobber" passages in Paul's letters, just as many British Bible scholars do, but aside from that he gives the best and most accessible background and cultural information that I know. Much of my material about Greek words and biblical backgrounds and culture come from Barclay.

The Rev. Sylvia Pennington, *Ex-Gays? There Are None*: Lambda, 1989.

Contact Evangelicals Concerned, founded by Dr. Ralph Blair, 311 East 72nd Street, New York, NY 10021 and at Web site www.ecinc.org.

See my Web site at www.truluck.com for links to "Ex-Gay Nomad" and "Ex-Ex-Gays" and to up-to-date information about the "Ex-Ex-Gay" movement.

Lesson 39

How to Include Everybody

† **Preparatory Bible Reading:** Acts 6:1-7

Assimilating widely diverse people into the new Christian fellowship was not easy. Growth in the early church created stress. The first serious conflict within the group of believers developed because some women were being left out and neglected because they were foreigners. This gave a great opportunity to demonstrate how to resolve conflicts within groups.

Face the Problem

Read Acts 6:1-7 for a short seven-verse study in good group dynamics. "While the disciples were increasing in number, a complaint [murmuring] arose on the part of the Greek speaking Jews against the native Hebrews, because their widows were being overlooked [neglected] in the daily serving ['deaconing,' the Greek word *diakonos*] of food."

The word "complaint" is the Greek word *goggusmos*, an onomatopoetic word that sounds like what it means. It expressed an undercurrent of hostility and smoldering resentment. Open anger had not yet broken out, but murmuring and muttering had started. This kind of mild resentment is easy to overlook and ignore, but resentment can build quickly into destructive and divisive hostility.

The first step in conflict resolution is to see the problem early before it gets out of control. The disciples were sensitive to the discontent of the people. They remembered what it was like to be left out and ignored. They responded with love and concern for solutions rather than blaming the people who were complaining or those who were serving. When people in religious groups feel slighted and left out, they often remain quiet, leave, and do not some back. When it is too late to do anything about it, people look around and say, "I wonder what happened to Sally?" How open and accepting are you to new people who come into your work, social life, or other groups? Do you know how it feels to be left out because of sex, race, age, education, income, sickness, or sexual orientation?

Jesus, as presented in the Gospels, was totally inclusive. Nobody was left out. The disciples recognized that discrimination based on sex, race, or religion was a deadly threat to their mission for Jesus. They moved as quickly as possible to find a solution.

Neglected and Overlooked

The word "neglected" is used only this once in the New Testament. The Greek word is defined as "overlook, neglect, leave unnoticed." This made me think of my favorite Liberace story. In a music video, Liberace came to the piano in his usual glorious costume of feathers and sequins, twirled around, flashed his famous smile, spread his arms, and said, "I didn't dress like this to go unnoticed!" Many lesbians and gays, however, do go unnoticed, usually on purpose. The closet is an escape from being noticed. You may not want people to know you are gay.

Liberace did not want to be noticed as being gay. He died of HIV/AIDS and has a memorial panel in the Names Project Quilt. After his death, his ex-lover sued his estate in a very public act of revenge. Yet Liberace had once gone to court to prove that he was not gay and won! The showman who worked hardest to be noticed did not want to be noticed as gay. Our human nature and fear of homosexuality keep us apart from one another. The Book of Acts tries to show that the Spirit of Jesus empowers unity in diversity. We do not by ourselves have enough in common to keep us together.

Including Everybody in the Solution

The first response of the twelve was to ask everybody to help solve the problem.

> The twelve summoned the multitude of the disciples and said, "It is not desirable for us to neglect the word of God in order to serve [*diakonos*] tables. But select from among you seven people of good reputation ["well-witnessed-to"], full of the Spirit and of wisdom [the Greek word *sophia*, meaning "practical good sense"], whom we may put in charge of this task. But we will devote ourselves to prayer and to the ministry ["deaconing," *diakonos*] of the word" (Acts 6:2-4).

People who suffer neglect and discrimination have to be part of the solution, or there will be no solution. Progress in unity requires teamwork. The twelve were the leaders. They no longer were called "the disciples," because all believers were "disciples." The twelve consulted the whole group. Nobody was left out in solving the conflict. This approach worked, for "the saying pleased the whole multitude" (Acts 6:4). Jesus had prayed for this kind of unity among his followers in John 17:20-26.

Being an activist in lesbian, gay, bisexual, and transgendered issues has made me very aware that I can speak only for myself. I cannot speak for women, for people of color, or for anyone else. My job is not to speak for others but to encourage and help them to speak for themselves. One of the main reasons for these studies is to encourage and equip you to speak for yourself and "to give a reason for the hope that is in you" (1 Peter 3:15).

I do not even speak for all gay men. I do not speak for Metropolitan Community Church. I speak only for myself. I hope and pray, however, that some of what you learn in this book will help you to develop more confidence and a sense of personal worth that will equip you to speak more effectively for yourself.

Characteristics of Problem Solvers

Credibility, the Spirit of Christ, and common sense were the characteristics of the seven people selected to be special agents for conflict resolution. They shared three characteristics of problem solvers.

Good reputation comes from the same Greek word as "martyr" and refers to those who live their faith even to the point of dying for what they believe. It is the same word translated as "witness." "Good reputation" literally means, "well witnessed to." Leadership requires acceptance and respect from those who are led. Spiritual leadership is earned, not bestowed. New Testament leadership always was based on evidence of the Spirit of Christ in the leader. The only power that spiritual leaders have is their influence. Nobody can force others to love and to act like Jesus.

Being Filled with the Spirit is the second quality of leaders. To be filled with the Spirit is to be filled with Jesus. Jesus promised to give the Spirit and said, "I will come to you" (John 14:16-18). "Filled" means that inferior, selfish motives and attitudes will be pushed out by being filled with the Spirit of Jesus. Paul made the contrast, "Do not get drunk with wine, for this is excess [the Greek *asotia*, meaning "without controls"]; but be filled with the Spirit" (Ephesians 5:18).

Often in the Book of Acts, the disciples duplicated the actions of Jesus. Jesus was inclusive; so were the believers, though it took them most of the first 15 chapters of Acts to get there. Jesus focused all attention on himself, "Follow me." All early preaching was about Jesus and his life, death, and resurrection. Jesus healed a cripple; so did Peter. Stephen was killed for his attack on the Temple and like Jesus, asked God to forgive his attackers and then committed his spirit to God (Acts 7:59-60).

Common sense is the third quality of good leadership. "Wisdom" is the Greek word *sophia* and means "practical or usable knowledge." To be "full of wisdom" is to be equipped to use knowledge sensibly and appropriately in practical service.

The seven leaders of reconciliation were to "wait on" or "serve" tables (Acts 6:2). "Wait on" is in Greek *diakonein*, from which the word "deacon" comes. *Diakonos* is a Greek word for "slave" and is made up of *dia* ("raise, go through") and *konis* ("dust"). It refers to the practical work of a slave "raising a cloud of dust" in hard work. *Diakonos* is probably best translated as "practical service." The same word is used of the twelve devoting themselves to prayer and the "ministry" (*diakonos*) of the word.

Practical service included preaching and teaching the gospel as well as serving tables fairly and without discrimination. Both were ministries of reconciliation in the service of Christ. Stephen was one of the first seven deacons who also proclaimed and taught the gospel of Jesus in Acts 6 and 7. He became the first martyr of the church. To be a deacon is to do whatever is needed at the time in order to serve Jesus and other people effectively.

The Touch of Love and Support

The whole multitude, not just the twelve, selected the seven deacons and brought them to the apostles, prayed for them, and laid their hands on them. The whole group was involved in each step of the healing process. "Laid hands on them" reflected a well-established tradition that expressed love, support, and identification of one person with another. It went back to the ancient Hebrew practice of the worshipper laying hands on a sacrificial animal to identify with it when it was offered as a gift to God. Only if worshippers also gave themselves to God along with the animal was the sacrifice meaningful. (See Numbers 8:10-12; 27:18; Deuteronomy 34:9; Leviticus 1:4; 3:2, 12, 13; Micah 6:6-8; and Psalm 51:16-17, where it is clear that sacrifices are meaningless without faith.)

Often the loving touch, being hand in hand, a pat, a hug, or a kiss can communicate more encouragement than words ever could. Jesus frequently touched people to identify with them and to give healing and hope. "Laying on of hands" was not a means of giving spiritual authority in Acts 6. The seven already had spiritual authority by being "of good reputation and filled with the

Spirit and wisdom." Laying on of hands by the whole group was saying, "We are with you in the work you will do on behalf of all of us. We love and support you and pray for you." Volunteers always need support and encouragement from the group to carry out their tasks. This powerful story in Acts tells how these simple and practical steps preserved unity in the church and led to greatly expanded outreach to new groups, including many priests.

Why People Fight in Church

A preacher once said, "Jonah had the dignity of being swallowed by a whale, while I am being nibbled to death by minnows!" Paul warned about destructive church conflicts, "You shall love your neighbor as yourself. But if you bite and devour one another, take care lest you be consumed by one another" (Galatians 5:14-15).

Why do people fight in church? Nothing undercuts the evangelistic and missionary outreach of the churches like internal conflict and competition for control. What lies behind the eternal struggle for power and control in many local churches? Why do many church leaders talk and not listen? What is the origin of the strong compulsion in church for people to take over and tell other people what to do and not do? Is it unresolved parent versus child conflict from the past? Why are some people quite willing to destroy their own church in order to have their way about insignificant issues like where the piano should be or who should or should not be allowed to play it?

How have the churches survived centuries of internal squabbling, division, and conflict? Have churches really survived for any healthy and redemptive function in the midst of generations of civil war? These are just some of the questions that lesbian and gay Christians have to ask as they seek to find and follow the will of God for their spiritual future. Does new understanding of God's unconditional, inclusive love for all people demand new forms of ministry and worship and community?

We stand at the threshold of a new millennium and unparalleled freedom and opportunity to start over with new beginnings as the gay and lesbian children of God. We can repeat the mistakes of the past or look with fresh eyes at the people around us and at ourselves. We can learn from the past and build on what has gone before us by being objective, open minded, and informed. We have a lot of choices to make. One of them is whether to fight each other or focus our energy under the guidance of Jesus in positive and loving service to each other and to the world around us. God helps us to make the right choices!

Questions for Study and Discussion

1. List the steps taken to solve the problem of neglect and discrimination against minorities in Acts 6:1-7. Which step was most important? Which step is most neglected today?

2. In what way is personal evangelism influenced by how we handle internal conflicts? What problem of conflict or discrimination has been most difficult for you? Why?

Additional Resources

Dietrich Bonhoeffer, *Life Together*: Harper, 1954.

Recent practical and useful studies about church conflicts include, Kenneth C. Haugk and R. Scott Perry, *Antagonists in the Church: How to Identify and Deal with Destructive Conflict*: Augsburg, 1988.

G. Lloyd Rediger, *Clergy Killers: Guidance for Pastors and Congregations Under Attack*: Westminster/John Knox, 1997.

Lesson 40

Group Dynamics According to Jesus

† **Preparatory Bible Reading:** Matthew 9:35 through 10:20; 20:17-34; Luke 6:1-38

Jesus is our guide to group recovery and healing. Jesus never heard the term "group dynamics," but he demonstrated all of the insights and skills in developing a recovery and spiritual support group that are currently accepted and followed today. Jesus is our best teacher. What was so special about how Jesus developed and led small groups?

The story of Jesus in the Gospels is intertwined with the story of the group of disciples who followed Jesus and who continued his mission and ministry when he was gone. You are involved in groups, even if you only talk to people on the Internet or on the phone. The crucial feature of the group that Jesus developed was that Jesus took the initiative to invite people to join him. Jesus was the center and reason for the existence of the group. Jesus gave only one consistent invitation, "Follow Me!" Any group that is patterned according to the Jesus group is centered in Jesus, listens to Jesus, memorizes what Jesus said, follows the Spirit of Jesus, and carries out the compassionate healing ministry of Jesus.

Teaching People to be Teachers

Jesus taught the people in his group with the view that they would duplicate and multiply his ministry and would themselves become teachers. At the end of the group program of Jesus, in the Great Commission, Jesus told the group members to "teach all people what I have taught you." The group was not an end in itself. The group existed in order that the people in the group could become equipped to go out and enable other groups and new disciples to follow the risen Jesus Christ and change the world!

> After Jesus was crucified and raised from the dead, an old story goes that Jesus came into the presence of God and the heavenly host. One of the angels asked Jesus what will happen next. "You lived the life of love, compassion, and healing like no other. You suffered and died for all people and you were raised from the dead by the glory of God. Now, how will the world ever know what you did?" Jesus replied, "I have left my friends to tell the world about me and to continue what I began." The angel said, "But Jesus, what if Peter goes back to fishing and Matthew returns to the tax tables, and all of the others neglect your mission and drift back into their former lives and do not continue your work, what is your other plan?" Jesus said, "I have no other plan."

Either you and I and other gay Christians will change the world for our own people, or our world will not be changed. The church has always been one generation away from extinction. What you and your group does now will determine the future. Jesus promised, "Truly, truly I tell you, whoever believes in me will do even greater works than you have seen me do, because I return to God" (to send my Spirit to you). Read John 14:1-31. Are we there yet?

A Varied and Inclusive Group

The Jesus Group was drawn from many ages, backgrounds, personalities, and points of view. We know that the group included women (Luke 8:1-3). Read these verses again now. Variety in the group was both a source of great learning and a cause for tension and stress that provided the setting for Jesus to teach what discipleship really meant.

The disciples included young people in their mid-teens, older professional people like Matthew the tax collector, and religious fanatics like Simon the Zealot, women like Mary Magdalene, and many others. It is obvious that Jesus saw far more potential in each person than they saw in each other or in themselves.

Conflict Resolution

The Jesus Group experienced daily conflict and learned how to handle conflict. A struggle among the disciples as to who was greatest or who should be in control was on-going. Jesus dealt with these times of tension on the spot as soon as he was aware of them. He used very simple, direct, and clear examples to deal with conflict. He defined true greatness by taking a child (the Greek word used means a child about two years old) in his arms. Jesus said that unless the people in the group turned (the same idea as "repent") and humbled themselves as this little child, they would not even see the realm of God, much less be leaders in it.

Recently I asked Edwin Warren, my sister's husband, what is the chief characteristic of a child. I asked because he is one of the best-known experts in California on early child care programs. He answered immediately, "A child is dependent." My sister, Jackque Warren, also an early child care specialist, agreed. She has written a college text, *Early Child Care in America*, in order to show how child care has developed and changed in the United States. A little child like the one Jesus picked up is dependent. What does that tell you about you and me and our role in a group? We are dependent, but on whom do we depend? God? Perhaps each other?

The Highest Rank in a Group

Jesus frequently had to remind his followers that the highest rank in his group was slave (See John 13). We follow Jesus and learn to do for people whatever they need. When Jesus washed his disciples' feet he showed that when you know who you are and your purpose in life you can stop along the way and be a servant whenever you are needed.

When the compassion that the Spirit has placed in your heart begins, you respond to people in need as if they were you. You take time to listen and get involved in the hurt and confusion of others. You do not let people suffer in fear, self-hate and self-rejection. With God's help, you find a way to be present in love and healing. "Compassion" means to feel yourself the hurt and suffering of another person as though it was happening to you.

A scene in the movie, "Airplane," has an hysterical woman who was out of control. There is a long line of people waited their turn to slap her, yell at her, and abuse her. It was a hilarious scene, until you realize that you have somehow seen that kind of scene in church!

Do Not Hurt People Who Are Asking for Help

Years ago in a small Baptist church where I was student pastor in Louisville, a woman Sunday School teacher came to me after the Wednesday prayer group meeting and whispered that she needed my prayers. She told me that she had suffered for a long time from depression and recently had to go back to her doctor for electric treatments. I assured her of my prayers and support. I asked her why she did not tell the group to pray for her. She said, "Oh no. I could not do that. They would criticize me for it!"

I was about to reply when another woman in the church came up and interrupted, saying, "What is this I hear about you, Joan, going back to that doctor. Don't you know that if you have faith in God you wouldn't have to go to a psychiatrist!"

That was one of the few times that I was truly flabbergasted by something in church. I said, "How could you say that to Joan! She is hurting and needs your love and support and not to hear condemnation and criticism!" She backed off a little and tried to be consoling. But it was crystal clear why Joan did not feel that she could safely tell her need to the group and receive the support that she needed.

Any group that is more social than compassionate and more concerned with looking good than with being available to others cannot really be following Jesus. Jesus always entered into the frame of reference of needy people and saw things from their point of view. Doing this, Jesus was able to draw wounded and oppressed people out of their self-pity and pain and introduce them to the God who truly accepted them, loved them, and was available to them to give them healing and hope. Remember that groups, like people, can be sick, abusive, and dysfunctional.

Groups Do Not Need to Be Tightly Controlled

Many leaders and group members are threatened by the freedom of spiritual recovery. Groups move along quite well without someone being in charge and running the show! The need to be in control is something that should be discussed by the group whenever it is obvious and interferes with the freedom of participation in the group. Jesus often let the dialogue and discussion of the group flow along and reveal attitudes and problems that the whole group could address in order to grow and learn.

One problem faced by spiritual support groups sponsored by churches is the persistent need that church leaders often have to be in control. What is really wrong with allowing groups to run themselves any way that they want to? They are going to do it anyway if the group is going to be a truly dynamic support and recovery experience. Nobody outside of a group really knows what the group ought to do. Trust the Holy Spirit to lead the people in the group to find and follow the leadership of Jesus for themselves. If they cannot, then someone telling them what to do will certainly not make them do the "will of God," whatever that is, in the group. Get to know how the Quakers do it. They know.

Part of the healing that takes place in the loving and accepting atmosphere of a Christ-centered group is the result of people feeling safe enough to let go and allow the Spirit to take over and control their ideas and feelings. Letting go not only means letting go of control over yourself but also letting go of trying to control others. A frequent act of control is to say to someone who is sad or angry, "You shouldn't feel that way."

Well, why not? If you feel sorrow or anger it is genuine for you. Who has the right to tell you what you should or should not feel?

A more helpful response to grief or anger would be to say, "How can I help you?" To say, "I know what you mean," or the vaguely omnipotent, "I see," is also an invasion of another person's emotional space. Only God "knows what you mean." Often the emotional person does not know himself or herself what they mean. Do not play God by being the "all knowing" and "all seeing" one. Let people be themselves without having to endure your opinion of what they should or should not feel. Learn to respond to people with nonjudgmental words like, "Tell me more," or just polite, noncommittal sounds. The inflection in your voice can be clearly judgmental even with a barely audible grunt, so be careful how you sound.

Learn that you do not have to say anything. Attentive listening can be redemptive and healing. Pay attention to other people and encourage them to be free to share as much or as little as they want to. Whatever you do, learn to listen; and listen to learn.

Questions for Study and Discussion

1. What did Jesus teach you about group dynamics in the way that he handled conflict among the disciples about who will be the greatest?

2. What attitudes and actions by Jesus helped you to understand your own group role better? Be specific. Look up the suggested passages from the Bible and find exactly what Jesus did and said that helped you.

3. What have you read that might help your group function more effectively?

Additional Resources

When I finished my doctoral dissertation on group dynamics in 1968, the world was already flooded with many books on groups. One problem was weeding through the mountain of literature to find really helpful sources. I went back to the seminary for my doctorate in part to try to understand small groups in the church. I found that nobody really perfectly understands groups. No two groups are alike and no group stays exactly the same even from meeting to meeting. You learn group dynamic by experience. Learn to listen to other people. That is the basic key to successful groups.

The best help in a book is probably Reuel L. Howe, *The Miracle of Dialogue*: Seabury, 1963.

Become familiar with some basic books on human relationships, like the entertaining and practical book by Eric Berne, *Games People Play: The Psychology of Human Relationships*: Grove Press, 1964.

Chapter 16

The Eleventh Step

Learn to Share Your Faith

Did someone help you to become a Christian? Have you ever helped anyone become a Christian? Have you shared with anyone else your experience of coming out as gay? These questions are important as you consider the Eleventh Step in recovery from Bible and religious abuse. Telling your good news can be fun. It is also a great challenge. These four lessons will help you think through and become better equipped to share your faith with other people. Write out your own experience with God and share it.

"Always be prepared to explain to anyone who asks you a reason for the hope that is in you, yet with gentleness and respect" 1 Peter 3:15. This verse was on the cover of my earlier book on personal evangelism in our community, *Invitation to Freedom* (Chi Rho Press, 1993, now out of print). Much of the material in *Invitation to Freedom* is also in this book.

"Jesus said, 'Follow me, and I will make you fishers for people'" (Matthew 4:19). Later, Jesus repeated his need for helpers, "Seeing the crowds, Jesus felt compassion for them, because they were distressed and downcast like sheep without a shepherd, and Jesus said to his disciples, 'The harvest is plentiful but the workers are few, ask God to send out workers into God's harvest'" (Matthew 9:35-38).

Read John 15:1-27 and John 17:18-23 as preparation for studying these lessons on finding and carrying out your mission of representing Jesus in your life and through your words.

Lesson 41

How Jesus Liberated Outcast People

† Preparatory Bible Reading: John 4:1-45

The first missionary to the Samaritans was a woman. This unnamed "woman at the well" was oppressed and outcast. Let's call her "Evelyn." She came to the well to draw water at the hottest time of the day when nobody else would be there. Evelyn wanted to avoid her neighbors, even though they were also oppressed and outcast Samaritans. She was condemned and rejected because of her lifestyle. She already had had five husbands and was not married to her present partner. Evelyn was an outcast among outcasts.

Read carefully through John 4:1-45 to gain a clear overview of this incident. Now let's look at the details. Jesus arranged to be available for a private consultation with Evelyn so that they could talk without interruptions. Often we can be insensitive to the need of profoundly wounded people to be protected from condemnation and rejection by others who do not understand or really care for them. Jesus was weary, but when he "sat thus by the well," he was in the posture of a teacher. Jesus was fully attentive. Some of the greatest teachings by Jesus were to a single individual. Never underestimate the significance of any person you meet and have the opportunity to help. You may not be able to change the world, but you may be talking to someone who can.

Jesus Listened

Jesus demonstrated the basic principle of effective counseling in conversation with Evelyn. Caregivers are teachers. My faculty supervisor in clinical chaplain training at Kentucky Central State Mental Hospital said, "You can teach mentally ill people only if you first sit at their feet and let them teach you." Jesus listened. He took Evelyn seriously and talked with her on her own terms. The first step in reaching out to anyone is to listen. All disciples are called and in training to become teachers. Jesus the teacher always began by listening.

Dr. Wayne E. Oates taught thousands of ministerial students and wrote dozens of books on pastoral care and counseling at the Southern Baptist Theological Seminary in Louisville, Kentucky. He was my teacher and friend. When I was preparing to teach a college course on pastoral counseling, I called Dr. Oates and asked him what part of effective modern psychotherapy was demonstrated by Jesus in the conversation with the "woman at the well" in John 4. Dr. Oates replied, "Everything!"

Breaking Down the Walls

Jesus took the initiative. He spoke to the woman. He asked Evelyn to do something for him, "Give me a drink of water." In this simple request, Jesus cut through layers of hostile tradition and personal pain to touch Evelyn's heart. Jesus broke the Jewish rules when he spoke to the woman. No Jewish rabbi would ever speak to a woman in public, not even to his own mother. Later, the disciples were amazed that Jesus talked to a woman.

Letting others do something for you is a gift to them. Evelyn suffered from abysmally low self-esteem. Jesus could have given her a beautiful lecture on her personal worth and God's love. She would not have believed a word of it, however, and would have been unmoved by any advice to feel better about herself. In a stroke of therapeutic genius, Jesus shocked Evelyn into beginning to recognize her worth as a person.

Evelyn replied with a question about why a Jew would ask a Samaritan woman for a drink of water. The Jews "have no dealings" with Samaritans. "Have no dealings" means literally "not to touch, handle, or use." Jews would not use a cup that had been touched by a Samaritan or any foreigner. A cup or bowl that had been touched by a Samaritan was "unclean" and useless to a Jew. Jesus had nothing to use for water. He had to drink from Evelyn's cup.

Who Am I and Who Are You?

Jesus engaged in creative and redemptive dialogue. Jesus and Evelyn talked about how they thought of themselves. As the conversation continued, Evelyn opened up not only to Jesus but also to herself. Jesus refused to be distracted by debating whether he was greater than Jacob. Who Jesus was spoke for itself. Jesus wanted to help Evelyn, not win useless arguments about other people. Your greatest credentials in helping other people are whom you are as a person, your genuine interest in and respect for them, and your willingness to listen with an accepting and nonjudgmental attitude.

John Powell wrote, "I can help you to accept and open yourself mostly by accepting and revealing myself to you" (*Why Am I Afraid To Tell You Who I Am?* Argus, 1969, page 16). How did Jesus demonstrate this kind of self-giving openness with Evelyn? Jesus began the conversation by admitting that he was a needy person also. He was tired and thirsty. So was Evelyn. They began on common ground.

Jesus accepted Evelyn's questions and answered them. Instead of imposing his own agenda on Evelyn, Jesus let her decide what was important to her and what she wanted to talk about. Jesus respected Evelyn, and she grew in respect for him. She recognized that Jesus was a prophet and was invited into the knowledge that Jesus was far more than a prophet. Jesus said to Evelyn, "I AM is the one speaking to you." To be "I AM" is to be God (Exodus 3:19). The word "he" is not in the Greek. This first absolute "I AM" by Jesus to identify himself with God in the Gospel of John was spoken to a despised and outcast foreign woman! See other "I AM" sayings on Bread (John 6:35); Light (John 9:5); Door (John 10:7); Good Shepherd (John 10:11); Resurrection and Life (John 11:25); Way, Truth, Life (John 14:6); and True Vine (John 15:1).

Healing Wounded People One at a Time

Let Jesus be your teacher as we begin this series of studies on how to invite others to experience God's gift of love, acceptance, and freedom. Sometimes we are discouraged in our care for others because we feel that we are spending too much time and energy with just one person and their seemingly endless needs. Jesus frequently devoted time and attention to a single individual. In the Gospel of John, Jesus is often pictured giving his full attention to one person at a time, Nichodemus (John 3:1-21); the lame person beside the pool (John 5:1-18); the woman accused of adultery (John 8:1-15); Mary at the resurrection (John 20:10-18); and Peter at the end (John 21:15-23).

Jesus recognized the "image of God" in every individual he met. He saw potential for greatness in the most unlikely people. Jesus also knew who he was. His self-awareness and confidence are greatly emphasized in the Gospel of John. Jesus was willing to accept rejected and wounded people and to listen and enter into dialogue with them. To "follow Jesus" is to become open and available to people who most need healing and encouragement. To 1 John 4:11, "If God so loved us, we also ought to love one another," we can add, "If God listens to us, we also ought to listen to one another." Listening is an act of love. Learn to listen without judgment, attentively without distraction, and with honest openness to learning something important from the other person.

From Fear to Evangelistic Fervor

Evelyn was afraid of people. She had many reasons for fear of what people might do to harm her. Evelyn was different. She did not fit in. Evelyn's life was a mess. We do not know why. We do not have to know. Jesus never tried to analyze or condemn people for their problems. He simply listened and then reached out to help. What a refreshing new approach to people! Why do more teachers, preachers, friends, and therapists not do it this way? The attitude of Jesus is called "nonjudgmental." The one person who had the authority to judge, did not. As Jesus said to the woman, "I don't condemn you" (John 8:1-15). "God did not send Jesus into the world to judge the world but that the world [you] might be set free [saved]" (John 3:17). How did so many people who claim to follow Jesus jump off the track and take off into the wilderness of judgmental, legalistic religion?

After her conversation with Jesus, Evelyn left her original purpose (she left her water pot) to go boldly to the very people she had carefully avoided. She wanted to share her newfound self-esteem and purpose in life that Jesus had given to her. Was this an example of how "perfect love casts out fear" (1 John 4:18)? Evelyn was suddenly an effective evangelist ("messenger of good news"). She gave personal testimony of her experience with Jesus. Her main concern was to invite the people of her village to come and see Jesus for themselves. Her mission was successful.

As a result of the "preaching" of Evelyn to her people, many believed in Jesus and requested that Jesus stay for a while. Jesus changed his plans and stayed for two days with the Samaritans. In John 4:27, the disciples saw Evelyn as a problem and were "amazed" that Jesus talked with a woman. "Amazed" means "to be surprised (shocked) by something you did not expect." Jesus, however, saw Evelyn and the Samaritans as a great opportunity for ministry.

Why do you think that the disciples usually failed to see people as Jesus saw them? What did Jesus gain from talking with Evelyn? (See John 4:31-35.) What did Jesus mean by "I have food to eat that you do not know about"? What made Jesus feel good about himself? When wounded relationships are healed, everybody feels better.

From Victim to Hero

Evelyn was afflicted, oppressed, rejected, and frustrated in her life and in her relationships. She had plenty of reasons to see herself as a victim and to be downcast and depressed. Her healing conversation with Jesus changed her attitude about herself and thereby changed relationships and her life. The greatest gift you can give to a wounded and broken person, gay or straight, is a strong boost toward self-esteem. Feeling that you are useless, rejected, and isolated from others is depressing. A sense of failure and frustration with life has made many of us vulnerable to low self-worth and depression and has led us to sabotage even our most cherished relationships. Have you ever done this?

The Rev. Elder Troy Perry, Founder and Moderator of the Universal Fellowship of Metropolitan Community Churches (UFMCC) and for 30 years a strong spiritual leader and activist in the gay community, was not always the strong hero he is today. Troy tells how after he was thrown out of the Pentecostal church as a pastor because of his sexual orientation, he became depressed. His first lover had left him. He was alone in the room. He took razor blades and slashed his wrists to "end it all," but a friend got him to a hospital before it was too late. Then Troy turned back to God and listened. God told Troy, "You are my child. I love you, and I don't have any stepchildren!" Then God told Troy to start a church for gay people. He did. The last time I heard Troy preach, one of his main points was, "When God speaks to you, listen and do it." Has God spoken to you through the story of Jesus and Evelyn? What does this story tell you about your own mission to reach out to others and how to go about doing it?

Questions for Study and Discussion

1. The approach of Jesus to Evelyn was simple, direct, and effective. Why do you think that so many preachers and counselors have ignored it and looked to other sources for guidance in how to help people?

2. What in the story of Jesus and Evelyn most struck you as something that you need to remember in your conversations with others? Why has this been a problem for you?

3. Why do you think that Jesus let Evelyn go to arouse the interest of the Samaritans instead of going himself or sending his disciples? The disciples bought back food. Evelyn brought back the whole village! List principles of

reconciling and healing conversation that you see demonstrated by Jesus and Evelyn in John 4.

Additional Resources

Read "Samaritans" by Th. H. Gaster in *The Interpreter's Dictionary of the Bible*: Abingdon, 1962, 1990, R-Z, pp. 190-197.

Lesson 42

Let Jesus Borrow Your Boat

† **Preparatory Bible Reading:** Luke 5:1-11

When I was professor of religion at the Baptist College in Charleston, Bob, one of my students, was very successful in helping other students turn to God and experience Jesus in their lives. The remarkable changes that were evident in the lives of students were all positive and healthy. Bob was a basketball star and an outstanding student leader. I asked Bob how he got so many students to talk with him about God. He said, "I never approached anybody to talk to me. I was just there, and they brought up the subject of God to me. They asked me to tell them what I had in my life that made me so happy. I always told them it was Jesus, and one thing led to another, and they decided that they wanted to have the same thing. They opened the door for me to share my testimony with them." Bob let Jesus borrow his boat.

The first step in discipleship is just being there. The invitation of Jesus to young fishers at the Sea of Galilee to follow him is given in all four Gospels. Luke gives details that demonstrate the meaning of discipleship and evangelism. For Simon Peter, discipleship began by being helpful. Peter let Jesus borrow his boat so that the crowd could hear and see Jesus.

> The crowds were pressing around Jesus and listening to the word of God. Jesus was standing by the lake of Gennesaret [Sea of Galilee] and saw two boats lying at the edge of the lake; but the fishers had gotten out of them and were washing their nets. Jesus got into one of the boats, which was Simon's, and asked him to put out a little way from the land. Then

> Jesus sat down and began teaching the multitudes from the boat. Luke 5:1-3

Jesus did not ask Peter to preach. He just asked him to let him borrow his boat so that the people could hear and see better. Peter could have refused. He was tired and busy. He had already fished all night and had caught nothing. Nobody would have blamed Peter if he had declined the request of Jesus. After all, other boats were there also. If Peter had refused, would we have ever heard of Peter again! But he agreed. Peter began the long road to being a disciple and preaching at Pentecost by the simple act of being helpful. He let Jesus borrow his boat.

Sitting to Teach

Jesus always sat to teach, for sitting was the traditional posture of confidence and authority. Jesus did the teaching. Later at Pentecost, the Spirit of Jesus filled Peter, and even then, Jesus did the preaching through Peter, using Peter's contact with the great variety of people who had come to Jerusalem. Recall Matthew 10:20, "It is not you who speak, but the Spirit of God who speaks in you." Jesus said, "I will give you a mouth and wisdom" to speak effectively for me (Luke 21:15).

The crowds had pushed Jesus to the edge of the lake. The Sea of Galilee is 600 feet below sea level and is like water at the bottom of a large bowl. The land slopes sharply down to the water's edge and makes a natural theatre. If Jesus sat on the land, few would see and hear him clearly. Jesus needed a vantage point to reach the crowd with his teachings. Peter's boat gave Jesus just the right point of contact with the people.

The beginning of discipleship is letting Jesus "borrow your boat" and use your contact with others in your life to share the good news of God's unconditional love for all people. You have a point of contact that nobody else has with some of the people in your life. Jesus will do the teaching, just let him borrow your boat to do it.

Sharing Jesus With Your Friends

You do not have to go anywhere for Jesus to borrow your boat. Let Jesus speak through you to the people who already are the closest to you. Your partner, best friends, family, and others you already know well are your best points of contact. The first person that Andrew told about Jesus was his own brother, Peter (John 1:40-41). At the college, I learned very quickly that the greatest influence on students is other students. Just as the greatest influence on gay men and lesbians is other gay people. Personal evangelism was part of several courses that I taught at the college. Many of the students shared their faith with their roommates, parents, best friends, and people that they saw every day.

Bob helped Allen, his roommate, become a Christian and encouraged him to get involved in a Bible study group. Allen joined Campus Crusade and later went overseas as a Crusade missionary. Allen transferred to another college and began to lead a Bible study in his dormitory. Shortly before Allen was to go overseas again to become the first Campus Crusade volunteer to go to China, I saw him and asked him what he had been doing at his new college. He said that he was leading a Bible study on his hall. I asked how many students attended. He said "60!" I was surprised and asked how they got so many people into his room. He laughed and said that they meet in a parlor at the end of the hall. Once again I was reminded that you never know what God will do in the life of somebody you take the time to talk with about Jesus.

Saying Yes to Jesus

Peter said yes to Jesus' request to borrow his boat. The next step was more difficult. Jesus asked Peter to go out into the middle of the lake in the middle of the day to catch fish. Peter knew this was all wrong. He was a professional fisher. Jesus told Peter to launch out into the deep water and let down the nets for a catch. Fish were never caught in the middle of the lake in the middle of the day. The Sea of Galilee is about 8 by 13 miles and roughly oval in shape. The lake is 700 feet deep! It is part of the great geological depression that runs along the route of the Jordan

River from Mt. Hermon to the Dead Sea, which is 1300 feet below sea level. Fish stayed far below the surface of the lake except at night when they fed along the shore. Fishing was always done at night along the shore. Peter trusted Jesus and agreed to do what Jesus told him to do even though he did not understand it. Peter was willing to do something that he had never tried before simply because Jesus asked him to do it.

Jesus said, "Put out into the deep water and let down your nets for a catch." Peter replied, "Master, we worked hard all night and caught nothing, but at your word, I will let down the nets" (Luke 5:4-7). Luke uses the term "master" ("boss," literally "one who stands over") for Jesus where the other Gospel writers use "teacher." Peter recognized both authority and knowledge in Jesus and responded with obedience. When the nets were lowered they pulled in so many fish that the nets started to break and they called for their partners in the other boat to help them. They filled both boats and the boats began to sink.

Being radically obedient to Jesus leads to success and creates the necessity for partnership in ministry. You cannot do it all by yourself. We need each other. Success in making disciples begins by listening to Jesus and doing what he tells you to do. You hear God through Jesus in the Gospels and through the Holy Spirit. Christ-centered Bible study goes hand in hand with evangelism and ministry. The keys to discipleship according to Luke 5:1-11 are your willingness to be helpful, to let Jesus use your contact with people, and to listen to Jesus and do what he tells you.

Dynamic Discipleship

Peter's reaction to these events was emotional and humble. The word used to describe Peter's feelings, "amazement," in the original Greek means "to be rendered immovable." Peter realized his own real limitations and need for Jesus when he saw what Jesus could do when given full control.

"But when Simon Peter saw that, he fell down at Jesus' feet, saying, 'Depart from me, for I am a sinner, O Master!'

Amazement had seized him and all his companions because of the catch of fish they had taken. They included James and John, sons of Zebedee, who were partners with Simon. Jesus told Simon, 'Do not be afraid. From now on you will be catching people.' So when they bought their boats to land, they left everything and followed Jesus" (Luke 5:8-11).

Jesus made a powerful and compelling impression on the young fishers. They "left everything" to follow Jesus. In Matthew 4:19, Jesus said to them, "Follow me and I will make you to become fishers of people." In other words, Jesus planned to make them become like him, for he was fishing for and catching people.

Unlikely Disciples

Jesus selected some of the most unlikely people to be his friends, learn from him, and continue his work. These first disciples were teenagers. Peter was probably 15 or 16 years old. These young men still lived at home and worked with their father and the hired help. The average age for marriage was 14 for women and 16 for men. Average life expectancy was only 25. Jesus was 30 when he began his work as a teacher. We usually imagine people in the Bible being much older than they were.

The one requirement for discipleship is that you be open and receptive to listen and follow Jesus. Jesus needed people with open minds. None of his disciples were already trained religious teachers or leaders. Do you wonder why? Peter and the others were energetic and impulsive boys. They were open to new ideals and willing to take chances. Jesus spent three years with them and they changed the world. You, too, can change your world. Lesbian, gay, bisexual, and transgendered people alienated by the traditional churches and abused and oppressed by religion can change the world. Jesus regularly called people who were profoundly aware of their limitations and yet who were willing to "take a chance on God" and do what Jesus asked them to do.

Jesus selected and invited women, teenagers, social outcasts, misfits, moral failures, and a great variety of others to join his mission to all people. For God to use you and me to share God's love and acceptance in the midst of the most abused and rejected people we know will take a miracle. Jesus offers that miracle when he says, "Follow me and I will make you to become like me and reach out to people."

The beginning of our discipleship is the same as it was for Peter.

- Be helpful.
- Be willing to do the small and seemingly insignificant things.
- Use what you already have.
- Let Jesus borrow your boat to reach the people you already know.
- Keep your eyes on Jesus.
- Realize your human limitations.
- Listen to Jesus and do what he says.
- Launch out into the deep and let down the nets.
- Do your part in planting and watering and "leave the results to God!" (See 1 Corinthians 3:1-23).

The Middle of the Lake in the Middle of the Day

When I went from the pastorate to teach at the Baptist College of Charleston, I felt that I had been sent into the middle of the lake in the middle of the day where nobody ever caught anything. I found, however, that a college is no different from any other gathering of people. I saw hundreds of students turn to Jesus and experience a personal new spiritual beginning with God in their lives. And I also saw many of those students learn to share their faith and win parents, brothers and sisters, friends, and even enemies to a fresh look and a new start in life with Jesus Christ. Many of them are pastors, missionaries, and evangelists today. The story of personal evangelism and spiritual renewal at the college is an epic in itself and should be told in full some day.

When I left the college in 1981 and found myself drowning in the middle of the lake in the middle of the day in the gay world of Atlanta, Georgia, I gave up for a while on ever having any ministry for Jesus again. I was wrong. God still has the power and the will to use any of us who are willing to be used to bring others to Jesus. In Metropolitan Community Church (MCC) and in other settings, I have seen the spiritual power and life transforming ministries of hundreds of gay Christians. Multitudes of lesbian and gay people have turned to Jesus and become Christians without fear and in freedom from oppressive and abusive religion. They have continued to be gay, of course, for they have no choice about that. But they do have a choice about following Jesus, and many thousands of gay men and women are following Jesus and serving God in quiet lives of ministry in thousands of traditional churches as well as in MCC, other gay churches, public activism, and bold outreach within the gay community. It is a good thing that "it takes all kinds," because we are all kinds, to the glory of God and in the service of Jesus.

Questions for Study and Discussion

1. What have been the greatest hindrances that have kept you from sharing your faith with others? How has this lesson helped you to overcome some of them?

2. What steps can you take to stay close enough to Jesus to hear what he tells you? See John 15:1-27 for a fresh look at how Jesus expects us to relate to him for the sake of our ministry of "bearing fruit" in our lives. What fruit is your life producing?

3. Take the time to read the Gospel stories that are parallel to Luke 5:1-11 in Matthew 4:18-22; Mark 1:16-22; John 1:29-51 and the final story in John 21:1-25. What do these stories tell you about God's call to you to share Jesus with the people that your life already touches?

Additional Resources

John J. McNeill, *Taking a Chance on God*: Beacon, 1988.

Lesson 43

How to Help Others Experience Jesus

† **Preparatory Bible Reading:** Acts 8:26-40

The Book of Acts is a handbook on "how to do it" for the followers of Jesus. How to help others receive Jesus Christ into their lives is outlined in Acts 8:26-40. Every principle of effective personal evangelism is played out in action in this familiar story of Philip and the Ethiopian eunuch. Read Acts 8:1-25 to see how Philip was led in a new direction for his work to take the gospel beyond Jerusalem to Samaria, where the people were considered to be foreigners and religiously unclean. Philip had great success in Samaria. Peter and John came from Jerusalem to help out.

In the midst of his successful beginning of making disciples of "all nations," Philip was told by an angel (messenger) from God to leave his success and go down to the barren desert road south of Jerusalem. Philip obeyed, just as Peter obeyed when Jesus told him to go to "out into the middle of the lake in the middle of the day" to fish and later when God told Peter in Acts 10 to go to the Gentile home of a Roman soldier to reach out to "the wrong people." The progress of the gospel over cultural, racial, religious, and geographical barriers is the dominant theme in the Book of Acts, which was written along with the Gospel of Luke by the only non-Jewish writer of the New Testament.

One person was traveling on the desert road. He was a high government official returning home to Ethiopia. He was a eunuch. (See what Jesus said about eunuchs in Matthew 19:10-12.) He was not yet a Jewish convert or a "proselyte," but he was interested in the Jewish God and was what was called a "God fearer." He was open minded and searching and was reading from Isaiah 53:7-8 in the Hebrew Bible.

Be Prepared

Philip was prepared and ready to share the story of Jesus with whomever God sent his way. "Sanctify [set apart] Christ as Sovereign in your hearts, always being ready to make a defense to every one who asks you to give an account for the hope that is in you, yet with gentleness and reverence" (1 Peter 3:15). The word "defense" is the Greek word *apologia* and means "to reply" or "to give an explanation." The word "account" (*KJV*, "reason") is Greek *logos* and is the "word" made flesh in John 1:14. Read 1 Peter 3:13-18 and 4:8-11 about maintaining a loving attitude while defending your faith under pressure.

When you are well prepared to share your faith, you will find that people will come along who are open and receptive to you. Maybe God brings them into your life, or perhaps they have been there all along and you just were not yet confident and ready to talk about Jesus. Here are some practical steps you can take to become prepared to share your faith.

Examine Your Own Experience with God

First, be clear about your own experience. Write it out. Tell yourself all of the details of how you became convinced of your need for God in your life, how you made a decision to turn to God or to receive Jesus, and how this has affected your life. Take all the time and space you need to "tell it all." Study Paul's personal testimony in Philippians 3:4-21 and 4:10-13.

In sharing your experience, take about a fourth of the time to tell how you came to see your need for God's help and a fourth of the time to tell what you did to invite Jesus into your life. Use half of your time to tell what is happening now as a result of your decision. Some people have tried to write out their experience with Christ only to realize that they did not have one. This frequently has led people to turn to God and invite Jesus into their lives in a refreshing new experience of faith. A pastor came to me after one of my workshops on sharing your faith and said, "I have an unusual prayer request. I want you to pray with me as I invite Jesus to come into my life. I have never done that. I want to do it now." We prayed and he invited Jesus into his life. Since then, he has continued in a growing and enthusiastic ministry of outreach to others. It is impossible to give away what you do not have yourself.

Once you have written out all of the details of your experience of letting God come into your life, reduce it to one page so that you can share your basic experience in about two minutes. You are the world's authority on your own experience! Be prepared to share it clearly and quickly. The more you share your faith, the stronger you faith will become.

Come Out as a Gay Christian

Coming out as a gay or lesbian Christian is part of your personal testimony. This may be the hardest part. Write out your experience of discovering that you are gay. Tell yourself all of the details that you can remember. Tell how you first came out to yourself and to others. Describe how you feel about being gay or lesbian and how it has affected your life. It will not be easy, but try to reduce it to one page. Be prepared to share briefly in about two minutes your basic story of what being gay and Christian means to you. You can become prepared to "give a reason for the hope that is in you" as a gay Christian, but it will take time to think it through and write it out. It will be worth the effort for what this exercise says to you and how it prepares you to share your truth with others.

You will be far more likely to do this preparation exercise if you are sharing these materials with a recovery and support group. Try to get involved with at least one other person in doing this so that you can talk and listen to each other about what you are doing.

Keep a daily journal of your experiences and ideas. This can help you to keep up to date your personal testimony of what is happening to you as a lesbian or gay Christian. I started keeping a daily journal in 1987 and only wish I had started it sooner. I read back over parts of it and am amazed at some of the idiotic things I have done! It makes me wonder why I repeat the same mistakes in relationships over and over. You can learn a lot about yourself by keeping a journal. I hope that you give it a try.

Your knowledge of the Bible that you are gaining by studying the lessons in this book will also help to prepare you to "give a reason for the hope that is in you." Learn thoroughly what you need to know to answer your own questions. This will prepare you to help others.

By Invitation Only

Helping someone else into an experience with God comes by invitation only. Read Acts 8:27-31. When Philip saw the eunuch on the desert road, the Spirit said to Philip, "Go up and join the chariot." That was a risky thing to do. Here was a high government official traveling through a barren desert area and probably surrounded by guards. He was the treasurer for the Queen, so he was undoubtedly well protected. Suddenly, an unknown man comes running up to the chariot. But God had told Philip what to do and God was protecting Philip. Here was a big step beyond going to "the middle of the lake in the middle of the day." It was like jumping into the lake when you cannot swim!

When Philip got close enough, he heard the eunuch reading Isaiah the prophet and said, "Do you understand what you are reading?" The eunuch's reply was, "Well, how could I, unless someone guides me?" Then he invited Philip to come up and sit with him.

All of the people that I have helped to receive Jesus have in some way invited me to share my faith with them. I do not know how to break down resistance to the truth of the gospel. God seems to do that through the work of the Holy Spirit. All that I have to do is to be ready to share my faith when I am invited to do so. I do not try to argue with the fundamentalists about homosexuality and the Bible any more. If someone asks, I will be glad to give the truth about the Bible and homosexuality.

Taking the initiative to try to get through to people who have already made up their minds against the truth is a tiresome and fruitless exercise. I am trying every day to remember to enter into the spiritual space of others by invitation only.

The way was open for Philip. He began where the eunuch was, listened to him, and followed his lead.

Listen and Learn

As in all sharing, the first step is listening. Philip began by listening and asking a question. The eunuch was already reading the Bible but without much understanding. Philip got to know him by being helpful and interested. He took the eunuch seriously, listened and built on what he was already reading in the Bible. We always have to start where the other person is.

Many people who are interested in turning to God for help know at least a little bit about the Bible. Some, of course, do not. It depends on the individual how much you will use the Bible in your sharing. When you use biblical material, keep it very brief.

When I do use a Bible in sharing, I often use a copy of *The Good News Bible* New Testament (available in inexpensive paperback). At the appropriate time, we turn to Romans 10:9-13 and I ask the person to read it. We discuss it if they have questions and I ask if they want to do what the passage suggests. If they do, I encourage them to pray and help them to pray if they want me to. Then I mark the places that we read and give them the New Testament to keep. Learn by experience what seems most comfortable to you. The only totally wrong way to do it is not to do it at all.

I have often been amazed at how effective some really inadequate approaches to sharing have turned out. Just about the worst approach to witnessing I have ever heard happened to a young man, Lacoste Munn, who was the assistant pastor of my home church. He told us that when he was in high school he went on a Boy Scout overnight hike with his troop. Walking along a country road, he looked up and a man in a car sped by, threw something out of the window, yelled, "Read this!" and kept going. Lacoste picked up what turned out to be a gospel tract. He forgot about it until his mother found it in his clothes when he returned from the hike the next day. That night he read it and was touched by what he read. He decided to pray and trust his life to God. Later, he experienced a call to the ministry, went to seminary, served in my hometown church, got his doctorate, and became Professor of New Testament at the largest theological seminary in the world! You can never evaluate the effect of your attempts to share, no matter how strange they may seem. God can take really weak material (us) and make powerful things happen.

When in Doubt, Talk About Jesus

The eunuch asked Philip, "Please tell me, of whom does the prophet say this? Of himself or of someone else?" Philip "Opened his mouth and beginning from this scripture he talked about Jesus to him" (Acts 8:34-35). Whatever else you do in sharing your faith, keep attention on Jesus. You want people to respond to Jesus, not to you.

A Definite Decision Leading to Joy

Offer the other person an opportunity to pray to receive Christ. The response may be "yes" or "no" or "let me think about it." Some kind of response can be suggested. The eunuch responded by making a definite decision to receive Christ and requesting to be baptized immediately. "Look! Water! What prevents me from being baptized?" (Acts 8:36). Philip baptized him and "they came up out of the water, and the Spirit of God snatched Philip away; and the eunuch saw him no more but went on his way rejoicing" (Acts 8:39). The passage concludes with Philip "continuing to proclaim the gospel in all the cities until he came to Caesarea" (Acts 8:40). The inclusive gospel moved on.

Individuals follow Jesus in their life in their own personal way. If we follow Jesus, we respect each person as an individual and do not pressure people into being like us or doing things our way.

"Friends Don't Let Friends Die Without Jesus" is the most sobering bumper sticker I ever saw. Do not push, but show your love by really listening to others. Learn to share your experience as a gay Christian. Just be yourself. Share your truth, and leave the results to God.

Questions for Study and Discussion

1. How do you view the role of personal evangelism in the gay, lesbian, bisexual, and transgendered community? Have you tried to share your faith as a gay Christian? What was the result?

2. How can you separate negative, legalistic fundamentalism from the liberating message of Jesus in sharing of your faith with others? In what way is the church a help or a hindrance to sharing your faith with others?

3. What are the characteristics of evangelical evangelism that have created problems for you in sharing your faith with others? How has the story of Philip and the eunuch shown you a better way to share your faith?

Additional Resources

William Barclay, *Turning to God: A Study of Conversion in the Book of Acts and Today*: Westminster, 1994.

When I completed my doctoral dissertation on "Small Group Evangelism in the Local Church" in 1968, the mountain of books on evangelism was already insurmountable. Only one still stands out, Samuel Southard, *Pastoral Evangelism*: Broadman Press, 1962. Dr. Southard challenged the Southern Baptist practice of "instant evangelism" and the abusive use of mass evangelism especially when aimed at children. He pointed out that in one year, Southern Baptist churches reported over 2,000 baptisms of children 6 years old and under. Dr. Southard was a Professor of

Pastoral Care and contributed greatly to my becoming more objective and healthy in my understanding of evangelism.

My doctoral dissertation is available from the Library of The Southern Baptist Theological Seminary in Louisville, KY, and from "Thesis Abstracts."

Your best resource for this lesson is you. Do the exercises suggested about writing out your own experiences.

Lesson 44

Resources for Sharing Christ

† Preparatory Bible Reading: Luke 24:44-53 and Acts 1:1-8

You can share only what you have received. When Jesus sent out the disciples in Matthew 10:8, he told them to do what he had been doing, "Heal the sick, raise the dead, cleanse the lepers, cast out demons; freely you received, freely give." You cannot give what you do not have. The first and most important resource you have in sharing Christ with others is your own personal experience.

Freely Give

Notice the intensity of Matthew 10:8. Jesus did not call disciples to go out and put on spiritual band-aids or tidy up the sick room. Jesus sent his people out to raise the dead! What has limited us in continuing the work of Jesus? Have we freely received all that Jesus has offered to us? You can give to others only what you have let Jesus do in your life. Your own recovery from abusive and oppressive religion is your best weapon to use in getting out the good news to everybody else.

Most people forget that the founder of Methodism, John Wesley was already a priest and a foreign missionary for the Church of England before he became a Christian. On a ship taking him to do missionary work in the colony of Georgia, Wesley became afraid during a storm. He noticed how calm and unafraid were a group of Christians called Moravians. When they finally arrived at land, Wesley asked their leader what was the secret of their calmness and peace during the storm. The leader simply asked, "Do you know Jesus Christ?" Wesley answered, "I know that Jesus is the Savior of the world." The leader responded, "True, but do you know Jesus has saved you?"

Wesley later wrote in his journal how that question bothered him. He could not answer it. He said that he started to answer that he was an ordained priest, but that was not the question. Later, on May 25, 1738, back in England, Wesley found his way to an Anglican "society" meeting on Aldersgate Street, London, and heard Luther's preface to the commentary on Romans being read. Wesley wrote, "About a quarter before nine, while Luther was describing the change which God works in the heart through faith in Christ, I felt my heart strangely warmed. I felt I did trust in Christ, Christ alone, for salvation; and an assurance was given me, that Christ had taken away my sins, even mine, and saved me from the law of sin and death."

From that experience, John Wesley went on the change the world as few others have done. If you do not know the story of John Wesley, ask a Methodist to tell you about him. Read his biography. Wesley could say from his own experience that one could be an ordained minister and a foreign missionary and not know Jesus Christ. Wesley also could say from his own experience how liberating and life changing the presence of Jesus had made his life.

Review Your Resources

At the end of Luke and the beginning of Acts, Jesus gave a clear summary of the resources that are available to his followers to continue his work. He gave them a clear understanding of the Bible in view of his life and work. He gave them a quick review of what he had accomplished in death and resurrection. He ordered them to wait until they were filled with the Holy Spirit before they did anything. Read and learn the content of Luke 24:44-53 and Acts 1:1-8. To ignore and neglect any of what Jesus said here is to doom your own mission to failure.

Most of all, the disciples were to be witnesses. You can be a witness only if you have seen and experienced something for yourself. This is why your own experience with Jesus is your most important resource. Paul drew upon his personal experiences with Christ throughout all of his letters to groups and to individuals.

The Personal Testimony of Paul

Read Philippians 3:4-21 and 4:10-13.

Philippians 3:1-3 gives the setting of Paul's personal testimony. Paul addressed specific needs and responded to the problem of false teachers who distorted the gospel by emphasis on the law. Testimony is always "in a setting," in a living situation that calls for your response. An effective testimony is given to answer real questions that matter to real people. Compare the situation of Paul's testimony to the setting of Philip with the eunuch in Acts 8:26-40.

- Philippians 3:4-6. **Life without Jesus.** Religious success without Jesus in his life was meaningless to Paul. Use about one fourth of your testimony to tell of life without Christ.

- Philippians 3:7-11. **What Christ means to me.** Use about one fourth of your testimony to tell of your experience of having Jesus come into your life.

- Philippians 3:12-14. **I am still growing.** Use about half of your testimony to tell what is happening in your life now with Jesus beside and within you.

- Philippians 3:15-17. **Notice my example.** The Greek work translated as "follow example" is the basis for our word "mimic." "Pattern" is the Greek word *tupos*, "type, sample" of the whole. See also Philippians 4:9; 1 Corinthians 4:16; 11:1; 1 Thessalonians 1:6-7; and 2 Thessalonians 3:7-9. Part of your testimony is your own life.

- Philippians 3:18-19. **Warning.** The Greek word translated as "appetite" is word for "stomach." See Romans 13:11-14. "Mind" is same as mind in Philippians 2:5.

- Philippians 3:20-21. **Emphasis on hope.** We are becoming like Christ. See 2 Corinthians 3:17-18; Romans 8:28-29.

- Philippians 4:10-13. **Contented in Christ.** The word translated "content" is *autarkes* ("self" and "rule") and means "self-sufficient" and therefore not dependent on outward circumstances for happiness, joy, and inner peace.

Your Testimony Is Unique to You

One sign of spiritual growth is our ability to learn from our own experiences and to relate with compassion to the experiences of others. Your testimony is always to some extent your personal response to another person. Your testimony for Christ includes listening, hearing, and caring as well as telling and sharing. Your testimony changes and grows as you change and grow.

You will probably be sharing most often with people like yourself who have suffered from oppressive religion and the abusive use of the Bible against them. Notice in Philippians 3:4-14 that part of Paul's personal experience was his escape from abusive and destructive legalistic religion. The theme of escape from abusive legalism runs through all of Paul's letters. How you found recovery in Christ from Bible abuse and religious oppression is a very important part of what you have to share with others. Review lesson 43 on how to write out your experience.

Learn from the Experiences of Others

One of the greatest values of sharing in any spiritual recovery and support group is learning from hearing other people tell their experiences. The experiences of other people help you to think through your own and realize that you are not the only one with problems. You also can grow from hearing others tell about their successes and progress in dealing with some of the same things that you face. This book would not have been possible without what I have learned from hundreds of people who have shared their experiences in spiritual recovery and support groups. No group remains exactly the same after even one person tells his or her story.

Write things down. If some of the things in this book make you think of experiences that relate to your own life, write them down in a notebook, your daily journal, or if all else fails, write in the margins of this book! But do write it down, you will not recall the details later. Write down the experiences of others that really speak to you. Make what you learn from others a part of your own resources for spiritual warfare.

Jesus Gives Extra Power

The Holy Spirit was given to the early believers to teach them and to help them remember all that Jesus had told them (John 14:26). Pray and ask for the Spirit of Christ to lead you, give you words, and prepare the way for you to share your faith with someone. Prayer is a spiritual resource for anything that you do for Jesus. Read John 3:1-17 to remind yourself that becoming a Christian is a new beginning that is an act of God. You do not argue people into following Jesus. Arguing, in fact, gets in the way.

Sometimes all you have to do is give a copy of the brochure, "The Bible as Your Friend," to someone and leave the results to God. Do not get in the way. Remember that the greatest resource that you have going for you is God! God wants people to enjoy freedom, forgiveness, love, joy, peace, and self-esteem more than you do. God came to earth in Jesus and suffered and died and was raised from the dead for **all** people. When you get out of the way, the miracle can happen.

Learning from Your Own Experience

The first time I used my brochure, "The Bible as Your Friend," to share with someone, I learned a lot and am still learning. I want to share with you some of what I learned. Peter visited Golden Gate MCC with a friend and asked for an appointment to talk with me. Peter said that he saw in me something that was missing in him. He said he was not clear what he wanted or needed or how to get it. The way was wide open to share the brochure with him.

With a silent prayer and some anxiety, I opened the brochure with Peter, each of us with a copy. We took a look at the first page on "What are the Facts?" I explained that in our community, a lot of damage has been done to us by the use of the Bible against us and we need to deal with more issues that others do. Peter read along and commented from time to time. He was very serious about discovering what he could have in Christ and how to get it.

Several times Peter mentioned that he had trouble believing. We discussed what it means to believe and why it is hard to believe. One person asked Jesus for healing and said, "I believe; increase my faith!" God gives you the faith you need.

We went on. At a few points, Peter asked questions, and I suggested that we finish the pamphlet then deal with other questions. He agreed, and we continued. I felt good about the selection of verses and the emphasis and explanations. Most of Peter's questions were answered as we read. When we got to the prayer and read it, Peter thought about it and then said he wanted to pray it.

We got on our knees to pray. I have generally done this in praying with someone to receive Christ. Kneeling is a physical action with great symbolic meaning to many people. It is one way to express one's willingness to let go and trust God. Peter prayed the prayer in the brochure. I prayed for God to help Peter find peace and I thanked God for what had just happened.

Peter said that as he waited to talk to me, an old song kept running through his head, "What a Friend We Have in Jesus." He said that he was deeply touched when he saw the title of the brochure was "The Bible as Your Friend." Peter was prepared for our conversation. Peter took some brochures to share with his friends. Peter never got well enough to come back to church and died a few months later.

Write out your personal experience with God. Review and add to it as you grow in your spiritual life and as you learn from your experience and that of others. Reduce it to one page and learn it so that you can share it with others clearly, quickly, and with confidence.

Steps to Using the Brochure, "The Bible as Your Friend"

1. **Carefully read the brochure.** Look up all of the Bible passages and read them in their context in your Bible. Note the setting for each passage and be aware of how the material has been made inclusive.

2. **Write out your own experience of faith in God.** Reduce your statement of your experience to a two-minute presentation or one page.

3. **Write out your experience of coming out as a lesbian or gay person.** Include how you came to accept yourself both as gay and Christian and how far and in what ways you have recovered from abusive and oppressive religion. Reduce your account of your coming out experience to brief one or two pages.

4. **Learn to share your personal experience of coming out and of becoming a Christian.** Remember that you are the world's authority on your own experience. "Be prepared to explain to anyone who asks you to give a reason for the hope that is in you, with all gentleness and respect" (1 Peter 3:15).

5. **Share your personal experience** of becoming a Christian and listen to the experiences of others in order to become better equipped to reach out to others.

6. **Read carefully** the experience of Philip leading the Ethiopian eunuch to Christ in Acts 8:26-40.

7. **Pray and be alert to opportunities** to share your faith with others. When you are ready, the opportunities will come. God's Spirit will set the stage. Other people will open the door for you to share with them.

8. **Use the brochure in your own personal way.** You can mail it, give it to someone, sit quietly while the other person reads it, read it to someone on the phone, go through it word for word together with someone, or share it in whatever way seems best to you at the time.

9. **Avoid being distracted and arguing along the way**, when you read through the brochure with someone. You can go all the way though the brochure and then come back to questions. The brochure usually answers most questions along the way.

10. **Follow up** with those who pray and invited Jesus into their lives. Bring them to your group. Introduce them to your friends. Encourage them to use the brochure and share their experience with others. Pray for them. Keep in touch with them.

Questions for Study and Discussion

1. What is the most helpful thing you learned in this lesson? Why?

2. What do you consider to be your most helpful resource in sharing your faith with others? How did you learn about it?

3. Have you attempted to share your faith with other people? If so, how did it work out? What do you want to change before you try to share your faith again?

Chapter 17

The Twelfth Step

Become a Freedom Missionary

Encourage others to accept and feel good about themselves. Develop and share with others your new joy and freedom. Grow through daily study and meditation.

> Heal the sick, raise the dead, cleanse the lepers, cast out demons: freely you received, freely give. . . . When they deliver you up, do not become anxious about how or what you will speak; for it shall be given you in that hour what you are to speak; for it is not you who speak, but the Spirit of God who speaks in you. . . . Make disciples of all people. . . . I am with you always, even to the end of the age.
>
> Matthew 10:8, 19-20; 28:19-20

Telling other people about your own experience of finding freedom from abusive religion and your joy and happiness in feeling good about yourself will help you to grow stronger in your own faith. As you encourage other people, you also will be encouraged to continue to grow, heal, learn, and recover.

Lesson 45

Good News for Outcasts

† Preparatory Bible Reading: Mark 4:35-41 and 5:1-20

Liberation from oppression and abuse can be highly dramatic. It is like release from slavery or being set free from prison. Freedom from fear can be like a resurrection from the dead. The deliverance of the most severely outcast person in the Gospels is told in Mark 4:35 through 5:20. Read this story and try to think of any similar experience of such total and dramatic change that you have ever seen in a person.

The disturbed man living in the tombs near a small Gentile town on the shore of the Sea of Galilee was completely out of control because of fear. His whole life and being were engulfed in pain and suffering. He is one of the most dramatically tragic figures in the Bible. He remains nameless. He was one of the many unnamed people who are known to us only because of their contact with Jesus. Let us give him a name. Let us call him Alexander. Perhaps his parents had seen great potential in their child and had named him for Alexander the Great. Alexander was gifted, brilliant, energetic and a born leader. He was a good public speaker and had a clear sense of purpose in life. Then something happened. We do not know what changed him, but something did.

He told Jesus that his name was "legion" for he was possessed by a legion of evil spirits. All that we know is that Alexander's terrible condition of fear was so great that he was filled with terror and he terrorized everyone who came too close to him. He was lonely and isolated. He tried to wound and destroy himself. He saw himself as a complete outcast and lived in the unclean desolate places of death and burial. Alexander was hopeless. Then he met Jesus.

Oppressed Within By Fear

Many gay and lesbian people have been so oppressed and abused by fear of who they are and fear of themselves that their lives have taken on the characteristics of this totally outcast man. Self-defeating and self-destructive behavior can develop from dramatically low self-esteem and from consistent pressure to see yourself as evil and an abomination to God. Most gay people try to mask their true feelings about themselves and hide as much as possible in the tomb of the closet. Loneliness, isolation, fear, mistrust of God and Jesus, rejection by others, self-destructive and suicidal behavior, separation from society and from logic and sanity, hopelessness that never lets up, and a pervading personal sense of doom drain all love, joy, peace, and meaning from life. This unfortunately and tragically is an accurate picture of the internal world of many gay, lesbian, bisexual, and transgendered people whom I have known and who have written mountains of e-mail to me in response to my Web site.

Perhaps Alexander was gay. If his name really was Alexander, he was named for the most famous homosexual of the ancient world. We have no way of knowing, of course, but what he experienced was the kind of trauma that comes from intense homophobia. Perhaps he was a very attractive, strong young man. We know he was very strong, because he could not be bound with chains, which he broke. His reference to his evil spirits as "legion" has caused some to suggest that Roman soldiers, who traveled in "legions," caused his condition. Perhaps when his homosexuality was known, some Roman soldiers used and abused him sexually and marked him as evil in his own eyes and in the eyes of all of his community. He was driven into the tombs both by his community and by his own inner turmoil.

Homosexuality does not make gays and lesbians depressed. Many gay, lesbian, bisexual, and transgendered people are depressed because of how they have been treated due to their sexual orientation. One preacher wrote to me to exclaim, "You do not mean to tell me that gays are depressed because the churches are mean to them!" My reply is, "Exactly!"

The Intense Suffering of Gay People

A very perceptive United Methodist pastor and Bible teacher, Dr. Edward W. Bauman, who for over twenty years conducted a Bible class on television in the Washington, D.C., area, was quoted in *Can Homophobia Be Cured?* by Bruce Hilton (Abingdon, 1992, on page 99),

"The thing that impressed me most, however, and moved me deeply was the discovery of the incredible amount of suffering experienced by homosexuals. For centuries the church refused to serve them Holy Communion. They were often stripped, castrated, marched through the streets, and executed. In Hitler's Germany, they were exterminated by the thousands in the furnaces and gas chambers.

"In our own country, gay persons are disowned by their families, ridiculed and rejected by society, made the object of cruel jokes, and forced to laugh at the jokes lest their 'secret' be revealed. They are barred from jobs and housing, often living in loneliness, seeking companionship in sordid places and in devious (and dangerous) ways. They have become the 'lepers' of our society. How many young people are there who lie awake at night, terrified by these 'feelings,' with no one to talk to?"

I have clipped out this statement and kept it in my Bible since 1992 as a reminder of where we are. Not much has changed since 1992. On page 69, Dr. Bauman said concerning the sin of inhospitality at Sodom, **"In the name of an erroneous interpretation of the crime of Sodom, the true crime of Sodom has been continuously perpetrated to our own day."**

Jesus Confronts the Face of Evil

Mark 4:35-41 sets the stage for the liberation of Alexander. Jesus traveled from the western side of the Sea of Galilee in a deadly storm to get to him. The disciples were terrified at the ferocity of the storm. Jesus was asleep in the boat. When the disciples woke Jesus, he calmed the storm and they arrived safely at the shore. People in the time of Jesus thought that evil spirits caused both the ferocious storm and the disturbed condition of the man in the tombs. Jesus made the dangerous trip across the stormy lake in order to reach just this one disturbed man. Jesus knew his potential for good. Jesus knew that he would become his first missionary to the Gentiles! Some of the very best clergy in Metropolitan Community Church (MCC) have come from just as unlikely backgrounds.

Mark 1:23-27 had already given a description of unclean spirits,

"At that point, there was in the synagogue a man with an unclean spirit; and he cried out, saying, 'What do we have to do with you, Jesus of Nazareth? Have you come to destroy us? I know who you are, the holy one of God.' And Jesus rebuked him, saying, 'Be quiet and come out of him!' And throwing him into convulsions, the unclean spirit cried out with a loud voice, and came out of him. And everybody was amazed and debated among themselves, 'What is this? A new teaching with authority! He commands even the unclean spirits and they obey him.'"

As in every story about unclean or evil spirits, the effect on the victim is self-destructive behavior. (See the Bible description of "evil spirit" causing King Saul's dementia in 1 Samuel 16:14-23 and 1 Samuel 19:9-10, 22-24.)

"When Jesus came out of the boat, immediately a man from the tombs with an unclean spirit met him. He lived among the tombs; and no one was able to bind him any more, even with a chain; because he had often been bound with shackles and chains, and the chains had been torn apart by him. Constantly night and day, among the tombs and in the mountains, he was crying out and gashing himself with stones. Seeing Jesus from a distance, he ran up and bowed down before Jesus and cried out with a loud voice, 'What do I have to do with you, Jesus, Son of the Most High God? I implore you by God, do not torment me!'" (Mark 5:2-7).

Jesus had already ordered the unclean spirit to come out of the man. (Mark 5:8.) Jesus responded to Alexander's outburst by quietly asking, "What is your name?" Alexander quietly answered, "'My name is legion for we are many.' Then he began to beg Jesus earnestly not to send them out of the country." Alexander's use of "we" and "them" as a reference to himself indicates to us the presence of a bipolar multiple personality condition that is well known by therapists today. We know that this condition can be brought about by extreme trauma.

Then in Mark 5:11-14, we hear about the herd of swine and the action of Jesus allowing the legion of unclean spirits to enter into the herd, which rushed into the sea and drowned. The local people were very upset about the economic loss of their pigs, which were unclean in the Jewish religion. Notice that the terms "unclean spirit" and "demon possessed" were used interchangeably.

Mark 5:15 is an extraordinary picture, "The man who had been demon-possessed was sitting down [Luke 8:35 adds "at the feet of Jesus" like a disciple], clothed and in his right mind." The people were filled with fear and demanded that Jesus should leave. "Sitting" was the traditional posture of teachers or disciples. It expressed an attitude of confidence and peace. The disciple at the feet of Jesus recalls Mary in Luke 10:39 and Paul "educated at the feet of Gamaliel" in Acts 22:3. Suddenly the local maniac had become a disciple of Jesus. "Clothed" was not only evidence of new dignity and modesty; clothing indicated the rank, class, occupation, and status of the individual. Alexander had found a new identity. He was no longer the wild thing in the mountains and tombs. He was seen as the child of God, which he had been all along. "In his right mind" is a word built on the Greek, *phrontos*, from which we get "frontal" as a word for part of the brain. It is the word used for the "mind" of Christ in Philippians 2:5. See also 1 Corinthians 2:16.

From Maniac to Missionary

Every word in the description of the liberated man carries great meaning and weight. The change was total and complete.

Alexander wanted to go with Jesus. He begged Jesus to let him follow him (Mark 5:18). Nobody would blame him for wanting to get away from his own people. But Jesus had better plans for him. Jesus wanted him to follow him by reaching out to others with the good news of liberation from abuse and oppression. Jesus said, "Go home to your people and report to them what great things God has done for you and how God had mercy on you" (Mark 5:19).

Armed only with his personal experience with Jesus, Alexander was sent out as a missionary to the hostile Gentile world. He went with great enthusiasm and success. "He went off and began to proclaim in Decapolis [the ten Gentile cities east of the Jordan River with Damascus as the capitol] everything that Jesus had done for him, and everybody marveled" (Mark 5:20). The same word "marvel" is used of the typical reaction of people to the mighty works of Jesus throughout the Gospels. Never underestimate what God can do with a person who is fully committed to following Jesus, and that includes you. See Mark 6:53-56 for the positive enthusiastic reception that Jesus received from the people when he returned later to this same place.

Share Your Freedom

Bob, a star athlete on the track team, spoke up at a meeting of students and faculty at the University of Oregon in Eugene in 1993. He responded to what I said about accepting yourself as a gay Christian. A heckler from the "ex-gay" ministry had come to the meeting and taken a lot of time to refute and ridicule what I said about God's love for gays and lesbians. Bob was well known and highly respected by the group. He raised his hand on the back row and asked to be heard. Everybody got very quiet.

Bob told how he had prayed for seven years for God to change him from being gay. Finally, after much prayer and tears, he said that he came to accept himself and feel good about himself as a gay Christian. He wanted everyone to know that he had found peace with God and freedom in Christ. After the meeting, a reporter talked with Bob and asked if he could print Bob's statement in the University newspaper. The reporter said he would leave out Bob's name so that he and the athletic department would not be embarrassed. Bob said "O.K."

Then Bob talked a while with some of his friends and came back to the reporter and said, "You can use my name." The reporter said, "That won't be necessary. The editor can work around it." Bob said, "You don't understand. I want you to use my name. I want to come out to everybody as a gay Christian!" The University paper printed his story the next week. Bob talked with me a few weeks later and told me how happy he was that he decided to come out and demonstrate his faith and his truth as a gay Christian athlete. He said that all of the response he heard was positive and supportive. He did mention, however, that the summer youth camp that he had always led each year did not want him back again.

Bob learned that becoming a convincing witness for freedom in Christ for gays and lesbians is not an easy mission. Bob will never know how many oppressed and frightened gay people in Oregon he encouraged by his public testimony of his own recovery from abusive oppressive religion.

Questions for Study and Discussion

1. Have you yet reached out to other lesbian, gay, bisexual, and transgendered people to encourage them to find liberation and freedom from destructive, sick religion? What success have you had?

2. What are the most destructive forms of homophobia that you have seen in yourself and in the gay community? Do you think that the picture in Mark 5:1-20 of the man living in the tombs and mountains is correctly compared to the persecution and suffering of gay people today?

3. What hope do you have for traditional churches using stories like Mark 5:1-20 to tell the truth about religious oppression and abuse of gays and lesbians and to call for a change?

Lesson 46

As You Go, Make Disciples

† Preparatory Bible Reading: Matthew 28:18-20, "The Great Commission"

What is your main purpose in living? Do you have a primary goal or a mission in life? Your answer can shape how you see yourself and other people around you. Someone suggested that most people aim at nothing, and hit it! Your self-image and sense of personal value depends a lot on whether you are bogged down or moving toward clear objectives. The Great Commission, which concludes the Gospel of Matthew, is the attempt of Jesus to offer a simple and clear purpose in the life of all disciples.

Miss Lottie Moon

The most famous Southern Baptist missionary was Miss Lottie Moon. Charlotte Moon was brought up in church and was a very assertive young woman in college. She once climbed into the rafters of the college chapel and tied cloth to the clapper on the bell to keep the bell from ringing to announce time for classes. She was a highly motivated scholar and learned New Testament Greek so well that for the rest of her life she read her "daily Bible readings" in the original language of the New Testament. She was one of the first women to receive a Masters Degrees in the United States. Her sister was one of the first women to receive a medical degree, but she could not practice medicine in America, and that is why she went to China. Lottie Moon went to China to be with her sister in 1873.

Lottie Moon became famous when she began to write regular reports to the Virginia Baptist State paper about the missionary work in China. Women were the only missionaries allowed into China at that time, because they could teach women and children. No men at all were allowed at first. Lottie Moon identified completely with the Chinese people. She adopted the dress, appearance, and customs of her Chinese friends. She left China to visit at home only three times before she died aboard ship in Kobe Harbor, Japan, waiting to return home on Christmas Eve in 1912. In 1888, Lottie Moon suggested that the Baptists should take up an offering for missions at Christmas as a birthday gift for Jesus. The idea caught on, and today, the Lottie Moon Christmas offering will provide almost half of the multimillion-dollar budget for the Southern Baptist International Mission Board.

Lottie Moon was far ahead of her time. When a man was sent to be the head of her mission, where woman missionaries did not even have a vote, she was so angry that she resigned and wrote the Foreign Mission Board to send her money for her passage back home. The Board did not even answer the letter. They just voted to change their policy and give equal vote to women on the mission field. What a woman! Lottie Moon was a powerful inspiration to many Baptists to be open to the call of missions as their purpose in life, even though most Baptists today do not know about her women's rights activism and revolutionary spirit.

The majority of Southern Baptist missionaries during these early beginnings were unmarried women whose zeal and determination led the most positive and inclusive part of the Baptist denomination's work at home and abroad. A number of retired Baptist women missionaries have been my friends, including Martha Franks, Bertha Smith, Olive Lawton, and Clifford Barrett, who was an active member of my church in Greenwood, South Carolina. I learned from all of them. We probably will never know how many of the unmarried woman missionaries in all denominations were lesbians, but some of them were.

The Rev. Elder Jean White is a lesbian and a former missionary to China for the Plymouth Brethren Church. She came home to London after being imprisoned and tortured for her Christian work in the People's Republic of China. She found the Metropolitan Community Church (MCC) in London, where she later became pastor and an outstanding effective leader in the Universal Fellowship of Metropolitan Community Churches both as an Elder and as a leader of gay and lesbian Christian ministries outside the United States.

The Great Commission of Jesus

> After the resurrection, Jesus said to his disciples, "All authority has been given to me in heaven and on earth. As you go, make disciples of all people, baptizing them in the name of God, Christ, and the Holy Spirit, teaching them to observe all that I commanded you; and behold, I am with you always to the end of the age" (Matthew 28:18-20).

The only imperative in the Great Commission is "make disciples." Go, baptize, and teach are linked to the one command, "Make disciples of all people [nations]." The disciples did not have to be told to go. They would be scattered into all parts of the world by many forces. Their command from Jesus concerned what to do as they went. The word "people" is the Greek word *ethnos* ("ethnic" comes from it) and means the people or "nations" of all the earth. It is also the word for "Gentiles" because there is no separate Greek word for "Gentile." At every level the mission of Jesus is totally inclusive. Nobody is left out.

What is Great About the Great Commission?

The greatest thing about the Great Commission is the one who gave it. Jesus was given "all authority in heaven and on earth." Stop now and read Philippians 2:1-11 for details of the basis for this authority. "Authority" is the Greek word *exousia*, which means to have the right to do something. It includes the idea of power but goes beyond power. Jesus earned the right to give orders to his followers and to empower them to act.

The commission comes from the one who demonstrated the unconditional love of God for all outcast, oppressed, misunderstood, rejected, and despised people. The commission did not come from any church, council, organization, or denomination. It is the mission of God through Jesus for the people of God. Nobody on earth can limit it. Nobody can take this mission from you. You did not initiate it, God did. Gay and lesbian believers share in this great commission. Do not let anybody talk you out of it. Do not abandon it or talk yourself out of it. This great commission can be the purpose that keeps you going through oppression and times of darkness and distress. It is your light at the end of the tunnel through jungles of sick and abusive religion. It can be the motivation in your life that equips you to "overcome the world."

A Commission that is Inclusive

The commission is great because it includes you and all people: make disciples of "all nations." Read the Great Commission with emphasis on "all," "always," and "you." The term "all nations [*ethnos*]" is the same as in Mark 13:17, "My house shall be called a house of prayer for all nations [Isaiah 56:7], but you have made it a den of robbers! [Jeremiah 7:11]." God's intention was to include everybody. Religion built walls to keep out the undesirables. Jesus broke down the walls, included everybody, and brought in alienated and oppressed people. Read Ephesians 2:8-22 for how walls are broken down in Christ. Sick religion divides and destroys. God's love includes the whole world and that includes you (John 3:16-17).

A Commission that Works

The commission is great because it is simple and complete. The principle of multiplication is there. If one person makes one disciple in one year, then each one makes one more disciple the next year for a total of four and this continues year after year, the total number of disciples in ten years will be 1,024, in 20 years it will be 1,048,576, in 30 years it will be 1,073,741,824, and in 35 years, about the time that the first written Gospel materials appeared, the number would be

34,359,738,368 or almost six times the current population of the world. If just the twelve of the disciples had followed the instructions in the Great Commission, the whole world would have become Christian within the lifetime of the first followers of Jesus. Why did it not? Why do Christians fail to make disciples of "all people" today? The Great Commission has not worked, because it has not yet been tried.

Making disciples takes time. We are in a hurry. We make converts. Evangelicals often practice a hurried up form of "instant evangelism" in which people are enticed to make a "decision for Christ" and then immediately included in the church as though they were fully matured disciples. They are not. The illusion of Christian maturity is not maturity, and it is not honest. Converts are not disciples.

Making disciples means teaching all things that Jesus taught. Learning, growing, recovery, and healing take time. Disciples learn to follow Jesus and take the time to teach and encourage others to become disciples. The desperate need for training in discipleship is the reason for the format of this book into 52 lessons that can be used for a year of weekly studies with time for extra study and discussion. Group discussion of the material is just as important as reading it.

Another reason that the Great Commission has not been tried yet is the simple fact that the traditional churches have systematically left out certain groups of undesirable people, such as gay people and other minorities. The Great Commission can never be complete so long as the churches reject the gay ten percent of the population along with other unwanted races, cultural and social outcasts, and anybody else who just does not fit in.

The Wake-Up Call of HIV/AIDS

The world eventually will not take seriously the religion that rejects its own gay children because of ignorance and prejudice based on flawed reasoning and inaccurate translations of a few isolated Bible verses. The Great Commission will never be carried out as long as the religious establishment refuses openly to accept and include lesbians and gay people and all others alienated and oppressed by religion. HIV/AIDS is a thunderous wake-up call to the world and to the churches. The question of accepting gay people as full members and ministers in local churches is not just an urgent and pressing issue of Christian compassion in the midst of the HIV/AIDS epidemic. It also is the overwhelming issue of the survival of Christian churches as credible representatives of the life and ministry of Jesus Christ.

Start Where You Are

The commission is great because you can start where you are right now. The first step in carrying out the orders of Jesus was "Wait!" "Jesus commanded them not to leave Jerusalem but to wait for the promise of God" (Acts 1:4).

"You will receive power when the Holy Spirit has come upon you; and you will be my witnesses in Jerusalem, and in Judea, and Samaria, and even to the remotest part of the earth" (Acts 1:8).

The next step after waiting and receiving the Holy Spirit was for all of the disciples to bear witness to the good news about Jesus to all of the many kinds of people who had come for the festival of Pentecost.

The first followers of Jesus began where they were. They waited and let the Spirit of Jesus guide and empower them. They then taught and began to make disciples of people who had come to them. They did not "go into all the world" until they first "made disciples" where they were.

Read all of Acts 1:1-8 and 2:1-4. Notice that Acts 1:1 speaks of the Gospel of Luke as the story of what "Jesus began to do and teach." The Book of Acts tells how Jesus continued to act and teach through the Holy Spirit in the lives of believers. The Book of Acts continues in your life as you enter in the mission of love and hope that Jesus began.

Starting at Home

Charles was a student in my first evangelism class at Baptist College. He learned to use the "WIN Booklet" (a Baptist evangelism tract) to share his faith at the rural church which he served as a student pastor. He helped several people become Christians. When Charles graduated from college, he asked me to pray for his father, who was not a Christian. Later in the summer, Charles told me he had some good news. He had shared his faith in Christ with his father and helped him to become a Christian. His father soon became a leader in his church.

In the seminary, Charles experienced the call to foreign missions and after finishing his degree, he went to Japan as a leader in evangelism and in teaching others to become disciples. Charles began personal evangelism at his rural church and at home with his father, and then he went out into the foreign mission field to continue what he had already started. Charles began where he was, and so can you.

Jesus Is With You Always

Jesus promised "I will be with you always to the end of the age." This was the "life verse" that kept David Livingston going through 42 years in Africa. Dr. Livingston was a Christian explorer, doctor, and teacher. He suffered with fever for over 40 years in Africa. His love for people was demonstrated in his life. When Livingston died, his heart was buried by his native partners in Africa. His body was buried in Westminster Abbey. "I am with you always to the end of the age," is engraved on his stone marker.

What keeps you going when you are tired and confused and worn out and tempted to give up? What keeps you going when nobody understands you and you wonder why everybody else seems to have a much easier life than you do? What keeps you going? Jesus never said your life would be easy, but he promised never to forsake you. He promised to be with you every step of the way.

Questions for Study and Discussion

1. What keeps you going when you are tempted to give up and quit?

2. Many other gay people have become discouraged, given up, and committed suicide. Why have you not done this?

3. What do you believe that God has called you to do with your life? How do you feel about doing it? Who has most tried to talk you out of doing God's will? Why?

Additional Resources

Myron S. Augsburger, *Invitation to Discipleship: The Message of Evangelism*: Herald Press, 1964.

Letty M. Russell, editor, *The Church with AIDS: Renewal in the Midst of Crisis*: Westminster/John Knox Press, 1990.

Lesson 47

The Bible as a Weapon for Freedom

† **Preparatory Bible Reading:** Amos 5:21-24; Micah 6:6-8; Jeremiah 31:31-34; John 3:1-17; Philippians 2:1-16

Mohandas K. Gandhi walked to the sea, made salt in defiance of unjust, oppressive laws, and set into motion the forces that brought independence to India.

Rosa Parks broke the law and was arrested in Montgomery, Alabama for not giving up her bus seat to a white man and set in motion the bus boycott that eventually galvanized the civil rights movement in the United States.

The Rev. Troy Perry and others began in 1968 to declare spiritual freedom from the tyranny of homophobic religion, and multitudes of lesbian, gay, bisexual, transgendered, and straight people have joined in the battle for gay human rights.

For the past 18 years, I have been part of the struggle for human, civil, and religious rights for gay people in Atlanta, San Francisco, Nashville, and on the Internet. I have seen and felt the tensions of unfair laws, abusive religion, and civil and religious disobedience. As a Metropolitan Community Church (MCC) pastor in San Francisco and Nashville, I have been part of our battle against homophobic Bible abuse and the religious terrorism that has been inflicted upon our people.

I have seen and experienced the self-defeating internal fear and confusion caused by the religious abuse and oppression of gay people. I have felt the anger of our community and have suffered along with many of our brothers and sisters from the craziness of our own people within and outside of the churches. It has indeed been a bumpy ride, usually without a seatbelt.

No challenge against entrenched ignorance, prejudice, and unfair social, religious, or political system is easy. The challenge is necessary, however, if we are to follow God's prophets and the example and teachings of Jesus. Read now all of 2 Corinthians 11:1 through 12:21 for Paul's story of what his attacks against the system cost him.

The Bible as a Weapon for Fairness and Freedom

The Hebrew Bible in the Law and the Prophets spoke out on behalf of acceptance, freedom, and justice for all people. Jesus used the Hebrew Bible to teach justice and love. He emphasized social justice and personal compassion in accordance with what the prophets had taught. Jesus, like the old prophets, set kindness and justice in contrast to religious ritual and superficial piety. This verse is an inscription on the Martin Luther King, Jr. memorial in a park in the center of San Francisco,

> I hate, I reject your festivals, nor do I delight in your solemn assemblies. Even though you offer up to me burnt offerings and your grain offerings, I will not accept them; and I will not even look at the peace offering of your fatlings. Take away from me the noise of your songs; I will not even listen to the sound of your harps. But let justice roll down like water and righteousness like a mighty stream.
>
> Amos 5:21-24

This last line is especially dramatic in the setting of the Martin Luther King, Jr. memorial where the visitor stands beneath a roaring waterfall to read it!

The priests and other religious and political leaders often hated prophets like Amos. They spoke for God to challenge unfair and oppressive abuse of power by the rulers, the rich, and the religious authorities. Jesus did the same. Jesus did not dilute any of the major prophetic teachings concerning God's steadfast love for all alienated and oppressed people.

People Come First

Jesus has been called the world's greatest humanist, because for Jesus, people always were more important than religion. Jesus not only saw clearly the abuses and pain caused by religion among his own people in the time of his ministry; he also recalled the awesome abuse and human misery caused by sick religion in the past. Jesus concluded his most eloquent rebuke of abusive religious leaders by saying, "You serpents, you brood of vipers, how shall you escape the judgment of hell!" (Matthew 23:33). Then later, Jesus reminded the people that God's prophets and teachers had always been rejected, beaten and killed in the past (Matthew 23:33-39). Jesus lamented that the people that he also was trying to reach with God's unconditional love and hope were rejecting him and his offer of love and truth, and then he concluded, "your house is being left to you desolate."

The prophet Micah condemned extravagant religious rituals and gifts that had even included human sacrifices in the Canaanite worship of Moloch. Evil, destructive religion is held in sharp contrast to love and justice,

> With what shall I come to God and bow myself before the God on high? Shall I come to God with burnt offerings, with yearling calves? Does God take delight in thousands of rams, in ten thousand rivers of oil? Shall I present my first-born for my rebellion, the fruit of my body for the sin of my soul? God has told you what is good; and what does God require of you but to do justice, to love kindness, and to walk humbly with your God?
>
> Micah 6:6-8

Even in the time of Jesus, many of the religious teachers viewed the requirement to "do justice, love kindness, and walk humbly with your God" as a summary of their over 600 laws reduced to a brief three-part commandment. Jesus was clearly saying to the leaders and to the people that he had come to demonstrate and live out what they already claimed to believe.

Laws Protecting the Weak

Life in Palestine in biblical times was harsh and fragile. Only the strong could survive. Hebrew laws and teachings protected people who were vulnerable because they were sick, poor, foreigners, old, young, widows, or orphans. Laws were developed to require compassion for the needy as well as fair and just treatment for those who could not protect themselves. No parallels to these compassionate laws have been found in other ancient law codes.

The five books of the Law contain many examples of rules for the compassionate treatment of alienated and oppressed people. The prophets and the prophetic writings consistently cried out for justice and compassion for all people and challenged unjust oppressive rulers and priests to repent and return to God. The reaction of leaders to such troublesome prophets was often to kill them, as Jesus was quick to point out in Matthew 23:37.

Compassionate treatment of weak and dependent people was so clearly demanded in the Law that Job's friends guessed that his great suffering was punishment for his mistreatment of the homeless, the hungry and thirsty, and widows and orphans (Job 22:1-11). When Jesus taught love and acceptance for outcast and rejected people, he built on the foundation of what the prophets had already done. Paul concluded, "You are no longer strangers and aliens, but you are fellow citizens with the saints and are of God's household, having been built upon the foundation of the apostles and prophets, Christ Jesus himself being the cornerstone" (Ephesians 2:19-20). Read all of Ephesians 2:1-22 for perhaps the most effective statement in the Bible about the freedom that Jesus has won for all people.

A New Heart

The prophet Jeremiah grappled with the issues of love and justice and wept over the oppression of his people. Jeremiah envisioned no hope for his oppressed people or their leaders to return to God. He saw hope for the future only in a new covenant and a new heart that God would give to the people. Stop now and read Jeremiah 31:31-34, a brief four verses that tell of a new heart, which was quoted in full in Hebrews 8:8-12 to show that Jesus fulfilled what Jeremiah predicted. Jesus talked at the Last Supper about the new covenant that he had come to establish (Luke 22:20). Jesus offers a new life, a new mission, inner peace, and a new commandment to "love one another as I have loved you." See also Ezekiel 36:22-32 for prophecy of a new heart and a new spirit.

Before you can be a force for fairness and justice in your own community, you have to experience for yourself the change of heart that Jesus offers in the gift of the Spirit. Do not settle for anything less. Rearranging the religious furniture does not really change where you live. As Jesus said to Nichodemus, who knew the Bible a lot better than any of us, "Do not be amazed that I told you that you must be born again" (John 3:7).

Read all of John 3:1-17. God loves the world. Our challenge to the world is based on our belief that God sent Jesus "not to oppress the world but that through Jesus the world might be set free." John 3:16-17 is in the context that assumes the necessity of the new beginning, the new heart, the new "birth" brought about by the Spirit of God. To edit out essential parts of the good news of Jesus is to become like the kind of Bible abusers that have distorted the Bible against us! Jesus offers real change within us as the basis for our freedom and our mission of liberation for others.

A New Creation

Paul said, "The love of Christ now controls us and in Christ we are a new creation. The old things passed away. Look! New things have come!" (2 Corinthians 5:14, 17). In Ephesians 4:24 and Colossians 3:10, Paul said that we have, "put on the new self." Hope for change is based on new life, "As Christ was raised from the dead by the glory of God, so we too might walk in newness of life" (Romans 6:4). Jesus gives to believers his own "mind" of truth and compassion. "We have the mind of Christ" (1 Corinthians 2:16). See all of Philippians 2:1-18 for details of what the mind of Christ means for the lifestyle of all believers.

The Bible can be a powerful weapon for love and justice. Learn to use it as Jesus did. Do not be intimidated by Bible abusers who use the Bible to judge and reject you. They are wrong. Jesus is our best hope for correcting the abusive use of the Bible. Jesus is our dependable example and teacher in restoring love and justice for people who have been oppressed and outcast by religion.

Laws and Attitudes

Laws do not change attitudes, people do. Laws to forbid and punish hate crimes and discrimination against people based on their sexual orientation are necessary, but they do not cure homophobia. The underlying religious basis for fear and hate against gay people must be faced and corrected with factual information and the truth about what the Bible does and does not say. For gay Christians to allow churches and church leaders to continue to distort the Bible against them unchallenged is a betrayal of the truth and an abdication of the call of Jesus to a ministry of love and justice. We need each other, and we need each other now!

Laws to protect weak and fragile people were bypassed by clever religious experts in the Bible. Jesus showed how some people used the law to avoid helping their own parents (Mark 7:8-13) and added, "You blind guides! You strain out a gnat and swallow a camel!" Legalistic religion feeds upon fear, ignorance, resentment, and hostility. Jesus liberates us from legalism and invites us to a new life and a new heart so that we want to "do justice, love mercy, and walk humbly with your God."

Follow Jesus into Freedom

Bible materials on how to invite Jesus into your life and experience a new beginning in your way of thinking, feeling, and seeing yourself and others are given in lessons 9, 42, and 43 of this book. Personally sharing your experience of new life in Christ is the most available method that you have to make a difference in individuals that touch your life. It also is your best chance to "change the world." Spiritual growth and preparation for reaching out to make a difference in the rest of your world can flow from doing the steps recommended in this book. Prayer, study, discussion in small groups, and applying what you learn to yourself can lead to personal growth in confidence and self-esteem, activism for social and political change, one-to-one personal evangelism, and ministry to the human need around you.

Do not miss out on the blessing! Be part of the solution, not part of the problem. Remember that any obstacle or pressure that you face as a gay and lesbian Christian has already been faced and conquered by Jesus.

"Since we have so great a cloud of witnesses surrounding us, let us also lay aside every hindrance and the failures and transgressions that so easily entangle us, and let us run with endurance the race that is set before us. Fix your eyes on Jesus, the author and finisher of faith, who for the joy set before him endured the cross, despising the shame, and has sat down at the right hand of the throne of God. Therefore consider the one who has endured such hostility by religious oppressors against himself; so that you may not grow weary and lose heart" (Hebrews 12:1-3).

Questions for Study and Discussion

1. What have you already done to become adequately informed about religious and spiritual issues that concern gay, lesbian, bisexual, and transgendered people? What have you done to become informed about political and civil rights issues faced by all gay people?

2. How have you acted to "right the unrightable wrong and dream the impossible dream" of changing the world's attitudes and treatment of gay people from oppression to fairness and justice?

3. How has the information in this lesson affected your thinking about activism for human and civil rights for lesbian, gay, bisexual, and transgendered people?

Lesson 48

Free At Last

† **Preparatory Bible Reading:** Romans 8:18-39

During the 1995 Universal Fellowship of Metropolitan Community Churches (UFMCC) General Conference in Atlanta, I visited the Martin Luther King, Jr. Center along with a large group of MCC people and especially my black lesbian Christian friend, the Rev. Carolyn Mobley, Associate Pastor at MCC of the Resurrection in Houston, Texas. She and I have been "growing up together" from the time we met in MCC Atlanta in 1981 until now. She has often been my teacher and encourager for over 18 years.

We honored the memory of Dr. King and recalled the contributions that he made to all of us in our struggle for self-respect, dignity, and freedom. His most famous speech, "I Have A Dream," still rings in my head and heart. We also long for the time when we shall all be able to shout with our brother Martin, "Free at last, Free at last, Thank God All Mighty, we are free at last!" The Apostle Paul cried out in such a shout of hope in Romans 8:18-39. If you ever memorize any of Paul's writings, memorize the eighth chapter of Romans.

We Have the Promise of God's Love

"God does not love homosexuals!" was shouted out by a gay man at a gay bar in San Francisco's Tenderloin District during a Celebration of Life that I was leading for a local drag queen who had died of HIV/AIDS. My opening statement in the brief service was to quote John 3:16-17 and announce that "God loves the world and so God loves homosexuals." I was not quite prepared to get an argument from the audience! When the man interrupted the service to shout that God did not love us, a lot of the patrons began to shout back, "Throw him out!" I said, "No, don't throw him out. Just calm him down!" They did and the service continued. Do you really believe that God loves you?

Perhaps the greatest thing going for us in our struggle for freedom is the assurance that God does indeed love us and we can depend on it. Jesus promised many things, but the main thing he emphasized time after time was that God's eternal and unconditional love is for you and me and for all people. We cannot earn God's love, for we already have it. We cannot deserve God's love, because while we were still in rebellion against God, Christ died for us (Romans 5:8). We cannot run away from God's love, for God is everywhere. We cannot control God's love, because God's love is free to all. You already have the freedom of God's love. So act on it, use it, live in it, move into it with all of your friends, rejoice in it, and share it. You already have the promise of God's love.

You Have the Promise of a New Life

In Jesus, you can start over every day. "If you are in Christ, you are a new creation. Old things have passed away. Behold, the new things have come" (2 Corinthians 5:17). "We have been buried with Christ by baptism into death, that as Christ was raised from the dead by the glory of God, so we too might walk in newness of life" (Romans 6:4). Expect new beginnings every day. Look for the miracle today, and one will always be there.

Recovering people learn to live "one day at a time," because that is all any of us have. As a recovering alcoholic, I am aware that every day is a new beginning and a gift from God. The first thing that I write in my journal each day is the number of years, months, and days that I have been sober. As I write this, it is nine years, eight months, six days (or 3,663 days). Sometimes I add the little note, "Thank God for one day at a time." If you also join me in recovering from abusive, destructive religion, you also make a fresh start every day and often several times a day. Life in

God's love is fresh every morning. Enjoy God, yourself, and the world and people around you.

You Have the Promise of a New World

All pain, confusion, and anxiety will pass away. "According to God's promise we are looking for new heavens and a new earth, in which righteousness dwells" (2 Peter 3:13).

Michael, a member of the Board of Directors at Golden Gate MCC, was close to death from HIV/AIDS. His doctor asked his partner, "Where is Glory? Michael keeps talking about wanting to go to Glory. Where is that?" Michael's partner laughed and said, "Michael wants to be with God, to go on to glory and be in heaven."

Later, as Michael was breathing through an oxygen mask, he said over and over, "Jesus loves me. Jesus loves me. Jesus loves me." Michael had been told all of his life that Jesus did not love him because of his sexual orientation, but he had fought the fight for freedom from abusive and destructive religion and with the help of God and many gay Christian friends, he had won. So Michael went to glory saying, "Jesus loves me. Jesus loves me." And so can you.

We Have the Promise of Winning the Victory

One of my favorite songs is "Victory in Jesus." I have heard that song sung with just about as much enthusiasm as is possible in many MCC worship services. Paul declared the promise of victory in Romans 8:37, "We know that in all things we overwhelmingly conquer through Christ who loved us." The *King James Version* translates it, "We are more than conquerors," and though we may lose battles, the war is over. Jesus has already won. In Christ, we are winners and the victory is ours.

Do not give up on a war that has already been won! I frequently have found myself in very vulnerable situations, partly because I am reckless and partly because I tend to trust just about anybody. I am codependent and gullible. Sometimes I seem to learn practically nothing from experience. Life has been and continues to be quite a trip! I have become used to hearing the sound of flying shrapnel coming at me from unexpected directions and have not always had the good sense to duck.

I have learned, however, that when God lets me get shot down, it is for a good reason, not to kill me but to teach me something or many things I need to learn. I do not give up or quit, but I do move on to another part of the battlefield and dig in again and continue to fight. Getting killed is not bad when you believe in resurrection. Every time that someone has succeeded in "killing" me, God has revived me and cast me back into the heat of battle with the promise that it will get worse! It always does. All of this has taught me totally to trust God. I do not know what is going on, but God does. If I let go and fight on with the sure spiritual weapons of love and truth; then God uses me in ways that I never quite understand and often am not even aware of.

I learned a long time ago that the real enemy is not people, but we are easily seduced by the real enemy into thinking so. Paul concluded his letter to the Romans with the promise that "the God of peace will soon crush Satan under your feet" (Romans 16:20). "Soon" (the Greek word *tachos*) is the same word as "speedily" in Luke 18:8 and "quickly" in Revelation 22:20. It means "quickly, at once, without delay." I am counting on this promise every moment of active duty that I serve in the mission of Jesus to help liberate us all from sick religion.

God is greater than Satan. "Satan" is the same word in Greek and in Hebrew and means "the adversary," which is a term for "the real enemy" and not a reference to people around you, your sexual orientation, or the way your parents treated you. Give Satan credit. Satan cannot defeat God, but Satan can stomp you flat. The most dangerous enemy is the enemy within. Pogo said, "We have met the enemy, and he is us." Our only hope of victory is in someone who is stronger than we are. Our hope is in God, who in Christ has already won for us. Face it, you cannot beat the devil! So do not try. Let God do it for you. You are called and trained to do what you can. Share your experience of

God's love with everybody you can touch as long as you live. When you do that, you are winning far more than you realize.

Nobody is Free Until Everybody is Free

As long as anyone around you is held in the grip of the crazy-making power of abusive, legalistic, judgmental religion, you cannot let up in your mission as a freedom fighter. Abusive religion always feeds on itself and multiplies. Abusive religion is like a virus that cannot be controlled by conventional means, because "conventional means" is one reason why the virus exists in the first place. If you want to see the religious abuse virus spring to life and take over like "the Blob," start a church. Remember the old joke, "They were having a fight and a church broke out!"

Remember that none of us will be free from the tyranny of sick and abusive religion as long as the original sin of trying to play God afflicts people who become addicted to religion. The "Emperor's New Clothes" is a joke because the emperor is naked. Religious vestments cannot hide the spiritual nakedness of clergy who say, "Sell what you have and give it to me." Jesus never said, "Sell what you have and give it to the building fund," did he? Maybe it is in there somewhere, but I cannot seem to find it. I realize that deadly abusive religion is far too serious to joke about, but if we do not learn to laugh at ourselves and see the absurdities around us, we will really lose it and adopt the "Daffy Duck" approach to handling stress. Laughing hysterically, we run away leaping and jumping into the distance with feathers flying in all directions.

The Promise of Freedom Not to Blame Yourself

Legalistic, judgmental religion is always looking for someone to blame for whatever is wrong. We can easily become caught up in the game of "Who is to blame?" In our low self-esteem and self-destructive victim mentality, we are all too willing to be "the one to blame." We can blame ourselves for just about everything that happens to us and to other people around us. We say, "I should have known better" or "I should have been more careful." We are reinforced by people around us saying, "You should have known better" or "You should have been more careful." This is not a very creative game, but it is a deadly game that chains us to our mediocrity and saps our energy and freedom.

Jesus shatters such games by telling us clearly, "You are not to blame. I have taken all of the blame for you and suffered, died, and been resurrected for you so that you can be free, have joyful fellowship with God, feel good about yourself, and have fun!" Remember that since you are not God, you cannot be blamed for everything that went wrong. You are not really that important. Get a grip. Others deserve some of the blame too. Truth and reality have a way of shattering most games and bringing us back to our senses.

Jesus sets you free from having to be the savior. You do not have to rescue every needy person you meet. Jesus already has taken care of that job. Your low view of yourself will just have to be repaired in some other way than by letting manipulative people use you to wipe their feet. Freedom in Christ sets you free from the fake responsibility of having to be in charge of every rescue operation you can find or invent.

Are You Ready for Real Freedom?

Jesus not only sets you free, Jesus also helps you to learn how to handle real freedom. We are tempted to retreat back into the comfort zone of letting someone else make decisions for us. It is hard work to think for yourself. Jesus gives you the Holy Spirit to encourage and empower you and to be your teacher so that you can be free from all forms of spiritual tyranny. You learn to work it out for yourself, or you can let someone else do it for you, but then your solutions are not really yours. If you live on the faith of other people, you feel like a hypocrite, because you are. Do you really want to be whole, healed, in recovery, and free? You really do have to answer that question. Yes or No?

Questions for Study and Discussion

1. Did you learn anything about yourself in this lesson? What do you intend to do about it?

2. How would you define freedom in Christ? Exactly how does abusive, legalistic religion affect Christian freedom? How has it affected you?

3. Have you tried to rescue people or organizations? What did you learn from your experience?

Additional Resources

A book that helped me to get a better grip on myself is, *Recovery from Rescuing*, by Jacqueline Castine: Health Communications, Inc., Deerfield Beach, Florida, 1989.

Gain some helpful insight into yourself and into abusive religion by studying Anne Wilson Scherf and Diane Fassel, *The Addictive Organization*: Harper, 1990.

Part VI

Beyond Recovery

Recovery is a never ending story. The scars of abuse always remain with us. Alcohol abuse, drug abuse, spousal abuse, parental abuse, and religious abuse all create tapes that remain in our psyche for life. Recovery never ends, because stress can trigger the tapes and play them again in our heads to distract us and undercut our feelings of well-being.

This does not mean that we never win. We win every day as we live one day at a time in recovery. God gives you whatever you need at the moment you need it. None of us ever grows beyond the need for God's help to remain sober, free, happy, and gay!

This final section of the steps to recovery intends to build on all that has gone before and help to equip you to continue to grow, recover, heal, learn, and share. Think of things that would help you to continue your freedom pilgrimage. Discuss these things with your group.

Keep learning. Keep your mind open to new truth. Give yourself the joy of learning from new and different sources. Begin to see things in a different light. You do not need to be afraid of what new and different people will let you learn from them. With Jesus in the center of your life, you have a powerful point of reference and an effective corrective to the abusive use of the Bible and religion against you. Let Jesus through the Holy Spirit equip you through prayer and new beginnings to grow in grace and self-esteem every day.

Many helpful resources are listed throughout this book and in the Bibliography and Special Studies at the end of the book. My Web site on "Steps to Recovery from Bible Abuse" at www.truluck.com will give you up-to-date resources and articles that relate to all of the material in this book.

Please let me know what you think will help you to keep moving ahead in your spiritual life. You can contact me through the publisher of this book or at the address given at the end of "My Story" in Chapter 2. You can help us to know where to go next to meet your needs. Please contact us and tell us what you think. Send e-mail requests to me, Rembert Truluck at rembert@slip.net to receive regular up-dates related to the "Steps to Recovery from Bible Abuse" Web site and giving new books, reviews, and other up-to-date resources.

Chapter 18

The Last Step

Give Yourself Time To Heal and Recover

"Love is patient and love is kind." (1 Corinthians 13:4)

Love yourself. Learn to be patient with yourself and others. Growth takes time. Give yourself and others the time and space needed for growth, healing, and recovery.

"Speaking the truth in love, we are to grow up in all things unto Christ."
(Ephesians 4:15)

"For freedom Christ set us free: therefore keep standing firm and do not be controlled again by a religious yoke of slavery. . . . The whole law is fulfilled in one word: You shall love your neighbor as yourself. But if you bite and devour one another, take care lest you be consumed by one another." (Galatians 5:1, 14-15)

The steps to recovery from abusive and oppressive religion are just a beginning. You can follow through in your own spiritual growth into self-esteem and effective spiritual living and sharing by finding or starting a spiritual support group. Be creative. Let God guide you into what works for you.

Lesson 49

Growing Up in Christ

† **Preparatory Bible Reading:** Luke 2:39-52; Hebrews 5:1-14; Ephesians 4:11-15; Philippians 3:4-14

When I wrote adult Sunday School lessons for the Southern Baptist Sunday School Board, I was told that adults read Bible study material on the level of 12-year-olds. I was not surprised. When I taught Bible courses at a senior college, I realized that nobody came to a college Bible course with the kind of background that was taken for granted in English, science, history, math, and every other subject. Some students in my survey of the New Testament had never seen a New Testament before they came to the class.

Throughout my life as a pastor and college professor in and out of the churches, I have been amazed at the low level of Bible knowledge and spiritual maturity that our churches are satisfied to maintain. The 60-year-old people in Sunday School class study the same Bible material in the same way as the class for 12-year-olds does. No new information about Bible background or how to translate the Bible culture and language into present realities is given in most classes. One college survey found that students who went to church said that they learned more new information in one college lecture than they learned all year in church and Sunday School. No wonder so many people abandon religion as they grow up and mature in every area of life except in their spiritual life.

Do Not Decide Things for Me

As gay people, we have had to work out our own sexuality without help or understanding from older people, adult authorities, religious leaders, or even from our peers. Few of us have any desire for other people to try to tell us what to believe about God or religion. We work out things for ourselves, just as we have had to work through everything about our sexuality and our deepest feelings.

My parents gave me freedom to learn and explore for myself. They encouraged me to pursue my personal interests and learn and grow. They gave me access to books, good music, many interesting people, and a loving and supportive home. I was very fortunate. Religion was never forced on me, but I was exposed to the Christian faith at its best in my home and in my home church. I am grateful I was given space and freedom to decide spiritual and cultural things for myself. Freedom to learn and grow includes the obligation to make the most of opportunities for education and learning. My parents supported and helped to finance my college and seminary education through four years at Furman University and three seminary degrees, including a doctorate.

During recent years, my parents accepted, supported, and encouraged me in my new directions of ministry in Metropolitan Community Church (MCC) and in my writing and publishing for gay and lesbian believers. My first book, *Invitation to Freedom*, was dedicated to them. For all of my life, I have been blessed with the freedom to decide for myself what I believe and what is important to me. All of us want to have the freedom to decide things for ourselves. Judgmental, legalistic religion is totally alien to the kind of freedom that learning, growing, healing, and recovery demand. Many gays and lesbians have had to struggle for the freedom to think for themselves and to be themselves. That freedom is not for sale or open for compromise with self-destructive religion. Either respect me as a person of value and good judgment or leave me alone!

This may sound harsh, but it is not. It is simply being fair to ourselves. It is also being honest. We really do want to grow spiritually. We expect to grow. We will grow some every day. With God's help, we will grow up in Christ.

Jesus Grew Up

One of the most remarkable stories in Luke's Gospel tells how Jesus as a twelve-year-old boy demonstrated his real humanity in development toward maturity. Read Luke 2:39-52. Read also 1 Samuel 2:18-26 and notice the parallels to the boy Jesus in the Temple. Luke 2:52 is quoted from 1 Samuel 2:26, "The boy Samuel was growing in stature and in favor both with God and with the people." Luke added "wisdom." Samuel was sent to a corrupt high priest and a discredited tabernacle to bring God's word of judgment and spiritual revolution. Jesus came also to challenge a corrupt religious system, to declare its impending doom, and then to go beyond Samuel to proclaim God's new word of hope and deliverance for all people.

Jesus was subject to his parents, but he remained in the Temple to talk and listen, to learn and to grow. His parents missed him and returned to find him caught up in the joy and excitement of exploring his own identity and a new and expanding world of opportunity that he had never experienced before. His parents were upset and they did not understand. His mother, however, accepted and respected the need of Jesus to learn and grow beyond her limited vision and abilities. She treasured in her heart the things that Jesus said. If she had a photo album, Mary would have put pictures of the trip in her family album to keep and to show to Jesus when he grew up.

As a human being, Jesus was more like you and me than he was different. He had a vision of the call of God, but he had to "increase" ("grow or make progress") in wisdom, physical stature (literally "age"), and in favor with (literally "before") God and people. To grow or increase obviously means that Jesus changed. He did not spring fully mature from the mind of God. Jesus came into the world just as we do. He was a helpless and dependent little baby. People often speak of the "virgin birth" of Jesus, but it was not the birth but the conception of Jesus that was an act of God through the Holy Spirit. The birth of Jesus was just like ours. Jesus grew up in a loving and caring environment. His mother loved and accepted him, but she did not understand him. He was different. He was not exactly like the other children.

You and I are different. We too are individuals with a calling and mission from God. We have our personal qualities and personalities, including our sexual orientation. Jesus saw his purpose in life as a call from God to be himself. You and I also are called by God to be ourselves and to honor, respect, and celebrate who we are as God's special lesbian and gay children. We also are different, but different does not mean bad or abnormal. Different means special and with a special mission in life that growing up to maturity will help us to see and to put into practice under the guidance and power of the Spirit of God, who made us what we are.

Does this seem to be too good to be true? Is real respect and acceptance of ourselves as God's special gay and lesbian children just too revolutionary to believe? Believe it! It is true. God made you just as you are and put you here for a good purpose. As Troy Perry says, "God didn't create anybody in order to hate them!" Jesus made it clear that God is not a vicious God who plays evil tricks on people. God is love, and in that love, you and I find serenity and hope even in the midst of a storm of misunderstanding and abuse from our society and the religious establishment, which falsely claims to speak for God.

Room to Grow

The parents of Jesus respected his need for room to grow. Even when Jesus was twelve years old, his parents recognized his need to have space to grow and explore being himself. Twelve years old is the age when Jewish boys were considered to become men. We delay our view of adulthood longer than any previous culture in history. We live so long today that you and I both know people who have made a career of going to school well into their 30's and 40's. Remember that in the time of Jesus, the average life expectancy was 25 years. What kinds of books were you reading and what kind of work were you doing when you were twelve years old?

We need room to explore new worlds and to expand our knowledge and to experience the rich variety of people and cultures in the world. Has your family or religion tried to restrict your freedom to learn and explore certain forbidden ideas and taboo subjects? Why is so much effort being made by certain religious groups to deny children the opportunity of learning about sexual orientation, scientific discoveries, and the variety of spirituality in the world? Our world today is more available than ever before through electronic communication. Many of our children, however, are being protected from the truth in the name of biblical literalism and flawed religion.

Religion that makes all of the decisions for us and tries to press us into a shape that does not fit is not the spiritual path that Jesus took. Following Jesus means being free to grow. Being free to grow is being free to explore and to make mistakes. Jesus taught his disciples to follow him, love one another, and listen to God so that they could be equipped to make their own decisions and be truly free.

We have found freedom in Christ in our spiritual support groups and have learned the joy of being given room to grow by being accepted and respected as the truly unique individuals that God made us to be. We learn to respect that freedom for all other people also. Part of the meaning of the inclusive gospel that leaves nobody out is our willingness to give to others their room to grow at their own pace and in their own individual ways.

Learning Obedience

Jesus grew by learning obedience through his sufferings. We often imagine a static Christ who is so perfectly consistent and so perfectly perfect that we cannot really identify with him at all. Read Hebrews 4:14-16 and 5:1-14 to see how Jesus was more like us than different. The word "perfect," *teleios*, means "mature" or "grown up." It means, "to reach a goal, to accomplish a purpose." This is why Jesus used a form of the word *teleios* on the cross when he cried out, "It is finished!" The word *teleios* was used in Matthew 5:48, "Be perfect just as God is perfect."

Grow to maturity. Reach the goal that God has for your life. This is why the word "sin" means "to miss the goal." See

Philippians 3:13-15, where Paul said that he was forgetting what was behind and pressing on to the goal that God had set before him in Christ Jesus in order that he and all of us might attain to be "perfect" or "mature" (*teleios*). Most of the time in the New Testament, the words "mature" or "perfect" are the Greek word, *teleios*.

Pressing on to Maturity

Growth to full maturity, "perfection" (*teleios*), is never over, just as recovery is never over. You grow as long as you live. We are "in recovery" as long as we recognize our need for God's help and continue to work our program of progress out of dependency into freedom. You never stop learning and growing. Read Paul's great statement of our growth from children to maturity as the purpose of all Christian ministries in Ephesians 4:7-15. Stop and read this passage now and think about what it is saying to you. The conclusion is clear, "We are to grow up in all things into Christ" (Ephesians 4:15). Maturity means becoming more like Jesus. In Christ, we learn to speak the truth in love.

In order to keep growing, we constantly let go of the past. We sometimes have to let go of negative and self-defeating relationships. We are tempted to hold on to old security blankets that do not really work but that we hate to leave behind. To grow, recover, and heal a lot of things have to be left behind in our progress toward maturity in Christ. Remember that the main thing Paul had to leave behind to follow Jesus was legalistic, judgmental religion (Philippians 3:4-14). Whatever you leave behind in order to follow Jesus will be replaced by something far better.

Your Leap of Faith

You will not stay as you are. You will either grow or regress. You will either continue to move forward in your trust that God loves and accepts you, or you will slide back into negative, self-defeating attitudes and unhealthy self-rejection. Taking part in a supportive, accepting, affirming small group for study and discussion can help a lot in your progress and growth. If Jesus had to grow, then so do we. We do not really have an option. We grow and live or stop growing and die.

Questions for Study and Discussion

1. What experiences have most helped you to grow toward maturity as a person and as a Christian? What experiences or people have most hindered your growth and recovery?

2. What has love had to do with your spiritual growth? How have suffering and pain helped you to grow?

3. How have you been able to help someone else grow in their faith in God and in their own self-confidence? How have you and others around you experienced growth in personal freedom and self-esteem?

Additional Resources

Get and use the book that helped me to deal with a profound personal loss, Iyanla Vanzant, *Acts of Faith: Daily Meditations for People of Color*: A Fireside Book, 1993. The Rev. Carolyn Mobley recommended this book to me when I needed it most. The book spoke to me and I believe it will speak to you.

Many Christians have been helped to catch a fresh vision spiritual growth and maturity by reading Watchman Nee, *The Normal Christian Life* (on Romans) and *Sit, Walk, Stand* (on Ephesians): Christian Literature Crusade, 1957.

Lesson 50

Growing Up in the Celebration of Life

† **Preparatory Bible Reading:** Matthew 11:28-30; John 3:16-17; 11:1-57; 14:1-27; 1 Corinthians 15:1-58; Romans 8:18-39

Instead of traditional funerals, gay and lesbian Christians often have celebrations of life. Ministers in Metropolitan Community Church (MCC) as well as many other clergy have led thousands of celebrations of life for people who have died from HIV/AIDS and for many others. The shift from funerals to celebrations of life is one of the greatest contributions to the spiritual life of our world by lesbian, gay, transgendered, and bisexual people.

During the almost 30 years I was a Southern Baptist minister, I do not remember ever hearing a joke or anything intentionally funny at a funeral. After 18 years in MCC, I cannot remember a celebration of life that did not contain humor, jokes, and occasionally a real knee-slapper! Humor and laughter are part of life, and a celebration of life is a lot more real and honest if the funny side of life is included. Humor was never planned. It just happened.

What Is a Celebration of Life?

A typical celebration of life might be held in a church, a funeral home, a gay bar, outdoors, or in a home. I have led them in all of these places. A celebration of life is informal and is always fitted to the individual and to the friends and family. Frequently people with HIV/AIDS plan their own celebration of life down to every detail of songs, reading, and who should lead. Usually a table is set up at the front to display things that were important to the deceased, including one or more pictures of the person whose life is being celebrated. Music often is lively and reflects the desires and interests of the person whose life is celebrated. My friend Crayne Kam's celebration of life in San Francisco featured three hula dancers. People dress up to come to a celebration of life. Some wear their best leather, really good drag (or really bad drag!), or whatever best expresses themselves.

The program is usually simple. A printed brochure often is provided with a picture and information about the person being honored. A word of welcome and an opening prayer begin the service, followed by music, either live or recorded, instrumental or vocal. Music often is a very important feature of celebration of the personality and life of a person. Brief meditations on encouraging and uplifting Bible passages might be included. My approach to using the Bible in celebrations of life is to quote brief familiar passages such as Psalm 23; John 3:16-17; and 1 Peter 1:3-9. A celebration of life is not the time to get into attempts at heavy theological or other explanations or speculations about religion. People are under emotional strain and need simple and clear expressions of encouragement and hope. People also need the opportunity to express themselves.

Telling It Like It Was

After these brief beginnings, the celebration of life moves into the main and most creative and helpful part of the experience. People are invited to talk about the person being remembered in the celebration. This can be a significant and healing time of emotional sharing. This is the time when a lot of funny things are shared. Some of the remembrances shared with the group are not intended to be funny, but they come across that way. Laughter is a way to relieve stress and tension. Laughter can be great therapy.

Some of the remembrances bring sadness and crying because of the profound sense of loss and grief that is shared with the group. Emotional support is given and received. Healing and encouragement can be important and lasting experiences during celebrations of life. Sharing may last for five or ten minutes or extend for an hour or more, depending on the mood and needs of the people in the group. The group really decides how long to share and whoever is leading can sense when it is time to conclude the sharing. A closing prayer or a song might conclude the service. Holy Communion is often included as part of a celebration of life. The person being honored and remembered along with friends and family determine the style and content of the celebration. A lot of creative new things are often included. No two celebrations of life are alike, for we respect and celebrate our uniqueness as individuals before God. We are all different from one another and we all have equal value, which is best honored and celebrated in ways that express our individuality.

Eating Together as Celebration

Most of the celebrations of life that I have seen concluded with a time of sharing food and fellowship. This might be in a home or church social hall or at a restaurant selected for the occasion. Eating together has traditionally been associated with ceremonies honoring people who have died. Eating a common meal is symbolic of sharing life in some form in most spiritual traditions.

Various features of celebrations of life have developed to meet the needs of people who are as diverse as the general population. Not having a common tradition to draw upon in times of profound loss and grief, gay people have created and developed their own emerging traditions for facing and dealing with the extraordinary pressures of the HIV/AIDS epidemic and its effects on individuals and groups.

New Forms for a New People of God

Some funeral homes have refused to handle the bodies of gay men who died of HIV/AIDS. Churches and pastors have refused to conduct services for gay and lesbian people. The HIV/AIDS epidemic has brought many gay and lesbian believers into head-on confrontations with the established churches. Mike Bussee called me when his partner Gary Cooper died of HIV/AIDS in 1991. Mike was one of the founders of Exodus International and had worked with Exodus along with his partner for five years before they realized they were hurting and not helping gay people. They also fell in love with each other and began a happy life together. Mike had told me he wanted me to lead Gary's celebration of life.

Mike announced to me, however, that Gary's family had asked their local Methodist pastor to lead the service; so Mike felt that would be appropriate and comforting for Gary's surviving family. Later, Mike told me what really happened. Just two hours before time for the service, the Methodist pastor called and told Mike that he could not perform the service. He had learned that Gary was in "the homosexual lifestyle" and he felt that if he led the service he would appear to condone and accept "the homosexual lifestyle." Mike was stunned. The pastor knew all along that Gary had HIV/AIDS and that Gary and Mike had been partners for over twelve years. Mike had two hours to find someone to conduct the service for Gary.

When Mike told me this, I asked why he did not just do it himself. He said he thought of it but was afraid that he would break down emotionally and could not continue. Then he told me that he called a close friend for advice. The friend said, "I don't have to look for somebody to do the service for you, Mike. I am an ordained minister. I will gladly do it myself." Mike's friend was Mel White. Mike and Mel had been friends for a long time. The celebration of life was just what Gary would have wanted, and Mel White went on to become one of the most effective forces for human rights and religious freedom that our community has seen so far.

New Ways to Celebrate

In Mark 2:18-22, Jesus and his disciples were celebrating at a wedding, and the Pharisees criticized Jesus for celebrating during a time that was ordinarily devoted to fasting. Jesus responded with his famous teaching, "No one puts new wine into old wineskins; otherwise the wine will burst the skins, and the wine is lost, and the skins also; but new wine belongs in fresh wineskins." Jesus linked the new freedom of his disciples to celebrate when others were fasting to the fact that they were in the presence of Jesus. Does the presence of Jesus in your life lead you to a new level of joy and celebration?

The use of the Bible and religion to abuse and oppress gay people has forced many people to search for new forms of spirituality that do not carry the sting of judgmental legalism. When traditional religion makes people in need "feel lower than a worm," as one woman put it, they look elsewhere for help and encouragement. The Universal Fellowship of Metropolitan Community Churches (UFMCC) was begun and has continued for over 30 years because the unmet need of lesbians and gay men for spiritual support in life's crises never ends. When religious leaders serve up vinegar and the bitter weeds of homophobic judgmental legalism instead of the bread of life, it is no surprise that many gay, lesbian, bisexual, and transgendered people have turned away from traditional churches and church rituals to find or create for themselves something better.

Many gay people began to look for a better way to deal with grief and bereavement when families would not even allow a gay or lesbian person's lover to attend the funeral service for their life partner. Such insensitive disregard for basic human need is so contrary to the compassionate attitude of Jesus that it is difficult to see how abusive religion has been able to convince people that homophobic, judgmental legalism has any connection at all with the Jesus of the Gospels.

Traditions of Grief and Mourning

Celebrations of life as healthy and healing approaches to dealing with grief and bereavement are helping a lot of people besides gay people. Increasingly now, I am seeing traditional church leaders conduct funerals in the style of celebrations of life. Mournful and sad traditions related to death and burial are deeply rooted in our common human experience. Jesus stopped a noisy funeral procession and raised up from the dead a young man who was being taken to the cemetery and restored him to his grieving widowed mother in Luke 12:11-17. Jesus turned a mournful tragic moment into a party by an act that foreshadowed his own resurrection and gift of life to all people.

This story came to my mind in 1958 when I was with a seminary study group in Cairo, Egypt. We heard screaming and yelling outside the hotel on the street below and looked down to see a funeral procession moving through the streets. As in the time of Jesus, people were buried on the same day that they died. The body wrapped in white cloth was carried and accompanied by a large crowd of people dressed in black and screaming their piercing cry of lament and sorrow, which was customary and appropriate as a means of showing honor to the deceased. It was like a sudden flash back through 2,000 years of human history to the time of Jesus and his revolutionary view of death and everything else.

Jesus expected his followers to be open and responsive to all human suffering and needs and to be creative and revolutionary in how they developed the forms and rituals of their new spirituality. Gay people have led the way in creating new patterns for celebrating holy unions for same-sex couples and have developed both celebrations of life and the Names Project Memorial Quilt to remember and honor those who have died. Rejection and condemnation by traditional church and community sources for comfort and support in times of loss and pain have driven gay, lesbian, bisexual, and transgendered Christians to find and follow paths that are truly new and exciting.

Love is the underlying motivation for holy unions, the Names Project Quilt, celebrations of life, and community services and support for people with HIV/AIDS. Love is of God, for "God is love." Remember, the most frequent comment that I heard from non-gay people at the showing of the Names Memorial Quilt in Atlanta in 1988 was, "There is so much love here!" In Christ, we learn to grow in our celebration of life and to build upon the good news of Jesus in the gospels as the basis for self-acceptance and self-esteem that sustain us in our steady progress toward full maturity.

Questions for Study and Discussion

1. Have you attended a celebration of life for a person who died with HIV/AIDS? What was it like? How did it affect you?

2. What unmet spiritual needs do you feel still need to be addressed more fully in the gay community? How could you be given more encouragement and support in times of crisis in your life?

3. How is facing life's common crises, such as marriage, serious illness, death and bereavement different for lesbians and gay men than for non-gay people in our society? What resources in books, other people, or groups have been most helpful to you in times of crisis?

Additional Resources

The Universal Fellowship of Metropolitan Community Churches (UFMCC) can provide up-to-date literature on holy unions, celebrations of life, and other related issues. See the UFMCC Web site (www.ufmcc.com) or write to UFMCC at 8704 Santa Monica Blvd., 2nd floor, Los Angeles, CA 90069 or call at 310/360-8640 for information.

Granger Westberg's *Good Grief* (Fortress Press, 1986) is still my favorite source of help to give to grieving people.

Lesson 51

Growing Up in Love

† **Preparatory Bible Reading:** Luke 10:25-37; John 13:34-35; 1 Corinthians 13:1-13

Spiritual maturity in Christ is measured in terms of love. "Above all, keep fervent in your love for one another, because love covers a multitude of sins. Show hospitality to one another without murmuring" (1 Peter 4:8-9). The word "murmuring," the Greek word *goggusmos*, is the same in Acts 6:1 where complaining developed about how some people were neglected in the serving of food to the needy. You can count on some of us to find a way to fight over love and how to show it.

Love is never fully mature and perfect. Love is like recovery from addiction. We once were addicted to self and self-destructive appetites. We are in recovery, and recovery takes time. We are on the road to recovery. We do not let go of the upward calling of God to mature love in Christ. We are on the right path, but we are not there yet.

Love as the Goal of Growth

Review the story in Luke 10:25-37 of the greatest commandment and the definition of neighbor in the adventure in compassion by a religious and social outcast. Then read again the New Commandment of Jesus in John 13:34-45 to love one another just as Jesus loved you. By our love for each other the world will be convinced that we are disciples of Jesus. Every use of "love" in John 13 is the Greek word *agape*, which is the love defined in the life of Jesus and in "God is love" in 1 John 4. Love is the quality that makes us most like Jesus and God. Read Matthew 5:43-48.

The only way that you can love as Jesus loved is to be filled with the Spirit of Jesus so that Jesus loves through you. It is not so important what you do as what you let Jesus do through you. Jesus said that we are to become fully mature like God is mature ("perfect," *teleios*) as the conclusion of saying that we are to love our enemies and be impartial and inclusive in our love just as God is inclusive and impartial in sending sunshine and rain for everybody. To be the children of God is to love, and to love is to be children of God.

How Does Your Love Level Measure Up?

Try a little experiment. Turn to 1 Corinthians 13 in your Bible. Begin at verse 4 and everywhere the word "love" appears, put in your name instead. Everybody laughed when I started the list in a college class one time by saying "Rembert is patient. Rembert is kind and is not jealous. Rembert does not brag and is not arrogant." The biggest laugh came when I read the final statement in 13:8 with my name in place of love, "Rembert never fails!"

You can have fun with this exercise in a group as each person reads 13:4-8 out loud with her or his name in place of "love." It will be amusing but also a sobering experience. It can help us not to take ourselves too seriously and at the same time realize that we have a lot growing to do to become like Jesus in our love. Most of the words that were used in 1 Corinthians 13:4-8 also were used in the Gospels to describe Jesus.

Wonderful Words of Love

Words to describe love in 1 Corinthians 13:4-8 were carefully selected and are filled with meaning. As in all of Paul's lists, the first and last items are especially important. They set the stage for the list and wrap up at the end with a big bang conclusion. The words are practical and not sentimental. They are realistic descriptions of love as seen in the life of Jesus and in the acts of God. Let's take a close look at each word.

"Love Is Patient"

Patient, the Greek word *makrothumei*, for "long" plus "anger," meaning that it takes a lot to make you angry. Patient describes God, "Do you think lightly of the riches of God's kindness and forbearance and patience, not knowing that the kindness of God leads you to repentance?" (Romans 2:4). See lesson 13 on "How Jesus Handled Anger." How do you handle your anger? The answer to that question is the first measurement of how much your love demonstrates the presence of Jesus within you. When you let your anger control you, you have not yet let the Spirit of Jesus control you.

Winning against anger and impatience are necessary steps to spiritual maturity in love. But how do we win? Watchman Nee tells in his book *The Normal Christian Life* (page 126) a story about his visit with an American Christian couple who asked him to pray for them about their problem. They explained that they were in a bad way, because they were very easily irritated by their children and during the past few weeks had both lost their tempers several times a day. They asked Brother Nee to pray for God to give them patience. Nee replied that he could not do it. He said he would not pray for their request because the prayer would not be answered. They were shocked and asked if they were beyond help. He said "No," and asked, "Have you ever prayed for patience? You have. But did God answer? No. Do you know why? Because you have no need of patience."

With that, the wife's eyes flashed and she became very upset and asked Nee what he meant. His answer was, "You do not need patience. You need Christ." He went on to explain that "God does not give humility or patience or holiness or love in separate little packets. God has already given us all that we need in giving Jesus to us. I will gladly pray for you to have more of Jesus in your life." This is a great and necessary key to every dimension of spiritual growth at every level. We grow in love and in everything else by having more of Jesus in our hearts and lives. As we look at each of the words that describe love, think of how the presence of Jesus within you makes them happen for you.

"Love is Kind"

The same basic word in Greek, *chrestos*, is used in Galatians 5:22 as fruit of the Spirit and in Matthew 11:30, where Jesus said, "My yoke is gentle," it means "well fitted." Kind is a word that describes the gentle and kind attitude that respects the feelings of others. Kindness helps us to accept others as they are and to respect their individuality without trying to force them to change to suit us. Kindness controls us when we "speak the truth in love." Truth not spoken in love is not heard as truth. When my family drove away after a visit with my parents, my father used to say, "Be kind to each other!"

"Love Is Not Jealous or Boastful or Arrogant"

These three negative words deal with attitudes that make us unattractive to others. Jealous, the Greek word *zeloi*, comes from the word for "hot" or "boil." We get the words zeal, zealous, and jealous from it. It means that when you love you do not get hot and upset when something good happens to somebody else instead of to you. To boast means to brag and show off. It means that you refuse to do anything unless you get credit for it. Arrogant means "puffed up" with your own importance. It really does mean "to be full of hot air!" See also 1 Corinthians 4:6, 18 and Colossians 2:18.

"Love Does Not Hide in Shame"

The Greek word is *aschemonei* and is the word for "indecent, unbecoming, unseemly" used in Romans 1:27; 1 Corinthians 7:36; 12:23; and Revelation 16:15. It refers to what is hidden or covered because of shame. Love is out in the open. Do you think this says something about our coming out of the closet?

"Love Does Not Seek Its Own Way and is Not Easily Provoked"

Read Romans 15:1-7, which begins, "We who are strong ought to bear the weaknesses of those without strength and not just please ourselves." Love leads you to put the interests and needs of others before your own. We usually call it love when we want others to meet our needs and not because we want to meet theirs. When we try to pressure someone else to do what we want whether that person wants to do it or not, we are not acting out of love. "Provoke" is the Greek word *paroxunetai*, and means "to urge on, to stimulate, especially to provoke to wrath, to irritate." The only other uses are in Acts 15:39; 17:16. It means something like, "Let's you and him fight!"

"Love Thinks No Evil"

The Greek word is *logizetai*, which is a term used in accounting and means that love does not keep a list of hurts and resentments. Love is able to forget the things that others have done to wound and hurt. To keep a list of wrongs suffered at the hands of others is to live imprisoned in the past. Part of love is letting go of the damage others have done to you. This is a healthy move toward maturity for you. Simmering resentments and nursing grudges can make us physically ill. Love sets us free to go on and live in joy and hope without having to drag along baggage from the past. I am sure you realize how important this is for gay Christians. Jesus offers us freedom and joy, but we can never enjoy life as long as we will not let go of all of the awful things people have done to us because of our sexual orientation. Let go and live!

"Love Does Not Rejoice in Unrighteousness But in the Truth"

Love never enjoys seeing somebody else getting hurt. Love never goes about listening and telling gossip about others. Love, however, rejoices in the truth. Living in the truth is never easy. Love means coming out of the closet for many gay people who are afraid of their own truth about themselves. Love means to stop living in denial about our addictions, even when we are addicted to sick and abusive religions. Love means letting Jesus set us free to be our true self. It is good to live in truth, but it is not easy. The truth will set us free, because the truth of God's love has liberated us. The question that has to be answered is "Am I ready for real freedom? Can I handle real freedom?"

"Love Bears, Believes, Hopes, and Endures All Things"

Love "all things bears, all things believes, all things hopes, all things endures." This is the order of the words in Greek. "Bears" all things means "to cover," the Greek word *stegei*, "to put a cover over something to protect it." Here it means "to cover, pass over in silence, keep confidential." Love "bears all things" by throwing a cloak of silence over what is displeasing in another person.

"Believes all things" does not mean that love is hopelessly gullible and will believe anything. That obviously is not the meaning. Believe and hope are closely connected. The two terms together mean that love says to the troubled person, "I believe in you. I have great hope for you. I am confident that you can become the person God has plans for you to be in Christ." Love means that in our relationships with others we "believe and hope all things" in an attitude of positive, supportive encouragement. Love never thinks of looking for opportunities to put down other people and say, "Ha! I told you so!"

"Love Endures All Things"

"Endures" is *hupomenei* in Greek, literally the two words, "super" and "remain." Love means to stand your ground no matter what happens or what others may do. It means to hold out and remain instead of running away. It is expressed in John 13:1, where "having loved his own who were in the world, Jesus loved them to the end (*telos*)." Jesus loved his friends until his mission was accomplished. Jesus did not run away or abandon those he loved. Jesus set the example of love in every way. To love is to stand firm and not give up on anybody.

"Love Never Gives Up"

The final word is *piptei*, meaning "to fall" and was used of a structure that collapsed or was ruined. It means "to become invalid, come to an end, fail." Love, like Jesus, never gives up. Love never quits loving. "Love is not love, that alters when it alteration finds." If we love only when we are loved, if our love is inconsistent, and if we love others only when they are loveable, we have a lot of growing up to do in loving one another as Jesus loved us. Love is the greatest gift, because when you love, you give yourself.

Questions for Study and Discussion

1. Think about what you mean when you say to someone, "I love you." My friend Dr. Roy O. McClain said, "I love you is never so meaningless as when it has to be said." What do you think that means?

2. How has our popular romantic vision of love in movies, novels, songs, and television distorted the meaning of love as it is presented by Jesus in the Bible?

3. What is the difference in the meaning of love according to Jesus and our romantic view of falling in love? What is the result of confusing the various meanings of love? Growing in love is a lifelong process. How far along the road to mature love do you think that you have come?

Lesson 52

Growing Up in Self-Control

† **Preparatory Bible Reading:** John 8:21-59; 1 Corinthians 9:16-27; Philippians 4:4-13

Self-control is the ultimate evidence of maturity. When I was drinking, the most destructive result was my frequent loss of control of my emotions and of my ability to think clearly. We all want to be free, but how can I become free from me? Paul's list of fruit of the spirit in Galatians 5:22-23 begins with love and concludes with self-control. The Greek term "self-control," *egkratein*, is formed from "self," *ego*, and "grip, grasp," *krateo*. It literally means "to get a grip on yourself." Many things can cause us to lose control, such as anger, fear, substance abuse, prejudice, ignorance, greed, abusive sick religion, and anything else that tries to take over and run our lives.

The first step in recovery from alcoholism is to admit that you have lost control of your life. Alcohol is in control. The first step in any recovery from addiction is to admit that you have lost control. Some addictions are more difficult to understand and admit than others. In codependency, you have to admit that you cannot really control other people.

Jesus in Charge

Read John 8:21-59. Throughout the Gospels, Jesus was pictured as totally in charge of his own life. In the Gospel of John, Jesus was seen to be always in control. He had authority to lay down his life and authority to take it again. His life was not taken from him; he voluntarily gave it up. He said that Pilate had no power at all over him except what God had given. Jesus declared that no harm could come to him until his "hour" had come. John 8:1-59 focuses on the experience and teachings of Jesus about being in control. Jesus pointed out to the people that they were in bondage to lies and distorted religious beliefs. They refused to listen. They were deep into denial about what was controlling them.

Who or what is calling the shots in your life? During the six years that I was drinking in Atlanta, I regularly denied that I had a drinking problem and really believed that I could quit at any time. Why did I continue to let alcohol control my life for almost seven years? I do not know. I probably will never know. You do not have to know why you are letting unclean spirits be in control of your life just as long as you recognize that you are not in control and need help.

A Remarkable Change in Life

When I served as pastor of a new mission church in Danville, Kentucky, as I was finishing my first seminary degree, I got to know Jay. His family came to the church, but he did not. He operated a used car business and was very successful. He was helpful and encouraging to me, but he rejected any effort on my part to share Christ with him. He gambled and drank a lot and allowed many unhealthy and negative forces to run his life. After I had moved away and began to serve a church in Greenwood, South Carolina, Jay called me on the phone to tell me his news. He had been very sick with headaches and had discovered that he had a brain tumor. He finally decided that he needed Jesus in his life and he became a Christian. He called me to tell me that my prayers for him had finally been answered.

Then Jay began to cry. He said that he was not crying for his own sake or his family, because they were all fine and well taken care of, but he was sad because he was not going to live long enough to tell all of his friends about how Jesus had changed him. The doctors had given him only a few weeks to live. When Jay became a Christian, he had given his testimony at the church and been baptized. Several of his drinking buddies and other friends turned to God and accepted Jesus into their lives. Jay's life was completely changed. He worked very hard to reach out to others to be a missionary of hope for every person that his life touched.

Jay had called me because he knew that I really cared about him and would be very happy to know that he had become a Christian. Jay said that he only wished he had turned to God sooner. I got another call about two weeks later to learn that Jay had died. His funeral was a community event that touched many people for Christ and led to others turning to God for help to make a new beginning. Jay finally had found the self-control that had been missing for most of his life.

A Vision of God's Control

A good way to catch a vision of the meaning of God's control in your life is to read through the Gospel of John and let the life of Jesus sink into your mind and heart. I know of no shortcuts to learning and growing in your knowledge of Jesus Christ as the pattern and guide for your life. Take whatever time necessary to learn and absorb the story of Jesus. Spend some time with the Gospel of John every day. The more of Jesus you have in your life, the more you will be free from unworthy negative forces in control of your life. Letting go and allowing Jesus to take over is the only way to get out of the way so that God can do the miracle in your life.

The Gospel of John emphasized the total obedience of Jesus to God. Jesus experienced self-control that gave him power and sustained him to triumph over all of the negative forces around and within his life. Jesus found perfect freedom through perfect obedience to God. Jesus said, "I am the way, and the truth, and the life; no one comes to God but through me" (John 14:6). When you follow Jesus, the way to God is the way Jesus experienced God through love, trust, and radical obedience. We come to God and experience God in the same way that Jesus did. Jesus is the road map and the clear guide to our experience with God. Each of us, however, becomes open to God and experiences God for ourselves in whatever way best fits us. This is the combination of freedom and self-control that characterized the life of Jesus.

Jesus made clear (in John 13 through 17) that your experience with God is personal and individual and unlike the experience of any other individual. You are not exactly like anybody else. In Christ, we learn to respect the differences in each other and to love each other and ourselves just as we are. Accepting yourself and others in love sets you free to be your true self and to be free to experience self-control in healthy spiritual growth toward maturity in Christ.

The Key to self-Control

Accepting ourselves and each other as persons with value to God, to ourselves, and to each other just as we are is the path to healthy spirituality and self-control. As soon as you start trying to run other people's lives you lose your freedom. You become obsessed and controlled by the temptation to play God and decide what is best for someone else. You are seduced by your good intentions to use your limited knowledge and power to try to force others to conform to your beliefs and convictions.

The problem of trying to play God, however, is obvious. You are not God. To play God is to abandon reality and to live in denial of the truth. You are set free from trying to play God and run other people's lives only when you learn to respect God, trust God, and let God be the one in charge, just as Jesus did throughout his life as set forth in the Gospel of John. God's control of your life sets you free from slavery to unworthy and destructive forces, such as legalistic sick religion that seeks to dominate us and take away our freedom in Christ.

Jesus never called anybody to submit in slavish, unswerving servitude to a system of doctrines, rituals, rules, regulations, and religion. Jesus came to set us free once and for all from destructive distortions of God's love and truth. In Christ, you have been set free. You are released from bondage. You are free to be yourself. Celebrate who you are. Explore your own uniqueness as a person. Jesus was free. Jesus celebrated who he was. Jesus found beautiful, consistent, honest self-control in his loving, obedient relationship with God. So Jesus invites you to share in his joy. Jesus wants you to be happy, "These things I have spoken to you that my joy may be in you and your joy may be made full" (John 15:11). You are not free to enjoy self-control as long as other people and unworthy attitudes are in control.

Compelled by the Gospel

Paul claimed to be under obligation to proclaim and teach the gospel. Read 1 Corinthians 9:16-27. Paul saw himself as a carefully disciplined athlete who had to sacrifice and train in order to win. Who is running your life? Are you in control or have you given control over to forces that are destructive and misuse you? Paul said that he was free from all, but he had voluntarily made himself "slave to all in order that he might win the more." Paul was free because he had given himself to Jesus Christ to guide and empower his life. "I have become all things to all people that I may by all means liberate [save] some" (1 Corinthians 9:22b).

We are free from the controlling forces of our lower nature because "the love of Christ controls us" (2 Corinthians 5:14). We are no longer slaves, but we are the children of God. Since we are related to God as beloved children, Paul asked, "How is it that you turn back again to the weak and worthless elemental things to which you desire to be enslaved all over again?" (Galatians 4:9). The "elemental things," the Greek word *stoichia*, are literally "things in a row," like ABC's and refers to our basic drives and appetites that can take control of our lives if we do not enter fully into God's gift of freedom in Christ (Galatians 4:3, 6-11; and 5:1).

Paul identified "elemental things" with legalistic, judgmental religion. Paul asked a very interesting question in the midst of his plea in Galatians 4 and 5 for believers to live in the freedom of Christ and not be enslaved again by sick abusive religion, "Have I therefore become your enemy by telling you the truth?" (Galatians 4:16). That is a very relevant question that we have to ask today. Why does anyone defend abusive, judgmental, legalistic religion when we can enjoy real freedom in Christ?

Finding Contentment in Christ

What does it take to rattle your cage? Are you easily bent out of shape by criticism from others or by neglect, ridicule, misunderstandings, dishonesty, and unfair treatment? All of us have our breaking point. We can take just so much pressure and abuse, and we explode. Can you usually tell when you are about to lose it and blow up under pressure? What do you do? Have you discovered any techniques for survival under pressure? I wish I knew good answers for all of these questions. We are all in the same boat. We all would like to discover the secret of how to "keep your head when all about you are losing theirs and blaming it on you."

Read Philippians 4:4-13 for a glimpse into the mind of Paul on contentment under pressure. This passage tells us how to ride out the storm and survive when the wind is against us, our boat is leaking, and we are out of strength and sinking fast. Paul said, "I have learned to be content in whatever circumstances I am" (Philippians 4:11). The word "content" was a key word in Stoic philosophy. "Content" in Greek is *autarkes*, from *auto* (self) and *arkeo* (rule) and refers to the state of mind in which one is unmoved by outside pressures and distractions. The Stoics used *autoarkes* to speak of reaching the goal of self-control in which an individual can remain calm and contented no matter what happens. Paul saw this "self-rule" as a gift of Christ, "through whom I can do all things" (4:13).

We can view the Bible as a weapon to abuse and hurt ourselves and others, or we can see it all through new eyes given to us by Jesus Christ. Jesus can give to us a fresh new perspective on the Bible that guides us to find and follow attitudes and examples that are healthy and healing and that lead us into love, joy, peace, and hope and on into full spiritual maturity and wholeness. Abandon Jesus, and you can find and follow biblical literalism into truly sick and abusive religion that oppresses and destroys the children of God. Jesus alone can overcome all of your addictions and controlling demons. You are free in Christ. Enjoy it.

Questions for Study and Discussion

1. Why have you been willing to let other people run your life? How does being dominated and controlled by abusive and oppressive religion feel to you?

2. How have you found success in gaining self-control in your own life? What has been your greatest obstacle to overcome?

3. What part of the Bible has been the most liberating for you? What in the Gospels has helped you most to let go of negative, unworthy, destructive forces in your life in order to find freedom and contentment instead?

Additional Resources

John J. McNeill, *Freedom, Glorious Freedom: The Spiritual Journey to the Fullness of Life for Gays, Lesbians, and Everybody Else*: Beacon Press, 1995.

Conclusion

Let Go and Live

Forgiveness is the basis for freedom in Christ. The Greek word for "forgive" is *aphiami*, which means to "let go, abandon." To forgive someone is to let go. To accept your own forgiveness is to let go. When God forgives you, God lets go of your faults and failures. Forgiveness, therefore, is freedom. This understanding of forgiveness reveals the meaning of the call of Jesus in Luke 24:47 to "proclaim forgiveness to all people" as God's invitation to freedom.

Abusive and oppressive religion has distorted the good news of freedom in Christ by convincing multitudes that the way of Christ is a tough, demanding, legalistic, judgmental journey through guilt. This book, *Steps to Recovery from Bible Abuse*, is an attempt to announce deliverance to the captives and open unseeing eyes so that love, truth, and freedom will prevail. Sharing Jesus Christ with others can be your part in the spiritual revolution that will change the world and free the slaves.

Sharing Your Faith With Gentleness and Respect

The Rev. Carolyn Mobley is a loving and caring minister who serves as associate pastor at Metropolitan Community Church (MCC) of the Resurrection in Houston. Carolyn has been my friend for over 18 years and has taught me a lot about the meaning of Christian ministry to all people. Carolyn visited Rosa in the hospital. Rosa is a lesbian in her 60's who grew up Roman Catholic. She has been rejected by her family and is hospitalized with a variety of serious illnesses. Over the course of several visits, Rosa asked Carolyn to share with her and help her spiritually. They went through the brochure, "The Bible as Your Friend," but Rosa was not ready to pray and invite Jesus into her life. She said that she felt unworthy.

Later, Carolyn took a communion set with her to visit Rosa. When Carolyn offered to share communion with her, Rosa said again that she was not worthy to receive it. Carolyn explained that taking communion was not based on being worthy but was simply a way for Rosa to invite Jesus to come into her life. Rosa said, "Yes. I want to do that." Carolyn and Rosa shared communion, which was Rosa's way of praying and inviting Jesus into her life. Carolyn demonstrated how to "give a reason for your hope in Christ, yet with gentleness and reverence." Flexibility and really listening to others can open many doors that seem to be closed.

Grow by letting go of ancient commitments and traditions that get in the way of being available here and now to the real people in your life. Forgive yourself and others by letting go of the icy death grip of the past on your life today. Let go and begin to live fully and with joy in Christ. Start having fun.

Are you having fun yet?

Appendices

Special Studies

These "Special Studies" provide background material and additional information and resources to illuminate the issues that are discussed in the Thirteen Steps and the 52 lessons in this book.

A. How I Lead Workshops and Groups

B. Homosexuality and The Bible

C. Challenging the "Ex-Gay" Industry

D. The Dynamics of Religious Abuse

E. A Gay Christian Response to Southern Baptists

F. How Do You Name God?

Special Study A

How I Lead Workshops and Groups

Most of what I know about small group spiritual recovery has come from leading workshops on "Recovery from Bible Abuse," facilitating small groups for many years, and my years of teaching group dynamics in many of my college courses. In recent years, I have had the privilege of leading workshops and small groups for many Metropolitan Community Churches (MCC) and other primarily gay congregations and groups.

I would like to share with you some of what I have learned about how to lead workshops and small group spiritual recovery in private homes and churches. As always, I will appreciate your feedback about this.

Building a nonjudgmental environment is essential for meaningful group discussion and dialogue. It is up to the leader or facilitator of the group to set this tone of freedom of discussion and mutual respect for every person present.

How I Lead A Workshop

1. Prepare
2. Arrange the seating in a circle
3. Get acquainted
4. Take frequent breaks
5. Present the main points
6. Listen
7. Stop at the announced time

1. The first thing that I do is to **prepare** in printed form ahead of time all of the material that seems to be important for the group. I see to it that we have enough sets of material for each person who will attend. I know that we never have enough time to cover all that is needed in the workshop; so the printed material gives incentive and information for further study after the workshop is over. I did this in my college classes so that we could spend as much time as needed for discussion and questions. People, not the material, are the main agenda in group dialogue.

2. **Arrange the seating in a circle** so that everybody in the group can easily see and hear everybody else. All studies of group work reveal that far more individual participation takes place in a circle than in rows. People remember best what they themselves say and what is said in answer to their questions. A circle encourages attention and participation by everyone present.

3. I begin a workshop by **getting acquainted**, asking each person to tell their name, their religious background, and what they hope to get out of the workshop. I take notes on what people say so that I will know each person's name and will have a better idea of the expectations and issues that concern the group. This often takes the first hour, but it is the best way I have found to start a group. During this time of sharing, people who have known each other for years learn important experiences, ideas, and attitudes about each other that they did not know before.

4. **Take frequent breaks**, at least every hour. This makes workshops possible! A bathroom break is necessary for most people, including me. Refreshments, such as coffee, other drinks, and cookies or other snacks are helpful. Often in a one-day workshop, a lunch break is taken in the middle of the day with simple food prepared ahead of time. Many variations on the breaks and refreshments are possible. The atmosphere of the group should be relaxed and informal so that a person can leave the group and return without fear of disturbing everyone else.

5. **Present the main points.** I try to cover in brief the main points and issues that the workshop has promised. Usually, after the time of getting acquainted, I give out the words and play

Harry Chapin's song, "Flowers Are Red." The words are included earlier in this book in Chapter 4. Read them and see why they are always appropriate for the beginning of any workshop.

6. **Listen** and encourage discussion. I always learn as much as I teach when I lead a workshop or small group. Twenty to thirty people can comfortably sit in a circle and engage in the dialogue of a workshop. For more intense dialogue and participation by each person, however, breaking into groups of six to eight people can be very helpful. Some of my college classes had 60 or more students in a study of such subjects as counseling, group dynamics, missions, evangelism, and preaching. We would spend some of our class sessions in small dialogue groups of six to ten people. We always learned better how to do this every time we tried it.

7. **Stop at the announced time.** I usually remain at the workshop as long as anyone wants to talk or ask questions. If the workshop is on Saturday or another weekday and is followed by Sunday worship services, some people may want to make appointments to talk with me later. I try not to wear people out with too much material and workshop activity at once. Most of the workshops begin at about 9:30 a.m. on Saturday morning and run until about 3:00 p.m. This means that lunchtime and several breaks are included.

A typical schedule for me when I visit a church is to have various types of group meetings or church services on Thursday and/or Friday evenings, the workshop on Saturday, and regular worship services (whenever they are usually held) on Sunday.

Workshops and other learning and growing opportunities are flexible and can be adapted to each situation. There are few "rules" of group dynamics that apply every time and every place. Groups change and develop like people do, and no two groups are ever exactly alike. **Listening,** really listening, and hearing what others are thinking and saying, is the key.

Special Study B

Homosexuality and the Bible

A. Learn the Facts About Homosexuality and the Bible
B. Hebrew and Greek
C. How I View the Bible
D. Translating the Gospels
E. What Bible to Read
F. Six Bible Passages Used to Attack Gay People

A. Learn the Facts About Homosexuality and the Bible

✓ Sexual orientation is not mentioned in the Bible.

✓ The original Bible languages of Hebrew and Greek have no words for "homosexual," "sex," or "romantic love."

✓ The Bible nowhere says that gays and lesbians can or should change their sexual orientation.

✓ The six Bible passages used against lesbians, gay men, bisexuals, and transgendered people are incorrectly translated and used out of context to hurt people not in the original text.

✓ The use of the Bible to condemn lesbians and gays violates scientific principles of translation and interpretation and is academically unsound, indefensible, irresponsible, and ignorant.

- ✓ The Bible in the original languages never condemns same-sex, romantic love as sin.

- ✓ The Bible gives positive support for same-sex, committed relationships in stories about Ruth and Naomi in the book of Ruth and David and Jonathan in 1 Samuel 18-20 and 2 Samuel 1.

- ✓ Bible translators and publishers who persist in using evil homophobic "translations from hell" to wound and destroy lesbians and gays must be challenged and corrected.

- ✓ Jesus never mentioned homosexuality. Distortion of the gospel into attacks on gay people demands a clear and effective response now.

- ✓ The Bible repeatedly demonstrates God's love, care, and acceptance of all outcast, rejected, misunderstood, and alienated people.

Sexual Orientation is not Found in the Bible

Our understanding of sexual orientation as we know it today did not exist 50 years ago, much less in biblical times. Only in 1973 did the American medical, psychiatric, and legal professions begin to recognize that homosexuality is an orientation and not a choice, illness, or crime.

Sexuality is seldom discussed in the Bible. The Bible view of the role of women as property, the absolute importance placed on having children to continue the family, the customs and demands related to marriage and inheritance, and an obvious demonstration of male dominance and control can be seen vividly described in Genesis chapter 38. In the Bible, all women were property that belonged to their father or husband.

Women were members of the covenant people of God only because of their relationship to their father, brother, or husband. Women could not carry circumcision, the "sign of the covenant," in their bodies. The Old Testament does not include a belief in "heaven" or a future time of reward and continued life. The only way a man could live on after his death was through his children ("seed"). No man was allowed to remain unmarried. Old Testament Hebrew does not have a word for bachelor.

Marriage in the Bible was not based on romantic love but on a legal contract usually entered by parents on behalf of their children. The average age for marriage in the time of Jesus was 14 for girls and 16 for boys. Average life expectancy was only 25 years. The Greek word for romantic love, *eros*, is never used in the New Testament, though it was the most common word for love in the Greek speaking world.

To read bits and pieces of biblical material into present day culture is to misrepresent the Bible and to distort its message of God's love in Christ for all people in today's world.

B. Hebrew and Greek

The original Bible languages of Hebrew and Greek have no word for homosexual. Old Testament Hebrew is a very primitive language. It is the first step beyond picture writing and is the first alphabetic language. It originally consisted only of consonants with no vowels written in the text. There is no "past, present, or future" in Hebrew. The Hebrew language had only about a 30,000-word vocabulary. Modern English has over 300,000 words. One Hebrew word could be used in dozens of different ways, and the meaning was determined by the context.

Each word was made up of three letters of the alphabet (consonants) and usually expressed some form of activity or action. Vowels were not included in written Hebrew in the earliest manuscripts. Vowels were developed over many centuries as tiny dots and strokes placed over, within, or beneath consonants by scholars, called "Masoretes." This "vowel pointing" attained the final form that is used today only several centuries after the time of Jesus. It is impossible to translate most Hebrew words exactly into modern English. Scholars come as close as they can and do a lot of guessing.

New Testament Greek was far more complex than Hebrew. Greek had a 250,000-word vocabulary and a great variety of words developed to express shades of meaning and degrees of feeling. Greek, for example, had four different words for "love." Greek had many verb forms that do not exist in English. Greek also includes over a dozen verb forms not found in Hebrew or in modern English to express variations on "past, present, and future." The Greek used in the New Testament also is different from both classical and modern Greek.

For many years, some scholars thought that New Testament Greek was a special language created by the Holy Spirit. A Greek lexicon published in 1866 listed 450 Greek words which occur only in the New Testament and nowhere else. Then, in the late nineteenth century, a collection of manuscripts was discovered from the time of the New Testament. Adolf Deissmann found a volume of Greek papyri from Egypt and was struck by the similarity to the Greek of the New Testament. These documents were bills of sale, personal letters, business and news reports that were written in exactly the same kind of Greek used in the New Testament. Deissmann's discoveries were published in *Bible Studies* (1895, 1897) and later in *Light from the Ancient East* (1908). For the first time, Bible scholars knew and could study the popular colloquial non-literary Greek of the first century. This was the "everyday" Greek, called *Koine* Greek, that was used in the New Testament. The *King James Version* was translated in 1611, long before the oldest manuscripts were discovered or the *Koine* Greek was known. The first English Bible that was published with this new knowledge of *Koine* Greek was the *American Standard Version* of 1901.

The reason that there are so many different Bible translations (about 30 major ones) today is because the exact meaning of many words is still in question, and even what should be included as original material is hotly debated by Bible specialists. [See the work of "The Jesus Seminar" and the book, *Honest to Jesus: Jesus for a New Millennium*, by Robert W. Funk (Harper San Francisco, 1996).] Other recent discoveries, like the Dead Sea Scrolls, add new information that throws light on the meaning of Bible words.

Biblical Hebrew and Greek Contain No Word for Homosexual

The word "homosexual" is made up of Greek *homo*, meaning "the same," and Latin *sexualis*, from which the English word "sex" is derived. The word "homosexual" has been in use to refer to people who have sex with others of the same gender for only about 100 years. According to the most recent edition of Merriam-Webster's *Collegiate Dictionary* (tenth edition), "homosexual" as an adjective was first used in 1892 and as a noun in 1902, "homophobia" was first used in 1969 and "homophobe" first used in 1975. The translation of any Bible word as "homosexual" is a mistake.

The Greek word in 1 Corinthians 6:9 and I Timothy 1:10 that is translated "homosexual" is *arsenokoites*, which is formed from two words meaning "male" and "bed." The word is not found anywhere else in the New Testament and has not been found anywhere in contemporary Greek of Paul's time. We are not sure what it means. It only appears in these two lists. The word is of obscure origin and uncertain meaning. It probably refers to male prostitutes with female customers, which was a common practice in the Roman world.

When early Greek-speaking Christian preachers condemned homosexuals, they did not use this word. John Chrysostom (AD 345-407) preached in Greek against homosexuality, but he never used this word for homosexuals. When he wrote homilies and preached on 1 Corinthians 6:9 and 1 Timothy 1:10, he did not mention gay people.

The Bible has no word in Hebrew or Greek that is the same as our word "sex." The word "flesh" means "human" and never means "sex." The Hebrew way of thinking about human nature continued to dominate the thought of the New Testament. Details of sexual practices were never given in the Old or the New Testaments. The only term that conveys the idea of "having sex" is the Hebrew term "to lie with."

Much of the New Testament thought was carried over directly from Hebrew terms and ideas in the Hebrew Bible, which had been translated from Hebrew to Greek about 250 years before Christ in the Septuagint (LXX) version of Scripture. Careful study of a tremendous body of historical material is necessary to sort out the exact meaning of Bible passages. Even more study is required to grasp and understand what the passages actually said in the culture in which they were written.

C. How I View the Bible

The Bible is a dominant force in our culture today. It is a source of comfort and encouragement for millions and a source of abuse and pain for millions of others. As a former Southern Baptist pastor and university Bible professor and now since 1981, an openly gay pastor, teacher, writer, evangelist, and community activist, I have had to face and deal with the Bible as both a blessing and a curse, a source of healing and a weapon of oppression.

Lesbian, gay, bisexual, and transgendered people are not the only people who are systematically attacked and oppressed by the abusive use of the Bible. Women, children, various racial groups, and other minorities also have suffered under the lash of religious and Bible abuse. This book and my Web site on "Steps to Recovery from Bible Abuse" are written from the point of view of a gay man and are addressed primarily to gay, lesbian, bisexual, and transgendered people. This is my world and my arena of personal experience and Christian calling.

I believe, however, that what I have learned about the Bible and how to use the Bible in positive and healthy ways is of value to all people of faith and not just for gay people. Many people who have been oppressed by the Bible and religion have understandably abandoned the Bible and no longer see any practical or spiritual value in the Bible. This is a good time to take a fresh look at the Bible and discover for yourself how you can be objective about the Bible and use it for spiritual and practical encouragement and help.

Give Yourself a New Bible

Changing the way you see the Bible and what it means can be like finding a new Bible that finally speaks to you and offers positive spiritual encouragement and help. For me, Jesus is the key and guide to a healthy objective use of the Bible. No two people experience Jesus and the Spirit of Jesus in exactly the same way, which leads to the kind of diversity and variety in life and ministry of individual Christians as described by Paul in Romans 12, 1 Corinthians 12, and Ephesians 4. These three Bible chapters set forth the principle of diversity within faith and open the door for individuals to experience Jesus and the Spirit of Jesus in ways that fit each person of faith.

The words "diversities," "varieties," and "heresies" used in the New Testament all are from the same Greek word, *hairesis* (1 Corinthians 11:19 and 12:4-7), which can mean either good or bad diversity. Without diversity (heresy), the church denies the freedom "for which Christ set us free" (Galatians 5:1) and the freedom that the Spirit brings (2 Corinthians 3:17). Paul said, "Work out your own salvation with fear and trembling, for God is working through you both to desire and to accomplish God's will" (Philippians 2:12-13). Thereby you celebrate and enjoy your individuality within the diversity that is God's gift to all people in Christ.

Biblical literalism and judgmental legalism are blinding and binding forces that work against discovering the liberating truth in Jesus and in the Bible as viewed by and through Jesus. The use of certain "proof texts" like 2 Timothy 3:16 to prove that the Bible is "the word of God" ignores the clear message of John 1:1-14 that Jesus is the word of God. The same kind of selective, ignorant, and out-of-context abuse of the Bible is employed to attack and condemn oppressed and outcast people.

Changing Forms and Shapes of the Bible

Dr. Clyde T. Francisco was a great scholar and teacher who taught me many of my Bible courses at Southern Baptist Theological Seminary in Louisville, Kentucky. He was my teacher and helped to supervise my Master's dissertation on "The Word of God in Isaiah 40-55," in which I demonstrated that the words "servant" and "word" both were used in the same way to describe the "coming One" (Messiah). Isaiah 40-55 provided a background for John 1:1-14 to identify the "Servant" (Jesus) as the "Word" of God.

After the *Revised Standard Version* of the Bible was published, it was condemned and rejected by many fundamentalists as evil and as a Communist book (because it had a red cover!). Dr. Francisco correctly said that the reason the average church person had problems with the *Revised Standard Version* Bible was because their pastors had never taught the people that the Bible has a history.

No version of the Bible looks today as it did originally. Many changes have been made in the way that biblical materials are packaged. The original manuscripts of the Hebrew Bible were written on scrolls that were rolled up and tied with a cord. Even in the time of Jesus, individuals did not own Bibles. The sacred scrolls were kept in a special box in the synagogue and taken out for reading by special teachers and students and for Sabbath services. Changing the form of the Bible materials from scrolls to stacks of pages came early in the history of the New Testament. Perhaps the greatest difference in the original manuscripts and our Bibles today is that both ancient Hebrew and Greek were often written with no space between the words, without punctuation, and without any division into chapters and verses.

Cardinal Hugo de San Caro of Spain first divided Bible materials into chapters in 1238. Robert Estienne first divided Bible materials into verses in 1551. No systematic plan was followed in either chapter or verse divisions, which often seem to be quite arbitrary. This means that until after the time of Martin Luther (1483-1546), no verse divisions existed. Luther's translation of the Bible from Hebrew and Greek into German, containing no verse divisions, was printed and widely used to fuel the fires of the Reformation.

The ancient manuscripts had no divisions into chapters and verses. Many of the chapter and verse divisions break apart complete thoughts and ideas that change the emphasis and thus the exact meaning from the original. Modern punctuation also serves to mislead the reader into separating ideas and breaking up the original ideas and emphasis in the text.

The Gutenberg Bible of 1455 was the first Bible printed from movable type in the Western world. This Bible was the Latin version that had been revised and translated by many scholars, including Jerome (347-419), who revised and translated the New Testament. It contains no verse divisions. It also contains brief passages that have never been found in any ancient Greek manuscript. One example is the "Trinity" verse in I John 5:8, "the Father, the Word, and the Holy Spirit, and these three are one. And there are three that bear witness on earth." This passage has never been found in any ancient manuscript.

The verse is in the Latin version, however, and when King James' translators came to it and did not find it in the Greek manuscript that they were using, they simply translated the Latin into Greek and used that as their basis for the English translation that is included in the *King James Version (KJV)* of the Bible! Other passages, including the last seven verses of the Book of Revelation, were also missing from the Greek text; so the scholars also translated them from Latin into Greek and then based the *KJV* on their English translation of the Greek that they had created with no ancient manuscript evidence.

These are only a few of the reasons why you will profit from using a carefully researched and translated modern language Bible like the *New American Standard Bible.*

The Bible does indeed have a history. Learn about it. The three-volume set of *The Cambridge History of the Bible* (Cambridge University Press, 1970) tells the details. Also see relevant articles in *The Interpreter's Dictionary of the Bible: An Illustrated Encyclopedia*, (4 volumes and a supplementary volume, Abingdon Press, 1962 and 1976). This is the best source I know for learning accurate information about the Bible.

Remember that the Bible had endured many years of history before Jesus used it, and he still found valuable spiritual resources in the Scriptures. God is still able to speak in any way God chooses to speak, and God speaks to those who are willing to listen. Jesus listened to God and heard in the Bible things that everybody else had missed. Jesus saw and demonstrated God's inclusive unconditional love for all people. The Spirit of Jesus can guide your open-minded study of the Bible and the working of God in your own life. Learn from every experience and every person that pass through your life. The Bible has a history, and so do you. How has your personal history shaped your use of the Bible? What is God trying to say to you today?

Reading Sex into the Bible

Western culture today is so dominated by vivid and explicit details of sexual practices and ideas that we all tend to read sex into just about everything that happens or that we read. To read sex into the Bible is to ignore what it does mean and to complicate and distort its message at many very important points. None of the 25 "works of the flesh" that Paul listed in Galatians 5:19-21 refer directly to sex, though many of the terms are translated in such a way as to imply a sexual meaning. These 25 "works of the flesh" primarily describe how people treat other people as things rather than persons and how attitudes of people cause divisive, destructive, and abusive behavior toward other people. Paul viewed the religion of judgmental legalism as a "work of the flesh."

D. Translating the Gospels

The four Gospels present particularly difficult problems for translators and interpreters. The rest of the New Testament, as far as we know, was originally written in the *Koine* Greek of the time of Christ, but the Gospels tell stories about Jesus and repeat teachings of Jesus that were first given in Aramaic. The Aramaic language is a form of ancient Hebrew, which is itself very difficult to translate. Aramaic is not used today except in various dialects by a few remote groups (*The Interpreter's Dictionary of the Bible*: I, pp. 185-190). A few brief portions of the Hebrew

Bible are in Aramaic in Ezra 4:8 through 6:18; 7:12-26; Daniel 2:4 through 7:28; and a gloss in Jeremiah 10:11 along with a few isolated Aramaic words. Many Aramaic words are scattered throughout the Gospels.

At first, the sayings and actions of Jesus were learned by memory and passed on to others orally. The rigid rules of Jewish teachers at the time of Jesus required that the teachings of a rabbi were to be memorized and passed on by word of mouth and never written down. The official body of rabbinical teachings, the *Mishna*, was not written down until after AD 90, over 50 years after the death of Jesus and 20 years after the destruction of Jerusalem and the Temple.

We have no evidence of original written Aramaic versions of the Gospels. At some time along the way, the Aramaic sayings and stories were translated from a language that is obscure and complex into *Koine* Greek, which is also obscure and complex, and were selected, organized, and written into the form of "Gospels." Then the Greek manuscripts after hundreds of years of copying and development were gradually assembled to provide the basis for modern English versions and many other translations.

Luke 1:1-4 states clearly that the material in the gospels had a long and complex history before being shaped into the present four Gospels,

> Inasmuch as many have undertaken to compile an account of the things accomplished among us, just as those who from the beginning were eyewitnesses and servants of the word [*logos*] have handed them down to us, it seemed fitting for me as well, having investigated everything carefully from the beginning [or "from their sources"], to write it out for you in consecutive order, most excellent Theophilus ["friend of God"]; so that you might know the exact truth about the things you have been taught.
>
> Luke 1:1-4

It is obvious from the statements in Luke 1:1-4 that the Gospels had a history before they were written in the form that appears in the English Bible today. The term "handed them down to us" in 1:2 is the same Greek word as "delivered up", which is translated as "betrayed" when the story of Jesus' being betrayed by Judas is told, Luke 22:4, 21, 48. The history of the development of the Gospel traditions about Jesus forms a massive growing body of scholarly biblical materials from the time of Jesus to the present. The best sources that I know about the cultural, historical, and linguistic setting of the Gospels are the many relevant articles in *The Interpreter's Dictionary of the Bible* (Abingdon Press, 4 volumes in 1962 and a Supplementary Volume in 1976).

We have few tools to help us know exactly what Jesus said and did and what was added or changed in the repeated telling of the stories in oral form. Whether or not Jesus knew and used Greek is still an open question.

The Gospels present challenges and problems at every turn in understanding the person and work of Jesus. The question, therefore, emerges, what can we be sure is genuine about Jesus in the Gospels? Many believers avoid the question by assuming that every word in the English Bible is inspired by God and is "the word of God" in every detail for today. Other believers want to know more about the history of the Bible and have used the rapidly emerging tools of science and scholarship to find a more clear and consistent view of Jesus that speaks with greater authority and relevance to them. Both groups and many in between seek and claim to follow the leadership of the Holy Spirit.

Nothing is more important for the followers of Jesus than being sure of what Jesus was and is like and being confident that one's vision of Jesus is true to the will and purpose of God. Give some thought to it. What do you believe about Jesus? Why? How do you act on that belief?

Jesus Was New and Inclusive

My own conclusion at this point in my studies and ministry is that the Gospels clearly demonstrate two consistent facts about Jesus. The first is that Jesus was always creative, new, and different. Jesus was revolutionary and challenged all of the ancient traditions and "made all things new." The main teachings and actions of Jesus in the Gospels are presented as something new that had never happened before in the forms and with the effects manifested in Jesus. The second is that Jesus was always consistently inclusive and accepting of all people, which itself was also brand new and unexpected. Looking for these two features of "new" and "inclusive" has led me to appreciate the underlying meaning of a lot of the stories about Jesus that did not seem clear before.

E. What Bible to Read

Many readers of my Web site have asked me what Bible is the least homophobic and translates the original languages most correctly. That is a difficult question. All current translations contain glaring mistakes in many places as well as in the anti-gay "clobber passages."

The most recent attempt in translation accuracy in wide use is the *New Revised Standard Version* (NRSV, 1989). It retained many translation mistakes and created some new ones. Its use of "sodomite" in 1 Corinthians 6:9 caused many outstanding New Testament scholars to ridicule the translation and point out that there is no such word as "sodomite" in the original languages. There is no totally accurate translation of even some of the Bible. The original *Revised Standard Version* (*RSV*, the New Testament first appeared in 1946) was the first translation ever to use the word "homosexual", which does not exist as a word in Hebrew or Greek. The *New Revised Standard Version* mistranslates 1 Corinthians 6:9 with "male prostitutes" for the Greek word *malakoi* (which literally means "soft") and "sodomites" for the Greek word *arsenokoitai* (which literally is "male bed").

The translation that I use now and have used from the time I finished my doctorate at the seminary is the *New American Standard Bible* (*NASB*, 1963). I found by experience that with the *NASB* I had to explain less often to my students that the original language was different from what they read in their Bible. The *NASB* (like all available versions), however, incorrectly translates the "clobber passages" used against gays. Students in my college courses used the *New American Standard Bible, Holman Study Bible Edition*, which includes good objective scholarly biblical study articles on history of the Bible, manuscripts, archaeology, etc. If you can find this edition, get it and treasure it. I cannot find it any more. Broadman Press, owned by Southern Baptist Convention, has bought Holman and does not now publish the edition that I used, as far as I know.

You can get a good easy to read text of the *NASB* with wide reference margins from a number of publishers. I greatly prefer Bibles with no elaborate notes and explanations. These notes usually are from a very biased point of view and can confuse a lot more than they help. When I was memorizing great portions of the New Testament, I found that the *NASB* was the easiest translation to memorize. One purpose of the translators as stated in the "Preface" was to make the material easier to memorize.

When you get a copy of the *NASB* be sure to read the "Preface to the *New American Standard Bible*" at the front. This brief preface gives helpful and important information about the translation. The *NASB* is a translation built upon the most accurate modern version, the *American Standard Version* (1901), which was the first translation to use the discoveries of the papyri that revealed that the Greek of the New Testament was a special form of Greek, *Koine* Greek (or common, everyday Greek) spoken in the time of Jesus. The *ASV*, however, is very difficult to read and was so exactly translated that a lot of the material is kept in the original word order and in syntax that are very hard to follow and is not clearly understandable to the average English reader.

The Good News Bible (New Testament, 1966; Old Testament, 1976 by the American Bible Society) is easy to read but contains strongly anti-gay translations. *The Living Bible* is incredibly inaccurate. It is a paraphrase that was begun by a book editor who did not know Hebrew and Greek and who simply put the New Testament in his own words to make it say more clearly what he believed. Many other popular translations that are strongly anti-gay are the *New International Version* (1973 by the International Bible Society), the original *Revised Standard Version* of 1946, and *The Amplified Bible*, which is full of errors and speculation.

This does not mean that the Bible is useless or that you cannot find spiritual instruction and inspiration in any Bible translation, including the *King James Version* (1611), which is still the most popular version of all. You simply must be objective in your use of the Bible and realize that the Bible is not God and not to be worshipped as if it were.

F. Six Bible Passages Used to Attack Gay People

(This material is given in the same form that it appeared in my Web site on "Steps to Recovery from Bible Abuse.")

The six passages are:

- **Genesis 19:5**
- **Leviticus 18:22 and 20:13**
- **Romans 1:26-27**
- **1 Corinthians 6:9 and 1 Timothy 1:9-10**

In preparation for each passage, read the entire chapter. For Romans 1:26-27 read the first three chapters of Romans. Read Genesis 38 for a clear picture of the Old Testament attitudes about women, sex, the necessity of producing offspring, the control of men over women, the double standard for men and women, and other sexuality issues.

Bring them out to us that we may know them. (Genesis 19:5)

The word "know" simply means know! No hint at homosexuality exists in the original Hebrew. No later Bible references to Sodom ever mention homosexuality as the sin of Sodom. Many modern translations add words to the text to create the lie that the people of Sodom were gay.

"Sodomy" is not a biblical word. Laws against sodomy not only violate the Constitutional guarantee of separation of church and state; they also use an incorrect and wrongly translated term for the laws. A "Sodomite" in the Bible is simply a person who lives in Sodom, which included Lot and his family. The term "sodomite" in the *King James Version* of Deuteronomy 23:17 and 1 Kings 14:24 is an incorrect translation of the Hebrew word for "temple prostitute." (See the recent book by Mark D. Jordan, *The Invention of Sodomy in Christian Theology*. University of Chicago Press, 1997.)

The average person assumes that the Bible clearly condemns male to male sexual intercourse as "sodomy" and that the city of Sodom was destroyed because of homosexuality, which is seen as the worst of all sins in the Bible. These assumptions are based on no evidence at all in the Bible.

No Jewish scholars before the first Christian century taught that the sin of Sodom was sexual. None of the biblical references to Sodom mention sexual sins but view Sodom as an example of injustice, lack of hospitality to strangers, idolatry, and as a symbol for desolation and destruction. See Deuteronomy 29:22-28; 32:32; Ezekiel 16:49-50; Jeremiah 49:18; 50:41; Isaiah 13:19-22, and Matthew 10:14-15. In Jude 7, the term "strange flesh" is the Greek words *hetero sarkos* ("different flesh" and from which the word "heterosexual" comes) and refers to foreign idols or people. It is not *homo* ("the same") flesh or people. *Sarkos* is never used in the New Testament as a word for sex.

The word "know" in Genesis 19:5 is Hebrew *yada*. It is used 943 times in the Hebrew Bible to "know" God, good and evil, the truth, the law, people, places, things, etc. It is a very flexible word, as are many Hebrew words. In Genesis 19:5, the word was used to express the request of the people of Sodom that Lot should bring out the strangers in his house so that they could know who they were. Sodom was a tiny fortress in the barren wasteland south of the Dead Sea. The only strangers that the people of Sodom ever saw were enemy tribes who wanted to destroy and take over their valuable fortress and the trade routes that it protected. Lot himself was an alien in their midst.

Lot's strange response to the request was to offer his young daughters to the men, an offer that seems to me to be far more reprehensible than any problem of sexual orientation. If the men were homosexual, why did Lot offer to give them his daughters? These hostile and violent people were heterosexual, and homosexual orientation had nothing to do with the incident.

Special note on *yada*: The Hebrew word *yada* "to know" is never used in the Hebrew Bible to mean exactly what we mean by "to have sex with." People have been conditioned to think that "to know someone biblically" means to have sex. The use of *yada* in Genesis 4:1-2 to say that Adam "knew" Eve and she conceived and gave birth to Cain is followed by saying that later she gave birth to his brother Abel without any reference to *yada*. Why? Simply because *yada* does not mean to have sex. It is a general term that describes many kinds of intimate relationships. I have studied all of the uses of *yada* in the Hebrew Bible, and my personal conclusion is that it never means what we mean by sexual intercourse. Just substitute a common slang expression for sexual intercourse instead of the word "know" in Genesis 4:1, and you will see how inappropriate the idea is. The writers of Hebrew Bible never thought or wrote in those terms. The Bible never gives any details about sexual acts. The only clear Hebrew term for sexual acts is the ambiguous term, "to lie with," which is left without any further explanatory details.

What Really Happened in Sodom?

To twist the story to say what it does not say is to miss what it does say. The story does not deal with sexual orientation or with homosexuality and has no bearing at all on the issue of

God's acceptance or rejection of gays and lesbians. The story of Sodom clearly teaches that evil and violent people who attack aliens and strangers whom they do not know or understand receive God's quick and terrible punishment.

The purpose of the story is to show that misunderstood, strange, or feared minorities in any community are in danger from violence by the majority when that majority is ignorant, ungodly, selfish, and afraid. The real message of Sodom is just the opposite of the claims of homophobic preachers and teachers. The gay and lesbian minority in our society today is more like the guests in Lot's house who were protected behind closed doors ("in the closet") than like the frightened mindless mob that wanted to expose, humiliate, and destroy people that they did not "know" and control.

Set the record straight! Genesis 19 is about the fear (like homophobia) and anger of a mob (like many misguided religious fanatics) directed against a small group of isolated strangers (like gays and lesbians today) in their midst. Sexual orientation is not the issue here or anywhere else in the Bible.

Read also the strange story in Judges 19:1-30 of the Levite in Gibeah, which was patterned after the story of Lot and the angels in Genesis 19. Jewish teachers before the time of Christ never saw either of these stories as having any connection with homosexuality or sexual orientation. Neither should we.

> You shall not lie with a male as those who lie with a female; it is an abomination. (Leviticus 18:22)

> If a man lies with a male as those who lie with a woman, both of them have committed an abomination and they shall surely be put to death. (Leviticus 20:13)

Both of these verses refer not to homosexuals but to heterosexuals who took part in the *baal* fertility rituals in order to guarantee good crops and healthy flocks. No hint at sexual orientation or homosexuality is even implied. The word "abomination" in Leviticus was used for anything that was considered to be religiously unclean or associated with idol worship.

Because these two verses in Leviticus (18:22 and 20:13) have been used more than any other Bible texts to condemn and reject gay and lesbian people, the following material is given to help you think objectively about traditional abusive use of the Bible.

The use of Leviticus to condemn and reject gay people is a hypocritical selective use of the Bible against gays and lesbians. Nobody today tries to keep all of the laws in Leviticus. Look at Leviticus 11:1-12, where all unclean animals are forbidden as food, including rabbits, pigs, and shellfish, such as oysters, shrimp, lobsters, crabs, clams, and others that are called an "abomination." You can eat some insects like locusts, but not others. Leviticus demands "you are to make a distinction between the clean and unclean animal and between the unclean and clean bird; and you shall not make yourself an abomination by animal or by bird or by anything that creeps on the ground, which I have separated for you as unclean" (Leviticus 20:25).

Leviticus 12:1-8 declares that a woman is unclean for 33 days after giving birth to a boy and for 66 days after giving birth to a girl and goes on to demand that certain animals must be offered as a burnt offering and a sin offering for cleansing. Nobody today who claims to be a Christian tries to keep these laws, and few people even know about them!

Read Leviticus 23 to see the detailed regulations concerning "complete rest" on the Sabbath day and demands of animal sacrifices to be carried out according to exact instructions. Leviticus 18:19 forbids a husband from having sex with his wife during her menstrual period. Leviticus 19:19 forbids mixed breeding of various kinds of cattle, sowing various kinds of seeds in your field or wearing "a garment made from two kinds of material mixed together." Leviticus 19:27 demands that "you shall not round off the side-growth of your heads, nor harm the edges of your beard." The next verse forbids "tattoo marks on yourself." Most people do not even know that these laws are in the Bible and are demanded equally with all the others.

Why do fundamentalists not organize protests and picket seafood restaurants, oyster bars, church barbecue suppers, grocery stores, barber shops, tattoo parlors, and stores that sell suits and dresses made of mixed wool, cotton, polyester, and other materials? All of these products and services are "abominations" in Leviticus. When have you heard a preacher condemn the demonic abomination of garments that are made of mixed fabrics?

The warning is given in Leviticus 26:14-16 that "If you do not obey me and do not carry out all of these commandments, if instead, you reject my statutes, and if your soul abhors my ordinances so as not to carry out all my commandments. . . . I, in turn, will do this to you, I will appoint over you a sudden terror, consumption, and fever that shall waste away the eyes and cause the soul to pine away; also, you shall sow your seed uselessly, for your enemies shall eat it up." The list of punishments and terrors that will come from not keeping all of the commandments continues through many verses.

Read what Jesus said about hypocrites who judge others, "Do not judge lest you be judged yourselves. . . . Why do you look at the speck in your brother's eye, but do not notice the log that is in your own eye? . . . .You hypocrite!" (Matthew 7:1-5).

If you have been led to misuse Leviticus and other parts of the Bible in order to condemn, hate, and reject people, you are on the wrong path. Jesus quoted only one passage from Leviticus, "You shall love your neighbor as yourself" (Leviticus 19:18). Jesus used Leviticus to teach love. Many false teachers use Leviticus and other writings to condemn, humiliate, and destroy. I know which approach seems truly Christian to me. Jesus never condemned gay people or even mentioned anything that could be taken as a reference to sexual orientation.

Any charge against gays and lesbians based on the life and teachings of Jesus has to be dismissed for a lack of evidence!

The use of Leviticus to judge and condemn anyone today is ludicrous and absurd in the light of the total content of the book. To call the content of the Book of Leviticus the "word of God" and try to enforce any part of it today is without support in the teachings of Jesus and in the letters of Paul.

Jesus chided his disciples for their lack of spiritual understanding. Jesus and his disciples had been condemned by the religious leaders because they did not wash and eat according to the Law. Jesus said, "'Are you too so uncomprehending? Don't you see that whatever goes into your mouth from the outside cannot defile you; because it does not go into your heart, but into your stomach, and is eliminated?' (Thus Jesus declared all foods clean.) And Jesus added, 'That which proceeds from within you, out of your heart, defiles you. Evil thoughts, abusive sex acts, thefts, murders, adulteries, deeds of coveting, wickedness, deceit, not caring, envy, slander, arrogance and foolishness, all of these evil things proceed from within and defile you'" (Mark 7:18-23).

Paul also rejected the absolute commands of Leviticus in Colossians 2:8-23, where he said, "If you have died with Christ to the elementary principles of the world, why, as if you were living in the world, do you submit yourself to decrees, such as, 'Do not handle, do not taste, do not touch!' (which all refer to things destined to perish with the using) in accordance with human commandments and teachings? These are matters which have, to be sure, the appearance of wisdom in self-made religion and self-abasement and severe treatment of the body, but are of no value against human indulgence" (Colossians 2:20-23). Paul declared in Colossians 2:14 that Jesus has "canceled out the certificate of debt consisting of decrees against us which was hostile to us; and Jesus has taken it out of the way, having nailed it to the cross."

Many people have answered the argument that most of the "abominations" in Leviticus referred to food by saying that the people back then knew that pork was unhealthy, and that is why pigs were declared to be unclean. If you follow that logic, you would declare anything that is unhealthy to be an "abomination." We know that cigarettes, alcoholic beverages, fatty food and many other things are unhealthy; so why are they not also called "abominations" and condemned by the Bible literalists with protests and pickets against cigarette machines, all liquor stores and bars, all fast food outlets, and any store that sells anything that is unhealthy? The reason is simple. The use of Leviticus to condemn and reject anyone is impossible to justify in the light of the facts.

The use of Leviticus to condemn and reject gay people is absurd, making literal, legalistic, bible-based religion look ridiculous.

To me personally, the message of Jesus Christ always has been good news for everyone. Personal evangelism has been my basic emphasis in the ministry since I became pastor of a small rural church in South Carolina in 1952 when I was nineteen years old. Our little church led the Baptist Churches of South Carolina one year in per capita baptisms. In all of my churches, both Baptist and MCC, my emphasis has been personal evangelism. What is your emphasis in your ministry? I personally have led hundreds of people to Christ and taught other hundreds of people to become effective in sharing Christ with others. During all of this time I have been gay. I have realized that I was gay since I was about ten years old. God loves me just as I am and uses me in ministry that fits me and my life as an individual. I pray that you find the same thing for yourself.

> For this reason God gave them over to degrading passions, for their women exchanged the natural use for that which is against nature. And in the same way also the men abandoned the natural use of the woman and burned in their desire toward one another, men with men committing indecent acts and receiving in their own persons the due penalty for their error. (Romans 1:26-27)

All of this refers to idolatrous religious practices that were common in the time of Paul.

Taking anything that Paul said out its context is like trying to drive a car blindfolded. You do not know where you are, where you have been, where you are going, or whom you just ran over and killed!

Paul's writings have been taken out of context and twisted to punish and oppress every identifiable minority in the world, Jews, children, women, blacks, slaves, politicians, divorced people, convicts, pro-choice people, lesbians, gays, bisexuals, transsexuals, religious reformers, the mentally ill, and the list could go on and on. Paul is often difficult and confusing to understand. A lot of Paul's writing is very difficult to translate. Since most of his letters were written in response to news from other people, reading Paul can be like listening to one side of a telephone conversation. We know, or think we know, what Paul is saying, but we have to guess what the other side has said. As 2 Peter 3:16-18 pointed out, we have to be on guard against using Paul's writings in unhealthy and destructive ways.

When I taught a college course in the Book of Romans, I decided to memorize Romans, as Augustine suggested. The effort paid off. Being able to visualize the message of Romans as a whole immediately cleared up a lot of Paul's thought that I had not been able to untangle before by traditional means of study. It helped so much that I continued to memorize the books of the Bible that I taught in college courses.

The theme of the first three chapters of Romans is, "The gospel is the power of God for spiritual freedom [salvation] for all who believe" (Romans 1:16). Paul showed that all people equally need and can have Jesus in their lives. Paul's gospel is inclusive, "There is neither Jew nor Greek, neither slave nor free, neither male nor female; for you are all one in Christ Jesus" (Galatians 3:28).

Romans 1:26-27 is part of Paul's vigorous denunciation of idolatrous religious worship and rituals. Read all of Romans 1:18 to 2:4 for the context of the verses.

Romans 1:26-27 contains some words used only here by Paul. Familiar words are used here in unusual ways. The passage is very difficult to translate. The argument is directed against some form of idolatry that would have been known to Paul's readers. To us, 2,000 years later and in a totally different culture, the argument is vague and indirect.

Verse 25 is clearly a denunciation of idol worship, "For they exchanged the truth of God for a lie and worshiped and served the creature and not the Creator, who is blessed forever. Amen." Paul at no point in his writing dealt with same-sex orientation or the expression of love and affection between two people of the same sex who love each other.

Paul wrote Romans from Corinth, the second largest city in the empire and the crossroads of world trade and culture. Pausanius observed at about the same time as Paul that there were over 1,000 religions in Corinth. The most prominent were the fertility cult of Aphrodite, worship of Apollo, and the Delphi Oracle, which was across the bay from Corinth. Paul's readers would have been aware of the religious climate from which he wrote Romans and would have understood Paul a lot better than we do.

The word "passions" in 1:26 is the same word used to speak of the suffering and death of Jesus in Acts 1:3 and does not mean what we mean by "passion" today. *Eros* is the Greek word for romantic, sexual love, but *eros* is never used even once in the New Testament. "Passions" in Romans 1:26 probably refers to the frenzied state of mind that many ancient mystery cults induced in worshipers by means of wine, drugs, and music.

We do not know the meaning of "burn" in 1:27, because Paul never used this particular word anywhere else, and it's origin is uncertain. The term "against nature" is also strange here, since exactly the same term is used by Paul in Romans 11:21-24 to speak of God acting "against nature" by including the Gentiles with the Jews in the family of God. "Against nature" was used to speak of something that was not done in the usual way, but did not necessarily mean that something "against nature" was evil, since God also "acted against nature."

One more word needs special attention. "Committing indecent acts" in Romans 1:27 is translated by the *King James Version* as "working that which is unseemly." The Phillips translation goes far beyond the evidence and renders it as "shameful horrors!" The Greek word is *askemosunen* and is formed of the word for "outer appearance" plus the negative particle. It speaks of the inner or hidden part or parts of the individual that are not ordinarily seen or known in public. "Indecent" in 1 Corinthians 12:23 referred to the parts of the body that remain hidden but are necessary and receive honor. 1 Corinthians 13:5 used the word to say that love does not behave "indecently."

This word for "indecency" was used to translate Deuteronomy 24:1 into Greek to say that a man could divorce his wife if he "found some indecency in her." The religious teachers argued endlessly about what "some indecency" meant. Some said it was anything that displeased the husband. Others were more strict and said it could only refer to adultery. In Matthew 19:1-12, Jesus commented on Deuteronomy 24:1-4, but he did not define the term.

Paul was certainly aware of the variety of ways that the teachers interpreted the word "indecency," and he used it in a variety of ways himself. To read into "indecent acts" a whole world of homosexual ideas is to abandon the realities of objective academic study and to embark on useless and damaging speculation that cannot be supported by the meaning of the word or by Paul's use of it elsewhere.

If Paul had intended to condemn homosexuals as the worst of all sinners, he certainly had the language skills to do a clearer job of it than emerges from Romans 1:26-27. The fact is that Paul nowhere condemned or mentioned romantic love and sexual relations between people of the same sex who love each other. Paul never commented on sexual orientation. As in the rest of the Bible, Paul nowhere even hinted that lesbians and gay men can or should change their sexual orientation.

The use of Romans 1:26-27 against gay people turns out to be a blunt instrument to batter and wound people who were not intended in the original text. Paul clearly taught throughout Romans, Galatians, and his other letters that God's freely given and all-inclusive love is for every person on earth. Notice what Paul said about judging others, "Therefore you are without excuse, every one of you who passes judgment, for in that you judge another, you condemn yourself; for you who judge practice the same things" (Romans 2:1).

Special Note on Romans 1:31: where the *King James Version* translated the Greek word *astorgous* as "without natural affection." This is one of the characteristics of people "with a reprobate mind" (*KJV* of Romans 1:28). The word for "reprobate" is more recently translated as "depraved" or "perverted" in order more neatly to fit the sexualizing of everything possible in the list. The literal meaning of "reprobate" (Greek *dokimon*) is "to fail to measure up" or "to fail to meet the test" and simply means that the list of things that follows is the result of a mind that has abandoned God. The word *astorgous*, "without natural affection," is used only here and in 2 Timothy 3:3. It has nothing at all to do with homosexuality or with sex. It is the Greek word for "family love" or "family ties" with the negative prefix. It refers to people who despise and reject their family members. Rather than being directed at gay people, it is a term that is directed at people who despise and reject their own gay and lesbian children and brothers and sisters! Modern translators, knowing this, usually render the word as "unloving," and the implication of some sort of "unnatural" or "perverted" affection is removed. Many more translation corrections are needed elsewhere!

> The unrighteous shall not inherit the kingdom of God. So do not be deceived; neither fornicators, nor idolaters, nor adulterers, nor effeminate, nor homosexuals, nor thieves, nor covetous, nor drunkards, nor revilers, nor swindlers, shall inherit the realm of God. (1 Corinthians 6:9)

> Law is not made for a righteous person but for those who are lawless and rebellious, for the ungodly and sinners, for the unholy and profane, for those who kill their fathers or mothers, for murderers and fornicators and homosexuals and kidnappers and liars and perjurers, and whatever else is contrary to sound (healthy) teaching. (I Timothy 1:9-10)

The Greek words translated "effeminate" and "homosexual" in the Corinthians verse do not mean effeminate or homosexual. The Greek word translated "homosexual" in Timothy does not mean homosexual.

These two verses contain completely wrong translations to create "homosexual ghosts" that do not really exist! Ghosts may not hurt you, but they can make you hurt yourself! The homosexual ghosts in 1 Corinthians 6:9 and 1 Timothy 1:9-10 were created by the inaccurate and intentionally misleading translation of two Greek words.

1 Corinthians 6:9 and 1 Timothy 1:9-10 sound very convincing in including lesbians and gay men in the most dreadful lists of depraved human behavior imaginable. The fact is that the word translated "homosexual" does not mean homosexual and the word translated "effeminate" does not mean effeminate!

The English word "homosexual" is a composite word made from a Greek term (*homo*, "the same") and a Latin term (*sexualis*, "sex"). The term "homosexual" is of modern origin and was not used until about 100 years ago. There is no word in biblical Greek or Hebrew that is parallel to the word "homosexual." No Bible before the *Revised Standard Version* in 1946 used "homosexual" in any Bible translation.

The word translated as "homosexual" or "sexual pervert" or some other similar term is Greek *arsenokoites*, which was formed from two words meaning "male" and "bed." This word is not found anywhere else in the Bible and has not been found anywhere in the contemporary Greek of Paul's time. We do not know what it means. The word is obscure and uncertain. It probably refers to male prostitutes with female customers, which was a common practice in the Roman world, as revealed in the excavations at Pompeii and other sites.

When early Greek speaking Christian preachers condemned homosexuality, they did not use this word. John Chrysostom (A.D. 345-407) preached in Greek against homosexuality, but he never used this word for homosexuals, and when he preached on 1 Corinthians 6:9 and 1 Timothy 1:10, he did not mention homosexuals. See the full discussion of this in John Boswell's book, *Christianity, Social Tolerance, and Homosexuality*, Appendix 1, "Lexicography and Saint Paul," pages 335-353.

"Soft" does not mean "effeminate." The word translated "effeminate" in 1 Corinthians 6:9 is the Greek work *malakoi* and means "soft" or "vulnerable." The word is translated as "soft" in reference to clothing in Matthew 11:8 and Luke 7:25 and as "illness" in Matthew 4:23 and 9:35. It is not used anywhere else in the New Testament and carries no hint of reference to sexual orientation. *Malakoi* in 1 Corinthians 6:9 probably refers those who are "soft," "pliable," "unreliable," or "without courage or stability." The translation of *malakoi* as "effeminate" is incorrect, ignorant, degrading to women, and impossible to justify based on ancient usage compared to the meaning of "effeminate" today.

This incorrect rendering of *malakoi* and *arsenokoites* as references to gender orientation has been disastrous for millions of gay, lesbian, bisexual, and transgendered people. This mistaken translation has enlisted a mighty army of ignorant religious fanatics against gay people and has turned many lesbians and gays against the Bible, which holds for them as for all people the good news of God's love in Christ.

Conclusion

Evil, homophobic Bible "translations from hell" must not go unchallenged. The use of these translations by ignorant religious bigots to incite fear and hate against gays demands a clear, academically sound, credible, and easily understood response. Every Bible word that has been incorrectly used to wound, alienate, and oppress people must be examined in detail and carefully exposed. God has called us to return the Bible to the oppressed and outcast people for whom it was written.

Three of the passages, Genesis 19:5, 1 Corinthians 6:9, and 1 Timothy 1:9-10 are incorrectly translated. The other three, Leviticus 18:22, Leviticus 20:13, and Romans 1:26-27 are taken out of their original setting of condemning idolatrous religious practices and wrongly used to judge and condemn people of the same sex who love each other. None of these passages refer to people of the same sex who love each other. None originally were aimed at lesbian, gay, bisexual, and transgendered people.

Even if God dictated every word of the Bible and every word is literally true in the original languages, there is still no condemnation or even discussion of homosexuality or sexual orientation in the Bible.

No words for homosexual or homosexuality as we understand the terms today exist in the Bible. The term homosexuality with the present day meaning of romantic and erotic love between people of the same sex did not come into use until less than 100 years ago. The concept of sexual orientation developed in scientific use only within the last 40 years.

Neither the Hebrew Bible, nor Paul, nor Jesus condemned romantic or erotic love between people of the same sex. They never discussed it. All Bible references that are used to condemn and destroy gay people are taken out of context, translated incorrectly, and used to hurt people not intended in the original setting.

Religious, academic, ethical, and polemical preoccupation with homosexuality in the Bible is a vast wasteland of ignorance and speculation that has darkened the minds of multitudes of people and created pain and death that the Creator and nature never intended.

Never underestimate the destructive power of ignorance.

Special Study C

Challenging the "Ex-Gay" Industry

A. The "Ex-Gay" Fraud

Sexual orientation is a given. The Bible never deals with sexual orientation. The concept of sexual orientation is a recent development. Nothing in the life and teachings of Jesus deals with sexual orientation. Jesus taught acceptance of ourselves and of others as having equal value to God. If Jesus is the guide to all Bible study for Christians, no basis exists in the life and teachings of Jesus to use the Bible as a weapon to attack and oppress gay people or anybody else!

Parents, Families, Friends, of Lesbians and Gays (PFLAG) is the oldest and most effective support ministry for lesbians and gays and their families and friends. The PFLAG Web site is filled with resources that are factual and helpful. It provides a much-needed response to the anti-gay religious fundamentalists who betray their claims to represent Christ by their open homophobia, and their misrepresentation of the Bible and rejection of scientific facts.

A three year study of "Calculated Compassion: How the Ex-Gay Movement serves the Right's Attack on Democracy" was published in October, 1998, as a report from Political Research Associates written by Surina Khan. This project was the joint work of The Policy Institute of the National Gay and Lesbian Task Force, and Equal Partners in Faith. This brief study is very informative and greatly needed. It brings up to date the facts about the political use of the "ex-gay" myth by the Religious Right. "Calculated Compassion" can be accessed from links on my Web site.

The Danger to Gays and Lesbians is Real

I do not think that some people who are committed to the "ex-gay fraud" realize how evil some dimensions of the whole movement against gay people really are. Dr. C. Everett Koop, while Surgeon General of the United States, was a strong advocate for HIV/AIDS education and effective treatment until his retirement. After he retired, Dr. Koop visited many churches and church conferences to appeal for understanding and help for gay and lesbian people. After months of this experience, Dr. Koop was interviewed in "Christianity Today" and said that he did not go to church much any more. He said that we need a stronger word than homophobia to speak of the hate towards gay people that he had found in the churches. He concluded that he knew many preachers and church leaders who hated homosexuals so much that if they had a button that would kill all gay people, they would push the button.

The attitudes that appalled Dr. Koop have been intensified in recent months. Dr. Koop's thoughts on this issue are included in the documentary "One Nation Under God," in which I appear along with Michael Bussee and Gary Cooper. Michael was a co-founder of Exodus. Michael and Gary worked with Exodus for five years before they woke up to the damage that they were causing and rejected the "ex-gay" myth. John Evans helped to begin the first "ex-gay" ministry in Marin County, California. John realized the human tragedy being caused by the "ex-gay" distortions of truth and turned against the whole movement when his best friend committed suicide because he tried to change from gay to straight and failed. Many others have stories of damage done to them by the "ex-gay" disaster.

The newspaper ads in the summer of 1998 promoting the Ex-Gay industry and religious groups that support it told only one side of the story. Michael Bussee says that after he and his partner Gary spent 5 years in counseling for Exodus, they knew of nobody who had really changed from homosexual to heterosexual but that he did know of great emotional damage, self-mutilations, suicides, and suicide attempts that had resulted from the Exodus ministries.

In any war, truth is one of the first casualties. This is war. Some feel that it is a "holy war" and will do anything to impose their false messages of hope and successful sexual orientation change therapy on the public. We cannot afford to stand by and not resist the evil that is being launched against us in an ever-increasing bombardment.

Homophobic Literature from the "Ex-Gay" Industry

My survey of this incredible flood of distorted science, religious lies, and self-serving propaganda by the enemies of gay, lesbian, bisexual, and transgendered people has been very disturbing. It has been a loud wake up call to the very real danger that we face.

This blending of religious speculation, prejudice, ignorance, and faulty psychology has created for gay, lesbian, bisexual, and transgendered people a deadly brew of lies and false hope. One Internet source for "Regeneration Ministries" lists over a hundred books and articles that promote the "ex-gay" teachings and programs.

One basic offer of Christianity has always been the forgiveness of sin. Yet there is no tangible evidence that anybody has ever received forgiveness from sins. Forgiveness is something that we accept and believe by faith with no proof whatever that it has happened.

Over many centuries, the churches have created countless strategies and formulas to make forgiveness seem to be tangible, from the confessional booth, penance, absolution, and the sale of indulgences to the emotional evangelism and the judgmental legalism and extreme scare tactics of modern apocalyptic prophets. Mixing this religious concoction with bad science and discredited psychology in the carefully prepared and packaged medicine of homophobic "ex-gay" advocates, therapists, and writers has unleashed on our people a plague of self-depreciation, self-doubt, and self-destruction that rivals any genocide of the past.

The Internet has made these lies and distortions by homophobic writers and webmasters easily available to vulnerable young gays, lesbians, bisexuals, and transgendered people in their search for information and encouragement. We have to do more. The truth that is contained in this book and in my Web site on "Steps to Recovery from Bible Abuse" and in the Web sites by PFLAG, UFMCC, Interfaith Working Group (IWG), Ex-Ex-Gays, and many others is one of our best weapons. My Web site gives Links to these and many others with very important and necessary up-to-date information.

Do whatever you can to let our people know that these and other Web sites are available.

Fight back with the truth. The truth is out there. The truth is within you. Tell your story. Find others who face the same pressures and misunderstandings that you face, and reach out with the truth and with the compassion in your heart so that you can be part of healing the real disease, homophobia.

It takes time to learn new and better ways of seeing yourself, your truth, your world, and the other people around you. I have always felt that the best way to move from fear into hope and from self-rejection into self-acceptance is by taking time to learn new information, to study and think, and to share in dialogue with others who are working through the same issues.

This process obviously takes a lot of time. It also requires a setting for dialogue that most of us cannot find. Technology through the Internet has begun to meet these needs in an explosion of new connections between millions of people who never even knew of each other's existence a few months, weeks, or days ago! Where do we go from here? Both ignorance and truth are packaged and offered on the Internet, which is like a great cyber-dumpster packed with trash, garbage, and some really good stuff. You have to be selective. Even a cow knows how to avoid the briars and eat the grass. What have you found that is truly informative and helpful to you? Have you made any progress in starting a spiritual recovery group for yourself?

I saw a bumper sicker recently, "It's a shame that ignorance isn't painful." Actually, it is. Ignorance is not bliss. Ignorance is a deadly plague that is killing our people.

Jesus asked the judgmental legalists,

> Why don't you understand what I am saying?
> It is because you are not listening to me.
> You are just like your real father, the devil,
> and you desire to do what your father wants.
> He was a murderer from the beginning and
> does not stand in the truth, because there is no truth in him.
> Whenever he speaks a lie, he speaks from his own nature,
> for he is a liar and the father of lies.
> But when I speak the truth, you do not believe me.
> (John 8:43-45)

B. Psychiatry and Medicine

The American Psychiatric Association (APA) voted in 1973 to remove homosexuality from its official list of mental disorders and declared that "homosexuality implies no impairment in judgment, stability, reliability, or general social or vocational capabilities." The APA resolved that, "The American Psychiatric Association deplores all public and private discrimination against homosexuals in such areas as employment, housing, public accommodations, and licensing, and declares that no burden of proof of such judgment, capacity, or reliability shall be placed upon homosexuals greater than that imposed on any other persons and urges the enactment of civil rights legislation at the local, state, and federal level that would offer homosexual persons the same protections now guaranteed to others on the basis of race, creed, color, etc."

The American Medical Association and the American Bar Association agreed in 1974 with this statement of the APA and added their approval of the Model Penal Code of the American Law Institute recommendation to legislators "that private sexual behavior between consenting adults should be removed from the list of crimes and thereby legalized." The American Psychological Association in 1975 also approved these declarations and "urged all mental health professions to take the lead in removing the stigma of mental illness that has long been associated with homosexual orientations."

Why have these conclusions by medical professionals been ignored, denied, and rejected by ignorant and prejudiced preachers and religious authorities and by many politicians?

News releases in October, 1998, announced the American Psychiatric Association Board's "unanimous decision to reject therapy aimed solely at turning gays into heterosexuals, saying it can cause depression, anxiety, and self-destructive behavior." Dr. Nada Stotland, head of the association's joint committee on public affairs, said, "All the evidence would indicate this is the way people are born. We treat disease, not the way people are.

"The very existence of therapy that is supposed to change people's sexuality, even for people who don't take it, is harmful because it implies that they have a disease. There is evidence that the belief itself can trigger depression and anxiety."

It is about time that the medical doctors who are specialists in mental and emotional health and illness spoke out in the midst the present storm of false propaganda in advertisements and books by the fast growing "ex-gay" industry. The American Psychological Association issued a similar warning in 1997.

The Associated Press article about this warning issued by the APA in Denver in October, 1998, was printed in the *San*

Francisco Examiner (Saturday, December 12, 1998) along with a lengthy article about the current debate of "Gay Marriage Policy" in Europe. The American Psychiatric Association was the first group of medical specialists to issue a statement recognizing homosexuality as a "sexual orientation" and not a disease (1973). Since that decision was made, the "ex-gay" forces have launched a relentless campaign of ignorance and misinformation to accuse the APA of giving in to gay activists instead of basing their decision on scientific and medical facts.

The "bottom line" was clearly stated by Dr. Stotland in October 1998, "during the psychiatric group's quarterly meeting there was no evidence that sexual orientation could be changed." We welcome this most recent announcement from the medical doctors who are the most qualified to speak about the false claims and dangers of the "reparative therapy" fraud perpetrated by the "ex-gay" religious/political industry.

A Personal Note

Almost 20 years ago, when I was a professor of religion at the Baptist College at Charleston, SC, I was urged to get psychiatric help to deal with my being gay. I went to three different outstanding psychiatrists including Corbett H. Thigpen, M.D., co-author with Hervey Cleckley, M.D., of *The Three Faces of Eve*, which was made into a movie staring Joanne Woodward, for which she won the Academy Award. Dr. Thigpen was head of the department of Psychiatry at the University of Georgia School of Medicine.

Dr. Thigpen had treated people in my church in Greenwood, SC, and I knew him well. His response to my request for help was that he and his team of 15 psychiatrists had found no way to change anyone from gay to straight. He said that he could treat me for two years, charge me a lot of money, and change my personality, but I would still be gay! He made it clear to me that sexual orientation could not be changed. The other two psychiatrists, both of them in Charleston, told me the same thing.

The "Ex-Gay" Push for Acceptance and Support

During 1998, homophobic religious and political forces accelerated and intensified their unrelenting attacks against homosexuals with ads in newspapers, magazines, and television. John Paulk along with his "former lesbian" wife Anne have become symbols of the "Ex-Gay" push for acceptance and approval of "reparative therapy" and religious transformation of homosexuals into heterosexuals. (See the cover story in *Newsweek*, August 17, 1998, about the Paulks.) Now John Paulk has published his autobiography to try to prove that he has been changed from gay to straight by religion. This book and books by Joe Dallas (former President of "Exodus") and others will have a devastating impact on young homosexuals seeking for help and encouragement in dealing with their sexual orientation.

The American Psychiatric Association, The American Psychological Association, The American Medical Association, and The American Bar Association since 1973 have all taken the position that homosexuality is a sexual orientation and is not an illness to be treated or cured.

My entire Web site on "Steps to Recovery from Bible Abuse" is a response to John Paulk's book and the fraudulent use of religion to give false hope and to raise money in the ongoing religious/political warfare being waged against gay people. John Paulk is on the staff of Focus on the Family in Colorado Springs, Colorado, (the powerful and rich political/religious organization owned and operated by James Dobson).

Paulk, with no formal theological or medical training, is "a homosexuality and gender analyst" at "Focus" and is North American Board Chairman of Exodus International, "a worldwide organization that provides assistance to men and women seeking freedom from unwanted homosexuality." The "Ex-Gay" industry is booming! John Paulk's credentials for his expert status in the "Ex-Gay Fraud" consist of his personal story, told in his recent book, published in July 1998, by Winepress Publishing.

The foreword to the book is by Joseph Nicolosi, Ph.D., author of *Reparative Therapy of Male Homosexuality*, which has been repudiated by the majority of psychiatrists, psychologists, and other medical professionals. Nicolosi has invented the term "homosexual condition" to use in place of sexual orientation. His incredibly prejudiced and judgmental attitudes against gay men become evident in the first few lines of his writing. His brief but pompous analysis of why John Paulk was homosexual would be ludicrous if it were not being set forth as through it were scientific and medical fact. Instead, it is dangerous, misleading, and false. Nicolosi's logic is like saying that gay equals crazy, and therefore all gays are crazy. My full review of Paulk's book is on my Web site, which also includes reviews of the 1996 books by Joe Dallas, former President of Exodus International, and by Jeffrey Satinover, M.D., who is a rabid promoter of the "ex-gay" cause.

American Psychological Association Warning

The American Psychological Association issued a warning on August 14, 1997, against the "psychological terrorism" of the Ex-Gay "reparative therapy" movement, which the APA declared reveals an "intense bias against gay people."

The warning said, "In the past ten years, Christian fundamentalists have enlisted a coalition of old-style psychologists, psychiatrists, and social workers who have become very visible in this country and internationally, and who have as a mission to 'help' gay people get rid of their sexual orientation. Our aim is not to try to stop them *per se* or interfere with anyone's right to practice, but we want to expose the social context that creates this market."

C. Truth Forever on the Scaffold
(first published in *The Second Stone*)

Bobby spent two years as a resident in a house run by an "Ex-Gay" program in Marin County across the Bay from San Francisco. He had been rejected and harassed by his religious parents and had fled from them and his oppressive rural home and religion to find help in the program that promised to change him from gay to straight. After two years of learning to reject and hate himself, he finally bailed out of the program and moved into the city. Bobby accepts himself as OK to be gay and Christian, but why has he also sought out a legalistic and judgmental gay church to attend? What are the long-term effects of the intense religious brain washing that he endured?

My experience with people who have survived the ex-gay movement both in San Francisco and in Nashville, Tennessee, where I served as Senior Pastor of Metropolitan Community Church (MCC) congregations, is that the lasting effects of abusive religion are as complex as they are unhealthy. In teaching recent study groups on Steps to Recovery from Bible Abuse, I have realized that the first step to "Admit that you have been hurt by religion" is far more difficult than it seems. Admitting that your religion has hurt you is like criticizing your grandmother! You have an emotional resistance to rejecting your childhood religion as abusive, and you therefore develop patterns of denial and become defensive about it.

Remember the reaction when Jesus told the people that "You shall know the truth and the truth will set you free" (John 8:31-59). The people said that they were already free and never had been slaves to anyone. Yet they had been slaves in Egypt, exiles in Babylon, the subjects of Greek rule for many years, and were under the oppressive control of the Roman army. They also were controlled by an oppressive and abusive system of religion that never let up in its pressures and demands of absolute conformity and blind obedience to the Law. The end of the discussion came when the people took up stones to kill Jesus because he pointed out that they were being hurt and destroyed by their own religion.

Deliverance from Denial

Recovery from any addiction begins with admitting that you are being controlled by something that is hurting you. It can be alcohol, drugs, codependency, or religion. Many of the people I have seen get out of the ex-gay movement still have difficulty staying away from abusive forms of religion, especially judgmental legalism. Like the child who defends abusive parents and hides their bruises and scars or the person who repeatedly goes back to an abusive partner, the abused gay Christian can develop a fatal attraction to abusive and oppressive religion to embrace and defend.

D. A Personal "Ex-Ex-Gay" Testimony

Thom, a high school friend of mine, sent me the following personal testimony. It speaks for itself.

A Personal Testimony by Thom C., 11/22/98

After twenty years of marriage, I left home, at my wife's request, because of my being "mentally homosexual." There had been few homosexual experiences – only a couple of encounters during my younger years. I was 53 years old and very much a believer in the biblical teachings of my Southern Baptist background, which included the belief that homosexuality was an abomination unto God. Therefore, having been "kicked out" by a wife who knew my thoughts as a result of reading my journal, I determined to get myself cured of this "leprosy" and located a group under the auspices of Exodus International which met weekly in Tampa at a church annex.

My first encounter with the group promised to be a frightening experience for me. I had never been around gay people and drove to the meeting with fear and trepidation, knowing, however, that what I was doing was "good." To my surprise, the participants at the meeting, both male and female, could have been members of my Sunday School class. I was greeted warmly. As I sat among the predominantly male group, I wondered why they did not look "different." They looked like me.

During the nearly three years that I participated in this group, I was never asked to have sex by any member of the group nor did I seek anyone sexually. The purpose of the group was to deliver one from homosexuality, and I took that commitment seriously. After all, I had an ex-wife and three children who were counting on me. Week after week I attended, saying nothing, but listening to stories of confession, repentance, recommitment. Finally, I was confronted and asked to tell my story, which I did. From then on, I felt accepted and looked forward each week to rejoining this group of fellow seekers.

One week I met Joey, a young professional dancer, who was dying of HIV/AIDS. The group prayed for Joey, and I realized I had had a superior attitude toward HIV/AIDS victims as I could not have been infected. The realization that these were not "bad" people turned my negativity and snobbery to sincere caring, and I visited with guys infected with HIV/AIDS several times with friends I had met in the group.

I did fall in love. My love affair was with a fellow younger than myself who paid much attention to me and confronted me regarding attitudes that he found were not Christ-like. I found myself drawn to this man but unable and unwilling to call it love. Nevertheless, I learned so much from him and discovered that he was trying to deal not only with his own gayness but with a father who had been murdered by a gay man whom he picked up. The experience left me breathless, as I had never truly been in love as I was with this man. It was a totally new and exasperating experience.

During my involvement with the group, I did everything I was instructed to do in order to change what was in my head, fasting, prayer therapy, confession, crying into my pillow, guilt, seeking to find the cause of my gayness. Most of the group that assembled was totally sincere and dedicated. Of that assemblage, I know now only two who are celibate and believe that homosexuality is a sin. One who has married a female has confessed to me his continued desires for companionship with males.

My assessment of the Exodus group is both harsh and kind. I think it was dangerous in that it refused to allow anyone to admit he/she is homosexual, which caused negative self-images and continual anguish. The fact is that only when I could utter the word "homosexual" about myself did I begin to experience healing. One young fellow in the group, who was married and had children, eventually killed himself. He had tried suicide many times. No one was allowed to discuss whether being gay could possibly be acceptable.

We were "sick" and had to be cured. God can do all things; therefore, God could change one's sexual orientation. When that did not happen, we were told to work harder, look for the sin in our lives preventing our change, and to pray "without ceasing." On the positive side, the group allowed me for the first time to meet in a church setting gay people whom I had avoided all my life and to learn that they were not perverts or abominations but people like me, seeking an understanding of themselves.

Frustrated at my inability to control my mind, at some point I addressed God and told Him that I was accepting myself just as He had created me — as a gay man. I was not going to continue fighting His creativity as I had come to believe I was acceptable in His eyes. At that point, I began a new life by accepting myself as a gay man. That acceptance has brought me great happiness and a new self-image that is positive, despite rejection by my dad and stepmother and my only brother. Most of the members of the group in which I was involved eventually dropped out and either have been or are involved in gay relationships, most very productively and healthily.

When I advised the group of my decision, I was asked to leave. Although I have written the leader telling him of my gratitude for his efforts on my behalf, I have never had a response.

Personal Note by Rembert Truluck: Thom and I grew up in the same Baptist church and were in high school together. We lost touch with each other after we went to college. Neither of us knew that the other was gay. Thom learned that I was gay and contacted me when I was Pastor of MCC Nashville. We have corresponded by mail and then by e-mail ever since. We still have not seen each other since high school days. Thom was the main influence on me to get on the Internet and begin to use e-mail. Thom's personal struggles with being gay and married with children have helped me to see more clearly the need to address and deal with the spiritual issues faced by homosexuals who are or have been married with children. Thom's experience with "ex-gay" distortions of religion and reality are also instructive. Thom's story is given here with his permission.

Special Study D

The Dynamics of Religious Abuse

A. Causes and Effects of Religious Abuse

We need more research and understanding of why sick and abusive religion has replaced the simplicity of the gospel of Jesus Christ in most traditional forms of the church. Totally committed religious legalists murdered Jesus. The virus of legalistic, judgmental religion is always fatal. It will kill you and your group if it is not cast out by the clear pure truth of Jesus. Jesus made only one demand, "Follow Me!" Everything that is truly Christian flows from that offer.

Homophobia is Demonic, Not Homosexuality

Perhaps the main thing that I have learned so far from my own experience and the struggles of others is that God loves us all the same and we can completely trust God's unconditional love and acceptance. We demonstrate our trust in God by letting go of everything else. Forsake everything, including religion, and follow Jesus. To follow Jesus you have to keep your attention on Jesus and not on people or organizations, churches, or anything else. Read the last seven verses of the Gospel of John for a plain declaration of the ultimate truth of Jesus Christ.

Low self-esteem and other characteristics of codependency are clearly demonstrated in sick and abusive religion. See the pioneering work on codependency by Melody Beattie, *Codependent No More*, Harper, 1987, and *Beyond Codependency*, Harper, 1989, where the codependent dynamics of unhealthy religion are spelled out.

Read how Paul viewed the abusive religion of his past compared to his present hope in Christ in Philippians 3 and 4 and meditate on what Romans 15:1-7 has to say about our acceptance of ourselves and each other. Also read *Ex-Gays? There Are None!* by the Rev. Sylvia Pennington, Lambda Christian Fellowship, 1989: Box 1967, Hawthorne, CA 90250.

A Personal Word

I know of nobody who has changed from gay to heterosexual. I know nobody else who knows anyone whose sexual orientation has been changed. I know many people who have been profoundly hurt and driven to self-destructive behavior because of attempts, including electric shock therapy, to change their sexual orientation. The "Ex-Gay" Movement is a fraud without any credible scientific research to support claims to change gay people into heterosexuals.

Liberation from Sick Religion

I have received thousands of e-mail responses to my Web site since it was first published on the Internet on September 14, 1997. Many people have written to tell me how much they have been helped to deal with their own abusive religion experiences. Others have written "hate mail" and even abusive and insulting personal attacks in their defense of homophobia and abusive religion.

A clear picture of sick and dysfunctional religion has begun to emerge. Merriam Webster's *Collegiate Dictionary* (tenth edition) includes in the definitions of "sick" the following, "spiritually or morally unsound or corrupt" and "mentally or emotionally unsound or disordered." The Greek word that is used for "sound" doctrine in Titus 1:9 and elsewhere literally means "healthy." Unsound doctrine means unhealthy teachings.

Sick religion hurts people. An underlying characteristic of sick religion is an arrogant, absolute certainty about everything. Sick religious leaders, churches, and denominations often pose as experts in every field of study, science, religion, psychology, politics, sociology, and everything else.

How to Recognize Sick Religion

1. Unhealthy religion claims to possess absolute truth.
2. Unhealthy religion claims that anyone who disagrees is evil.
3. Unhealthy religion sets people against each other for religious reasons.
4. Unhealthy religion demeans and belittles people and makes them feel shame and guilt if they do not comply with religion as seen by the dominant group.
5. Unhealthy religion requires obedience to beliefs and practices that are not logical.
6. Unhealthy religion refutes and rejects the findings of modern medicine, science, and psychology without knowing the facts.
7. Unhealthy religion teaches self-destructive behavior unhindered by the evidence.
8. Unhealthy religion demands absolute allegiance to a particular party or group.
9. Unhealthy religion talks a lot but does not listen. It offers to engage in dialogue but refuses to give the other side a fair opportunity to respond.
10. Unhealthy religion demonstrates a closed mind and uncompromising judgment of all opposing views.

My own observations as a counselor, pastor, religion and Bible teacher, and writer for the past 46 years have shown me that sick religion produces mental, physical, emotional, and social dysfunction and stress but denies that religion is the cause of the problems.

Our Enemy is Ignorance

Dr. John A. Broadus was one of the best-educated and most brilliant Baptist leaders of his age, one of the founders of The Southern Baptist Theological Seminary, and the author of seminary textbooks. Dr. Broadus was preaching at a small rural church in South Carolina. After church, one of the local people was criticizing and disputing what Broadus had said and finally said, "Dr. Broadus, don't you think that God can do without your education?" Dr. Broadus replied, "Yes, I believe that God can do without my education, and furthermore, brother, I believe that God can do without your ignorance." Recent religious attacks have brought gay and lesbian people and their supporters together to resist and fight the common enemy, which is ignorance, not people.

When Gideon (Judges 7) led a small force to victory against a much larger army, the key to success was sudden fear and panic among the enemy soldiers that led them to fight and kill each other in the darkness. Attacks against gay people have not divided us, instead they have made us more united and stronger. The enemy is being fragmented and turned against itself as it flounders about in the darkness of ignorance and fights itself.

Newsweek reported that almost 1000 people responded to a cover story about "The Uproar Over Sexual Conversion" (August 17, 1998). Most of the letters were from gays and lesbians who rejected the anti-gay claims in the story and refuted the spurious claims of homosexual cures by telling their own stories.

Addiction to sick and abusive religion demonstrates the same kind of denial and habitual lying that are characteristic of alcoholism and drug abuse. Be aware of the symptoms of sick religion. Resist getting caught up in sick and abusive religion yourself. Take a fresh look at your own spirituality.

B. Going Beyond Abuse

The vicious cycle of the death and rebirth of sick and destructive religion deserves far more attention and careful study than it has received so far. Just finding a church that says it is acceptable for you to be gay is not enough. The whole abusive and oppressive system of church and traditional religion demands radical examination in the light of the truth of good news from Jesus Christ. The main theme of the Gospels is that Jesus came to set us free from all slavery and abuse by religion, ourselves, our society, and our past.

We do not yet know the long-term effects of religious brain washing both in and outside of the "ex-gay" movement. Some of the results seem to be an ongoing uncertainty about spiritual life and values along with a strong tendency to revert to legalistic, judgmental attitudes that are destructive of self-esteem and are used to invalidate other people.

The dynamics of oppression usually lead the oppressed to become the oppressors whenever they can gain the upper hand over others. Oppression is a "crazy making" environment that warps our perception of reality and truth. Extreme, long term, and dedicated attempts to cast out the "evil and unclean spirits" of sexual orientation from gay, lesbian, bisexual, and transgendered people leave deep invisible scars that we are only beginning to recognize and try to heal.

Paranoid delusions emerge as unhealthy and self-deprecating forces at work in individuals who have been convinced that something is desperately wrong within them and that they cannot change. When these delusions and fears are projected on other people, they create barriers and lead to fear, isolation, loneliness, and a retreat from the believer's freedom in Christ. Frequently new legalisms and a fresh set of judgmental demands develop to control and abuse the person who has broken out of the "ex-gay" grip. Internalized and horizontal homophobia is a powerful destructive force in the gay world, especially when it emerges as self-destructive religion.

Healing Powers

Compassion, love, joy, peace, acceptance, patience, gentleness, kindness, faithfulness, self-control (fruit of the Spirit of Christ in Galatians 5:22-23) give hope for healing and peace even for those whose greatest torment has been religion itself. My experience with small groups who share regularly in a home setting and who create an environment of nonjudgmental acceptance has convinced me that such home groups offer one of the best settings for recovery and healing from sick and abusive religion. Recovery, healing, learning, and growing take time. The people who have suffered a lifetime of religious abuse and the dedicated ignorance of the ex-gay ministries do not recover instantly or without help. We all need a little understanding.

C. Why Homophobic Legalists Do Not Listen

Legalism is an idolatrous religion. Legalistic, judgmental religion is based on absolute commitment to biblical literalism, the conviction that every word of the Bible is literally true and every statement in the Bible has equal authority as the word of God. This approach generates most of the religious opposition to civil and human rights for lesbian, gay, bisexual, and transgendered people. Biblical literalism is the basis for the rejection of gay people as an abomination to God and therefore unacceptable to God and to God's churches and people. It is the basis for rejecting same-sex marriage and the ordination of gay clergy. It is the reason for denying gay and lesbian couples the right to adopt children. It is the primary obstacle to opening the mind of America to the facts about sexual orientation and the truth about what the Bible does and does not say about homosexuality.

Facts About Legalism

Legalism is a distortion and denial of the gospel of Jesus Christ as given in the four Gospels and expounded in the rest of the New Testament.

Legalism is a mental disorder that masquerades as religion. Suspicion and fear are the chief characteristics of paranoid delusions and legalism. The severely suspicious person creates a rigid legalistic system that organizes and dominates all of life. This rigid legalistic system is their protective shield to keep other people at a distance. Any question or attack on any part of the system is viewed as a threat to the person. This personal legalistic system is defended at all cost.

When I was a chaplain intern at Central State Hospital, Kentucky, during my doctoral program, I met a patient who was severely paranoid schizophrenic. We spoke to each other in a friendly way every day. Then one day he was sitting at a table and invited me to talk with him. I listened as he told me how he was a prisoner at the hospital so that they could perform experiments on him against his will. He went into detail to spell out his fears and to tell me how he was being watched and manipulated by the hospital staff. I listened for about thirty minutes. Afterwards, he would not speak to me again and avoided me. I "knew too much" and though I had not questioned his paranoid views, I was now the enemy and could not be trusted. I have experienced some of the same kind of behavior in far too many church leaders not to take seriously the pathology of suspicion and fear in legalistic religion.

Paranoid delusions are based on fear and an exaggerated view of one's importance. When a person sees a group of people talking and thinks "they are talking about me," the subtle implication is, "Where two or three are gathered together, there am I in the midst of them." One way to handle severe anxiety and fear is to develop the delusion that you are God and people are trying to take away your power. This kind of pathological thinking is not at all rare in churches and religious leaders.

Homosexual orientation is not a mental disorder. Legalism Is.

Legalism based on biblical literalism is the foundation of many programs of financial support for religious institutions and churches. Fund raising demands and tithing techniques are often built upon distortions and inappropriate applications of biblical teachings about giving to the poor while clear teachings about accepting and loving outcast and unattractive people are ignored completely. The legalistic system that brings in the money is untouchable. Any threat to any part of the system is perceived as an attack on God.

Institutional arrogance is one deadly product of legalism. The tightly wound coils of legalistic demands command absolute obedience and service to the institution that represents the legalistic system. Churches, colleges, schools, political movements, television and radio ministries, and various campaigns and programs demand and get sacrificial support from people who are convinced that these institutions are the "work of God" and have the right to require every resource that members and supporters might possess.

Until we lesbian and gay people can successfully challenge and change the dominant legalistic systems based on biblical literalism in this country, gays, lesbians, bisexuals, transgendered people, and many other religious outcasts will never be free from abusive, oppressive religion. When religious leaders are committed to legalism, they see truth as threat and love as limited and conditional.

Our only hope is the conversion of religious leaders from legalism to Jesus plus nothing. We have to begin by being willing ourselves to follow Jesus plus nothing else. It takes a lot of spiritual confidence and courage to let go of all other "weapons" and trust only Jesus in a mortal conflict that determines our survival. Where will we find that confidence and courage? That is up to you.

Special Study E

A Gay Christian Response to Southern Baptists

A. **How Southern Baptists Have Changed**
B. **Baptists Declare War on Gay People, June 7-11, 1998**
C. **Gay and Lesbian Strategies for Spiritual Warfare**
D. **What Jesus Said about Family Values**

A. How Southern Baptists Have Changed

Jesus in the Gospels defined his ministry by who he included that previously had been left out. See the first hometown sermon that Jesus preached in Nazareth and notice the response in Luke 4:17-30. When the people rejected the inclusive message of Jesus, he left town. When Southern Baptists defined themselves by who they left out (lesbian, gay, bisexual, and transgendered people) in changing the bylaws of the Southern Baptist Convention to exclude any church that accepted openly gay and lesbian members, Southern Baptists ceased to be Christian (Christ-like). They also forced pastors, staff, and church members into the closet of denial and oppression about sexual orientation. To force people to lie about who they are is spiritually unhealthy and ultimately self-defeating.

Southern Baptists include 16 million members and are the second largest religious body in the United States, second only to the Roman Catholic Church. The over thirty other Baptist denominations draw much of their literature and program materials from the Southern Baptist Convention Sunday School Board and other agencies.

Southern Baptists Have Denied Their Own History

For over 150 years Baptists have believed and taught soul freedom of the individual and have respected and supported the autonomy of the local church. Recent actions by the Southern Baptist Convention have rejected and repudiated these great principles of the historic Baptist tradition. The Convention's call for Baptists to boycott Disney was a blatant rejection of principles for which Southern Baptists have stood for many generations as well as a way to show the world their new, mean, legalistic, judgmental spirit.

A conservative political takeover has changed Southern Baptists. Seminaries and other institutions have been undermined. The erosion of objective academic credibility of once great schools and boards has made Baptists the object of scorn and ridicule in the scholastic world. Some institutions have already lost their accreditation. Even the "mother seminary" in Louisville, Kentucky, has had accreditation suspended and has been discredited in the eyes of the rest of the academic world, which this seminary once led.

Baptists Deny the Bible That They Claim to Follow

Southern Baptists in their attacks on gay people ignore the facts about biblical translations and other evidence that refutes their anti-gay position. Baptist Greek scholars know, like all others do, that the Bible has no word for "homosexual" in the Old Testament Hebrew or the New Testament Greek. Yet the same incorrect translations and out-of-context use of only six verses to attack and condemn gay people continues in this so-called "Bible believing" denomination.

On January 31, 1999, these six "clobber passages" that are used to attack gay and lesbian people were studied for the first time as the basis for anti-gay Southern Baptist Sunday School lessons. This incredibly negative development has led me to begin writing a series of *Gay Sunday School Lessons* to tell the truth and to help gay people and other oppressed minorities to know how to follow "the real Jesus" who loves and accepts us just as we are.

Baptists Deny Jesus

In their attacks on gay people, Baptists ignore the fact that Jesus gives no basis for religious gay bashing. Jesus never mentioned sexual orientation or even hinted at the idea of homosexuality. Jesus never said, "Hate the sin and love the sinner." That slogan was invented by homophobic fundamentalists and is never used except to condemn gay and lesbian people. If Jesus is the guide to understanding all Scripture, why do Baptists not let Jesus guide them in fighting the abusive and mistaken use of Bible passages to condemn and destroy gay and lesbian people?

Baptists Deny Reality

Baptists deny reality in their support for so called "Ex-Gay" ministries that try to use religion to change the sexual orientation of people. Scientists, medical doctors, psychiatrists, attorneys, psychologists, and other professional groups have taken a clear stand against the abusive use of "reparative therapy" to try to change gays to straight. There is no reliable evidence that a person's sexual orientation can be changed. All of these failures will be corrected if Baptists turn back to Jesus.

Repent! Turn away ("repent") from your homophobic lifestyle of legalistic, judgmental religion that denies God's unconditional love and grace for all people. ***Shame!*** For betraying the spirit and legacy of John A. Broadus, Richard Furman, and George W. Truett. ***Shame!*** For retreating from soul freedom, autonomy of the local church, and separation of church and state. ***Shame!*** For claiming to follow Jesus yet teaching ignorance and prejudice. ***Turn back to Jesus*** as the only way to truth and life for individuals and churches.

One of my friends recently asked me to point out what parts of the New Testament Southern Baptists have ignored in their attitude of condemning and rejecting gays. My first response was, "just about all of it!" But upon reflection, these passages seem to be the most obvious ones,

Matthew 7:1-5
John 3:16-17; 10:10; 12:47; 13:34-35; and 17:20-23
all of Acts 10, especially verses 28 and 34
1 Corinthians 13
2 Corinthians 10:3-5
all of Galatians, especially Galatians 2:11-21; 3:1-5; 3:23-28; 5:1; 5:14-15; and 5:22-23
all of Ephesians, especially chapter 2
Philippians 2:1-13
1 Peter 3:15
2 Peter 3:14-18
1 John 3:13-21; 4:7-19
and most of all, Romans 15:1-7

What do you think?

See the Web site for "Rainbow Baptists," the combined ministry of Internet support for American Baptist and Southern Baptist gays and lesbians. Also see Keith Hartman's book, *Congregations in Conflict: The Battle Over Homosexuality* (Rutgers University Press, New Brunswick, New Jersey, 1996). Hartman's book tells the story of Baptist and other churches struggling within their denominations to include God's gay children in membership and ministry.

B. Baptists Declare War on Gay People, June 7-11, 1998

(This is a special update that was added to my Web site on June 13, 1998, in response to the meeting of the 1998 Southern Baptist Convention in Salt Lake City.)

Southern Baptists on June 7-11, 1998, in Salt Lake City, have declared war on gay people and women and on Jesus Christ and the inclusive and accepting teachings of Jesus. They have declared war against the clear teachings of Jesus about family values in Mark 3:31-35. They have tried to turn back the clock of progress for gay and lesbian rights and for women's rights and equality.

During the week when the President of the United States called for equal pay for women, the largest evangelical church in the country called for women to retreat back into being submissive to their husbands, and then denied the gift of Jesus to women to be disciples, apostles, preachers, teachers, and prophets. Southern Baptists have declared war on their own people, including many of their own denomination and church leaders and their families, and on their own history and traditions. They have bowed down and worshipped the two false gods of biblical literalism and judgmental religious legalism in their growing service and submission to the new idolatry of homophobic fundamentalism. They have given their full support to the emerging anti-gay religious/political industry that has condemned, rejected, wounded, and destroyed many of their own families and leaders.

In renewing their call for Baptists to boycott Disney, Baptists have lied about the success of the Southern Baptist Convention boycott of Disney, claiming that they have hurt Disney at a time when "Disney's revenue, earnings, and amusement park attendance all set records last year." The leader of "ethics" for Southern Baptists, Richard Land, said that the head of Disney, Michael Eisner, "wouldn't be attacking us if we were not bothering Mickey's Empire." It did not seem to occur to Richard Land that Eisner attacked Southern Baptists because they are wrong and not because the boycott was working.

The Southern Baptist Convention has changed radically from what it was when I was active in it. The Southern Baptist Convention's "Baptist Faith and Message" was first approved in 1925 as a clear statement of the founding Baptist principles of the priesthood of all believers, soul freedom, religious liberty, local church autonomy, and separation of church and state. In Salt Lake City, the Convention perverted this great "Baptist Faith and Message" by adding false teachings that condemn and reject gays and lesbians and reduce the role of women from partners in life and ministry back to the submissive role of property and slaves for men that Jesus came to correct 2,000 year ago.

This new "Baptist Faith and Message" is a declaration of war against truth and has laid a foundation for violence against lesbians and gays that is accelerating at an alarming rate. Recently in a high school only a few miles from San Francisco, students vandalized the school and painted anti-gay signs on the walls in what the police are calling a "hate crime." Where did the students get encouragement and support for these hate crimes? They got their inspiration from the evangelical religion that they see on television and hear from their own preachers and politicians. A 19-year-old student in Orlando, Florida, who committed vandalism by destroying rainbow flags that the city had displayed in honor of gay pride said that he had acted in response to the public attacks on gays and the city of Orlando by the Rev. Pat Robertson.

The horror of the murder of a black man in Jasper, Texas, last year by three white racists, who tied the man to the back of a pickup truck and dragged him to death over country roads simply because of the man's race, shocked the nation. The same kind of ignorance and hate that motivated such a crime, motivates the unrelenting gay bashing that gay people experience on a daily basis. A lot of the gay bashing that oppresses gays and lesbians comes in the form of verbal abuse from church pulpits and denominational decisions that glibly characterize gays as "the abomination of God."

Remember the Bible definition of "abomination," "Six things that God hates, yes, seven that are an abomination to God, haughty eyes, a lying tongue, and hands that shed innocent blood, a heart that devises wicked plans, feet that run rapidly to evil, a false witness who utters lies, and one who spreads strife among the family" (Proverbs 6:16-19). No mention of gays or sexual orientation. This description of abominations is a description of **homophobia** and not **homosexuality**.

C. Gay and Lesbian Strategies for Spiritual Warfare

It is time for all gay and lesbian people to prepare to defend ourselves in the developing religious wars. This is a time of spiritual warfare and a threat to our survival. What strategy is available to us?

1. Fear Is Our Greatest Enemy

First, fight fear! Fear makes you vulnerable. Fear is a crazy making environment to live in. Fear makes you nervous. Fear clouds your mind and judgment and causes you to make mistakes. To live "in the closet" is to live in fear of being discovered as gay. Fear makes you over-react to people who "get too close" and then you create pressures and problems of misunderstanding with your own family and friends and at work.

Face and deal with your fear. The most destructive fear is the internalized fear of homophobia, in which you have been conditioned by religious lies and distortions to believe that you really are an abomination to God and a worthless human wretch. You can run away from the schoolyard bully or the hateful family members who despise you, but you cannot escape from the bully within that ridicules you for your God-given sexual orientation and tries to destroy you. The most evil crime of modern religion is the teachings that turn young gay and lesbian people against themselves and that contribute to the self-destructive attitudes and behavior that make suicide the leading cause of death of gay and lesbian teenagers. (See recent studies by PFLAG and others that are available on Web sites given in my Web site links. See also the statistical reports by the U.S Government Centers for Disease Control in Atlanta.)

Violence against gays and lesbians reaches its most horrible expression, not in attacks by street gangs or even in the hellish punishments devised by homophobic parents against their own children or in the diabolical methods of gay "reparative therapy," but in the suicides of gay and lesbian people. Many gays and lesbians are depressed but not because they are homosexual.

They are depressed and suicidal because of the way they have been treated by churches, parents, families, and society for being gay. To drive a child of God to suicide has to be an evil act that is in a special class by itself. "Perfect love [Jesus] casts out fear, because fear causes pain" (I John 4:18).

2. Come Out and Tell Your Truth

Invisible means vulnerable. Tell your parents that you are gay and request them to meet with the pastor of your church to ask him to stop the anti-gay attacks because they are hurting you. This will take courage. But what else stands a chance of changing the prevailing destructive situation? I know of one Southern Baptist Church in which a new pastor preached a strong sermon attacking homosexuals. Soon after the sermon, some of the leaders of the church went to the pastor to tell him that the sermon hurt a lot of leaders in the church who had gay children whom they loved and accepted. The pastor never mentioned homosexuals in his sermons again. He remained as pastor of the church for 25 years. I know that this story is true, because two of the church leaders were my parents, and the pastor became my friend.

3. There is Strength in Numbers

Find other gay and lesbian people to know as friends and to find and give support and acceptance to each other. This goes also for the parents and friends of gays and lesbians.

Find PFLAG, a local Metropolitan Community Church (MCC) or other accepting and affirming spiritual group, or start your own recovery group.

4. Knowledge Is Power

One of our greatest weapons in the "holy war" of regaining our rightful place in our world is knowing the truth. "The truth will set you free." Learn what the Bible really says and does not say about homosexuality. "For though we are human, we do not fight according to human methods, for the weapons of our warfare are not human, but mighty before God for the destruction of fortresses. We are destroying speculations and every lofty thing raised up against the knowledge of God, and we are taking every thought captive to the obedience of Christ" (2 Corinthians 10:3-5).

5. Develop Your Own Spiritual Life

Traditional churches may be of little help to you in building a strong spiritual life that will sustain you throughout the war. A great wealth of inspirational and informative resources for spiritual recovery and growth can be found in the "Resources" section and throughout my Web site and in the Annotated Bibliography at the end of this book. Get busy and learn what you need to know in order to recover, heal, learn, and grow spiritually. Pray. Share with other seekers like yourself. Read devotional material that you can trust and that really speaks to you. Do not be afraid to reach out to new and unfamiliar resources and to take "the road less traveled" to find freedom from fear and spiritual oppression and abuse.

6. Keep Healthy

It is hard to hold your ground during battle if you are not healthy. Pay attention to your body. Be aware of how you feel, what you eat, and what you do that is healthy and positive for your life both physically and emotionally. If you need medical help, get it. Be sensitive to the health of others around you. Help one another to be well and healthy. With God's help, let go of habits and addictions that are harmful to your mental and physical health. If you need help in recovery, find it.

7. Love Yourself

Healthy self-esteem and a clear sense of self-worth are the necessary foundation for winning your part of the war. Jesus said, "God notices even one sparrow who falls to the ground, and you are of greater value than many sparrows" (Matthew 10:29-31). Jesus never said you were worthless. Jesus said repeatedly that you are a child of God and God loves you just as you are.

Love yourself. "The love of God has been poured out into our hearts by the Holy Spirit, who was given to us." How can you love your neighbor as yourself unless you truly love yourself?

Jesus responded to deceit and violence with the double-edged sword of truth and love. Jesus won. Jesus was non-violent and taught and demonstrated love for his enemies. You and I are called to follow Jesus and not to give up on love as our most powerful weapon. Be consistent. Love yourself, your friends, and your enemies. By this you show that you also love God.

D. What Jesus Said About Family Values

"Traditional Family Values" has become a powerful political slogan and an anti gay weapon that cannot be ignored. Did Jesus talk about family values? How can Jesus lead us into a Christian gay and lesbian understanding of family values? Jesus expressed great respect for family values. Luke 2:39-52 tells how Jesus as a child respected his parents and remained subject to them. Even then, however, Jesus recognized that God was a higher authority in his life.

Jesus revealed to his parents that he was different and that he had a special mission in life that they did not understand. When his parents found Jesus in the Temple, they were surprised and said exactly what a lot of parents say to gay children when they come out to them, "How could you do this to us! We have been looking for you sorrowing [literally, "in great pain"]." Jesus did not apologize to his parents for "coming out" and acting on who he really was. He simply said that he had to be his true self and left it at that. His mother loved and accepted Jesus even when she did not understand him. We need more mothers like Mary.

Jesus rebuked his mother for telling him what to do and then did it anyway in John 2:3-11. Later, Jesus provided for his mother by telling his beloved disciple to take care of her. Yet Jesus also taught that following him was more important than usual family obligations, "Another of the disciples said to Jesus, 'Sovereign, let me first go and bury my father.' But Jesus said to him, 'Follow me; and let the dead bury the dead'" (Matthew 8:21-22).

Jesus Challenged All Traditions

Parents selected children's mates. Women were property and had no freedom in choosing their partners. Jesus elevated women from property to persons to partners in ministry and respected and honored little children, all of which was new. Jesus set into motion many freedoms we assume today.

Your Union With Christ

The word "forsake" used by Jesus to tell his followers that they should forsake everything else in order to be his disciples is the same word used for forsaking father and mother in order for the human partners to "become one" in marriage. Jesus set loyalty to him in contrast to traditional family values,

> Everyone who has left houses or brothers or sisters or father or mother or wife or children or farms for my name's sake, shall receive many times as much, and shall inherit eternal life. (Matthew 19:29)

Same-sex committed couples who are bound to each other by their love can joyfully look to Jesus for guidance and strength for living. Their love for each other, their service to Christ in their personal lives and their ministry of acceptance and encouragement to others can help everyone redefine family values more in keeping with the example and teachings of Jesus. Gay couples can challenge the rest of the world to put Jesus at the center of marriage instead of focusing on law, custom, procreation, and social pressure.

Going Beyond Tradition

Everything that Jesus did was new. His new understanding of family was revolutionary. The traditional family ties of the time of Jesus were challenged and replaced by ties to Jesus and to doing the will of God.

When the mother and brothers of Jesus came to get Jesus, the crowd told Jesus that his mother and brothers were looking for him. Jesus answered by asking, "Who are my mother and my brothers?" And looking about on those who were sitting around him Jesus said, "Look! Here are my mother and my brothers. For whoever does the will of God is my brother and sister and mother" (Mark 3:31-35).

You do not choose your biological family. Jesus sets you free to choose who will be closest to you and who will most influence your life. What kind of choices have you made in selecting people to be in your life? Your freedom in Christ includes your freedom to decide who your circle of closest friends will be. Freedom to choose your "family" implies your obligation to choose wisely. You can destroy your freedom by making bad choices.

Jesus carefully selected his closest friends. God will help you do the same.

Jesus Makes All Things New

Jesus gave a "new" commandment that his followers should love one another just as Jesus loved them. The only way that you can follow that commandment is to have Jesus in your heart and mind. Whenever the Spirit of Jesus comes into your life, the first evidence is your love for people. "The fruit of the Spirit is love" (Galatians 5:22).

Loving one another includes loving your biological family also. Jesus did not reject traditional family values of his time. He went beyond them to define all values in relation to himself. Jesus calls you to a radical letting go of everything in order to follow only Jesus. The bottom line in everything for Jesus was, "follow me."

Have you experienced Jesus in your life?

Showing how ignorant and prejudiced the radical homophobic fundamentalists are about family values is not enough.

We agree, "Hate is not a family value." Jesus invites us to define everything in the light of God's inclusive and accepting love demonstrated for all people in the life and work of Jesus. The first step in your successful challenge to the hate-filled, homophobic purveyors of "traditional family values," is to connect with Jesus in whatever way best fits you and to follow Jesus.

Special Study F

How Do You Name God?

(An earlier version of this study was included in my 1993 book, *Invitation to Freedom*, published by Chi Rho Press and now out of print.)

Jesus has liberated us from abusive religious language. This brings up an important issue of biblical translation and interpretation. Jesus used new names for God and filled old names with fresh new meaning. Inclusive language in Bible translations is a recent and still developing phenomenon. It has been highly controversial in many religious groups. Jesus can be our guide to what the Bible really means about everything. Jesus ignored and transcended all of the old taboos about male and female roles. He called women to be disciples and broke down the traditional barriers that separated people because of race, sex, religion, class, sexual orientation, local customs, and fear of the unknown.

Read about how God gave God's name to Moses in Exodus 3:5-15.

A missionary was asked why Christians use so many different names for God. "You call your God by many names, like God, Lord, Jesus, Christ, Father, Creator, Redeemer, Savior, King, etc. How do you know what name to use?" The missionary thought for a few moments and answered, "We call our God by the name of what we let God do for us. If we let God comfort, protect and guide us, we say Father. If we let God forgive our sins, we say Redeemer. If we let God set us free from fear and oppression, we say Deliverer. I suppose we give God that name of what God does."

No two people are alike. Each of us experiences God in ways that are appropriate to us as individuals. If our faith is based on experience and not just on religious ideas, if our hope is based on the evidence all around us of God's love and power and not on speculation, and if our love springs from our hearts made new in Christ and not from religious conditioning, then we call God by many names.

God Who Acts

Moses asked God to give the name to use when Moses represented God to the people. God replied, "I Am Who I Am [in Hebrew, *hayah sher hayah*]. Tell them that I Am [*hayah*] has sent me to you" (Exodus 3:13). The holy name *YHWH* (*Yahweh*) is built on *HYH*, which is the verb "to be." Biblical Hebrew had no written vowels. The vowel pointing was added later. We do not know the original vowels in *YHWH*. The vowels that create Yahweh are a guess. The Hebrew word *adoni*, "Lord," often was used in place of *YHWH* to avoid using the holy name. The word Jehovah is a modern creation from the consonants of *YHWH* with the vowels of *Adoni*. The word "Jehovah" does not exist in the Bible.

G. Ernest Wright wrote a Bible history titled *God Who Acts* and later with Reginald H. Fuller, another book, *The Book of the Acts of God*. These two books by a highly respected biblical scholar and archaeologist viewed the Bible as "a record of God's actions in human history." Wright based his life work on his belief that "I Am Who I Am" means that God reveals the name of God through what God does.

Wright would interpret the name as "I Am Who I Will Show Myself to Be by What I Do," or perhaps more simply, "I Am What I Do." This means that the name of God is constantly being revealed by the acts of God. Jesus said in John 14:9 that if you see Jesus, you see God, and then Jesus linked his actions with the actions of God. Jesus explained in John 5:36 that the actions of Jesus reveal the presence of God. The theme of "the word of God made flesh to dwell among us" is found throughout the Gospel of John. Trace the use of "I Am" for Jesus in John 4:26, 35; 8:23; 9:5; 10:7, 11, 14, 36; 11:25; 13:13; 14:6; and 15:1.

We say, "Actions speak louder than words." The Bible teaches that God's actions are words. This means that the name of God is constantly developing and emerging with fresh meaning as we experience the activity of God. Jesus taught that God could not be imprisoned in a building or in a set of rules. Jesus sets us free to call God by whatever name speaks most clearly to us as individuals. As Eric Rust, a great theology professor, said, "You can't put God in your pocket." God is not discovered at the end of an argument but in experiencing the presence of God in action.

Jesus as the Way

When Jesus said, "I am the way, the truth, and the life, and nobody comes to God but by me" (John 14:6), Jesus was not saying that believers should create a new idolatrous religion out of how they imagined Jesus must have looked or acted. No basis exists in the Gospels to make pictures, stained glass windows, and statues of "Jesus" that represent billions of dollars of investment. How did we lose sight of the invitation of Jesus to "sell what we have and give it to the poor, and come follow me" (Mark 10:21)?

Jesus was saying in John 14:6 that if you experience God in your life, you relate to God in the same way that Jesus did through radical trust and obedience. "Believe" and "follow" were used interchangeably in the Gospel of John. The presence of God in our lives reveals the love and life of God in and through us to others. We shine as lights in the world.

All of this would be quite obvious if we had not been conditioned by abusive, legalistic judgmental religion that long ago abandoned the simple "way, truth, and life" of Jesus. Legalism conveniently forgot that Jesus said God is seen in the faces of people around us and not in the Temple, the rituals, or the holy garments, which Jesus rejected.

Multiple Images of God in the Bible

Begin with the third word in the Hebrew text of the Bible, "God" (Hebrew, *Elohim*), which is never translated literally. ("In beginning, God created the heavens and the earth" Genesis 1:1) *Elohim* is the plural of the Hebrew word for god. *Eloh* means "god." *Im* is the plural. The singular "God" is an interpretation. The word means "gods" and yet it is never translated that way. *Elohim* is the most frequently used name for God in the Hebrew Bible. Scholars explain that the word is in the plural to express "the plural of majesty" as in "Let us make people in our own image and after our likeness" (Genesis 1:26). But is this true? Is not Genesis rather making clear that the person of God is plural and in exists in perfect unity, love, and harmony? God intended that people made in the image of God should inhabit, subdue and have dominion over the earth and live in peace and harmony with each other, with nature, and with God. God is to be seen as perfect unity in diversity as we learn more every moment about the vastness and complexity of God's Creation.

Sexuality in the Image of God

Genesis 1:27 says, "God created *Adam* [the Hebrew word used for "humanity," which comes from the word for "dirt" or "dust"] in God's own image. God created him in the image of God; male and female God created them." This fluid use of the words "him" and "them" is typical of biblical Hebrew. The main point of Genesis 1:27 is that human beings in their sexuality are "in the image of God." God includes far more than we have experienced or imagined. God reveals to us whatever we are ready to receive. God is not limited, but we are.

Jesus sets us free to be individuals. You are not called in Christ to let religion press you unwillingly into a pattern that does not fit you. See all of Romans 12 and 1 Corinthians 12. "Varieties" of gifts, ministries, and works (1 Corinthians 12:4, 5, 6) is Greek *diaresis* from the same root as "heresy." Jesus respected our variety and individuality as persons and said, "My yoke is gentle [well fitted], and my demands are light [not burdensome]" (Matthew 11:30). Whatever certain passages might imply, the Bible says that your sexuality is not only a gift from God to be celebrated and enjoyed; it is an expression of the plural nature and being of God.

Human Images of God in the Bible

Anthropomorphic images of God abound in the Bible, which speaks of God's back, hand, face, eyes, etc. These human features are not just primitive ideas that should be discounted as irrelevant today. The New Testament teaches that God was revealed most perfect when "the word of God became flesh" in Jesus of Nazareth (John 1:14). The word of God came most perfectly to people not as words but as a human being.

Read carefully Philippians 2:1-18, where Paul drew upon the Genesis ideas of "image" and "likeness" to draw a dramatic contrast between the disobedience of *Adam* and the obedience of Jesus. The result of trust and obedience of Jesus was the new name of "ruler" (Greek *kurios*) that was lost in Genesis 3. God's humans were to have dominion over the earth and subdue it. Because of their grasping after equality with God, the first humans lost their dominion over the earth and became slaves to the earth instead.

The comparison of Adam and Jesus was a persistent theme in Paul's letters. See Romans 5 and 1 Corinthians 15. Human characteristics of God cannot be discounted as primitive and out of date. The Bible views Jesus of Nazareth as an open window on God. Jesus said, "God is spirit and those who worship God must worship in spirit and in truth" (John 4:24). This means at least that God is more than we can imagine God to be. See Isaiah 55:6-11 and 2 Peter 3, where the greatness and glory of God are shown to be beyond our imagination and far beyond anything that we can grasp.

In Matthew 22:30, Jesus said that after resurrection we do not marry and we are like the angels in heaven. Jesus did not, however, say that we lose our individuality or our gender identification. In fact, the main point of Jesus in Matthew 22:23-33 was that a woman's primary identity is not "whose wife she will be" but it is her own value as an individual before God. Jesus completely rejected the prevailing view of women that a woman had identity only in relationship to whom she married. This meant that a woman who had been married several times had a hopelessly confused identity. Jesus challenged and changed the way that God's people were to view women as also God's children with equal value before God with all of God's other children.

Female Images of God in the Bible

The biblical image of God includes gender orientation. Activities of God in the Bible reveal both male and female functions. God as "mother" is implied in every one of the 15 uses of "Father" for God in the Hebrew Bible. This is of great significance in understanding what the word *abba* and "father" in prayer and especially in the Gospel of John mean. In the Garden of Gethsemane, Jesus called out to God as *abba*, which was an affectionate and respectful Aramaic term used by children as an equivalent to our term "daddy." In Mark 14:36, Romans 8:15; and Galatians 4:6, *abba* is accompanied by "father."

As far as we know, Jesus was the first to address God in prayer as "Father." See the use of "Father" in Matthew 6:5-15 for the model prayer and in John 17 in the prayer of Jesus for his followers. On the cross (Luke 23:46), Jesus quoted Psalm 31:5 and prayed, "Father, into your hands I commit my spirit." Jesus added, "Father," which is not in Psalm 31:5.

Joachim Jeremias is the biblical scholar most associated with research into the meaning of *abba* and the title of "Father." See the collection of Jeremias' articles in *The Prayers of Jesus*, (SCM Press, 1967) and the article on *abba* by Gerhard Kittel in the *Theological Dictionary of the New Testament*. Jeremias pointed out that "Father" was used for God only 15 times in the Hebrew Bible and 170 times in the Gospels. All of the references to God as "Father" in the Hebrew Bible describe mothering functions of nurture and care, as in Hosea 11:1-11. See also Psalm 103:13-14. Read Hosea 11:1-11.

Jeremias concluded that the use of "Father" in reference to God as Parent encompassed what the word "Mother" signifies for us today. God's "compassion" in Hosea is Hebrew *ruhamah,* which is the Hebrew word for the mother's womb. See Hosea 2:19, 23; and 11:8. See also Hosea 1:6-9; and 2:1, where *ruhamah* was made into names. Hosea was quoted 40 times in the Gospel of John.

The thinking of Jesus was saturated with the ideas and images of God in Hosea. The view of God in Hosea as "Mother and Father" is implied in the Gospel of John whenever Jesus used "Father" for God. To be true to the spirit and attitude of Jesus, God as "Father" should always be rendered as "Mother and Father." Terms like "Sovereign" and "Creator" are not adequate substitutes for "Father" in light of the Hosea background that is clearly evident in the Gospel of John and elsewhere. "Mother and Father" is what Jesus meant by *abba* and "Father" and that probably is the way it should be read. God is both mother and father in the role of parent of the nation and the individual in Hosea 11:1, "Out of Egypt I have called my son" (quoted about Jesus in Matthew 2:15). Jesus as the "Son of God" was both the individual and the nation. Jesus was the new beginning of the people of God. The Bible pictured God in many activities, but Deuteronomy 6:4 declared, "Listen, O Israel, the Ruler our God is One." This One God has many names. God still demands, "Have no other gods before me."

Women Leaders in the Church

See Lesson 30, "How Women Disciples Changed the World," for details about women as disciples and leaders in the early beginnings of the church. Dr. Nancy Hardesty helped me gain a better perspective on inclusive fellowship that accepts women as having equal value and importance as men in all levels of ministry. Her book is filled with useful historical facts as well as her own personal story, (*Inclusive Language in the Church*: John Knox Press, 1987).

The argument that God and Jesus are male and therefore can be represented only by males has no basis in the New

Testament. The biblical account of the beginnings of Christianity includes women on an equal standing with men. To obscure this truth through sloppy and misleading translations and selective out-of-context interpretations is to deny the fullness and completeness of the gospel and to contribute to the body of "translations from hell" that have plagued lesbian and gay people, women, youth, racial minorities, and many others alienated and oppressed by religion.

Paul declared clearly, "There is neither Jew nor Greek, neither slave nor free, neither male nor female; for you all are one in Christ Jesus" (Galatians 3:28). Today in our diverse multi-cultural world, we would expand this truth and say, "We no long-er are separated by race, sex, age, social class, religion, sexual orientation, ethnic origin, or any barriers and walls that have been raised to divide us, but we all are one in Christ Jesus."

What Is Your Personal Vision of God?

Remember that the purpose of this study is to encourage you to think and learn facts that will equip you to make your own decisions as an informed individual. "The heavens declare the glory of god; and the firmament shows God's work" (Psalm 19:1). "Firmament" (Genesis 1:6-8) is Hebrew for "a reflective polished metal surface" that was like a mirror to reflect all that God has created in, on, and above the earth. God is revealed in all that God has made. Recall the many uses of nature in the Bible to speak of attributes of God.

Jesus ministered primarily to the common people, to "country people," in contrast to the rich and the self-righteous rulers and guardians of tradition. The word "pagan" is from Latin and French words that mean "country people" or "people of the land." The word "pagan" has taken on an unfortunate judgmental religious meaning not originally intended. The attack by Jesus on established religion and his appeal to the country people to "follow me" could be called a "new paganism." The role of ordinary people, animals, plants, and forces of nature for communicating God's truth by Jesus in his parables and other teachings in the Gospels is obvious.

What About Crystals?

A crystal is a rock. One of the most useless recent controversies in some churches is the argument over crystals being used as religious symbols. When Jesus gave Simon a new name that would express his role as the first person to realize who Jesus really was, Jesus called him Peter (the Greek word *Petros*, "rock"). This was a nickname. We would call him "Rocky." This was no arbitrary term of endearment and fun. Rock is one of the most significant symbols for God throughout the Bible. Rock is right up there with "light" and "power." A rock represented strength and stability.

God was called the Rock in Deuteronomy, "The Rock! God's work is perfect, for all of God's ways are just; a God of faithfulness and without injustice, Righteous and upright is God" (Deuteronomy 32:4). "You neglected the Rock who begot you, and forgot the God who gave you birth" (Deuteronomy 32:18). "God is my rock" (2 Samuel 22:2-3, 32-33). God is rock and fortress in Psalm 18:1-2, 31, 46; 19:14; 31:2-3; 62:2; 71:3; and 42:9, "I will say to God, my Rock, why have you forgotten me?" Compare this to Psalm 22:1. God is called a "rock" far more often than a "light" in the Hebrew Bible.

The Law was written on tablets of stone (Exodus 34:1) and in Christ was written on human hearts (2 Corinthians 3:3). Water for survival and life came from the rock in the wilderness in Numbers 20:11; and Exodus 17:6 and then was fulfilled in Christ in 1 Corinthians 10:4 and John 7:38-39.

The Messiah is called the chief stone in Psalm 118:23 and Matthew 21:42. Isaiah 8:14 and 28:16 spoke of a stone of stumbling and a chief cornerstone that were fulfilled in Christ. In 1 Peter 2:4-8, Christians are "living stones." John the Baptist said that God could raise up the true children of Abraham "from these stones" (Matthew 3:9). When Pharisees rebuked the followers of Jesus for shouting at the entry of Jesus into Jerusalem, Jesus said, "If these are silent, the stones will cry out!" (Luke 19:40). The first evidence of the resurrection was the stone rolled away from the tomb.

A rock is one of the most persistent spiritual symbols of God and the work of God in the Bible. A crystal is simply a beautiful rock. Perhaps a crystal is a better symbol for God than most of the religious objects that have been accumulated to replace Jesus with "stuff" and to try to convince people that Jesus meant to say, "Sell what you have and give it to the building fund."

We worship stones already, but the wrong ones. We honor and worship the bricks and stones of impressive buildings that Jesus rejected and condemned. Remember that Jesus said of the Temple, "Not one stone will be left standing on another until it is all destroyed." The building had become a symbol of division and exclusion. Jesus came to destroy the kind of legalistic, judgmental religion that neglects people and glorifies buildings. 1 Peter 2:4-8 says that people are the stones, the building of God.

Use whatever name for God best expresses your personal experience with God. If you have met the God of Jesus, you have encountered the God who loves you, created you as you are in the image of God, and liberated you from sick religion. Now you can love yourself, God, and other people. Call God by the name that best indicates what you have let God do for you.

Freedom to Invite Others to Be Free

Effective personal evangelism springs from enthusiasm about your personal experience with God. Your testimony of how God came into your life and set you free is a personal story that is uniquely yours. You are the world's authority on your own experience. You are free in Christ to experience God in whatever ways are most meaningful to you. Do not let anyone take that from you.

Read 1 Corinthians 9 for Paul's discussion of how his freedom in Christ obligated him to be "all things to all people" that he might by all means liberate some (1 Corinthians 9:22). An essential part of our invitation to freedom in Christ through personal evangelism is our freedom to listen, take others seriously where they really are, adapt our approach to each individual, and respect people who are different just as we want them to respect us.

Are You Free Yet?

Many inclusive issues are not yet settled, and probably many never will be settled to the satisfaction of all of us who are open to new directions and ideas about who God is and how to relate to and represent God. That is as it should be. We maintain our respect for the individual experiences of others as we remain open to new truth that can break forth in our lives as we experience God working within us to will and do God's good pleasure (Philippians 2:13). When God touches your life, expect the unexpected.

The truth will set you free. Think for yourself. Make your own decisions about who God is for you. Jesus liberates us to be our true and best self as individuals. To compromise that freedom is to deny the Spirit of Jesus in us. Do not let others pressure you into religion that does not fit you, for that makes you a hypocrite, which is worse than no religion at all. If you are ready to stone me as a heretic, take a look at the stone in your hand and think of God. She still loves you anyway.

Questions for Study and Discussion

1. Have you written out your personal experience with God? What name for God has emerged from your experience with God?

2. What in the Bible best helps you to put into words your experience of the acts of God? Reading the Book of Psalms will expand your vision, stir your emotions, and stimulate your imagination about God. Find and read the Psalms that Jesus used in the Gospels to express his relationship with God. What does Jesus' use of Psalms and other biblical materials tell you about how Jesus viewed God?

Additional Resources

Works by Virginia Ramey Mollenkott have been helpful to me.

Virginia Ramey Mollenkott (with Letha Scanzoni); *Is the Homosexual My Neighbor? A Positive Christian Response*, Harper, 1978; revised and updated in 1994; *The Divine Feminine: Biblical Imagery of God as Female*: Crossroad, 1983, and *Sensuous Spirituality: Out from Fundamentalism*: Crossroad, 1992.

Mollenkott gives a helpful overview of her conclusions about inclusive terminology for God, "I dislike the word Goddess because in our social context that word implies the presence of a second All-Encompassing Being, which is surely a contradiction in terms and logic" (*Sensuous Spirituality*, page 11).

See my Web site for up-to-date resources on spiritual issues related to women and to gay, lesbian, bisexual, and transgendered people and others who have been abused and oppressed by religion.

ANNOTATED BIBLIOGRAPHY

I do not recommend very many books. Few books on issues related to the Bible and homosexuality are carefully researched and well written. Many other books could be included, and many more are included in the suggested readings at the end of most lessons in this book. I recommend the following,

Boswell, John. *Christianity, Social Tolerance, and Homosexuality: Gay People in Western Europe from the Beginning of the Christian Era to the Fourteenth Century.* University of Chicago Press, 1980. The most thoroughly researched of any treatment of the subject of church history and homosexuality along with the Bible and homosexuality printed so far.

Boswell's last book, *Same-Sex Unions in Premodern Europe.* New York: Villard Books, 1994.

Aarons, Leroy. *Prayers for Bobby: A Mother's Coming to Terms with the Suicide of Her Gay Son.* HarperSanFrancisco, 1995. A powerful and deeply moving true story that is being planned as a movie.

Bawer, Bruce. *Stealing Jesus: How Fundamentalism Betrays Christianity.* Crown Publishers, Inc., 1997.

Also by Bruce Bawer, *A Place at the Table: The Gay Individual in American Society.* Poseidon Press, 1993.

Booth, Father Leo. *When God Becomes a Drug: Breaking the Chains of Religious Addiction and Abuse.* G. P. Putnam's Sons, 1991.

England, Michael E. *The Bible and Homosexuality*, Fifth Edition: Chi Rho Press, 1998. First published in 1977, this brief frequently revised study by the former pastor of MCC San Francisco has been widely used in UFMCC congregations as part of new member training and information for inquirers.

Enroth, Ronald M. *Churches that Abuse*. Zondervan: A Division of HarperCollins Publishers, 1992.

Glaser, Chris. *Come Home! Reclaiming Spirituality and Community as Gay Men and Lesbians*. (Published in 1990 by Harper) This book is now available in a completely revised and expanded (five new chapters) edition published 1998 by Chi Rho Press.

See also Glaser's *Uncommon Calling: A Gay Man's Struggle to Serve the Church*. Harper, 1988; *Coming Out as Sacrament*. Westminster John Knox, 1998; *Coming Out to God: Prayers for Lesbians and Gay Men, Their Families and Friends*. Westminster John Knox, 1991; *The Word is Out: Daily Meditations on the Bible Reclaimed for Lesbians and Gay Men*. Harper, 1994.

Gomes, Peter J. *The Good Book: Reading the Bible with Mind and Heart*. New York: William Morrow and Company, Inc., 1996.

Johnson, David and Jeff VanVonderen. *The Subtle Power of Spiritual Abuse: Recognizing and Escaping Spiritual Manipulation and False Spiritual Authority Within the Church*. Minneapolis: Bethany House Publishers, 1991.

Jordan, Mark D. *The Invention of Sodomy in Christian Theology*. Chicago: The University of Chicago Press, 1997. This recent study is carefully and thoroughly researched. The material is even harder to read than Boswell, but it is worth the time and effort to learn a lot of things you don't already know.

Hartman, Keith. *Congregations in Conflict: The Battle Over Homosexuality*. New Brunswick, New Jersey: Rutgers University Press, 1996. A lively telling of the stories of the Rev. Jimmy

Creech, Dr. Mahan Siler, and others who have led their churches to affirm and celebrate gay and lesbian holy unions.

Haugk, Kenneth C. *Antagonists in the Church: How to Identify and Deal with Destructive Conflict.* Minneapolis: Augsburg Publishing House, 1988.

Hilton, Bruce. *Can Homophobia Be Cured?* Abingdon Press, 1992. A clear and well-informed brief treatment of issues related to homosexuality and the church.

Helminiak, Daniel A. *What the Bible Really Says About Homosexuality.* San Francisco: Alamo Square Press, 1994. A well-written overview of the main issues related to the Bible and homosexuality. See also Dr. Helminiak's Web site with same name as the book.

McNeill, John. *The Church And The Homosexual*, 1976, revised and enlarged 1988, *Taking A Chance On God*, 1988, and *Freedom, Glorious Freedom!* 1994. All from Beacon Press, Boston.

Also by Father McNeill is a practical and reliable work. *Both Feet Firmly Planted in Midair: My Spiritual Journey.* Louisville: Westminster John Knox Press, 1998. John McNeill's Web site is at www.johnjmcneill.com.

Oates, Wayne E. *When Religion Gets Sick.* Philadelphia: The Westminster Press, 1970. This excellent study of sick and abusive religion has recently been republished and is of great value. See the Wayne E. Oates Institute Online.

Perry, Troy D. *The Lord is My Shepherd, and He Knows I'm Gay*: Universal Fellowship Press, 1972, 1994; and (with Thomas L. P. Swicegood) *Don't Be Afraid Anymore: The Story of Reverend Troy Perry and the Metropolitan Community Churches*: St. Martin's Press, 1990. These two books by the Founder of the Universal Fellowship of Metropolitan Community Churches are very important in understanding where we are now and where we have been. Most valuable, however, is this telling of the personal story of a gay man struggling to find and follow the will of God and succeeding.

Piazza, Michael S. *Holy Homosexuals: The Truth About Being Gay or Lesbian and Christian* (revised edition): Sources of Hope Publishing, Dallas, Texas, 1997. Michael Piazza is senior pastor of the largest gay and lesbian church in the world, the Cathedral of Hope MCC in Dallas, Texas. Michael tells his story and shares his vision and ministry of hope for homosexuals.

Ritley, M. R. *God's Gay Tribe*: Beloved Disciple Press, 1994. This brief book helped me when I was experiencing a time of "wandering through the wilderness" and I needed the clear vision of how to survive the trip through the wilderness. This is the best Christian meditation on "coming out as a spiritual journey" that I have found.

Scanzoni, Letha and Mollenkott, Virginia Ramey. *Is the Homosexual My Neighbor? Another Christian View.* Harper San Francisco, 1978, 1994. Revised and updated. The first, and still one of the best, treatment of the problems created by the use of the Bible as a weapon against gay people.

Stuart, Elizabeth. *Religion is a Queer Thing: A Guide to the Christian Faith for Lesbian, Gay, Bisexual and Transgendered People*. Cleveland, Ohio: The Pilgrim Press, 1997.

Spong, John Shelby. *Why Christianity Must Change or Die: A Bishop Speaks to Believers in Exile*. HarperSanFrancisco, 1998.

Weinberg, Dr. George. *Society and the Healthy Homosexual.* St. Martin's Press, 1972, 1983. Recently Revised. This book invented the term "homophobia."

White, Mel. *Stranger at the Gate: To Be Gay and Christian in America*: Simon and Schuster, 1994. This book is by a former ghostwriter for many famous fundamentalist preachers like Jerry Falwell, Pat Robertson, James Kennedy, Billy Graham, and others. Mel tells his story of closeted gay life and spiritual struggles that have led him into a powerful ministry of activism for homosexuals in today's homophobic fundamentalist holy wars against gays.

Wilson, Nancy. *Our Tribe: Queer Folks, God, Jesus, and the Bible*: HarperSanFrancisco, 1995. This creative and practical book by the First Vice-Moderator of UFMCC and pastor of the "Mother Church" of MCC in Los Angeles is well worth your time. Nancy has been a powerful leading force in MCC for inclusive language and practice and for ecumenical outreach to all other branches of Christianity.

Great Classic Books for You to Read

These books have helped me personally to shape my views on God, Jesus, and my call to ministry. They have special relevance to the material in this book. All of them are well worth your time. Most of them have had many publishers.

Bonhoeffer, Dietrich. *Life Together* (helpful in understanding the dynamics of small group and individual ministry), *The Cost of Discipleship*; and his most influential work, *Letters and Papers from Prison*.

Brother Lawrence. *The Practice of the Presence of God.*

Howe, Ruel L. *The Miracle of Dialogue*: Seabury Press, 1963.

Kierkegaard, Soren. *Attack Upon Christendom*, *Edifying Discourses*, *Purity of Heart is to Will One Thing* and other books and writings by the "first Christian existentialist."

Powell, John, S.J., *Why Am I Afraid to Tell You Who I Am?* and *Why Am I Afraid to Love?* (I used these two exciting and creative brief books in most of my college ministerial courses at Baptist College.)

Robinson, John A. T. *Honest to God* (1963) and *The Honest To God Debate*, edited by David L. Edwards (1963). These books were a bombshell in the field of theology when they first came out. Robinson was already Bishop of Woolwich and a famous and respected biblical scholar when he wrote *Honest to God.*

Thurman, Howard. *Jesus and the Disinherited* (1949). This brief book by a great African American scholar and teacher had a profound effect on my thinking when the Rev. Carolyn Mobley gave me a copy in 1981 in Atlanta. Read it with great profit.

Tillich, Paul. *Dynamics of Faith*, *Biblical Religion and the Search for Ultimate Reality*, *The Shaking of the Foundations*, and many other books, lectures, and a three volume *Systematic Theology.* Do not miss out on the life and work of this great American thinker and theological pioneer. Tillich, Bonhoeffer, and Kierkegaard profoundly influenced Bishop John A. T. Robinson in his brave new approach to spirituality in *Honest to God.*

Additional resources are also included at the close of most lessons and chapters in this book.

This selective book list is far from exhaustive, but it represents books that have been of special help to me and that I can confidently recommend to you. Many other works by Randy Shilts, Eric Marcus, James B. Nelson, Malcolm Boyd, William Countryman, and others are important for understanding our own history and religious roots, but space does not permit mentioning all of them.

Review the other books published by Chi Rho Press at www.ChiRhoPress.com.

See my Web site for links to resources on the Internet and for regular updates and additional resources and bibliography that will help you to keep up-to-date with current information and research, www.truluck.com.

If you want to receive my e-mail updates on issues related to this book, please send e-mail to rembert@truluck.com and request to be added to my mailing list. Most of my updates are included in my Web site.

Index of Bible References

Bible references, special translations, and explanations used in each unit of "Steps to Recovery from Bible Abuse" are listed below. All of the translations and paraphrases are by the author and are based on the original Hebrew and Greek with special reference to the *New American Standard Version.* For printed copies of most of the key Bible passages, see the author's web site at www.truluck.com

Because ancient Hebrew and Greek are subject to many possible translations that depend on the cultural conditions 2,000 years ago and that have to be interpreted in view of cultural information and attitudes today, some of the author's translations of a passage may vary from one use to another in view of what the present application and clarity demand.

Full Text of Preparatory Bible Readings

The full text of Dr. Truluck's translation and paraphrase of key "Preparatory Bible Readings" suggested at the beginning of each of the 52 Lessons can be found in his Web site on "Steps to Recovery from Bible Abuse" at www.truluck.com. Go to the "Twelve Steps to Recovery" section of the Web site and click on the Bible passages listed with the title of the Lessons given at the end of each Step. The full text of the passages will appear on the computer screen.

Using www.truluck.com in conjunction with this book greatly expands the resources available to the reader and allows for key Bible quotations to be found easily in carefully researched translations that take into consideration both the historical cultural setting of the original manuscripts and the present rapidly developing world of the new millennium. The Web site also provides up-to-date information and additional content based on future studies and current events.

The Web site is revised and updated each month.

The Bible References in Special Studies A, B, C, D, and E are given in the lessons in this book and in the author's web site at www.truluck.com, where key passages are printed out as links.

Updates related to these Special Studies are also included in the Author's web site. To receive Dr. Truluck's e-mail updates on current issues and events, look at his web site www.truluck.com and send an e-mail request to be added to Dr. Truluck's e-mail list. Questions or comments can be sent by e-mail to rembert@slip.net.